Windows NT®
Terminal Server
and Citrix MetaFrame

New Riders

New Riders Professional Library

Windows NT®
Terminal Server
and Citrix MetaFrame

New Riders

201 West 103rd Street
Indianapolis, Indiana 46290

Ted Harwood

Windows NT® Terminal Server and Citrix MetaFrame

Ted Harwood

Copyright © 1999 by New Riders

International Standard Book Number: 1-56205-944-0

Library of Congress Catalog Card Number: 98-87722

Printed in the United States of America

First Printing: December, 1998

00   5

Trademarks

All terms mentioned in this book that are known to be trademarks or service marks have been appropriately capitalized. New Riders Publishing cannot attest to the accuracy of this information. Use of a term in this book should not be regarded as affecting the validity of any trademark or service mark.

Windows NT is a registered trademark of Microsoft Corporation.

Warning and Disclaimer

Every effort has been made to make this book as complete and as accurate as possible, but no warranty or fitness is implied. The information provided is on an "as is" basis. The author and the publisher shall have neither liability nor responsibility to any person or entity with respect to any loss or damages arising from the information contained in this book.

Publisher
David Dwyer

Executive Editor
Al Valvano

Acquisitions Editor
Amy Michaels

Development Editor
Juliet MacLean

Managing Editor
Sarah Kearns

Project Editor
Lori Morency

Copy Editor
Daryl Kessler

Indexer
Tina Trettin

Technical Reviewers
Craig Cumberland
Schyler Jones

Proofreader
Jeanne Clark

Production
Laura A. Knox
Steve Balle-Gifford
Liz Johnston
Louis M. Porter, Jr.

Contents

About the Author

Ted Harwood is a senior network engineer for Davocom One in Miami, Florida. He specializes in the design and implementation of LAN, WAN, and thin-client solutions. Harwood is a Microsoft Certified Systems Engineer (MCSE), Novell Master Certified NetWare Engineer (MCNE), and a Certified Citrix Administrator. He also holds a B.S. in Computer Information Systems from the University of the State of New York. When not working, Mr. Harwood enjoys spending time with his wife and baby boy. He can be reached at `tharwood@davocom.com`.

About the Technical Reviewers

Craig Cumberland has been involved in the IT industry for over seven years. He received an undergraduate degree in Philosophy and Business from Texas A&M University while employed as a Research Computing Engineer and a Masters of Business Administration from Indiana University, focusing on Strategy and Technology. After graduating, he established a computer consulting firm in Bloomington, Indiana, specializing in network infrastructure design.

Currently he is employed at Microsoft as a Server Operating Systems Product Manager, working on various products, including Windows NT Server 4.0; Windows NT Server 4.0, Enterprise Edition; and, most recently, Windows NT Server 4.0, Terminal Server Edition. Current duties include development of capacity planning information for Terminal Server; production of the Terminal Server Architectural Overview white paper, Reviewers guide; and development of OEM Server Partner Co-Marketing programs. He is also a happily married golfer with three cats.

Schyler Jones is a Microsoft Certified Systems Engineer and Citrix Certified Administrator with thirteen years of experience working with multi-user and PC LAN systems. He has been involved with a number of application deployment and desktop replacement projects using WinFrame and Terminal Server. Schyler is a member of the Virtual IS Team at the Taylor Group in Bedford, New Hampshire, a Microsoft Solution Provider Partner and a reseller for Great Plains Software. The company specializes in business software implementations and frequently uses WinFrame and Terminal Server to deploy mission-critical applications. He can be reached via email at `sjones@taylornet.com` or you can visit the company's Web site at `http://www.taylornet.com`.

Dedication

To Karen, my love, and Justin, my joy.

Acknowledgments

You hold in your hands the final product of an effort contributed to and supported by many people. My heartfelt thanks goes first, and always, to my wife. Without her untiring support, this book would not have been completed. I also owe deep gratitude to both her family and mine for all of their help along the way.

I would like to thank all those at Macmillan Computer Publishing who helped in the production of this book, especially Amy Michaels and Julie MacLean. Amy's can-do attitude and faith were what got the project started and carried it through to successful completion. Julie's logical insight and intelligent guidance were invaluable in the writing of this material.

Finally a great deal of gratitude is owed to the outstanding technical editors on this project, Craig Cumberland and Schyler Jones. Their constructive commentary and technical assessments were essential in ensuring the accuracy of the writing on such a new product.

Tell Us What You Think!

As the reader of this book, *you* are our most important critic and commentator. We value your opinion and want to know what we're doing right, what we could do better, what areas you'd like to see us publish in, and any other words of wisdom you're willing to pass our way.

As the Executive Editor for the Networking team at Macmillan Computer Publishing, I welcome your comments. You can fax, email, or write me directly to let me know what you did or didn't like about this book—as well as what we can do to make our books stronger.

Please note that I cannot help you with technical problems related to the topic of this book, and that due to the high volume of mail I receive, I might not be able to reply to every message.

When you write, please be sure to include this book's title and author, as well as your name and phone or fax number. I will carefully review your comments and share them with the author and editors who worked on the book.

Fax:	317-581-4663
Email:	newriders@mcp.com
Mail:	Al Valvano
	Executive Editor
	Networking
	Macmillan Computer Publishing
	201 West 103rd Street
	Indianapolis, IN 46290 USA

Introduction

Microsoft's Windows NT Server 4.0, Terminal Server Edition is a very powerful implementation of thin client technology. With Terminal Server, Microsoft has basically taken the standard Windows NT Server 4.0 operating system and rewritten it to distribute Windows NT 4.0 desktops to remote Terminal Server clients. By using thin client technology to distribute these desktops, Terminal Server greatly extends the reach of the Windows applications that run on it.

Citrix MetaFrame 1.0 is an add-on product for Terminal Server. MetaFrame adds many important features to Terminal Server, including load balancing, application publishing, and support for non-Windows clients such as UNIX, OS/2, DOS, and Macintosh.

In this book, we will be discussing these two products in detail, giving you the information you need to know to integrate them effectively.

Who This Book Is For

This book is mainly for system administrators and consultants who are responsible for integrating a Terminal Server thin client solution into their networks. This book provides you with real-world solutions and advice that will help you when you need it the most. The material is technical and covers a wide range of expertise—it assumes a basic understanding of Windows NT Server 4.0 operation, along with a solid understanding of the various Windows workstation operating systems, such as Windows 95 and Windows NT Workstation 4.0.

How This Book Is Organized

Windows NT Terminal Server and Citrix MetaFrame is organized into four main parts. Each part covers a general Terminal Server topic. Each of those parts is then further divided into chapters that cover specific aspects of the topic. They are organized as follows.

Part I: Overview of Terminal Server and MetaFrame

The first part is a technical overview of Terminal Server and MetaFrame. The chapters in this part will provide the necessary introduction for those who are new to NT thin client technology or who want a better understanding of all its varied aspects.

- Chapter 1, "Introducing NT Thin Clients," introduces the thin client computing model, its many variations, and how they differ from the NT thin client model of Terminal Server. You will examine how Terminal Server works and distributes NT desktops using thin client technology. You also will find out about the different types of thin clients available, including Windows-based Terminals, Net PCs, network computers, and more.

■ Chapter 2, "Planning for Terminal Server," is where you are introduced to the many applications for which Terminal Server is best suited, along with the applications for which you would want to use other solutions.

■ Chapter 3, "Terminal Server Architecture," covers basic Windows NT Server architecture and how Terminal Server extends and changes it.

■ Chapter 4, "Terminal Server and MetaFrame," covers the many technical advantages of the Terminal Server add-on product MetaFrame by Citrix.

Part II: Installation, Configuration, and Administration

The second part is the core of the book. Here is where you will learn what you need to know to get Terminal Server and MetaFrame up and running on your network.

■ Chapter 5, "Installing Terminal Server and MetaFrame," guides you through installing both Terminal Server and MetaFrame, pointing out key differences between a Terminal Server installation and a similar Windows NT Server 4.0 installation.

■ Chapter 6, "Creating the Connections," covers the connections that have to be set up for each of your remote users.

■ Chapter 7, "Creating Users and Groups in Terminal Server," instructs you on the differences between a Terminal Server user and a standard NT Server user. This chapter shows you how to properly set up your Terminal Server users.

■ Chapter 8, "Using Logon Scripts," shows you how to use scripts with your Terminal Server, such as logon scripts and Application Compatibility scripts.

■ Chapter 9, "Installing Clients," guides you through installing both the Terminal Server and ICA client software on the most common operating systems.

■ Chapter 10, "Installing Applications on Terminal Server," gives you guidance on the technically challenging topic of how to integrate your applications into Terminal Server's multiuser environment.

■ Chapter 11, "Securing the Server," shows you what steps you should take to secure your Terminal Server.

■ Chapter 12, "Administering the Desktop and Server," looks at the important aspects of administering Terminal Server desktops.

■ Chapter 13, "Measuring Performance," is a very important planning chapter that will help you ensure that your Terminal Server hardware is adequate for its intended purpose. It will also help you establish a performance baseline to measure against future needs.

: Real-World Terminal Server and MetaFrame Solutions

hapters in this book make up a solutions guide for Terminal Server and
Each of these chapters covers a specific type of Terminal Server or
solution in detail.

■ er 14, "Terminal Server and Remote Access," covers how to implement
the most popular uses for Terminal Server—remote access to corporate
computing resources.

■ Chapter 15, "Terminal Server and NetWare," is a very important chapter for
administrators who will be integrating Terminal Server into primarily NetWare
networks.

■ Chapter 16, "Terminal Server and the Internet," explores topics such as Web-
publishing applications with MetaFrame and accessing your Terminal Server
across the Internet.

■ Chapter 17, "Terminal Server and Wide Area Networks," examines two major
issues in wide area networking—WAN access to Terminal Server and WAN performance.

■ Chapter 18, "MetaFrame and UNIX Clients," is for those who want to run
Windows applications on their UNIX workstations. This chapter shows you how
to integrate Terminal Server into a primarily UNIX network.

■ Chapter 19, "MetaFrame and Macintosh," discusses issues such as integrating
Terminal Server into Macintosh networks and running Windows applications
with the Macintosh workstations.

■ Chapter 20, "Application Publishing and Load Balancing with MetaFrame," discusses how, for many corporations, these features are the most important features
that MetaFrame offers. This chapter goes into these critical features in-depth.

Part IV: Appendixes

The appendixes cover some additional topics of interest that are beyond the scope of
the main material.

■ Appendix A, "The History of Terminal Server," puts Terminal Server into a historical context, providing details of both its history and prospective future.

■ Appendix B, "Windows-Based Terminal Manufacturers," lists some of the many
manufacturers of Windows-based Terminals, a new class of thin client device.

■ Appendix C, "Disaster Recovery Kit," has forms for recording important
Terminal Server information in case you need to rebuild it.

■ Appendix D, "Terminal Server Resources," lists useful Terminal Server–related Web
sites that you can go to for further information about thin client technology.

Conventions Used

Throughout this book, certain conventions are used to convey the material in a standard and understandable fashion.

Referring to Terminal Server and MetaFrame

Both Terminal Server and MetaFrame are referred to many times in this book. Because MetaFrame is an add-on product to Terminal Server, there are certain topics that only apply to MetaFrame.

MetaFrame   When you see this symbol in the margin, it indicates that the text in this section refers only to MetaFrame. The plus sign in the symbol indicates that you must first install the add-on MetaFrame product before you will be able to use the features that are being discussed. You will also see this symbol at the heads of chapters that cover MetaFrame-only topics. Particular sentences may also be noted as "MetaFrame-only" in the text.

Because MetaFrame adds on to Terminal Server's basic features and does not change them, most Terminal Server features discussed in the book apply to both Terminal Server alone and Terminal Server with MetaFrame. If a particular sentence or paragraph applies to just Terminal Server without MetaFrame, it will be referred to as "Terminal Server-alone."

Notes and Tips

Three special conventions have been used to indicate real-world tips, notes for WinFrame administrators, and author's notes.

Real-World Tip

Real-world tips are asides taken from the real-world experience that apply to the topic at hand. They may also cover special topics or considerations that come up in the daily use of Terminal Server.

Note for WinFrame Administrators

Many features of Terminal Server and especially those of MetaFrame are already familiar to WinFrame administrators. Notes for WinFrame administrators cover special considerations with Terminal Server of which WinFrame administrators need to be aware.

Author's Note

Author's notes are general notes that cover information related to the topic at hand.

I

Overview of Terminal Server and MetaFrame

Introducing NT Thin Clients

ICROSOFT WINDOWS NT SERVER 4.0, Terminal Server Edition (or Terminal Server for short) is designed to distribute Windows NT desktops by using thin-client technology. Although the desktops appear to the client as if they're running locally, all the application processing is actually happening at the Terminal Server. This departure from the standard PC computing model, where applications normally run locally, is one of the primary reasons why corporations choose Terminal Server over other solutions. As you'll see in this chapter as well as those that follow, putting the responsibility for processing back into the computer room makes a lot of sense for many types of applications.

This chapter first defines the thin-client computing model and explains its advantages. Next, it describes how Terminal Server works within this model and how it competes with other thin-client solutions, such as Java. Finally, the chapter ends with descriptions of the many different types of thin-client choices you have with Terminal Server, such as Windows-based Terminals (WBTs) and Net PCs.

The Thin-Client Computing Model

The *thin* in "thin client" means simply that the client is small. Although a thin client is normally less than a few megabytes in size, it's often as capable as a workstation with an operating system taking up several hundred megabytes. This capability is due to the fact that thin clients act as interpreters, leveraging the processing capabilities of powerful remote hosts by viewing, controlling, and interacting with applications that are running on them (see Figure 1.1). With Terminal Server, application processing is handled entirely by the server, not by the client; only the application display is sent across the wire to the client. In a Terminal Server environment, applications execute entirely on the server.

One of the main advantages of thin clients is how easy they are to port to different hardware and operating systems. Because the client piece is small, very little processing code needs to be written. Software publishers can easily port the client code to just about any platform. This means that applications that run on top of thin-client technology do not have to be rewritten for the applications to run on new operating systems. Only the thin client underneath needs to be rewritten.

The various Terminal Server clients, including the ICA client with MetaFrame, are great thin-client solutions. In this section, you'll learn how Terminal Server uses thin-client technology to distribute NT desktops to its users. We'll then cover the advantages of Terminal Server as a thin-client solution over other types of thin-client solutions such as Java. This will give you a good overview of the current state of thin-client technology and where Terminal Server fits in.

How Terminal Server Works

Terminal Server can be divided into three parts for better understanding: the desktop server, the protocols, and the thin client (see Figure 1.2). Terminal Server is a server of NT 4.0 desktops to remote clients. The Terminal Server operating system has been written to run multiple NT 4.0 desktops or sessions simultaneously at the server. Using specialized thin-client protocols, Terminal Server packages these desktops and then sends them across the network to the clients. Each client's job is to display the desktop for the user and return user interaction with the desktop to the Terminal Server. Terminal Server is, therefore, a remote control solution. Basically, Terminal Server clients remotely control their individual desktops running on the server.

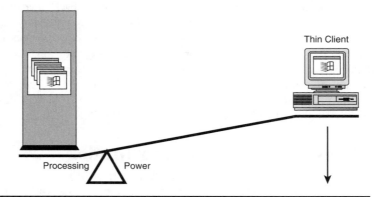

Thin Client

Processing   Power

- Thin clients with very little processing power can leverage the processing capabilities of a much more powerful server.
- With thin-client technologies such as Terminal Server, processing occurs at the host.

Figure 1.1   The thin-client model.

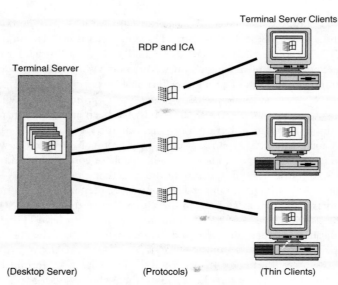

Figure 1.2   The desktop server, protocols, and thin clients.

The Desktop Server

The Terminal Server operating system is based on Microsoft's Windows NT Server 4.0. With the purchase and integration of key thin-client technology components from Citrix, Microsoft has created a thin-client edition of its flagship operating system (see Appendix A, "History of Terminal Server," for more details). For those who have worked with Windows NT Server 4.0 before, you'll find that the majority of the operating system has remained the same. However, although most things may look the same, key parts of NT Server's underlying architecture have been changed to support the multiuser environment of Terminal Server. In Chapter 3, "Terminal Server Architecture," you'll learn exactly how the architecture has changed from the original NT Server 4.0 operating system.

The Protocols

With Terminal Server and MetaFrame come two special-purpose, thin-client protocols—RDP and ICA, respectively. These upper-layer protocols are what carry the NT 4.0 desktops to the clients and pass back user interface commands to the server.

> **Note for WinFrame Administrators: WinFrame, MetaFrame, and TS**
> Terminal Server is based on the NT Server 4.0 operating system in a very similar fashion to the way WinFrame 1.x is based on NT Server 3.51. You'll find that you can directly relate many of the concepts with WinFrame to MetaFrame and Terminal Server. The differences between Terminal Server and MetaFrame will be discussed in detail in Chapter 4, "Terminal Server and MetaFrame."

Microsoft's RDP, which stands for *Remote Desktop Protocol*, is based on the T.120 multichannel conferencing protocol series defined by the International Telecommunications Union (ITU). Microsoft has already been using the T.120 protocol series for over a year in its NetMeeting videoconferencing product. Microsoft has basically extended this protocol series to meet the needs of a multiuser Terminal Server environment.

Citrix's ICA (Independent Computing Architecture) protocol comes only with the Terminal Server add-on product MetaFrame. ICA has been around for many years and has become the *de facto* standard in the thin-client industry.

Both ICA and RDP are very efficient thin-client protocols, designed to work well over low-bandwidth connections. They are both capable of compression and encryption.

ICA and RDP currently differ mainly in the underlying protocols they support. Because both ICA and RDP are upper-layer protocols, they need to rely on transport protocols underneath, such as TCP/IP, to carry them across the network. RDP currently only works on top of TCP/IP. This means you first must have TCP/IP communication established between the client and the server for RDP to be able to communicate. ICA will work on top of TCP/IP, IPX, SPX, NetBIOS (NetBEUI), and direct serial and modem connections. As you'll see in Chapter 4, "Terminal Server and MetaFrame," you have a variety of client and protocol choices with MetaFrame.

The Thin Client

The thin clients are responsible for re-creating the NT 4.0 desktop for the user from the information they receive from the server. They also take the mouse movements and keyboard input of a user, package them using either RDP or ICA, and send them back to the server.

Two types of thin clients work with Terminal Server. The first is the Terminal Server client (or RDP client). This client, written by Microsoft, comes with Terminal Server. It can be installed and run from most Windows operating systems, including Windows for Workgroups, Windows 95/98, Windows NT, and Windows CE. It uses RDP to communicate with the server and, therefore, currently only works with TCP/IP.

The second client is the MetaFrame client (or ICA client). This client is only available after installing Citrix's MetaFrame add-on product. Citrix has gone to great lengths to port this client to as many operating systems as possible. Using the ICA client, you can run Windows applications from all versions of Windows as well as many versions of UNIX, Macintosh, and more. Refer to Chapter 4 for a complete list of the operating systems with which the ICA client currently works.

> **Note for WinFrame Administrators: The MetaFrame Add-On**
> The ICA client included with MetaFrame 1.0 is backward compatible with the ICA client for WinFrame 1.7. This means you can access both WinFrame 1.7 and MetaFrame servers from the new client. It's also forward compatible, so your existing WinFrame clients can still access their server if you upgrade to MetaFrame. MetaFrame includes an automated client distribution tool that makes this transition easier.
>
> RDP and ICA are not compatible protocols. If you install Terminal Server without adding MetaFrame, you'll have to change all your current clients to RDP clients. If you're going to upgrade a WinFrame server or incorporate Terminal Server into an existing WinFrame environment, it's recommended that you purchase and install the add-on MetaFrame product.

Terminal Server as a Thin-Client Solution

Now that you understand how Terminal Server works, it's time to focus on the advantages of Terminal Server over other thin-client solutions available today. This will help give you a better understanding of the many different variations of thin clients that exist and how Terminal Server measures up against them. Here's a list of Terminal Server's advantages:

- *Terminal Server runs Windows applications.*   The primary advantage of Terminal Server over most other thin-client solutions is that it's designed to run with Windows applications. Any Windows applications that work under Windows NT will generally work well on Terminal Server. Most current thin-client technologies, such as Java, require you to write entirely new applications in their native language. Because Terminal Server can run Windows applications, it can run Java apps through a Windows-based, Java-enabled browser such as Internet Explorer.

- *The client is very small.*   Both the RDP and ICA clients are less than a few megabytes each. The thinness of the client means great savings in both processing power and memory. You don't need a huge processor on the client or a lot of memory to run the Terminal Server client. This means that even legacy PCs, such as 386 PCs, can run 32-bit Windows NT applications by leveraging the processing power of the Terminal Server. As you'll see in the section on Windows-based Terminals, the thinness of the client also means that you can now feasibly run Windows applications on a much wider variety of devices.

- *Terminal Server is highly reliable.*   The underlying multiuser technology, provided in large part by Citrix, has been around already for several years. Citrix has tested this technology in thousands of different environments. Terminal Server also supports the Windows NT API. This tightly controlled and standardized programming interface has been tested and used by developers around the world for several years.

Java as a Thin-Client Solution

There are some key differences between Java and Terminal Server that you need to be aware of. Refer to Figure 1.3 while reading through the following differences:

- *Java is an interpreted language, not just a user interface protocol like ICA or RDP.* Unlike Terminal Server clients, part of the application processing occurs on the client, not the server. A Java applet or application can be written so that either the client or the server shares the major processing load of the applet or application. Typically, the server takes on the work.

- *Java is a new language.*   For companies to make use of Java, applications have to be written from scratch. This is a key difference. With Terminal Server, you can run almost any of the millions of Windows applications already available. With Java, relatively few applications are currently available. You may likely have to develop your own.

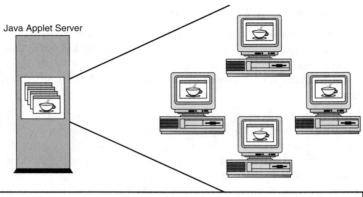

Java Applet Server

- Java applets are downloaded by Java clients and run locally on the client's Java Virtual Machine.
- Processing is distributed, since clients run the applets, not the server.
- Java applets can be large and take up significant bandwidth during busy times while clients download applets from the server.
- Clients have to have significant resources, such as memory and processing power, in order to handle business applications written in Java.

Figure 1.3   The Java thin–client solution.

- *Java is struggling to be standardized.*   Although standards have been defined, their implementations sometimes differ. In the real world, this has often led to Java applications that do not work well across different Java clients.

- *Java applications must be downloaded to the client.*   A typical full-function, business Java applet can be larger than 2MB, depending on its complexity. When users first access a Java application, the entire application needs to be downloaded to them. This process taxes the network, especially in the morning when everyone is getting in and downloading their applets for the day. The large amount of bandwidth necessary often makes Java a poor solution for remote access and WANs.

Other Thin-Client Solutions

Although Java is Terminal Server's main competitor in the thin-client arena, many other examples of thin clients are in existence today. Although not always considered thin-client solutions, these systems share many salient features with Terminal Server's implementation of thin-client technology.

Web Browsers

Although Web browsers were originally intended for the display of information across the Internet, they have become much more interactive in recent years. Using languages such as Perl, CGI, ActiveX, and Java, programs can be designed so that users with Web browsers can interact with remote hosts. These programs have served many corporations well, especially in the area of electronic commerce. Large volumes of transactions can be supported using a Web interface.

The main disadvantage of these applications is their expense. Commercial quality Web applications can be very expensive to purchase or develop.

As you'll see in Chapter 4, MetaFrame offers an alternative to typical Web-based applications by allowing you to publish Windows applications on your Web servers. This means your remote users or customers can run Windows applications on your Web server across the Internet using most any popular Web browser.

X Window

In the early '90s, the UNIX community came up with an application interface called X Window, which put a GUI interface on UNIX. An application written properly to the X Window API can, with little modification, run on any UNIX platform with X Window loaded.

In an X Window environment, you typically have several X Window terminals running graphics sessions on a UNIX X Window server. This setup is very similar to a Terminal Server environment in that only screen updates and user interface commands go across the network between the X Window server and the X Window terminal or client.

As compared to ICA or RDP, the X Window protocol generally takes up more network bandwidth per client. This means that although X Window works well on a LAN, it's not as good a solution for WANs or remote access as Terminal Server is. Although many X Window applications have been written, the majority of software companies are dedicating their resources to developing Microsoft Windows–based applications. The lack of application support makes it difficult for administrators to integrate X Window into their corporate environments or to implement corporate-wide applications on X Window.

Types of Terminal Server Clients

A large variety of devices can connect to Terminal Server. What you choose depends on your needs as an administrator as well as the needs of your users. This section explains the advantages and disadvantages of your different Terminal Server client options.

Windows-based Terminals

Windows-based Terminals represent the next step in the evolution of the terminal. They are terminals that are designed primarily to run Windows applications remotely on Terminal Server. Windows-based Terminals normally have Microsoft's Terminal Server client and/or Citrix's ICA client preloaded in the firmware. In situations where you currently use terminals or terminal emulation, using WBTs with Terminal Server is an excellent choice. WBTs are well suited for task-oriented workers. The following are some of the many advantages of Windows-based Terminals compared to other Terminal Server clients, such as PCs:

- Like text-based terminals, WBTs are very easy to install and inexpensive to maintain.
- With WBTs using Terminal Server, users can run most Windows applications they can run on a PC.
- WBTs are less expensive than PCs.
- Processing power is not wasted because WBTs are relatively inexpensive and require only enough processing power to update the screen and communicate on the network.
- There are fewer problems with theft because WBTs require a network and Terminal Server to function.
- Because WBTs have no local hard drive, all user data resides on the Terminal Server. User data is, therefore, safer and more secure than if left on a user's hard drive in the work area. Daily backups can easily be taken of all user data, and data access is controllable through NT security.

For a listing of some of the many manufacturers of Windows-based Terminals, refer to Appendix B, "Windows-Based Terminal Manufacturers."

Portable Windows-based Terminals

One of the most interesting innovations in the Windows-based Terminal market is the portable WBT. These devices can normally be held in one hand, and they often come with touch sensitive screens. They communicate back to the Terminal Server using wireless communications such as radio waves or infrared.

The portability of this new class of device adds greatly to the number of potential uses for WBTs, making WBTs a great solution for portable information gathering and display. Take, for example, a hospital. Hospital employees, such as nurses and doctors, need quick access to patient records and status. Using portable WBTs, these employees can have instant access to a Windows-based patient database while they're taking their rounds. Patient status information can be entered using a touch pad stylus. Because real-time patient data is now being entered into the hospital's computer system, doctors can analyze the data more quickly and in ways not possible with paper-based patient records.

The Net PC

In April of 1997, Microsoft, Intel, HP, Dell, and Compaq came out with the Net PC standard v1.0. This standard was mainly in response to the Network Computer initiative by IBM, Sun, and Oracle.

The main distinction between a Net PC and a standard one is that a Net PC is specifically designed to be centrally manageable. With Wakeup on LAN support, an administrator can turn on a Net PC remotely to manage it. Each Net PC is also required to have the capability to provide its serial number or identifying information across a LAN in a format that will work with central management software (using SNMP, for example). Despite the changes required for it to be centrally manageable, a Net PC can still run all the applications that a standard PC can.

The Net PC is also designed as a higher-end alternative to Windows-based Terminals. Even though using Windows-based Terminals is an ideal solution for certain task-oriented workers, some users need more resources. Take, for example, an accountant who makes extensive use of a spreadsheet package, such as Excel. For large calculations, it would be better and faster to run them locally than to tax the resources of a Terminal Server. With a Net PC, the accountant can run Excel locally and all other applications remotely.

You'll likely find that many of the enhancements recommended by the Net PC standard have already been incorporated into the PCs that you're buying today. Although computer manufacturers do not always tout their PCs as Net PCs, the Net PC movement was partly responsible for some of their enhancements. The following lists explain the required and optional components of a Net PC.

Here's a list of the required components:

- Minimum 133MHz Pentium equivalent or comparable processor (such as RISC).

- Level 2 cache of 256KB or greater.

- 16MB RAM (32MB recommended).

- All hardware fully detectable (ACPI) and configurable via software.

- OnNow. This stipulates that the OS must have control of the state of all the hardware. For example, this allows the OS to spin down a hard drive for power savings.

- Wakeup on LAN support (after January 1, 1998). This important capability allows central management packages such as SMS to "wake up" a computer so that it can be managed. With this technology, for example, a central application distribution program could roll out an application across the network to several hundred PCs at night. The program first sends a wakeup packet to these PCs, which may have been turned off. Once the PCs are running, the application can be distributed to them.

- A sealed case, designed to prevent users from installing their own equipment or to prevent thieves from stealing internal components.

- Plug-and-Play hardware.

- Adherence to management standards.

- Internal hard drive.

- USB support.
- Unique system ID structure. This is a unique product serial number that's accessible centrally through a management platform. It is important so that each computer can be identified and inventoried centrally.
- DHCP and TFTP. Extensions to DHCP are available to allow automatic configuration of the Net PC across a network. By using TFTP, you can also download a boot image from a central server.
- Mouse and keyboard.

Here's a list of the optional components:

- Upgrade capabilities for the RAM and CPU. The specification stipulates that both the RAM and CPU need to be upgradable; however, these can't be accessible to the end user.
- Lockable CD-ROM and floppy drives.
- Audio cards.
- Graphics accelerator cards.
- Serial and parallel ports.

Network Computers

The Network Computer (NC) is based on a hardware operational standard released by IBM, Sun, and Oracle in May, 1996. It basically defines a network device capable of interpreting Java applets and working with most major Internet standards. The original intention of the Network Computer was to solely run Java applications, not Windows applications. However, Network Computers can be made into Terminal Server clients using MetaFrame's Java-based ICA client. If you intend to only run Windows applications on your clients, you're better off using Windows-based Terminals instead of Network Computers. If, on the other hand, you need to run both Java applets and Windows applications on your thin-client devices, Network Computers may be what you need.

Network Computers compete directly with Windows-based Terminals. Like Windows-based Terminals, Network Computers are designed to have a small footprint and run a thin client. The key difference is that the amount of memory and processing power necessary to run most Java apps on Network Computers is much larger than that necessary to run either the ICA or RDP Terminal Server thin client. As Java applets grow in complexity, so will their hardware requirements. Terminal Server clients' processing and memory requirements are much less likely to change because they do not process applications locally. The additional memory and processing power necessary, along with the need to support the major Internet protocols, also means that Java NCs are generally more expensive than Windows-based Terminals.

Most major Internet browsers, including Netscape Communicator and Microsoft's Internet Explorer 4.0, also include Java interpreters out of the box. By loading one of these free browsers onto a PC and adding a network card, you have basically just created a Network Computer! Many companies find that adding network cards and browsers to their existing PCs is a much better investment than buying Network Computers if they need to run Java applications.

Personal Computers

Whether or not you choose PCs to implement a Terminal Server thin-client solution can depend on a lot of factors. Because many corporations already have personal computers on nearly every desktop, PCs are often the thin client of choice. By installing Terminal Server thin clients on your existing PCs, users can run their applications using less network bandwidth than if they ran the same applications locally. This makes it feasible to distribute your corporate Windows applications to PC users in remote offices using low-bandwidth WAN or modem connections. Because the thin client runs as just another application on the users' desktops, they can still run their other applications locally.

Using Terminal Server to distribute new applications to PC users is also much easier than having to locally install new applications one PC at a time. You only have to install an application once on Terminal Server to make it available to all its clients.

Because of the low processing and memory requirements for Terminal Server clients, you'll be able to run them on many of your existing legacy PCs. This economical solution works well for more frugal corporations that want to take advantage of their existing stock of legacy PCs instead of purchasing new thin-client terminals.

Using a personal computer running the Terminal Server thin client is an especially good option for the power user. Those who need a lot of processing power, such as developers and graphic artists, are generally better off running their main applications locally instead of on Terminal Server. This is beneficial for the administrator, because the servers and network will be less taxed, yet they can still distribute applications to these users via Terminal Server. This is also better for power users, because they can control the speed of their critical applications by buying more powerful PCs.

For many situations, the extraordinary local processing power and numerous features of PCs may be overkill. This is especially the case for task-oriented usage. For task-oriented personnel, such as those doing data entry, PCs have more features than they really need. They also have more components than terminals and are therefore more expensive and difficult to maintain.

In comparison to terminals, PCs are also not nearly as secure. Users can easily and inadvertently load viruses or troublesome applications onto their PCs. Applications and user data often reside locally on PCs, instead of centrally, where they can both be backed up.

2

Planning for Terminal Server

AN IMPORTANT PART OF PLANNING a Terminal Server solution is determining how and where it can be used to the greatest advantage. Because Terminal Server can easily be applied incorrectly, proper planning is essential to ensure that the solution will meet your company's and your needs. This chapter discusses the advantages of the Terminal Server product over other solutions, comparing the life cycle of a typical PC purchase to that of a Windows-based Terminal (WBT). Next, this chapter covers ways to think about your corporation's or client's needs in terms of Terminal Server solutions. The chapter ends with a discussion of situations in which Terminal Server should and should not be used.

Terminal Server and Total Cost of Ownership

The Total Cost of Ownership (TCO) of today's PCs goes far beyond the initial purchase price. According to a report by Zona Research on total computer costs over five years, only 13% of TCO is accounted for by the initial purchase price of the computer. The largest percentage of the cost, 55%, is due to network administration.

To compare the major costs of using a PC network to using a Terminal Server, take a walk through the life of a typical PC network. In this scenario, you are a network administrator for a large company. The scenario shows how administration is made easier with Terminal Server and how deploying Terminal Server can save you money.

- **The Initial Purchase**

   PC   Your company buys a PC ($1200–$2200) for a new user or for upgrading the computer of an existing user.

   Terminal Server   Your company buys a WBT ($500–$1200) for the same user. If you had older, unused PCs, you could also save money by installing them as Terminal Server clients. The hardware requirements are fewer for a Terminal Server client than for most modern operating systems.

- **Installing or Upgrading the Computer**

   PC   The technical department spends an hour or two unboxing the PC, installing the corporate software, setting up the user on the network, and installing the PC on her desk. If this is an upgrade, the tech support individual spends a few more hours transferring data and application settings and making sure the user has the applications and capabilities she had before.

   Terminal Server   The tech support department spends half an hour unboxing the Terminal, setting up the user on the network, and installing the Terminal. Upgrades are rarely necessary, unless the user needs a bigger monitor. Upgrading takes less than a half hour because data and applications are stored centrally—all the tech needs to do is connect the Terminal to the network.

- **Virus Removal**

   PC   Because the PC reports that it has a virus, you go to the user's desk, do a virus scan, and find that the user has infected his PC. You clean the PC and all of the floppies.

   Terminal Server   Virus protection is done at the server. Because WBTs do not use floppies, the most likely source of infection is email. The boot sector and all system files are locked using NTFS, so viruses will have a difficult time causing significant damage. By running virus protection software, the administrator is notified immediately upon infection and the server is scanned periodically.

- **Software Upgrades and Rollouts**

   PC   When a rollout of a new client occurs, you and a group of technicians go from PC to PC and install the client from a network share. If users experience problems, such as missing files as a result of the rollout, you must go to their desks to resolve the problems.

   Terminal Server   Application installation for all of your users can be done from your desk. Most applications can be installed in multi user mode, so you must install applications only once, and they are distributed to each of your users when they log in.

- **Hardware Problems**

   PC   Suppose a user can't remove a floppy from the drive. After a half-hour of fiddling with it, the user finds that the label had gotten stuck badly in the drive. You need to take the entire machine to get the floppy drive replaced or cleaned out. Perhaps, then, someone else calls in with a hard drive that won't boot. You find that the hard drive is dead and replace it with a new one. Because the new drive does not have anything on it, you spend an hour or two formatting the drive, installing the operating system, gathering the correct drivers, and installing user applications.

Terminal Server   The main points of failure on a WBT are the monitor, keyboard, and mouse. If any of these fail, they can be replaced very quickly and easily. If the server fails, however, everyone is affected. Because of this, it's important to invest in high-reliability hardware options such as RAID 5. If a RAID 5 drive fails, in many systems it can be replaced while the system is running without losing any data or causing downtime.

■ Software Problems

PC   A user's application keeps giving her GPFs. All your other users are running the same application with no problems. You reinstall the application and the problem disappears.

Terminal Server   The protected environment of Terminal Server keeps applications and users separate. Still, it is important to maintain tight control of the applications they can run. By using the Shadow feature you can remote-control any user's session to assist him with a software problem, without leaving your desk.

■ Data and Hardware Security

PC   Consider the following security issues:

> A user has been storing documents on his hard drive, and now they are lost. He will have to re-create the documents.

> Unbeknownst to you, a user is secretly copying product design documents and other mission-critical information to a Zip drive. The next week she quits to work for a competitor, taking the Zip disks with her.

> Your PC storage room has been broken into. Some equipment and memory are missing.

Terminal Server   Applications and data are all backed up centrally. Because data is not stored locally, there is little chance of user data loss.

> Windows-based Terminals have no local storage, so pilfering large amounts of company data is not an easy task. The auditing feature on NT also allows you to track data use down to a file level.

> Windows-based Terminals are not as valuable on the street as PCs because they require a network server to operate. The cases are also often sealed.

■ Remote Access

PC   To give a user remote access from home, you must request that a phone line be installed, and order and install remote access software and a modem. When other users see that user's ability to remote access the network, they begin to request remote access also.

Terminal Server   You can set up remote access for hundreds of users by installing and configuring a modem bank for the server. Because users share a bank of modems and phone lines, you do not have to dedicate a phone line per user, saving your company money on phone costs. Terminal Server is also an excellent solution for remote access needs because it has very tight, centralized security.

■ **WAN Access**

PC   When a user relocates, you must move his PC to a remote branch. Because many of the user's programs were run from the server, you need to reinstall them locally. Some of the user's financial applications require access across the WAN to corporate data; for the user to work at an acceptable speed, you must install an expensive, fast WAN link.

Terminal Server   By providing better functionality, using less network bandwidth, Terminal Server can save the company a lot of money on WAN fees. Terminal Server works very well across a WAN. Because you are remote-controlling a session running at corporate, only screen updates must go across the line. A user can use a WBT to run applications from corporate, or run some of the applications locally and the corporate applications from Terminal Server. Either way, the bandwidth required would be minimal compared to that taken by running an application at corporate without using Terminal Server.

■ **User-Created Problems**

PC   Suppose a user finds a screen saver at the local computer store that is much too tempting to resist. He installs the $19.95 screen saver, which eats up so much memory that mission-critical apps crash regularly on that machine. The user complains to you about the crashing, but doesn't inform you about the screen saver. After a half-hour of searching for the problem, including a virus scan and scan disk, you discover the screen saver and remove it.

Terminal Server   With Terminal Server, users can easily be prevented from installing their own applications. By using policies, you can lock down the desktop tightly.

■ **Hardware Obsolescence**

PC   You spend a lot of time doing the "computer shuffle." The president complains that the PCs at the local computer store are twice as fast as what's on his desktop. After you upgrade his PC, he requests you give his old computer to his secretary. You spend several hours installing all the correct apps for the president, cleaning up his old PC, installing apps for the secretary, moving data, and moving the PCs. (Meanwhile, the secretary's old computer is too old for anyone else to use, and ends up in storage.)

Terminal Server   Because the processing occurs at the server, with Terminal Server, user's WBTs are far less likely to become obsolete. The president may want a bigger monitor. If so, replacing his terminal and giving the old one to his secretary is only a few-minute job.

As you can see, the cost in terms of your time in a PC-only environment can quickly add up. By establishing a network using Terminal Server, you can use this time more productively by implementing solutions that would make your company more competitive and your job more interesting. It is important to keep in mind, however, that Terminal Server is meant to fill a particular need, not to replace every PC in your organization. As you will see at the end of this chapter, there are several situations in which a PC is better suited than a WBT to solve a computer problem.

Integrating Terminal Server into Your Environment

Businesses want solutions that integrate well with their current computer environments. Under many thin-client models, such as X Window, the choice of clients is limited. Terminal Server, however, works well with a wide variety of clients, especially with MetaFrame installed. Figure 2.1 shows some of the many types of clients Terminal Server and MetaFrame both work with. This makes a Terminal Server solution much easier to integrate into a wide variety of computer environments.

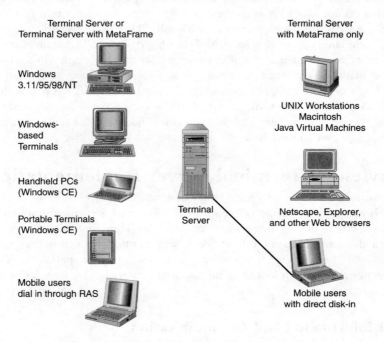

Figure 2.1   Terminal Server and MetaFrame clients.

You can access Terminal Server from most Windows-based clients, including Windows for Workgroups, Windows 95/98, Windows NT, and Windows CE. By installing MetaFrame, you can access Terminal Server from a much wider variety of clients and equipment, including the following:

- *X Window Terminals*   By running the X Window client on UNIX workstations, you can distribute Windows applications to these users.

- *Java-enabled Computers (Network Computers)*   This client adds Windows capabilities to your Network Computers and other Java Virtual Machines.

- *UNIX Workstations*   Native UNIX clients are available from Citrix for several UNIX platforms, including IBM's AIX, SCO, SGI, Solaris, SunOS, and HP/UX. For Linux fans, remember that Linux runs X Window and Java-enabled browsers.

- *Macintoshes*   Both new and old Macs can run Windows programs using the Terminal Server client.

As you can see, you can quickly turn your heterogenous computing environment into a more homogenous one. Because Terminal Server client is merely a small application, users do not have to give up their existing programs in order to run it. If your company is like most, you probably have the "Dungeon of Obsolescence." This is the dark and covert room to which all of your legacy PCs and equipment are banished. Terminal Server integrates well in environments that have legacy PCs. This old equipment makes decent terminals, which can be deployed by simply dusting them off, installing a network card, and loading the Terminal Server client. A 386 with 8MB of RAM, a VGA monitor, 100MB hard drive space, and DOS has enough processing capability to run the thin client, and thus run any Windows 32-bit application at speeds rivaling a Pentium machine.

Overview of Terminal Server Implementation

Many companies already have a huge legacy of computer choices that have been made and which you currently support. To implement a Terminal Server solution, you need to spend some time finding answers to a few concerns. Think in terms of your company's global, departmental, and job-level needs. Keep in mind that one of the greatest advantages of Terminal Server is that it extends the reach of your applications. The following sections take a fresh look at some common concerns to see how Terminal Server can address them.

Global Information and Communication

What are your company's global information and communication needs? This is where solutions like email, intranets, and other global means of communication come into play. Terminal Server's cross-platform support opens up many possibilities. From heterogeneous to homogenous, Terminal Server allows you to spread your existing investment in global communications software to all your users. For example, your email client may not have been made available for all your UNIX platforms. With Terminal Server and MetaFrame, however, you can run Windows-based applications, such as an email client, on most major UNIX platforms.

Departmental Communication

What are your company's departmental communication needs? Each division within a company generally has a specific set of interdivisional communication and information needs. For example, a research and development division might need access to detailed technical diagrams and specifications of their products, but members of this division run everything from Macintosh to Sparc Stations. Without much effort you could write a database application for Windows, which you could then distribute to all of the machines in the research and development department through Terminal Server.

Job-Level Communication

What are your company's job categories and what are their communication and information needs? Job categories tend to run across departments. For example, several departments in a company may have secretaries, executives, technical personnel, and data-entry personnel, and each of these general jobs has specific information needs. By implementing a TS solution particular to a given job category, it is likely that you can decrease you administrative tasks. Perhaps data-entry personnel need to enter data into mission-critical databases. They also may need access to email, and company policies and procedures. As an administrator, you are tasked with fulfilling these needs, but you also don't want to increase your administrative burden. For this situation, a Windows-based Terminal running a limited suite of apps is a great solution.

Top Ten Terminal Server Solutions

Terminal Server will not cure all of your computer woes. There are, however, situations in which Terminal Server is the ideal solution, just as there are situations in which TS is not well suited. The following is a short list of the "top ten" ideal uses for this product.

1. *Replacing text-based terminals* Terminal Server is a great solution for upgrading your existing terminals. Many companies such as banks need to give employees access to mainframes and mini-computers, but also want them to be able to take advantage of the capabilities of modern Windows applications such as email. Terminal Server puts your investment in Windows-based applications and legacy host computers together on one desktop.

2. *Extending the use of legacy equipment*   The closet full of old PCs you might currently be thinking of getting rid of could make excellent Windows-based Terminals. Terminal Server will squeeze new life out of your old computers by giving them the capability to run like new.

3. *Making your heterogeneous environment more homogenous*   Terminal Server greatly extends the reach of your Windows applications. You have probably experienced the need to run a Windows application on a non-Windows platform, or have waited months for a software company to release clients for all your operating systems. With Terminal Server, you can immediately extend any Windows application across all of your different types of clients.

4. *Remote access*   With Terminal Server, your mobile work force can dial in and access a Windows desktop running on your network. From the desktop, mobile users can run any application. This gives users easy and secure access to tons of applications and data.

   As an administrator, this solution is more secure and much easier to manage than running a proprietary dial-up client or having users dial in with a remote desktop control package. Suppose a mobile user with a laptop installs a program that wipes out a critical DLL in one of his remote client applications. This application originally took you 20 minutes to install from CD-ROM. To fix the problem, the user either ships the laptop to you, or you send him the CDs and talk him through the installation process over the phone. Either way, the troubleshooting involves a lot of time for both of you. With Terminal Server, however, the client is "thin" and easy to reinstall. Each mobile user can be given an installation disk for the Terminal Server client in case it needs to be reinstalled, and because the DLLs for the applications that users run remotely reside on the Terminal Server, they are normally locked from modification by a user.

5. *Branch office access to corporate applications*   Terminal Server is great for extending the reach of your corporate applications to branch offices. Many companies find this useful in the accounting department. Sales data from branch offices is often either faxed or emailed in raw form to the corporate office, where workers manually type the data into the corporate accounting package. By giving secured access to this accounting package to one or two desktops at branch sites, a company can divide the data-entry workload and achieve near real-time sales results.

6. *Public access terminals*   Because terminals can be locked so tightly and so easily and because of their ease of management, they are great solutions for kiosks, information terminals, research machines, and other means of distributing information publicly. Even inside a corporation they have great possibilities. Many legal firms have libraries where legal assistants and lawyers can do research. A few Windows-based Terminals could be put in the library to run a checkout application, legal research program, library database, and Internet browser.

7. *Customer service*   Terminal Server clients make very flexible point-of-sale terminals. Terminal Servers are a great solution for point of sale, where sales representatives need access to special information. For example, a realty office could use Windows-based Terminals to display its database of homes to buyers. A central database could be updated regularly with pictures of the homes available, their interiors, and their features. Queries could be quickly done against this database to generate a list of prospective homes. Other pertinent real-estate applications could also be distributed to employees' desktops, such as a mortgage calculator or contract form-maker. Terminals with home information could also be made publicly available in the lobby, so buyers could do their own searches.

8. *Task-oriented workers with low processing requirements*   Task-oriented workers are those who only need access to a small number of applications, which they use extensively in their work. Examples of task-oriented workers are data-entry and customer service personnel, receptionists, and secretaries. Terminal Server is a good solution for these workers, whose processing requirements are not high. If their applications do a lot of number-crunching, it would be best to run those apps locally and not on a Terminal Server.

9. *Harsh environments*   Windows-based Terminals are a good solution for harsh environments. Because they are relatively inexpensive and simple, they are easy to replace. They are also resistant to pilfering. Examples of this application would be terminals on a factory floor, in a machine shop, or on the workbench.

10. *Hand-held devices*   Hand-held devices used for data entry are a great way to use Terminal Server. These devices would be connected to the server using infrared or radio-wave technologies. Hand-held devices can be used for gathering experiment data in a lab and as inventory devices for use in a warehouse.

Situations in Which Not to Use Terminal Server

There are many situations in which you would *not* want to run Terminal Server exclusively. If you still need to distribute applications to these users from Terminal Server, a Net PC or high-end workstation running the Terminal Server client is a good option. Following is a list of five common situations in which use of Terminal Server is not recommended:

1. *Applications requiring heavy calculation*   Users who often run processor-intensive applications, such as developers and spreadsheet power-users, would significantly tax the resources of the server. Having them run their applications on Terminal Server can be done, but they will take up a large piece of the processing time, leaving less for other Terminal Server users. This quickly becomes an unreasonably expensive option, compared to running the same processes on the users' PCs.

2. *Applications using animation*   Because the only thing that goes across the wire are screen updates, if your screen is changing constantly, you will bog down the network with these updates.

3. *Publishing/drawing programs*   Publishing applications, such as desktop publishers, CAD applications, image editing, and drawing programs, are better run locally than off a Terminal Server. These applications place a burden on both the processing time and network bandwidth available.

4. *Unstable network*   Without a network, your users are dead in the water. If you frequently have network outages, are low on network bandwidth, or have users who can't take any downtime you should either consider other options or take steps to increase the reliability of the network before implementing Terminal Server.

5. *Users requiring the capability to work locally*   Some users may need to work after hours or on weekends, when the network may be down for maintenance. If you have users who regularly work late, make sure they have PCs capable of running their applications locally. Otherwise, *you* may end up staying late to do your network maintenance and upgrades.

It takes some planning to ensure that Terminal Server 4.0 and MetaFrame are used to their fullest capability and to meet the needs that they are best suited for. Terminal Server offers a great solution for providing your users with headache-free access to low-end applications such as data entry. On the other hand, for power-users, it can be a poor choice because their heavy processing needs will overtax the Terminal Server. When deciding how best to implement Terminal Server, always keep the final users and their application needs in mind.

3

Terminal Server Architecture

I T IS TIME TO BEGIN your exploration of the core architecture of the Terminal Server operating system. Because Terminal Server is based on Windows NT Server 4.0 you will find that, for the most part, their architecture is very similar. For those who are already familiar with the intricacies of Windows NT Server 4.0, the chapter begins with a discussion of the main differences between Windows NT Server 4.0 and Terminal Server. You will learn how, in the Terminal Server Edition, key components of NT Server 4.0 have been rewritten to support a multiuser environment.
For those who want more, this discussion is followed by a much more detailed coverage of Terminal Server architecture. This information is fundamental to your understanding and administration of the Terminal Server product.

Architectural Differences Between Terminal Server and NT Server 4.0

Before you get into the details of both NT Server 4.0 and Terminal Server 4.0 architecture, spend a moment learning the differences between the two. The fundamental difference is that Terminal Server architecture supports multiple sessions or desktops running at the same time, whereas NT Server 4.0 supports only one—the console. Each session running on Terminal Server must be isolated from the actions of all other sessions. Terminal Server handles this need by assigning each new session a unique Session ID. The Session ID is used to keep track of and keep separate each session's resources.

Although many components of the NT Server 4.0 architecture have been modified in Terminal Server, the three most significant components that have changed are the Object Manager, Win 32 subsystem, and the Virtual Memory Manager.

Differences in the Object Manager

The Object Manager is responsible for creating, managing, and deleting operating system and application objects. In the multiuser environment of Terminal Server each session must keep its objects separate from those of the other sessions. To keep them separate, Terminal Server appends the Session ID onto the end of each object that is created within the session.

Using the query object Terminal Server command, you can actually see this process in action. The query object command shows you a list of all current objects on the system. The list is usually rather long so you may need to dump it to a text file (query object > objects.txt).

The following output shows two of the many objects in the object list. Note the :1 and :0 that have been appended to the object names. These are the Session IDs of the sessions that these objects belong to. Had Terminal Server not kept these identical object names unique, using the Session ID number, they could not have been created.

```
C:> query object
.....
\BaseNamedObjects\NDDEAgent:1                    Semaphore
\BaseNamedObjects\NDDEAgent:0                    Semaphore
......
```

Differences in the Win 32 Subsystem

The Win 32 subsystem mainly handles graphical display requests and other Win 32 API calls for applications running on Terminal Server. On NT Server 4.0, a single instance of this subsystem is created, when the server is first booted, by the Session Manager (smss.exe). This instance handles the graphical display of the NT Server console desktop. Because Terminal Server must keep track of multiple desktops simultaneously, each session created on it must be assigned its own Win 32 subsystem.

As with the Object Manager, Terminal Server distinguishes the processes running in the different Win 32 subsystems using the Session ID. In this way, Terminal Server is able to keep all of the desktops running on it separate.

> **Real-World Tip: Gaining a Deeper Understanding with NT Utilities**
>
> Many of the concepts of Terminal Server architecture can be difficult to grasp and remember unless you can actually see them in action. Fortunately, there are several utilities, such as the query utility included with Terminal Server, that help you see what is actually going on inside. Not only are these invaluable learning tools, but they double as great troubleshooting tools. From time to time I will highlight where you can use a particular tool to gain a deeper understanding of the topic at hand.

Creating the Separate Win 32 Subsystems

Much like NT Server 4.0, when Terminal Server first boots, the Session Manager (`smss.exe`) starts a Win 32 subsystem for the console. Under Terminal Server, the console is always assigned Session ID 0. After the console processes are started, the Terminal Server service (`termsrv.exe`) instructs the Session Manager to start up two idle instances of the Win 32 subsystem to wait for client connections.

By going into the Task Manager on your Terminal Server (Ctrl+Alt+Del, Task Manager) and selecting the Processes tab, you can actually view the instances of the Win 32 subsystem that have been loaded (see Figure 3.1). The key user mode process in the Win32 subsystem is the Client Server Run-Time Subsystem process (`csrss.exe`). The CSRSS handles some of the non-graphical Win 32 API functions. Every instance of CSRSS also starts an instance of the WINLOGON process (`winlogon.exe`), which is responsible for the initial handling of the client logon. Note in Figure 3.1 that there are multiple instances of the CSRSS and WINLOGON processes and that each is assigned its own Session ID (ID column).

Differences in the Windows Manager and Graphics Device Interface

The Windows Manager and Graphics Device Interface (GDI) are the kernel mode portions of the Win 32 subsystem responsible for windows management and the handling of Win 32 API graphics calls. They both run as part of the `win32k.sys` system file. Because they are both part of the Win 32 subsystem, there is a separate instance of them running for every session.

The main difference between NT Server 4.0 and Terminal Server is with the GDI. Under NT Server 4.0, the GDI interacts directly with the video display driver for the server console. Suppose you are running Microsoft Paint at the server console. When you draw something in Paint, the Paint program makes a Win 32 API call to display

Figure 3.1   Processes in Task Manager.

what you are drawing onto the screen. This API call is eventually passed to the GDI. The GDI then instructs the video driver what to display by using standard video driver interface commands.

Although this technique works fine for server console display on Terminal Server, it does not work for remote terminal sessions. On Terminal Server, the GDI display commands must be packaged and sent across the network for display on the remote terminals. Terminal Server and MetaFrame both handle this through virtual display drivers. Both the RDP and ICA protocols have their own virtual display driver. Each remote session on Terminal Server runs its own instance of one of these drivers. The driver captures the video driver interface commands from the GDI. These commands are packaged up by the protocol and sent across the wire for display on the remote client.

Differences in the Virtual Memory Manager

The final major difference between NT Server 4.0 and Terminal Server 4.0 is in the Virtual Memory Manager. The Virtual Memory Manager maps virtual addresses used by processes into actual physical locations in the computer's memory. Each process running on Terminal Server is given up to a 2GB virtual address space within which to work. Because each process's space is kept track of separately, this NT Server 4.0 architectural convention works well with Terminal Server.

The difference occurs within the 2GB virtual address space used by the operating system itself. Because all processes running on server need access to certain areas of this operating system memory, the processes would conflict in a multiuser environment. The main culprit is actually the kernel mode component (win32k.sys) of the Win 32 subsystem. NT Server 4.0 was designed to run only one instance of this subsystem, which it loaded into the operating system memory space so that processes running on the console could have access to it. Because the arrangement of much of the operating system memory space was fixed, Terminal Server had to use a special technique to run multiple instances of the Win 32 subsystem.

To solve this problem, Terminal Server assigns each session its own virtual Session Space. Any memory calls to the Win 32 subsystem memory range by a particular session are redirected to that session's Session Space by Terminal Server. This redirection keeps each session's Win 32 subsystem memory separate from that of the other sessions.

> **Note for WinFrame Administrators: User and Kernel Mode**
>
> For those familiar with the architecture of NT Server 3.51 and WinFrame 1.x, it may seem strange to talk about user and kernel mode components of the Win 32 subsystem. Under NT 3.51 and WinFrame the Win 32 subsystem ran entirely in user mode. One of the main architectural differences between NT 3.51 and NT 4.0, and thus between WinFrame 1.x and Terminal Server, is that significant portions of the Win 32 subsystem have been moved to kernel mode to improve efficiency.

Windows NT Design Goals

For those who want to know more about Terminal Server architecture, you will note that this section starts at the beginning, with the development of the operating system it is based on. The design goals of the NT operating system are a large part of the reason why NT was originally chosen by Citrix for its multiuser product WinFrame, and why Terminal Server, which evolved from WinFrame, is possible.

When the development team for Windows NT was first formed in 1989, its mission was to design an operating system to meet the following design goals:

- *Extensibility*   For an operating system to be extensible, it must be modular with well-defined interfaces for applications to plug into. The extensible nature of NT is what makes Terminal Server possible.

- *Robustness*   An operating system must protect itself and other running applications from applications that "misbehave." This is especially important in the multiuser environment of Terminal Server, in which several users can be running several applications at once on the same system.

- *Scalability*   For an operating system to be used by major corporations, it must be scalable. You should be able scale from serving a handful of users to several hundred users on one server, by simply adding more hardware (processors and memory).

- *Portability*   The operating system must work with multiple hardware architectures and be able to be easily ported to new ones.

- *Compatibility*   NT must work with applications from several different operating systems, including OS/2, POSIX, DOS, and Windows 16-bit.

- *Performance*   Although feature-laden, the operating system still must maintain a competitive level of performance.

These design goals were met by using a highly modular architecture. The next section shows how Terminal Server takes advantage of this modularity to work within a multiuser environment.

Components of the Terminal Server Architecture

The goal of this section is to provide a thorough understanding of the underlying structure of Terminal Server. You will find that a thorough understanding of the operating system's operation at this level will help you to better troubleshoot Terminal Server and optimize its performance.

This section starts with the Terminal Server architecture diagram shown in Figure 3.2, and as you proceed through this section, the function of each part of the diagram is explained. As each part is described, refer back to the architecture diagram to see how a specific part fits in with the whole architecture.

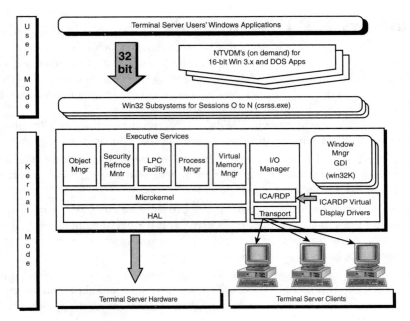

Figure 3.2   Terminal Server architecture.

Components of the Terminal Server operating system run in one of two modes: user or kernel:

- *Kernel mode*   In kernel mode, an application has direct access to the hardware. Examples of kernel mode applications are the HAL, Microkernel, Virtual Memory Manager, and device drivers. Because the applications are running in kernel mode, the system is not protected from them, and as a result, they must be written and tested very carefully. One poorly written application can lock up or crash the entire system.

- *User mode*   In user mode, an application can access hardware and operating system resources only through the Win 32 subsystem. This layer of isolation provides a great amount of protection and portability for applications. Examples of applications running in the user mode are DOS applications, Windows 3.x (16-bit), Windows 32, POSIX, and OS/2. If a user mode application crashes, the crash affects only the process the application is running in. By using Task Manager, you can simply delete the frozen process. All other applications continue to run without interruption.

The underlying difference between kernel and user mode has to do with the processor privilege level. Kernel mode is often referred to as *privileged mode*. On most modern processors, including Intel and Alpha, you can run an application at different privilege levels. On the Intel processors, there are four privilege levels or rings in which applications can run: 0–3. In reality, kernel mode refers to programs that run at privilege level 0. These programs have unrestricted access to all hardware and memory in the system. Programs running at privilege level 0 can set the privilege level for programs that they call. In contrast, user mode refers to applications and subsystems that are set by the kernel to run in privilege level 3. In this mode, applications are "boxed-in." The processor allows them to work only within their own memory areas. The processor also restricts them from directly accessing I/O, such as disk drives, communications ports, and video and network cards. To access these devices, applications must make a special gated call to a kernel mode program that handles the hardware.

Kernel Mode Components

A description of the components that make up Terminal Server must start at the heart of the operating system and work outward. The following sections first describe the Microkernel and HAL in detail and their relation to each other. These are the core components of the operating system. Next the Executive Services, which run in kernel mode, are covered.

Microkernel

Notice in Figure 3.2 that many of the modular components of the Terminal Server operating system are built around a Microkernel. The Microkernel is a small and very efficient program that handles the core functions of the operating system.

The Microkernel's primary job is managing the operating system's workload. As a manager, the Microkernel takes the tasks assigned to it by the applications and divides the work between the server's microprocessors. In a multiprocessor system, the efficiency of the Microkernel is critical. Without an efficient Microkernel, some processors become overburdened while others remain idle.

The Microkernel actually resides in either `ntoskrnl.exe` or `ntkrnlmp.exe` in the `SYSTEM32` directory. The `ntkrnlmp.exe` file is the multiprocessing version of `ntoskrnl.exe`. It is specially written to handle multiprocessor synchronization.

Processes and Threads

Terminal Server applications and the operating system itself divide their work between processes and threads. An understanding of the basics of how applications, processes, and threads interact is key to understanding how the Microkernel works. This knowledge is also important when administering Terminal Server. You need to know what processes and threads are when you use tools such as Performance Monitor, Task Manager, and the Terminal Server Administrator.

- *Processes*   A process is a program under control of the NT operating system that in essence is given its own room in memory and resources to work with by the operating system. When a process is started, an address space is set up for it. A process has its own variables and can request from the operating system its own access to the hardware below it. The operating system keeps track of what each process is doing by assigning it a unique process ID. Furthermore, Terminal Server keeps track of the processes that each session is running by assigning them Session IDs.

  When an application is run, it can request that the operating system start up as many processes as it needs to do its tasks. Most applications run with one or two processes.

■ *Threads* For processes to get any work done, they divide their work into threads and have the operating system execute them. A thread is a piece of executable code that can be run on a single processor. The Microkernel works by dispatching these threads to the processors based on their priorities.

HAL

The *Hardware Abstraction Layer (HAL)* is what the Microkernel communicates through when it needs to send threads to the processors or I/O devices. The HAL shields the Microkernel from the differences in the hardware below it. Suppose you are using a Micro Channel Bus instead of a standard PC bus, or various types of multiprocessor arrangements. For each of these machine specific setups, a HAL is written, normally by the manufacturer. The HAL translates the standard HAL requests that the Microkernel makes into code that the processors and I/O devices can understand. In this way, the HAL provides a uniform interface for the Microkernel to use the capabilities of different hardware platforms.

The HAL is also used by many device drivers to access the hardware. The HAL shields these drivers from the differences in the structure of the hardware below them by providing a uniform interface.

Real-World Tip: Processes in Action

One of the many ways to see processes in action is to use the query process utility:

1. Log on as administrator to Terminal Server.

2. Go to the command line and run **query process** *.

You will see a list of all processes running on the system, to whom they belong, and what their process IDs and session IDs are.

Run your favorite program and look at the processes again using the query process command. Notice the new processes that are created when your program opens.

You can also see processes in action by using the Terminal Server Administrator tool (described in Chapter 12, "Administering the Desktop and Server") and Task Manager (as shown in the earlier "Differences in the Win 32 Subsystem" section). You can also measure many performance parameters of the operating system by process by using Performance Monitor (described in Chapter 13, "Measuring Performance").

Real-World Tip: Viewing Available HALs with UPTOMP

The HAL is implemented in the hal.dll. Notice on the Terminal Server CD under the I386 directory that several files start with HAL (HAL*.*). When you first install Terminal Server, you have the option of picking your processor. At this point, the appropriate HAL is expanded, renamed hal.dll, and put in your SYSTEM32 directory.

If you have the NT Server 4.0 Resource Kit, available from Microsoft, run the Uni to Multiprocessor utility (uptomp.exe) from the Start menu, by selecting Resource Kit 4.0, Configuration. By using this utility, you can view a description of the various HALs on your install CD.

Executive Services

There are seven primary Executive Services. These are the basic kernel mode components that the applications running in user mode use through the Win 32 API:

- Object Manager
- Security Reference Monitor
- Process Manager
- Virtual Memory Manager
- Local Procedure Call Facility
- I/O Manager
- Windows Manager and Graphical Device Interface

Refer to Figure 3.2 for a general idea of how these components relate. The Executive Services are all kernel mode components that provide the operating system services that are used by the applications running on Terminal Server. The following sections describe each of the kernel mode components in detail.

Object Manager

One of the most important components in the Executive Services suite is the Object Manager. Because Windows NT is an object-oriented operating system, most of its resources are treated as objects. The Object Manager is in charge of creating, tracking, protecting, and deleting system objects. The Object Manager is responsible for objects used in both kernel mode and user mode. As described in the section "Differences in Object Manager," the Object Manager keeps track of both global objects that are used by all sessions and session-specific objects that applications running in a particular session create.

To truly appreciate the importance of the Object Manager, you must understand what objects are. Nearly every time an application accesses a file, displays something on the screen, communicates with a device, or accesses most operating system resources, it does so through an object. Objects have three main components: properties, methods, and handles.

- *Properties* Used to provide information to applications and users about the object.
- *Methods* Used for controlling objects.
- *Handles* Used by the operating system to identify which object an application is referring to.

The following are examples of some of the objects under Windows NT:

- Port objects
- Memory objects
- Process objects
- Thread objects
- File and directory objects

Suppose an application needs to access a file on the hard drive. The application would access the file through a file object, as shown in Figure 3.3, which has properties such as file name, file size, date of creation, current status, and attributes. These properties allow the application to gather information about the object. To do something with the object, the application must use a method. Examples of file methods are create file, delete file, open file, read file, and close file. To keep the file object unique, the operating system assigns it a handle. The handle is used by any applications that reference the file object.

Security Reference Monitor

For an operating system to be secure, not every application or user can have access to all resources on the system. This is especially important with Terminal Server, in which several users can access the same resources remotely. For example, if the operating system is not protected, a single Terminal Server user could accidentally delete a critical system file that everyone needs. The Security Reference Monitor provides both authentication and auditing services to protect your server from instances like this. NT security works through access control lists (ACLs) and security IDs (SIDs).

- *SIDs* Every user and group in the security database has a unique identifier called a SID. An example of a typical SID is S-1-15-50-101. This unique number is associated with the user or group until it is deleted. Even if another user or group is created with the same name the newly created user or group is assigned a different SID.

- *ACLs* Every Windows NT object has an access control list (ACL). An ACL is made up of access control entries (ACEs). The ACE contains the SID of a user or group, along with their security rights to this object.

When a user logs on to Terminal Server, an access token object is created for him that lists his SID, the SIDs of all the groups that he belongs to, and special privileges such as the ability to set system time.

In Figure 3.4, you see the access token object for the fictitious user John.Smith. Note that the object contains all of the SIDs for all of the groups that John.Smith belongs to. This object acts like a set of keys to unlock the system resources. When John.Smith tries to access the Office 97 directory, the Security Reference Monitor retrieves the ACL for this directory, compares it to the SIDs in John.Smith's access token object, and grants him Read and Execute rights to that directory.

Figure 3.3 Accessing a file through the file object.

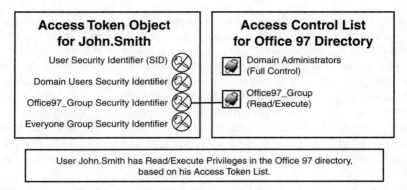

Figure 3.4   Access tokens and ACLs.

Another example is an accounting database file with an ACL that allows the Accounting group full access, but restricts the Management group to read access. When someone in the Management group logs on, she receives an access token object that includes the SID for the Management group that they are in. When she tries to access the accounting database file, the Security Reference Monitor checks the ACL for the file and finds that the Management group has only read access to the database. The user is then allowed to open the database with read-only access. If the user tries to write to or delete the database, the Security Reference Monitor prevents this action.

Another important function of the Security Reference Monitor is auditing. Suppose the accounting database in the preceding example is set up for strict auditing. When someone tries either successfully or unsuccessfully to access the file, such as an attempt to delete it, the Security Reference Monitor records the attempt.

Process Manager

In the earlier discussion about the Microkernel, processes are described as being part of applications and having threads. The Process Manager keeps track of all processes running on the system and their associated threads. The Process Manager also handles the opening and closing of processes and threads.

Every process is assigned a security access token when it first starts. The Process Manager works closely with the Security Reference Monitor to ensure that the process goes through security checks before accessing protected objects.

Virtual Memory Manager

The applications that run on your Terminal Server need memory to hold their data and code. The Virtual Memory Manager is responsible for keeping track of this memory and assigning it to your programs.

In older operating systems such as MS-DOS, there was a set amount of memory available and only one program was loaded into it at a time. Under Terminal Server there can be several users simultaneously running multiple applications at the same time on the same server. For these applications to work together properly, they are each given their own block of virtual memory. Applications are allowed to access only their own memory and are blocked from accessing others' memory. In this way, each application runs in its own protected space in the Terminal Server's memory.

Each process running on your Terminal Server is allocated 4GB of virtual memory. The first 2GB block is for user programs and the second 2GB is reserved for operating system storage. This is a lot of memory. Few machines will have even close to this amount available. The magic of the Virtual Memory Manager is that although you may not actually have this amount of memory, to your applications it *appears* as if this amount is available. If you have a program that runs out of room, the Virtual Memory Manager swaps other portions of memory to the hard disk to make room for the running application. To your application, the memory still appears as one contiguous space.

Although the memory assigned to your program appears contiguous, the actual physical locations in memory where the program is stored does not have to be. The Virtual Memory Manager divides the memory and hard drive space available into 4KB pages It handles assigning these 4KB pages to your programs to actual physical memory locations, as shown in Figure 3.5. Because programs are starting and stopping all the time on your server, without the Virtual Memory Manager there would be gaps of available memory left unused after a program releases it. The Virtual Memory Manager fills in these gaps when programs make new requests for more memory.

The Virtual Memory Manager also provides very important performance information to your system. On Terminal Server, having the right amount of memory to handle all users and applications is critical. If there is not enough memory, the response time slows down tremendously for all users because the Virtual Memory Manager must swap out memory to disk to make room. In Chapter 13, you learn how to use Performance Monitor to effectively monitor how much memory you are using, and how much you need.

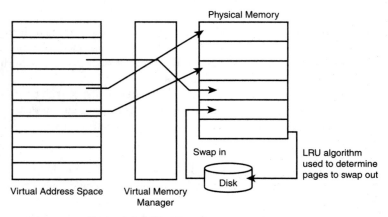

Figure 3.5   The Virtual Memory Manager.

Local Procedure Call Facility

The Local Procedure Call Facility (LPC) handles the client/server communication between applications and subsystems and between processes. It handles only those calls that occur locally. The actual request is sent to the Win 32 subsystem, which in turn sends the request to the appropriate Executive subsystem for display. This level of complexity is hidden from the application, which must only call the procedure and receive a response.

Terminal Server makes extensive use of LPCs. The Terminal Server service (`termsrv.exe`), which handles most of the background administration necessary on Terminal Server, uses LPCs to communicate with other processes. For example, when new connections need to be made, the Terminal Server service calls the Session Manager (SMSS) to create idle connections that wait for new users who need to log on.

I/O Manager

The I/O Manager handles all input and output to your system's devices, and as such it is probably one of the busiest subsystems. I/O Manager handles data input and output from all of the following and more:

- Hard drives using NTFS or FAT
- CD-ROMs
- Floppy drives
- SCSI devices such as scanners, or removable storage such as a JAZ drive
- Serial and parallel ports
- Tape drives
- Mouse and keyboard
- Network cards

The I/O Manager includes a cache manager that handles caching all disk and network input/output. Caching can improve performance greatly during heavy disk access by caching or copying data that it reads from the disk drive into memory. The next time this data is accessed, it is taken from memory instead of the disk, which results in much quicker access. Caching is also beneficial during writes. A process can write to the cache by using the *lazy write* service. Rather than the process having to wait for the disk to finish processing before sending it more data to the disk, the process simply writes additional data to the cache. The next time the processors are not busy, the cache is written to disk; meanwhile, the process can carry on uninterrupted.

Whether you are connecting your clients to the Terminal Server via the network, serial ports, or modems, the I/O Manager is the main Terminal Server subsystem that they will interact through. Because of this, it is important that you keep up with new releases of I/O drivers so that you always have the most up-to-date and efficient versions.

Windows Manager and Graphical Device Interface

The Windows Manager and Graphical Device Interface (GDI) are responsible for handling all Win 32 API video requests by applications. They are the kernel mode components of the Win 32 subsystem. These components are covered in detail in earlier section "Differences in the Win 32 Subsystem."

How the Windows Manager and GDI relate to the Win 32 subsystem is diagrammed in Figure 3.2. Note that there is one instance of the Windows Manager and GDI (win32k.sys) for every session running on Terminal Server.

User Mode Components

So far, the discussion has focused on kernel mode components. The applications the users are running are in user mode. For Terminal Server to support as many types of applications as it does, it has subsystems that emulate the native environments that these applications would run in. There are environment subsystems for DOS, Windows 16-bit, POSIX, and text-based OS/2 applications. All of these subsystems are designed to basically convert the foreign application's calls into calls that Terminal Server's native environmental subsystem, the Win 32 API, can understand.

Win 32 Subsystem

The Win 32 subsystem handles most Win 32 API calls. All user mode applications communicate with the Terminal Server operating system through this API. Because Terminal Server is a strictly controlled operating system, all interaction between applications and hardware must occur through the Win 32 API. Applications that try to improperly bypass the operating system and access hardware directly are shut down or stopped by Terminal Server. This level of application security brings a great amount of stability to the operating system. Even poorly written applications do not have the ability to lock up the entire operating system with an improper direct hardware call, such as a direct disk write. This is very important for Terminal Server because it typically is running several applications at once for several users.

The Win 32 API, supported by the Win 32 subsystem, is an object-oriented set of functions and procedures that allows the application to control all aspects of the operating system. Because the Win 32 API for NT is very similar to the one for 95, in general, Win 32 applications can run on either API without modification. One of the main advantages of an API is the layer of isolation it provides to the operating system. As long as the Win 32 API stays the same, the entire kernel can be rewritten, and Win 32 applications would still run.

The Win 32 subsystem can be divided into two subsystems: the Executive and the Console. The Executive subsystem resides in the kernel mode; it is made up of the Windows Manager and GDI. The Executive handles the majority of the graphics related Win 32 API calls. The Console runs in the user mode and provides text window support, hard-error handling, and shutdown. The system file that makes up the Console is Client Server Runtime Subsystem executable (`csrss.exe`).

DOS and Windows 16-bit Applications

To run DOS applications, you need a converter to take the application's device calls and convert them to Win 32 API calls that Terminal Server can understand. The module that does this is the NTVDM or NT Virtual DOS Machine. The NTVDM simulates a DOS environment for DOS applications. It provides simulation for the following:

- Standard DOS 21 Interrupt services
- ROM BIOS calls
- Device calls, such as to the keyboard or video

When a DOS application runs on Terminal Server, it is assigned three threads. The first thread is the one in which the application runs. The second thread provides a heartbeat to simulate timer interrupts for the MS-DOS applications. Many DOS applications rely on the timer interrupt to time various procedures and to control the execution of programs. The third thread is for console I/O.

Although you can run DOS applications on terminals attached to Terminal Server, there are disadvantages:

- You can expect a 10–25% decrease in performance of a typical DOS application due to the Win 32 translation. This extra processing time for translation reduces the amount of processing time available for other users of the Terminal Server. You cannot run as many users concurrently if all users are running DOS applications.

- Users cannot run DOS applications full screen unless they are using the DOS-based client. Because Terminal Server comes with only Windows-based clients, you cannot run DOS applications full screen unless you purchase the MetaFrame add-on and use the DOS-based client.

- 16-bit Windows was originally designed to be basically a graphical operating system that runs on top of DOS. Because it was designed to run on top of DOS, many Windows 16-bit applications rely on DOS system calls, such as interrupt 21. For 16-bit Windows applications to run under Terminal Server, Terminal Server runs them on top of the NTVDM. This provides the DOS environment that they need. Consequently, you face the same decrease in performance with Win 16 applications as you do with DOS.

- Windows 16-bit applications must also make Windows API calls, such as to manipulate graphic objects on the screen. To do this, Win 16 applications must use a converter to convert Win 16 API calls to Win 32 API. That conversion is performed by the Win 16 on Win 32 or WOW exec. Like the NTVDM, the WOW takes its effect on system performance. You still must have more memory and processing speed to run 16-bit Windows applications than for a similar Win 32 applications. Because of the significant performance hits, it is not recommended to run DOS or Win 16 applications with Terminal Server, if you have the choice.

4

Terminal Server and MetaFrame

ONE MAJOR QUESTION ON THE MINDS of many administrators is whether or not they need MetaFrame, the add-on product for Terminal Server from Citrix. Out of the box, NT Server 4.0, Terminal Server Edition is a very powerful product. It may already have all the features you need for your network. If this is the case, MetaFrame is a luxury more than a necessity. However, many administrators absolutely need the extra features that MetaFrame offers. This chapter explores these features in detail and the solutions that they are intended for.

Understanding MetaFrame

MetaFrame is an add-on product from Citrix that you install on your existing Terminal Server. As you are shown in Chapter 5, "Installing Terminal Server and MetaFrame," the installation process is very simple. You install it from the server console using the MetaFrame CD, which normally takes less than 10 minutes.

The MetaFrame installation adds many features to the base Terminal Server operating system, but does not change the base features. Your existing Terminal Server clients are still able to connect just as they did before MetaFrame was added. You can take advantage of the new features offered by MetaFrame only by installing MetaFrame's ICA client software on the client workstations. This client software is included on the MetaFrame CD. In Chapter 9, "Installing Clients," you learn how this is done.

Citrix is working constantly to provide support for the widest range of client operating systems. Compared to Terminal Server, MetaFrame currently supports a much wider variety of clients. Out of the box, Terminal Server allows you to connect to it from the following Windows operating systems:

- Windows NT 3.x, 4.x, 5.x (both Intel and Alpha), Server, and Workstation
- Windows 95 and Windows 98
- Windows for Workgroups 3.11
- Windows CE (built into many Windows-based Terminals)

If you have non-Windows clients on which you want to run Windows sessions, you must purchase the MetaFrame add-on. With MetaFrame, you can run Windows terminal sessions on all versions of the Windows operating system plus the following:

- *Macintosh*   Client is available for 68030/040 and Power PC-based Macintosh.
- *UNIX*   Currently there are clients available for the following versions of UNIX and above: HP-UX 10.20, Sun Solaris 2.5.1, SunOS 4.1.3C, IRIX 6.2, OSF 1.32, and IBM AIX 4.1.
- *DOS 3.3 and above*
- *OS/2 v2.1/3.0/4.0*
- *Web browsers*   Both Microsoft's and Netscape's browsers have been tested with MetaFrame. There are both MIME-based and Java Web Clients.

Keep in mind that the list of clients supported by MetaFrame is growing constantly. For the latest list of clients supported by the product, check out Citrix's Web site at www.citrix.com.

In the sections that follow, you learn about the features that are available when you install MetaFrame. Each subsection describes one new feature, what it is intended for, and how it compares with any similar feature available in the base Terminal Server product. Remember that these features are available only after you have installed MetaFrame on the server and have changed the clients to the MetaFrame ICA client.

Multiple Protocols

Both RDP and ICA, the two protocols used on Terminal Server, rely on an underlying transport protocol to carry them across the network. Microsoft's RDP protocol supports two types of protocol transports, TCP/IP and TCP/IP across RAS for remote access.

In contrast, MetaFrame's ICA protocol works on top of IPX/SPX, NetBIOS (NetBEUI), and TCP/IP. ICA supports RAS for remote access, but RAS is not necessary because it also supports dial-in asynchronous connections directly into MetaFrame. If you have an environment in which you do not want to be limited to just TCP/IP, or you need support for direct dial-in connections to the Terminal Server, then MetaFrame may be for you. For more information about the RDP and ICA protocols, see "ICA and RDP," near the end of this chapter.

Direct Connections

For users familiar with plugging terminals directly into the server, or who already have a serial terminal wiring infrastructure in place, MetaFrame supports direct serial connections. It also supports direct video and keyboard connections into special multiuser video and keyboard interface cards by using the DirectICA technology.

Automated Local Device Redirection

For many people, the automated local device redirection capabilities of MetaFrame are important. When you log on to MetaFrame, by default, your local drives and printers become incorporated into your Windows terminal session.

With Terminal Server alone, a client can access his local drives and printers by using standard NT device sharing. MetaFrame, on the other hand, supports automatic redirection of the clients' Windows printers, local drives, LPT ports, COM ports, audio, and clipboard.

- *Printers*   You can print to any of your local printers from any Windows program running on MetaFrame. Your printers automatically appear as `[Computer Name]#[Printer Name]` in the Printer Control Panel in MetaFrame after you log on. This nomenclature differentiates them from the printers that were already set up on the server before you logged on.

- *Local drives*   You can see your local drives, such as your C: drive. This means you can easily access data on your local drive from any program running on MetaFrame. Because the server's C: drive and your local C: drive use the same letter, MetaFrame offers you the option during install to move the server's drives later in the alphabet, starting with M:. This way, your local drives retain their original drive letters when you log on. The `\\CLIENT` UNC server is created by MetaFrame to represent your local resources. You can map drives to your local resources simply by mapping them to `\\CLIENT\[Drive or Port name]`.

- *COM and LPT*   The COM and LPT port redirection allows you to use your local COM and LPT ports with a program running on MetaFrame. This is often important if you are running DOS applications on MetaFrame. Because DOS applications cannot print to Windows printers, the only way for them to print is through the LPT or COM ports.

- *Audio redirection*   Multimedia applications running on MetaFrame can play sounds and music on your local speakers. MetaFrame gives you control of the audio quality and thus the amount of bandwidth it takes for sending the audio across the network to the clients. This feature is intended primarily for LAN environments in which network bandwidth is not much of an issue. Client computers can play 8- or 16-bit mono or stereo .WAV files at 8, 11.025, and 44.1KHz.

- *Clipboard redirection*   Gives you the ability to cut and paste from applications running on MetaFrame to applications running locally.

Accessing Client Drives and Printers with Terminal Server

With Terminal Server alone, if you want to be able to print to your local printers or work with data on your local drive, you must first share them on the network. When you log on, you will need to map drives to these shares and create printers in Terminal Server for the workstation's shared printers. This means that you must establish Microsoft networking and file and print sharing services on your client and be able to see the server across the network.

Shadowing

One justly heralded feature is *shadowing*. With shadowing, MetaFrame allows an administrator to basically remote control any user's Terminal Server session. This is very handy for remote technical support because you can see the user's desktop and troubleshoot a problem by simply shadowing his or her session.

Publishing and Embedding Applications

Application publishing is a very powerful MetaFrame feature. Instead of your users having to log on to a desktop and then run their applications, with MetaFrame you can simply select their applications from a list that you publish.

With application publishing, you can also restrict which users or groups are allowed access to individual applications. Finally, you can even embed applications on your Web server. Remote users can then run your applications by using standard Web browsers.

Pooled Anonymous Users

MetaFrame's pooled anonymous users are primarily intended for use for web access to embedded applications. One anonymous user for each licensed connection is automatically created by MetaFrame when it is first installed. Anonymous users do not require a password. They are given certain restrictions by default: There is a 10-minute idle timeout, disconnected sessions are logged off automatically, and the user cannot change the password.

When an administrator publishes an application, she can decide whether to require an explicit user logon or allow anonymous logons. If anonymous logons are allowed, MetaFrame does not require a user name or password when a user attempts to run an application from his Web browser; instead MetaFrame logs the user in automatically as the next available anonymous user.

This is more of a convenience feature than an advantage, intended primarily for embedded Web applications. You can also create anonymous logons manually with Terminal Server alone.

Seamless Windows

Seamless Windows works only with published applications and only for network connections to MetaFrame. In addition to providing a uniform appearance for your applications, seamless Windows takes up only one connection on MetaFrame, no matter how many application sessions have been opened. This allows for the seamless integration of multiple published applications onto your users' desktops.

Persistent Caching

MetaFrame supports persistent caching across sessions of commonly used screen graphics, such as icons and bitmaps. This feature can speed initial client access to applications because the MetaFrame client "remembers" the graphics used in previous sessions and does not require all of them to be sent again across the wire. This feature requires the use of local drive space at the client and can be turned off if this presents a problem. Terminal Server alone also supports caching, but it dumps the cache after the session is logged off.

Automatic Client Update

MetaFrame is set up to automatically update your client software with the latest version as your clients log on. The administrator can distribute new versions of a client to all users of the server by simply installing the new client at the server.

TAPI Support for Direct Asynchronous Connections

With WinFrame, you had to detect and define your own modems both at the server and at the dial-in clients, even if the modems were already defined. Because modems and modem speeds are constantly changing, the supported modem list became out of date quickly. To fix this problem, you would often have to manually edit .INF files with the settings for your particular modem.

With MetaFrame, this problem has been resolved. MetaFrame works with existing modems that are already defined on the user's desktop or on the server, by using TAPI support. Even DOS or Win 16 clients can read modem settings from standard Windows 95/NT modem configuration files.

Option Pack Features

There are some additional features available with MetaFrame that require you to purchase and install feature option packs after installing MetaFrame. Although these option packs can be too expensive for some, these features are indispensible for others. The following is a description of the two main option packs currently available for purchase: load balancing and SecureICA.

Load Balancing Option Pack

Load balancing is a very important feature for large networks with many users. *Load balancing* makes the most efficient use of your servers by evenly distributing the users across them, based on the reported load by the servers. Load balancing is also a good solution for high availability. If a server goes down, or is taken down, users can log back on to the next available server.

With load balancing, you publish your applications across groups of MetaFrame and WinFrame 1.7 servers called *server farms*. When users try to access the applications on the server farm, they are automatically placed onto the server with the least current workload. If any of the servers are found to be constantly over- or underutilized, the administrator can use the Load Balancing Administration tool to adjust the criteria by which the server reports its current load to the server farm. The reported server load can be adjusted using the following criteria:

- Number of current users versus licensed users
- Number of current users versus a set maximum number of users, pagefile usage
- Swap file activity
- Processor utilization
- Number of sessions and memory load

Load Sharing Using DNS Round Robin

It is important to point out that there is an alternative to load balancing that works with both Terminal Server and MetaFrame, called DNS round robin. *DNS round robin* is a load-sharing solution often used in the world of web and FTP servers. Basically, you create several name records (A records) on your DNS server for the same host name, each with the IP address of one of your Terminal Servers. When a client requests the host name, the DNS server returns the next IP address in the list in round-robin fashion. In this way, users are evenly distributed across the servers in the DNS round-robin list. Of course, your DNS server first must be able to support round robin. Most versions of BIND support it, as does Microsoft's DNS services, which are included with both Terminal Server and NT Server 4.0.

Be aware, however, that there are some disadvantages to this technique as compared to the MetaFrame load-balancing solution described previously. The main disadvantage is that round robin is a *load-sharing*, and not a *load-balancing*, solution; it does not take into account the current load on the servers before assigning new users to them. To avoid overloading a particular server with DNS round robin, you must ensure that the servers in your server farm are of similar capacity and that you monitor them carefully.

SecureICA Option Pack

The SecureICA Option Pack enhances the security of your MetaFrame server by offering strong encryption (up to 128 bits) of the communications between the client and server. Although Terminal Server alone supports up to 128-bit encryption to RDP clients, RDP can support only Windows-based clients.

The SecureICA Option Pack comes with an installable server component and special SecureICA clients for DOS, Windows 16-bit, Windows 32-bit, and most common web browsers.

One of the most common uses for the SecureICA Option Pack is for remote access across the Internet to corporate applications that you have published on your web server by using MetaFrame.

ICA and RDP

When comparing Terminal Server to MetaFrame, you might find that you are actually comparing RDP and ICA. Microsoft's RDP and Citrix's ICA are the core protocols that allow Terminal Server technology to work. They are both specially designed to package, carry, and deliver Windows desktops and other client information across a network in an efficient manner. The following sections cover the basics of the two protocols.

Microsoft's Remote Desktop Protocol

The Remote Desktop Protocol (RDP) is the default protocol for the Terminal Server operating system. RDP is based on the International Telecommunication Union's (ITU) T.120 protocol series. The T.120 protocol series was designed to handle video conferencing and application sharing across networks. Microsoft has already implemented the T.120 protocol in such products as NetMeeting. Building on their past experience with T.120, Microsoft made modifications to the base protocol in order for it to work well for packaging the desktops running on Terminal Server for distribution across the network.

When you first install Terminal Server, you might notice that the option to install TCP/IP is forced on. The reason for this is that RDP needs TCP/IP to transport it across the network.

Citrix's Independent Computing Architecture

The Independent Computing Architecture (ICA) protocol is the key piece of the Citrix MetaFrame add-on. ICA can run over TCP/IP, NetBEUI, IPX/SPX, and asynchronous connections. Like RDP, ICA also works by packaging up the Windows desktops running on Terminal Server with MetaFrame and having them delivered to the clients.

Many of the features that MetaFrame adds to Terminal Server are actually the result of features within the ICA protocol. ICA supports a wide range of client redirections and is thus what makes possible such MetaFrame features as audio, printer, and file redirection.

Author's Note: ICA Versus RDP

Many administrators want to know flat out which protocol is the fastest: ICA or RDP. Both Microsoft and Citrix have carefully optimized their respective protocols for high performance over low-bandwidth connections. The truth is that, over a networked TCP/IP connection, both protocols perform similiarly. This assertion is supported by the results of two extensive performance tests, one done by Compaq and one by HP on their own servers. The results of these tests can be obtained at either of these URLs:

http://www.compaq.com/support/techpubs/whitepapers/ecg0680698.html

http://www.hp.com/netserver/techlib/perfbriefs/index.htm

Even with the results of these tests, several questions still remain on the performance differences between ICA and RDP. Which is faster over a modem line, for example: RDP on RAS, or ICA using direct dial-in? The full answer to this type of question may never be tested; instead, the deciding factor for choosing MetaFrame over Terminal Server alone should be based on the features covered in this chapter. This is what is known, and what is important.

Installation, Configuration, and Administration

Installing Terminal Server and MetaFrame

T HE KEY TO ANY SUCCESSFUL Terminal Server installation is proper planning. This chapter begins with a discussion of how to plan for both large and small Terminal Server implementations. This includes the major decisions you must make when installing Terminal Server. This discussion is followed by details of the installation process of Terminal Server and how it differs from standard NT Server 4.0 installation. The chapter ends with coverage of the installation of MetaFrame. Because MetaFrame is an add-on product, you must have Terminal Server installed first.

Planning the Installation

You will find that the actual installation process for Terminal Server is very similar to that of NT Server 4.0. This can deceptively lead you to believe that the decisions you need to make are based on similar reasoning. This is not true! Terminal Server (TS) may look and act like NT Server 4.0, but it is an entirely different animal with very different hardware and resource needs. Before going any further, you must understand the following differences between NT Server 4.0 and TS that are important to installation.

- *File security* Security is always important. Under TS, you must be especially careful that you have a secure file system. With NT Server 4.0, you gave access to your server's data by using shares and then assigned rights for users to the share or the directories beneath it. Because users access the server across the network, they can see only what you decided to share with them. In TS, however, users not only have access to shares, but they also can run applications off of the server's local hard drive. If you are not meticulous when implementing your server's file security, users could destroy critical system files or accidentally save confidential files in public rather than private areas. For this and several other reasons that will be covered shortly, you should choose NTFS over FAT for your file system during the installation.

- *Reliability* Server reliability is critical in a multiuser environment because all application processing occurs at the server. In a standard NT server environment, if your server went down, your users may still be able to work locally, their documents still in memory on their PCs. With Terminal Server, the computing environment is more like that of a mainframe. If the mainframe goes down, everyone's terminal goes dark and no one can work. Imagine how frustrated you would be if you were typing in a large document when all of a sudden your Windows Terminal screen went black and your document was lost. In this chapter, you learn the steps you can take to help ensure the reliability of your Terminal Server.

- *Performance* You should take a close look at the hardware resources you will need to support your users. Because all application processing occurs at the server, Terminal Server normally requires more server resources per user than standard NT Server. You are given specific guidelines in this chapter for determining the hardware you need.

Making Choices for a Secure System

One of your main concerns when first installing TS should be file security. The main decision you need to make on file security at this point is the format you want to use for your operating system partition. You basically have two choices during the installation: FAT or NTFS. It is strongly recommended that you install the operating system on a NTFS-formatted partition. When TS is installed on NTFS, the install program applies important default security rights to the partition, which helps prevent future users from damaging critical system files. With the original NT Server 4.0, there are several reasons you may have chosen to format the system partition as FAT instead of NTFS. The following section explains the main differences between FAT and NTFS and the reason why choosing NTFS during installation is important.

Differences Between NTFS and FAT

There are many differences between NTFS and FAT. The most important overall difference is that NTFS is an object-oriented file system. Although this may not immediately seem important, NTFS's object-oriented design is what makes its robust file security possible. Important security features such as auditing, file level security, and directory level security are not available with FAT because it is not an object-oriented file system. Although you can apply share-level security to a FAT partition, this does not offer any security from Terminal Server users, who have the same access to the partition as if they were sitting at the server console.

Every file and directory on NTFS is considered an object with properties. The following are some of the many properties that can be associated with a particular file or directory:

- Attributes, such as hidden, read-only, and system
- File data
- Audit settings, such as whether file access or deletion is audited
- File and directory access control lists (ACL), which list which groups and users have what access to the file or directory
- File name, date, and time of creation and last access

Another important advantage of NTFS being object oriented is that it is extensible. Developers can add additional properties to the file system to support new types of access. For Terminal Server administrators who have Macintosh users on their network, this is especially important. Microsoft's Macintosh services for NT extend NTFS by adding additional properties that support Macintosh files. In this way, your Macintosh users not only can run Windows sessions off your Terminal Server, but they can also save and retrieve files from it by using AppleTalk.

Converting to NTFS

Some administrators choose FAT instead of NTFS during installation because a FAT partition can always be converted later to NTFS using the `convert drive` command (`/fs:ntfs`). Although you can convert a FAT partition to NTFS later, Terminal Server does not apply any of the security detailed in Table 5.1 when you do it. This is a very important distinction: When you choose NTFS for your system partition during installation, a dialog box appears near the end of the installation process, indicating that security is being applied to the NTFS partition. At this point, all the rights are assigned to the system directories. If you convert FAT to NTFS after installation, no rights are assigned. By default, everyone has full access to everything on the partition! The recommendation is to always select NTFS during installation, rather than after.

Table 5.1 **NTFS Default Rights**

Server System Director	Everyone	Administrators	Server Operators	System Account
C:\	Chg	Full		Full
C:\Program Files and below	Chg	Full	Chg	Full
C:\TEMP	Chg	Full	Chg	Full
C:\USERS	List	RWX		Full
C:\USERS\DEFAULT	RWX			Full
C:\WIN32APP	Read	Full	Full	Full
C:\%System Root%	Read	Full	Chg	Full
C:\%System Root%\Config	Read	Full	Chg	Full
C:\%System Root%\Cookies	Read	Full	Chg	Full
C:\%System Root%\Cursors	Read	Full	Chg	Full
C:\%System Root%\Desktop	Read	Full	Chg	Full
C:\%System Root%\Fonts	Read	Full	Chg	Full
C:\%System Root%\Help	Chg	Full	Chg	Full
C:\%System Root%\Inf	Read	Full	Chg	Full
C:\%System Root%\Media	Read	Full	Chg	Full
C:\%System Root%\Nwspool	Chg	Full	Chg	Full
C:\%System Root%\Profiles	Chg	Full	Chg	Full
C:\%System Root%\Profiles \Administrators		Full		Full
C:\%System Root%\Profiles\All users	Read★	Full		Full
C:\%System Root%\Repair	Read	Full	Full	Full
C:\%System Root%\Shellnew	Chg	Full	Chg	Full
C:\%System Root%\System	Read	Full	Chg	Full
C:\%System Root%\System32	Read	Full	Chg	Full
C:\%System Root%\System32\Config	List	Full		Full
C:\%System Root%\System32\Dhcp	Read	Full	Full	Full
C:\%System Root%\System32 \Drivers and below	Read	Full	Full	Full
C:\%System Root%\System32 \Inetsrv and below	Read	Full	Full	Full
C:\%System Root%\System32\LLS	Read	Full	Chg	Full
C:\%System Root%\System32 \OS2 and below	Read	Full	Chg	Full
C:\%System Root%\System32 \RAS	Read	Full	Full	Full
C:\%System Root%\System32\Repl	Read	Full	Full	Full
C:\%System Root%\System32\Repl \Export and below	Read	Full	Chg	Full

Server System Director	Everyone	Administrators	Server Operators	System Account
C:\%System Root%\System32 \Repl\Import and below	Read	Full	Chg	Full
C:\%System Root%\System32\Viewers	Read	Full	Chg	Full
C:\%System Root%\System32 \Spool\Wins	Read	Full	Chg	Full
C:\%System Root%\System32\Clients	Chg	Full	Chg	Full
C:\%System Root%\System32\Lserver	Chg	Full	Chg	Full
C:\%System Root%\Application Compatibility Scripts	Read	Full	Chg	Full

Read = Read-only access

RWX = Read, write, and execute

Change = Read, write, execute, and delete

Full = Read, write, execute, delete, change permissions, and take ownership

★ Individual users are given full access to their own profile directories. They only have read access to the others.

Speed—FAT Versus NTFS

FAT is generally considered faster than NTFS on partitions smaller than 500MB because of the additional overhead imposed by the NTFS disk structures. For this reason, many NT administrators make a small FAT system partition and a large NTFS data partition. With Terminal Server, however, this is not recommended. The difference in performance, if any, is minimal compared to the security problems that could occur by not having file and directory level security on your system partition. Normally you are better off making a system partition larger than 500MB and formatting it by using NTFS.

Drive Size—FAT Versus NTFS

FAT partitions on Terminal Server can currently be up to only 4GB in size. This limitation is quickly reached with today's drive sizes. NTFS, on the other hand, has a practical size limit of 2TB (terabytes). Because NTFS can handle much larger drive sizes than FAT and is considered more efficient on larger drives, the following is recommended: Make your server into either one large NTFS partition or into two or more smaller NTFS partitions—one for the operating system and applications and the others for data and users. One thing many administrators may not realize is that you have a 4GB limit during setup on the size of the NTFS system partition. Because NT copies files to the FAT partition before it converts the partition to NTFS, you are limited to 4GB because of the FAT 4GB (1024 cylinder) limit.

Running Applications on NTFS

Some administrators choose FAT simply because they are most familiar with it. They may also have had experiences in the past in which applications did not seem to run correctly on NTFS. If you find that you have a problem running a particular application on NTFS, it is much more likely that the user does not have sufficient rights to run the application than that application simply will not run on NTFS. Application problems due to NTFS are very rare.

To isolate the cause of an application problem, first try running the application as an Administrator equivalent with full rights to the applications and operating system directories. If this works, then NTFS is definitely not the culprit. Take a closer look at the files your application needs access to. You can use Table 5.1 to isolate the rights your application needs to the operating system directories, if this is where the problem is occurring.

Another possibility is that you tested the application on a compressed NTFS partition. Some timing-sensitive applications may not work on compressed drives. Try testing the application again on an uncompressed NTFS directory or partition. Also give the software publishers a call and see if they have had similar problems and know of a better solution. If you still find that your application will not run on NTFS or runs better on FAT, leave space during installation for a 500MB or smaller FAT partition from which you can run this application. Make sure you still install your operating system on a NTFS partition to maintain its security.

Emergency Recovery—FAT Versus NTFS

With Terminal Server, if one of the critical boot files is missing or you have a corrupted driver, you may not be able to start the operating system. Because FAT is not as secure as NTFS, you can boot from a floppy and have full access to the system partition files. The administrator can then replace missing or corrupted files by copying them from the installation CD.

With NTFS, you can still replace any missing files by booting from the install floppy disks and selecting Emergency Recovery from the main installation menu. The emergency recovery process scans your hard drive for any missing files and prompts you for their replacement.

Real-World Tip: Sidestepping Partition Size Limitations

You can circumvent this limitation by using one of the many third-party partitioning utilities such as Partition Magic by PowerQuest (www.powerquest.com). The ones that work with NTFS normally allow you to expand NTFS partition size without losing any data. You can create a 4GB NTFS partition during install to have all the important security applied automatically, and then expand later it to the size you want.

It is also a very good idea to make an emergency recovery disk during the installation of Terminal Server. You will be presented with this option part way through the install. The emergency recovery disk contains the Registry and other critical system settings files that you will need to recover your server.

Making Choices to Improve Reliability

Reliability is key to a Terminal Server installation. Not only do you need to take steps to prevent downtime, but you also must be able to quickly bring the server back up in case of an unexpected problem. If users are using Windows-based Terminals (WBT), when Terminal Server goes down they will not be able to work at all. Thus it is critical, especially in environments with large numbers of WBTs, that Terminal Server be as reliable and supportable as possible.

For your server to be as reliable as possible you must start with reliable hardware. Also, it is very important to document your installation to ensure that it can be repeated easily. The following section covers some of the issues involved with choosing reliable hardware as well as good techniques for documenting your installation.

The Hardware Compatibility List

You need to be very careful when selecting hardware for Terminal Server. Hardware drivers are written in the kernel mode, and thus have direct access to many of the operating systems resources. If you have ever experienced the *blue screen of death,* a blue-colored error dump screen produced after an unrecoverable error, you know how helpless you can feel with hardware related problems.

Hardware problems can often become manifest as intermittent lockups. Your server will be working fine all day with no problems, and suddenly your phone lights up with calls from users complaining they can no longer access the server. When you take a look at the server you see the blue screen or a server lockup and are forced to reboot to bring your server back up. To prevent this from happening with Terminal Server, you must make some important decisions before installation even begins.

Before installing Terminal Server, always make sure that the hardware you choose for Terminal Server is on the Windows NT Hardware Compatibility List (HCL). You can find the Hardware Compatibility List at www.microsoft.com/hwtest/hcl (see Figure 5.1). Do an advanced query for Windows NT 4.0.

> **Real-World Tip: Booting from a Floppy**
> There are some third-party utilities available for NTFS that allow you to boot from a floppy and work with your system partition files. One excellent utility is the ERD Commander, available for purchase at www.sysinternals.com. The full read-write version of this utility allows you to boot from a floppy, access your NTFS partitions, and use the DOS-like commands.

Because Terminal Server is based on NT 4.0, the HCL for Windows NT 4.0 applies. To get their products on this list, hardware manufacturers must subject their equipment to rigorous testing by using Microsoft's own testing utilities. Although this testing does not completely guarantee that you will have no problems with the hardware, it is a good start. It is also important to note that only servers whose hardware is in the HCL are fully supported by Microsoft.

If a driver for the device you have chosen was not included on the original Terminal Server CD-ROM, you can find the driver that was tested with the device on this web site. There will be a disk icon (refer to Figure 5.1) that you can click to go to the driver download page. It is highly recommended that you start here before any Terminal Server installation. Do a search for all of the hardware you plan to use for your Windows Terminal Server, including the following:

- *Server model*   The HCL includes compatible, tested server models from a wide variety of server manufacturers. There are often important notes on BIOS levels and their compatibilities on the HCL list. If you are using a multiprocessor system, make sure that you have the correct HAL for your system.

- *Video adapters*   Video adapters are a frequent cause of blue screens of death. Make sure your adapter is on the list. Many video driver adapters, which you will need during installation, are available from the HCL Web site.

- *Network cards*   During installation it is important to have the correct network card drivers. You cannot finish the install process without loading drivers and having them available for at least one network card.

- *Storage devices*   Ensure that your hard drive controller is on the compatibility list and that the driver is included with the standard NT installation. If it is not, you must download it and have it available for the installation process.

- *Modems*   If you are using MetaFrame with dial-in client access or Terminal Server with RAS, make sure your server modems and communications card are on the HCL. If the modem is not on the list, you must obtain the latest modem.inf file from the manufacturer and merge it with the [Term Server Dir] \SYSTEM32\RAS\MODEM.INF file after Terminal Server is installed. More details on modems are provided in Chapter 14, "Terminal Server and Remote Access."

Real-World Tip: Install Processors First

Always install all of the processors before you install Terminal Server, and make sure you choose the multi-processor version of the HAL for your system. You may have to reinstall the entire operating system if you add processors at a later time and your system currently has the single-processor HAL installed.

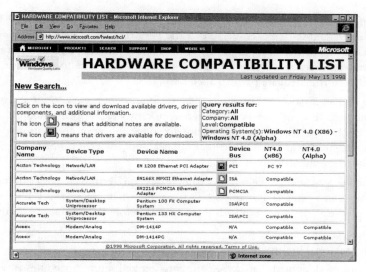

Figure 5.1 Microsoft's Hardware Compatibility List Web site.

Choosing RAID Systems

One of the most critical choices of hardware in terms of reliability is your storage system. In general, RAID (Reliable Array of Inexpensive Disks) storage systems can provide the highest level of reliability if you choose the correct RAID level. Most administrators choose RAID level 1 (mirroring) or 5 (disk striping with parity).

RAID can be implemented with either software or hardware. The Terminal Server operating system supports three levels of RAID—0, 1, and 5—out of the box. However, because of the performance hit taken by the overhead of implementing RAID, it is recommended to go with a hardware-based RAID solution. This is especially true of RAID level 5, in which the parity of every block written to the hard drive has to be calculated.

Documentation During the Planning and Testing Stage

Documentation is a very important factor in your server's reliability. Your server documentation should start before you begin the initial work with the server. Documentation is important in every part of a server's life including the initial planning stages, installation, and maintenance.

When you first begin to plan and test your Terminal Server network, you should document the many decisions that need to be made and the criteria by which you made them. Planning and testing involves several important steps. From each step, you should create a document to record what was decided during that step. While the particular steps may vary depending on your environment, here are some suggested documents for common planning and testing steps:

- *Network Design Document* Having both physical and logical network design documents is important for making future network troubleshooting easier.

- *Performance Testing and Baseline Documents*   One of the most important parts of planning and testing is ensuring that the performance of your Terminal Server is adequate. Chapter 13, "Measuring Performance," covers performance testing in detail. Before putting your server into production be sure to read that chapter and perform adequate performance testing.

- *Application Installation Document*   The techniques necessary to install an application onto Terminal Server can differ significantly from normal application installation. It is very important to document your application installations thoroughly. Chapter 10, "Installing Applications on Terminal Server," covers application installation in detail.

- *Naming Standards Document*   As you create your Terminal Server and its users, groups, and printers, it is important to follow a naming standard. The best time to produce a naming standards document is before the servers are set up.

Documentation During Installation

A good time to document hardware configuration and setup procedures is while you are installing a Terminal Server. Appendix C, "Disaster Recovery Kit," provides a collection of forms to help you do this called the Disaster Recovery Kit (DRK). You will need these in case of a major server failure. Even for regular maintenance this documentation can be handy. Make copies of the DRK forms and start filling them in during the server installation. You will have to enlarge the forms in order to make them fit well on 8 1/2" × 11" paper. When the installation is finished, make sure all the driver disks you needed are labeled and put into a binder along with the server documentation. Keeping all of the pieces you will need for a reinstallation in one location will save you a lot of stress and aggravation in an emergency.

Documentation After Terminal Server Is Installed

Controlling and documenting any changes or maintenance is very important with Terminal Server after it has been installed. Log forms are located toward the end of the DRK. Make several copies of these pages and put them at the back of the aforementioned binder. Require those who do maintenance on the server to sign the log and write down a description of what was done. If a lot of your maintenance is done remotely, you may instead want to create a log file on the server. This could be just a simple spreadsheet or text document that is filled in every time maintenance is done.

Imaging

One excellent technique for increasing the reliability of your server is by imaging it with imaging software such as Ghost. *Imaging* involves making a complete copy of your server's hard drive data after your server and all of its applications have been installed. If your server ever fails, you can quickly rebuild it using this image. This works well in situations where users store most of their data remotely and use

Terminal Server mainly just to access that data. This situation also works well for server farms (see Chapter 20, "Application Publishing and Load Balancing with MetaFrame," for more information about load balancing and server farms). In these situations, the data on the Terminal Servers themselves is not likely to change.

Imaging can also be a good technique for installations. After you have created the initial image of a working and tested server, you can copy the image to your other servers instead of installing Terminal Server and its applications from scratch. Of course, to copy the image, your servers all must be of the same model and capacity, or else this procedure likely will not work. This procedure also makes troubleshooting problems much simpler because you know the software patch level is exactly the same on all servers.

Making Choices for High Performance

Performance on a Terminal Server is a critical issue. Because everyone is sharing from the same performance "pie," the pie has to be large enough to give everyone a piece. Maintaining performance at the level needed involves a lot of decisions. Some of these decisions are obvious, such as having enough hardware and processing capabilities. Some are less obvious. The key steps required to ensure satisfactory performance on a Terminal Server are as follows: Start out with powerful enough hardware, test that hardware thoroughly by using real-world performance testing techniques as outlined in Chapter 13, and simplify the server to ensure that it is running only the processes that need to be run.

Terminal Server Hardware Requirements

Remember that Terminal Server clients are thin clients. Because all of their processing occurs at the server, the server needs to be "thick." Your Terminal Servers should be some of the most powerful servers in the server room. The four critical types of hardware that affect your Terminal Server performance the most are the processor, memory, network, and drive array. The requirements discussed in the following sections are minimums for running Terminal Server.

Processor

Processing power is normally the biggest bottleneck with Terminal Server. Having enough processing power for your users is critical for ensuring that they have adequate performance. How much processing power you need will varies greatly depending on how many users you have, what their applications are, and how actively they use them. Because of the large number of variables involved, it is best to start with a highly scalable system that can handle several processors. You then need to do extensive performance testing (outlined in Chapter 13) that will simulate normal, real-world user activity with the applications you intend to run on the server. The following are some general guidelines for choosing your processors. These guidelines are presented to give you a general idea of what kind of performance to expect when making your initial hardware planning. They do not supplant the need for thorough performance testing, however.

- Currently, you can expect to be able to support between 10 and 45 users per processor. The number you can actually support will vary widely depending on how many users you have, how heavily they use the server, and the type of processor and server you choose.

- Terminal Server has been shown to scale well across multiple processors. If you find that you can support 20 users comfortably on a single processor, you will likely find that with two processors your server can support between 30 and 40. Note that the more processors you run concurrently, the more overhead your server will incur managing them, and the fewer additional users each new processor will support.

- The size and speed of the internal cache on your processor can make a big difference. For this reason, try to choose processors such as the Pentium II, which has a large and fast internal cache.

- You should always choose a Pentium or higher Intel processor or an Alpha processor. Note, however, that Alpha processors are not supported by MetaFrame.

Memory

Memory is the next most important part of your server's performance. Memory normally will not cause a bottleneck with the server if you plan your memory requirements well. As with processor requirements, the amount of memory your server needs depends greatly on the applications your users use. It also depends on how many applications your users normally have open at the same time. For single-application, task-oriented users, the memory requirements are much less than for power users who may have several applications open simultaneously on their desktops.

Real-World Tip: Additional Capacity Recommendations

Many more resources are available to you for helping estimate the capacity you will need before making the initial purchase. One very good source of capacity recommendations is your server's manufacturer. Both HP and Compaq have performed extensive performance testing on their servers with Terminal Server. Microsoft also has done significant performance testing, the results of which can be found at the following sites:

```
http://www.hp.com/netserver/techlib/perfbriefs/index.htm
http://www.compaq.com/support/techpubs/whitepapers/ecg0680698.html
http://www.microsoft.com/windows/downloads/bin/nts/tscapacity.exe
```

Because of the many variables involved, it is important to perform real-world user simulation testing before implementing your Terminal Server.

The documented absolute minimum amount of memory you need with Terminal Server is 32MB. Although this is the documented minimum, you are best off starting with two to four times this amount as the minimum for your server. To this minimum number add between 5 and 15MB per user depending on the applications that they run. While this rough estimate will get you started, you should still do your own performance testing. Chapter 13 covers how to determine the amount of memory used per user. Also refer to the real-world tip in the earlier "Memory" section for studies that have more information about memory requirements.

Network

Planning your network is a very important part of Terminal Server installation. Without adequate planning your Terminal Server users may suffer dismal performance due to lack of network capacity.

Network planning is especially important for WAN access to Terminal Server. In general you can expect an average of anywhere between 10KB and 25KB of network bandwidth utilization per user. This will vary significantly depending on the graphical activity of your user's applications. It is still important to test these numbers to ensure that they are correct for your environment. Chapters 13 and 18 ("MetaFrame and UNIX Clients") get into specific techniques for ensuring that your WAN has adequate capacity for your needs.

Compared to all of the choices you need to make during server installation, choosing a high-performance network card for your server is very important. Always use a 32-bit network adapter. A PCI-based network adapter is currently your best bet. Using a 100Mbps network adapter connected to a high-speed switch is an excellent choice for Terminal Server networks.

Drive Array

The performance of your drive array can often play an important role in the performance of your Terminal Server. This depends a lot on how heavily your users will be using the server's hard drives. If you are running a database off the Terminal Server, such as a local accounting application or database, drive use will likely be very heavy. In this situation, it makes the most sense to invest in as high a performance drive system as is available and practical for your server.

Real-World Tip: Using Auto-sense

The auto-sensing feature available with many of today's network adapters is a common source of problems. You may find that the auto-sense only sets your server at 10Mbps instead of 100Mbps or that it causes network connection problems. It is always best to "lock down" your server's network cards at the highest speed possible on your network. Also, using full instead of half duplex can greatly enhance the speed. Full duplex is available with many high-performance switches. You might also consider locking the auto-sense feature of the switch or hub on the port that the server is attached to. Refer to the manufacturer's instructions for information about these devices and how to "lock down" the auto-sense feature.

If most of the applications your users will be using access data across a network, such as mainframe terminal emulators or client/server databases, then drive performance will not be as much of a factor.

Gaining Performance by Simplifying Your Server

Performance can be ensured by simplifying your server. The key is to run only what is absolutely needed. The guidelines presented here are general recommendations that should help improve your server's performance. Depending on your situation, you may or may not be able to implement them all.

- Terminal Server is such a flexible and robust operating system that it is tempting to load several services onto it at one time. Any production Terminal Server, especially one that will be supporting a large number of users simultaneously, should be run as a dedicated server that is a member of a domain. This means you should normally choose other servers for running your back office products. It also means you should not run it as a Primary or Backup Domain Controller (PDC or BDC). These options unnecessarily consume system processing time.

- Reliability is another reason not to load multiple services on top of Terminal Server. The more services you load, the greater the chance that a software bug will either down your server with the dreaded blue screen of death, cause a memory leak, or hoard your processing resources and bring your server to a crawl. In the real world this unfortunately happens more often than not. If you absolutely must have a service running, be sure you know which one it is and how to uninstall it. If your users complain of a server slowdown, try disabling the service for a short time while watching your processor and disk cache utilization in Performance Monitor. You might need to add more resources to your server to handle the application and your users at the same time.

- In general it is best to back up your server remotely across a high-speed link, rather than load complicated and bulky backup software locally. If you do load backup software locally, go with a tape drive and SCSI card that have been tested to work with your choice of backup software. Because tape and SCSI card drivers are kernel level software, they are a potential source of serious problems. The built-in NT Backup utility is an excellent choice for simple local backup.

- One of the biggest concerns with running backup software locally is the amount of processing and memory resources that backup software tends to need during backups and restores. Backups should be done at off-peak times, such as at night. If you have to do a restore of a set of files for a user, also try to do the restore during off-peak times. With some backup software, even a small restore can rob significant processing power and memory from the rest of the applications running on your server.

- Try not to store too much data on the server itself. This results in a large backup and restore window. In case of hardware failure, you want to be able to bring up your server as quickly as possible. It is recommended that you save space for only your applications, operating systems, and user settings directories. Data should be stored on other servers and accessed with shares. Of course, with databases and other data-intensive applications, it may be necessary to keep the data locally.

- As mentioned previously, running your server as a member of a domain instead of as a PDC or BDC is also important, especially with large domains. Domain logon attempts, security checks, and PDC-to-BDC synchronization can take up significant processing resources.

- Finally, as mentioned in the earlier "Making Choices to Improve Reliability" section, it is best to use hardware level RAID instead of Windows NT software level RAID. This is especially the case with RAID 5, which would take up processing time by calculating the parity.

Top Ten Installation Tips

This chapter has discussed many of the decisions you will need to make when installing Terminal Server. Now it's time to summarize those decisions in a top ten list.

1. *10 to 45 users per processor; 64 to 128MB minimum plus 5 to 15MB memory per user*   These are good guidelines to start with, but they do not supplant proper performance testing.

2. *Use only hardware that is on the Hardware Compatibility List*   It is important to verify that your hardware is on the Hardware Compatibility List (www.microsoft.com/hwtest/hcl). The list is also a good starting point for collecting the drivers you will need for installation.

3. *Make sure all processors and other hardware, such as NIC cards, are installed prior to installing the operating system*   Prior to installation, check in your BIOS to ensure that the system has detected all installed hardware and that the interrupt levels do not conflict. In general, on most systems you want to avoid using the cascade interrupt (2/9).

4. *Gather together the drivers for your hard drive adapter card, NIC card, video card, and HAL prior to installation*   The install process forces you to load a hard drive adapter, network card, video card, and HAL. If the drivers are not included with Windows NT's base set of drivers, you will need to have the driver disks in hand.

5. *Use NTFS for system partition. Do not use FAT and then convert to NTFS later*   At the end of the installation process, a default security setup is applied to your NTFS partition. If you choose FAT for your system partition, this security is not applied, even if you later convert the partition to NTFS.

6. *Documentation starts here*   Start documenting your server during the initial installation. The forms in the Appendix C, "Disaster Recovery Kit," provide you with a good starting set of documentation.

7. *Use hardware level RAID 1 or RAID 5*   Using RAID greatly improves your server's reliability. Using the software level RAID that comes with NT can tax your processing power.

8. *Simplify the server*   Your Terminal Server should be as dedicated as possible to serving Windows terminals to your users.

9. *Use a high-speed network adapter and lock your speed, transceiver, and duplex options*   A slow network adapter can easily become a bottleneck. Manually force your speed, transceiver (AUI, BNC, or RJ-45), and duplex options rather than having the card auto-detect them.

10. *Prepare for fast recovery*   Keep together your installation documentation and driver disks near the server to speed disaster recovery.

Installing Terminal Server

Up to this point this chapter has focused on the many planning decisions that you need to make prior to installing Terminal Server, such as acquiring adequate hardware for your intended use. It is time to cover the installation itself. This section first goes over the different installation options you have available and then covers the installation itself.

Installation Options

There are two supported installation options with Terminal Server.

- *Fresh install*   Starting with a fresh install onto a formatted hard drive is the surest bet for a successful installation. If you are making a dual-boot machine for testing, install Terminal Server last. Dual-boot machines often share the Program Files directory. Terminal Server comes with its own version of many files under Program Files. By installing Terminal Server last, it will overwrite any existing files under these directories with its own versions.

- *Upgrade install from WinFrame 1.6 or 1.7*   Upgrading an existing WinFrame 1.6 or 1.7 machine to Terminal Server is fully supported by Microsoft and Citrix. You will need Citrix's MetaFrame add-on product to retain all the original functionality and the ability to communicate with your existing Citrix clients. MetaFrame is installed after you finish the Terminal Server installation. All of your installed applications and users are migrated to Terminal Server 4.0. You must add the TCP/IP protocol to your server, if you weren't using it before. When the installation is complete be sure to test all your applications thoroughly.

Many administrators try an upgrade from an existing Windows NT Server 3.51 or 4.0 to Terminal Server. This option is not supported and not recommended. As Chapter 10 illustrates, when an application is installed on Terminal Server, many unique things happen in order for it to work in a multiuser environment. If you do decide to upgrade from an existing NT server, you must reinstall all of your applications. Make sure when you do reinstall the applications that you follow the techniques described in Chapter 10.

Terminal Server Install Media

The installation process for Terminal Server is very similar to the installation for standard Windows NT Server 4.0. The first step begins with deciding what media will be used to install Terminal Server. There are three primary methods available: CD-ROM, network installation, and server image.

Terminal Server CD-ROM

The simplest installation method by far is booting off the CD-ROM. This method is supported by most major servers today. If your server does not support bootable CD-ROMs, you can use the boot floppies instead. If you are upgrading an existing Citrix server, simply run `winnt32.exe` from the install CD-ROM.

You can also install from a CD-ROM by booting into good ol' DOS, loading the CD-ROM driver and running `WINNT /B` from the CD. If this option works the best for you, it would be a good idea to make a CD boot floppy. Simply format a floppy disk to be bootable. Next, copy the drivers for your CD onto it so that they load up when you boot to the disk. Copy basic utilities such as FDISK and FORMAT to the floppy disk. Keep this disk by the server. If you ever need to reinstall from scratch, you can use this disk to do it.

Network Installation

An alternative method for large rollouts is doing a network installation. With a network installation, you have a lot of control over the automation of your NT Server installation. If you are rolling out several Terminal Servers or would like to have a means of quick recovery, network installation is the way to go.

There are three steps in performing a network installation. First, you must copy the install CD to one of the servers on your network. Because the install CD is large, you must have available several hundred megabytes of space. If you are using only Intel (D:\I386) or only Alpha (D:\Alpha) processors, you can delete the directory for the other. Second, you need to create a network boot disk. The network boot disk is a bootable DOS disk that contains the `FORMAT` and `FDISK` commands, and also has enough drivers to attach to the network server that you have the copy of the CD on. Finally, you must perform the install. This involves booting from the disk, creating and formatting a partition for Terminal Server on your new server, and logging on to the network so that you can access the installation files.

Server Image

A server image can be the fastest installation method of all. Although a server image is discussed in detail in the earlier section "Making Choices to Improve Reliability," you may not realize the many options you have for this type of installation. Many people simply create an image of one of their fully installed servers, using imaging software such as Ghost, and copy it to a CD. In this way, all you need to create a new server is a bootable disk with the CD-ROM drivers for your servers and a copy of the imaging software. This is a very simple, fast, and effective solution. By booting off the disk and loading the image onto your server from CD, you can have an entire server rebuilt in under a half hour.

Another option is putting the server images on the network. In this way you could load one image for each model of server that you have. Using a network boot disk, you can boot into the network from the server and quickly load the correct image for your server from the network.

The Installation Process

For those who have installed Windows NT Server 4.0, the process for installing Terminal Server is nearly identical. The install is still started by using either winnt.exe or winnt32.exe, booting from the Terminal Server CD-ROM, or with the install floppies, which leads you to the character-based portion of the install. During this part, your initial hardware is detected and an initial set of files is copied to your server. The server then reboots into the graphical portion of the setup, where the installation is finished. The next few sections cover this installation process.

Starting the Install

The installation process can be started in any of three ways. The first way is to run winnt.exe from DOS or winnt32.exe from Windows NT or WinFrame 1.x. These install files are located in the D:\I386 (Intel x86) directory on the Terminal Server CD-ROM. The options for these files have not changed since Windows NT Server 4.0. Most administrators choose the /B option to avoid having to use install floppies. The second method is to boot from the Terminal Server CD-ROM. This is one of the fastest and easiest ways to install Terminal Server. The third method is to boot from the install floppies included with Terminal Server. This option is available for those who do not have a server capable of booting from CD-ROM.

Character-Based Stage

Next, you are taken to the character-based stage of the setup. During the character-based stage, the critical components of your PC necessary for the GUI install are detected. This includes components such as the keyboard, video adapter, CPU type, hard drive adapter, and mouse. Also you either select or create the partition on the hard drive where Terminal Server is to be installed. This portion of the setup is identical to the Windows NT Server 4.0 character-based setup. The following list briefly covers the steps involved in the character-based setup.

1. At the Windows Terminal Setup screen, press Enter to begin the install.

2. The install program attempts to detect your storage devices and lists them. Make sure it detects all of your drive controllers correctly. Press S to specify additional devices or Enter to accept those listed and continue.

3. Read the Microsoft License Agreement and press F8 to accept.

4. The install program performs a search for previous Windows NT Server installations and lists them. Highlight the installation you want to upgrade and press Enter or press N for a new install. If you are upgrading from WinFrame 1.6 or 1.7, highlight the WinFrame installation and press Enter.

5. The install program displays the detected keyboard, processor, video adapter, and pointing device. Verify that these have been detected correctly. If not, highlight the incorrect component, press Enter, and select the correct one from the list. Highlight the No Changes line and press Enter to continue.

6. Select the partition in which Terminal Server is to be installed from the list shown and press Enter. You can also press D at this point to delete a partition or press C to create a new one if necessary.

7. Select the directory for the Windows NT operating system files (\WTSRV is the default).

8. The install program gives you the option of checking the hard drive for corruption; press Enter to scan it.

At this point, the install program copies an initial set of operating system files to the hard drive. After the copy is finished, you are prompted to remove any floppy disks and reboot. You are now ready to move on to the next stage of the installation process.

Real-World Tip: Checking the Computer Component

One of the most important things to check at this point is the computer component, which indicates that HAL will be used by the operating system. If you have a multiprocessor system, make sure the install program detected to correct HAL. Refer to your server's manufacturer for the correct one. The following list shows which HAL or computer component types are available on the standard install. If your server is not listed, obtain the HAL driver from your server's manufacturer and install it.

AST Manhattan SMP
Compaq System Pro Multiprocessor
Corollary C-Bus Architecture
Corollary C-Bus Micro Channel Architecture
IBM PS/2 or other Micro Channel PC
MPS Multiprocessor Micro Channel PC
MPS Multiprocessor PCMPS Uniprocessor PC
NCR System 3000 Model 3360/3450/3550
Olivetti LSX 5030/40
Standard PC
Standard PC with C-step i486
Wyse Series 7000i Model 740MP/760MP

GUI-Based Setup

After rebooting the machine you are taken to the graphical portion of the setup. All the devices you detected in the character-based portion of the setup should now be working, including your mouse, keyboard, video adapter, and processors. In the GUI-based portion of the setup you are finishing up the installation.

1. Click Next at the initial Windows NT Server Setup screen.

2. Enter your Name and Organization and click Next.

3. At the Registration window, enter the CD-Key, normally located on the back of the CD cover, and click Next.

4. At the Licensing Mode screen, select the licensing mode you will be using and click Next. This screen refers to the Client Access Licenses that you have purchased for Terminal Server.

5. At the Terminal Server Desktops screen, elect the number of Terminal Server desktops you have purchased licenses for and click Next. Remember that according to Microsoft's current licensing scheme with Terminal Server, each desktop requires a Windows NT Workstation license.

6. Enter the Computer Name for the Terminal Server and click Next.

7. Enter the Server Type: PDC, BDC, or stand-alone server. Remember, as covered previously, for performance reasons it is usually best to set up all of your Terminal Servers as stand-alone servers and join them with an existing domain.

8. At the Administrator Account screen, enter the initial password for the Administrator and click Next.

9. Select whether or not you want to create an Emergency Rescue Disk and select Next.

10. At the Select Components screen, select the software components you want to have initially installed and select Next.

11. Select to install Internet Explorer 4.0 and click Next. This is a new option compared to NT Server 4.0.

12. Click Next to skip past the Windows NT Server Setup information screen.

13. Select whether the server is wired to the network and/or has remote access to the network and click Next.

14. Select whether to install the Internet Information Server (IIS) and click Next. (You can install IIS after Terminal Server has been installed if you wish.)

Real-World Tip: The Default Components

You might notice that the default set of components selected at the Select Components screen differs from standard Windows NT Server 4.0. The default selection is usually adequate. By default, games, wallpaper, and the Open GL and standard screen savers are not installed. It is best to not have these installed on Terminal Server. If these are installed on your server, they will be available to all of your users. Because these components are all graphically intensive, they are likely to cause performance problems if your users start using them.

Installing the Network

At this point, the installation process varies according to what options you have selected. If you indicated that your server is wired to the network, the installation first guides you through detecting and installing your network card, network protocols, and network services. If you indicated that your server has remote access to the network, you are also guided through installing the Windows NT Remote Access Service (RAS). The steps presented in the preceding sections are identical to what you would follow with Windows NT Server 4.0.

Finishing Up

After the network components have been installed and the network has been started, the install process continues with the final choices that need to be made. You are guided through choosing the time zone and selecting and testing your video adapter. A final set of files are copied to your server. At this point, the default NTFS security, described in the earlier section "Making Choices for a Secure System," is applied to the file system.

Terminal Server is now installed! When you reboot the server you are asked to log on for the first time. If you will be using MetaFrame, it is time to install it.

Installing MetaFrame

MetaFrame installs as an add-on option to Terminal Server. After Terminal Server has completed its installation, you can install MetaFrame from the server console. The steps that follow guide you through the installation and the choices that need to be made.

Real-World Tip: Installing Network Cards

If you are installing a multi-port communications adapter such as a Digiboard or Rocketport, the driver for these adapters usually installs as a network adapter. Terminal Server does not normally automatically detect these types of cards.

When you get to the point of the installation where you are installing the network card, you must have the driver disk for your communications adapter and manually install it. It is important to install it at this stage, especially if you will be using it with RAS, which is installed right after the network install.

Author's Note: Installing IE4

If you select to install Internet Explorer 4.0, Terminal Server reboots, logs on automatically into NT, and installs Explorer. After this installation is complete, you can reboot the server and log on normally.

1. Insert the MetaFrame CD-ROM and run `D:\I386\SETUP.EXE`. Click Next at the Welcome and Setting Up MetaFrame screens to begin the initial install of the product files.

2. At the MetaFrame Licensing screen, select Add Licenses. The screen shown in Figure 5.2 appears.

   This is the Citrix Licensing tool. If you need to add more licenses at a later time, after MetaFrame is installed, you can find this program under MetaFrame Tools in the Start menu.

3. Enter the license code from the back of the CD-ROM or from your license document. A typical Citrix license number follows the following format: XXX-XXXX-XXXX-XXXX-XXXXXX. It is a good idea to write down these serial numbers and keep them next to your server. The Disaster Recovery Kit in Appendix C has a place where you can record them. You will need these numbers if you ever have to reinstall.

4. Click OK to acknowledge the warning message and keep installing License Packs until you have installed all of the ones you have bought.

   You must activate these licenses when the install is finished. Citrix gives you 35 days to do this. See the next section, "Registering MetaFrame," to learn how to activate the licenses.

5. At the TAPI Modem Setup screen, select Add Modems if you will be adding modems for direct dial-in to your MetaFrame server; if not, click Next.

6. Read the instructions at the Client Drive Mapping screen carefully (see Figure 5.3) and press Next to continue.

7. At the Server Drive Reassignment screen, select whether you want to reassign the drive letters for your server and with which letter to start (see the following Real-World Tip).

The installation of MetaFrame is now almost complete. After the server reboots, you can use MetaFrame immediately. You should, however, take the time now to register MetaFrame.

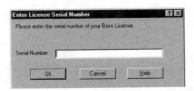

Figure 5.2   Citrix Licensing tool.

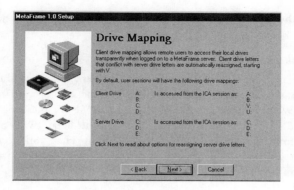

Figure 5.3   Client Drive Mappings.

Registering MetaFrame

Citrix tightly controls the licensing of the MetaFrame product. In order to use the product after 35 days, you must activate all of the MetaFrame licenses that you installed. Activating the licenses involves connecting with Citrix, receiving an activation code, and activating the licenses with the code.

Registration Methods

The first step is to register MetaFrame and receive the activation code. There are five methods to do this. For the first three methods, described in the next three sections,

Note for WinFrame Administrators: TAPI Support

One advantage of MetaFrame is its TAPI support. Basically, after you add a modem to your Terminal Server, all TAPI-enabled programs, such as MetaFrame, can use it. This is a big improvement over WinFrame, where you had to add modems to every program that used them using that program's proprietary method. Notice that the Add Modem dialog box is the same one used when adding a modem to the server through Control Panel|Modems.

Real-World Tip: Mapping Drives

When you log on to MetaFrame it , by default, creates drive letters in your MetaFrame session that are mapped to your local drives. This allows you to copy to or access them from programs running on MetaFrame.

Without reassigning drives when you log on to MetaFrame, the C drive you see in Windows Explorer is the C drive of the MetaFrame server. MetaFrame , by default, reassigns the C drive of your local machine to the V drive instead. Some people prefer to have their local C drive appear as C on the MetaFrame and have the MetaFrame drives be remapped to other letters. If so, choose to remap the server drives at this point. Be aware that this process is not reversible. You may also cause problems due to the difference in drive mappings across servers, such as logon scripts that fail.

you must run the Activation Wizard (select MetaFrame Tools | Activation Wizard from the Start Menu) as shown in Figure 5.4.

Registering with a Web Browser

If your MetaFrame server is connected to the Internet and you can browse Web sites from the server, then the simplest method is to use the Web browser to register. Run the Activation Wizard from the desktop or from the MetaFrame Tools group in the Start menu, and select Activate with Web Browser. Your default Web browser is launched and connects to Citrix's registration Web site. Here you are guided through entering your registration information. At the end of the registration you receive the activation code for the license that you registered.

Registering by Using TCP/IP Across the Internet

You can also register across the Internet by using Citrix's ICA client across TCP/IP. To ensure that this method will work, first try pinging www.citrix.com from the command prompt. If you do not receive a response, your server may not be fully connected to the Internet and this registration method will not work.

To register using TCP/IP, run the Activation Wizard and select Activate over the Internet. You are prompted to install the ICA 32 client first. This is necessary because you are actually registering with a Citrix MetaFrame or WinFrame server across the Internet. After the ICA 32 client is installed, it automatically attempts to connect to one of Citrix's registration servers. You then must enter the registration information. When you are finished, you receive the activation code.

Registering by Using a Modem

If you have a modem directly attached to your MetaFrame server, using it is one of the easiest methods for registering. From the Activation Wizard, select Activate by Modem. Just as in registering using TCP/IP, you are guided through installing the ICA 32 client

Figure 5.4   Activation Wizard.

first. The Activation Wizard then dials one of Citrix's registration servers using the client, where you can register the product and receive the activation code.

Registering by Fax or Phone

One of the advantages of using the preceding methods is that they are supported 24 hours a day, seven days a week, and you receive your activation code immediately. If you have problems registering by any of the preceding methods, you also have the option of registering by fax or phone. To register by fax you must fax in your Activation Data Form, included with MetaFrame, to the number on the form. To register by phone you must leave a voice mail message with your registration information at Citrix's Telephone Activation number, listed in the "Support Services" section of the Release Notes. Expect a three- to five-day turn-around time before you receive your activation code.

Activating MetaFrame

Now that you have received the activation codes for all of your licenses, it is time to activate them.

1. Run the Citrix Licensing tool, which is located in the MetaFrame Tools group in the Start menu.

2. Highlight the license you want to activate and select License, Activate License from the main screen.

3. Enter the activation code for that license in the window shown in Figure 5.5.

4. Repeat these steps for all the licenses you need to activate.

Congratulations! The MetaFrame and Terminal Server installations are now complete.

Figure 5.5   Entering the activation code.

6

Creating the Connections

IN CHAPTER 5, "INSTALLING TERMINAL SERVER and MetaFrame," you learn how to install both the basic Terminal Server product and MetaFrame. Now you are going to start filling in the details of what you need to know after the products have been installed. This chapter begins by going over one of the first things you need to check after installing Terminal Server—the connections that are available to your client. *Connections* are processes that have been set up for your Terminal Server clients to connect to. Connections receive incoming users and allow them to access Terminal Server services. Even though your initial connections are created by default, you need to be aware of what connections are, how to create them when needed, what connection options are available, and how to set their access permissions.

Connection Basics

Connections are the means by which your clients connect to your Terminal Server. Imagine that they are docks in a busy port. You have to have enough docks or your ships will have nowhere to land! In the same way, you must have enough connections on your Terminal Server for all of the clients who will attach to it.

Connections are defined by making connection entries using the Terminal Server Connection Configuration Tool. There must be one connection entry for every protocol combination that you want connections to be available for. With Terminal Server alone there is only one protocol combination possible—RDP over TCP—and thus only one type of connection entry. With the addition of MetaFrame you also get the ICA protocol, which runs on top of many different protocol transports, such as TCP, IPX, SPX, direct serial connections (asynchronous), dial-in modem connections (asynchronous), and NetBEUI (NetBIOS). For every ICA protocol combination you need, such as ICA over TCP, there must be a connection entry defined in the Terminal Server Connection Configuration Tool.

The following section discusses the basics that you need to know to set up a new connection on your server. Because of the wide variety of configuration options that are available with connections, the many options are covered in detail later in their own sections.

Connection Configuration Tool

To work with the connections and connection entries on your Terminal Server, you need to use the Terminal Server Connection Configuration Tool, which is located in the Start menu under Programs | Administrative Tools. When you first start this tool, it lists the connection entries that have currently been created for your server. With this tool you can create, delete, modify, and rename connection entries.

During the installation of Terminal Server and MetaFrame, the respective install programs will automatically create the initial RDP and ICA connection entries that your clients must have to connect to the server. Take a look at Figure 6.1. This snapshot was taken from a MetaFrame server loaded with IPX/SPX and TCP/IP, right after the initial installation of Terminal Server and MetaFrame. Notice that several connection entries have been defined automatically: ICA over IPX, ICA over TCP, and RDP over TCP. One initial connection entry has been created for each protocol combination currently available on the server, by their respective install programs.

This initial setup works well for most situations. Because the initial connection entries are set for "unlimited" connections, you do not have to worry about manually increasing the number of connections if you add more licenses. Terminal Server automatically keeps track of this for you by making connections available up to the number of licenses you have available. Generally there are only a few situations in which you would want to change this initial setup:

- *Adding or deleting protocols* If you add or delete protocols from the server, you must add or delete the related connection entries with the TS Connection Configuration Tool.

- *Changing options* There are many options that you may want to change for each connection entry. These options are covered in detail later in the chapter.

> **Note for WinFrame Administrators: Understanding Connections**
>
> All of this discussion of connections may initially seem confusing for those familiar with WinFrame. Connections are basically the Terminal Server equivalent to the WinStations you are used to with WinFrame. Instead of creating WinStations with the WinStation Configuration Tool, in Terminal Server you create connections with the Terminal Server Connection Configuration Tool.

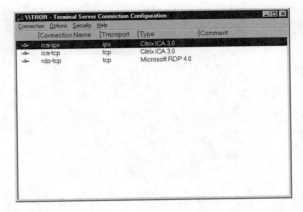

Figure 6.1   The Terminal Server Connection Configuration Tool.

■ *Adding/removing modems from your server (MetaFrame only)*   Although network connection entries are defined once for every protocol combination, you need to define connection entries individually for each modem with which you want your remote clients to be able to directly dial in to MetaFrame.

Creating Basic RDP Connections

Creating connections is a relatively easy process. This short subsection covers how to set up a basic RDP connection entry by using the Terminal Server Connection Configuration Tool. The many more advanced options that you can set are covered in their own sections later in the chapter. Here is how to set up the entry:

1. Open the Terminal Server Connection Configuration Tool. It is located in the Start menu under Programs | Administrative Tools.

2. From the Terminal Server Connection Configuration window, select New from the Connection menu or press Ins on the keyboard to create a new connection.

3. From the New Connection window, select Microsoft RDP 4.0 as the connection type from the drop-down list next to Type. Note that this window changes depending on what connection type is selected. Figure 6.2 shows the New Connection window that you see for an RDP connection.

Note for WinFrame Administrators: Automated Connection Creation

You will find that many aspects of connection creation have been automated with Terminal Server as compared to WinFrame 1.x. The availability of "unlimited" connections is a new feature. With WinFrame you had to manually define how many connections you needed to make available to your clients. Although "unlimited" connections does not mean you can use more connections than you are licensed for, it does mean that their creation is automated. Also, rather than creating all of the connections in memory at startup, as WinFrame does, Terminal Server creates connections as needed.

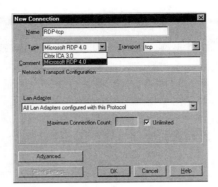

Figure 6.2   RDP New Connection window.

4. Fill in the Name and Comment sections. If you are assigning different protocols to different adapters, it is a good idea to specify in either the name or comment to which network adapter this protocol applies.

5. Select from the drop-down list under Lan Adapter the Lan adapter to which you want the RDP protocol bound. By default, RDP is bound to All Lan Adapters configured with this Protocol.

6. By default, the Maximum Connection Count is set for Unlimited connections. If you want to limit the number of RDP connections, uncheck the Unlimited box and fill in the maximum number of RDP connections you want to allow.

7. If you want to change the advanced options, such as autologon, timeout settings, encryption, and initial program, click the Advanced button. These settings are covered in detail later in the chapter.

8. Click OK to create your connections.

After the RDP connection is created, you are immediately able to attach to your server by using RDP clients, up to the maximum number of connections you defined or are licensed for.

Creating Basic ICA Connections (MetaFrame Only)

MetaFrame

Because of the many more protocol transports available, the decisions involved in creating ICA connections are a little more complex. This subsection covers the setup of a basic ICA connection entry and then covers the advantages and disadvantages of the many transports available for ICA connections.

To set up an ICA connection entry using the TS Connection Configuration Tool, follow these steps:

1. Open the Terminal Server Connection Configuration Tool located in the Start menu under Programs, Administrative Tools.

2. From the Terminal Server Connection Configuration screen, select New from the Connection menu.

3. Select Citrix ICA 3.0 for connection Type.

4. Select the Transport that you want for the connection (async, IPX, SPX, NetBIOS [NetBEUI], or TCP). See the section that follows for more information on choosing your protocol. Figure 6.3 shows the New Connection window after selecting TCP. As with the RDP New Connection window, the window changes depending on the protocol and protocol transport selected.

   For the network transports to work, you must have already installed the protocol by selecting Network, Protocols from the Control Panel. The transports that are available, their descriptions, and the server protocols you must have loaded for them to work are covered in the following section.

5. Fill in the Name and Comment. Because many different types of ICA connections can be made, it is a good idea to be descriptive in the comments.

6. Either set the Maximum Connection Count to what you need or leave it set to Unlimited.

7. (For network connections) If you plan to assign this connection to a particular network adapter instead of all of them, select the correct LAN adapter from the drop-down box under Lan Adapter.

8. (For asynchronous connections) Select the modem this connection is for from the drop-down list next to Device. Figure 6.4 shows the New Connection window for async connections.

Figure 6.3   ICA New Connection window (TCP/IP).

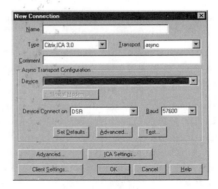

Figure 6.4 New ICA Connection window (async).

9. Click the Advanced, ICA Settings, or Client Settings button to set these options, which are covered in detail in "Connection Options," later in the chapter.

10. Click OK to create the connection.

After your ICA connection is created, you can use it immediately.

ICA Protocol Transport Choices

You have several protocol transport choices with an ICA connection. Perhaps you are wondering which one you should choose and why. The following is a list of each of the choices available and their advantages and disadvantages:

- *Async (Asynchronous protocol)* This protocol supports all types of asynchronous access to the server through standard asynchronous communications ports, such as COM1 or COM2, or multi-port communications cards, such as a Digiboard. Async supports both standard modems and null modem direct cable connections. Async connections are ideal for directly connecting to MetaFrame.

- *NetBIOS* The version of NetBIOS that is referred to with Terminal Server connections is the one that rides on top of NetBEUI (NetBIOS Extended User Interface). It is a very simple protocol with low overhead. NetBIOS is not routable and is a good choice only for small networks or test environments.

Real-World Tip: Asynchronous Connections

Recall that in network connections, you define a connection once, and as many clients as you have license for can connect to it. In contrast, with asynchronous connections, only a single device can connect to one connection at a time. You must define a new connection for every modem attached to your server. One easy way to create new asynchronous connection entries is to use the copy feature.

To copy a connection, highlight the asynchronous connection you want to copy and select Copy from the Connection menu. This creates a new copy of this connection.

- *IPX*   This is a routable protocol commonly found on Novell networks. IPX is an ideal choice if your clients currently only use IPX.

- *SPX*   SPX works at the Session layer, above IPX. Because with SPX a session is established between clients and server, the link tends to be more stable than IPX alone. It also means that there is extra protocol overhead that can degrade performance. SPX is routable. Generally IPX is a better choice for Terminal Server unless you are having lost connection or timeout problems.

- *TCP*   This is the most widely supported protocol. You will find most clients support TCP. This protocol is well designed for WANs and is routable. In general, TCP/IP is the best choice for a networking protocol as long as your clients have support for it.

Connection Options

The real power of connections is the connection options that are available. To see the different options, double-click on one of your connection entries. When the New Connections dialog box appears, you will see buttons for Advanced, Client Settings, and ICA Settings (if MetaFrame is not installed, only the Client and ICA buttons are available). Click any of these buttons to open a dialog box in which you can select from the related options.

Connection options apply to all users that connect by using a particular connection entry, such the entry for RDP over TCP shown in Figure 6.1. There are options for things such as AutoLogon, Initial Program, Audio Quality (ICA), Timeouts, and more.

The following sections describe the different connection options you have available. Because these options can often be controlled on different levels, the first section considers the differences between configuring these options at a connection, user, and client level. The section following that describes the purpose of the options available after clicking the Advanced, Client Settings, and ICA Settings buttons.

Configuring Options at Different Levels

To understand how options are set, you must first understand the difference between setting options at a connection, user, and client level. If you are already familiar with WinFrame, the differences between these levels will be familiar to you. While the different configuration levels are being explained, take a look at Figure 6.5.

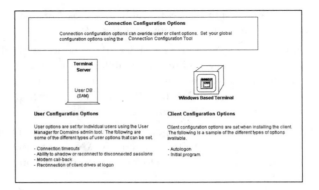

Figure 6.5   Connection, user, and client configuration options.

Setting Options at a Connection Level

Options set at the connection level are global options for a connection type. They are what this chapter is all about. If you want to set an option that affects all users who connect to the server using a particular protocol combination, setting them at the connection level using the TS Connection Configuration Tool is the way to do it. Connection options, such as Shadowing, override whatever has been set on either a user or client level.

Setting Options at a User Level

Many of the same options that can be set on a connection level, such as Timeouts and Initial Program, can also be set on a user level. User-level options are set by using the User Manager for Domains administrative tool. These options apply only to the user that you set them for. These options and how to set them are covered in more detail in Chapter 7, "Creating Users and Groups in Terminal Server."

Setting Options at a Client Level

Many of the connection-level options can also be set at the client level. Client configuration options are set by using the client software. Client configuration options allow you to set up AutoLogon or run a particular application when the session is first started (Initial Program setting), for example. Just as with user-level options, client options can be overridden by connection-level options.

Take, for example, the Initial Program setting. Suppose you want to set up a particular client so that it automatically runs a particular application upon logon. You would set up the Initial Program option on the client. If instead you wanted all users to run a single application when they log on using a particular connection, you would set up the Initial Program at the connection. Client-level options and how to set them are covered in Chapter 9, "Installing Clients."

Advanced Options

You can get to the advanced options by selecting the connection entry you want to modify, pressing Enter, and then clicking on the Advanced button in the New Connection dialog box. The Advanced Connection Settings dialog box appears with its wide variety of advanced options. Advanced options are settable for both RDP- and ICA-based connection entries. The following list briefly describes the different advanced options that are covered in the following subsections. Study Figure 6.6 as the options are being described.

- *Logon option*   Allows you to enable or disable logon ability to the connection.

- *AutoLogon option*   Enables you to define a username and password by which all users of this connection automatically log on.

- *Timeout settings option*   Lets you define idle and disconnect timeouts for users who attach to this connection.

- *Security option*   Allows you to select the level of encryption enforced for users of this connection.

- *Initial Program option*   Launches a particular application for all users of this connection.

- *Miscellaneous advanced options*   Provide other advanced options such as enabling or disabling user wallpaper.

Logon Option

Logon ability for all users using this connection entry can be enabled or disabled with this option. This is a good way to disable the logon ability of users while doing maintenance. If you need to disable the logon ability of a single user, you should use User Manager for Domains instead.

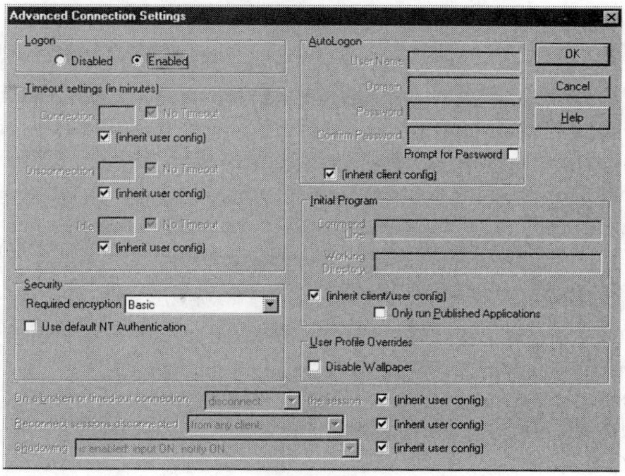

Figure 6.6   Advanced Connection Settings dialog box.

AutoLogon Option

By default, the connection inherits whatever AutoLogon option has been set up at the client level. If you override this option and fill in the AutoLogon information here, then all clients who use this connection will automatically logon using the username, domain, and password you entered.

Although this defeats the logon security of the Terminal Server, it can be useful in some situations. Perhaps your clients are running a client/server or a terminal emulation application from Terminal Server, which requires them to log on to a remote host. Rather than force the users to log on twice (once to Terminal Server and then again to the remote host), you can set up AutoLogon to Terminal Server. Remember that if you enable AutoLogon at the connection level, you cannot log on, using that connection, as anyone else!

The AutoLogon option can also be useful if you are configuring an asynchronous connection. Remember that if you configure a network connection, it applies for everyone who connects to the Terminal Server using that network protocol combination. If, instead, you configure an asynchronous connection for AutoLogon, that configuration applies only to the users accessing the server from that particular serial port or modem. By using the AutoLogon option, you can set up a modem bank or bank of Windows-based Terminals (direct serial connections) that log on to the Terminal Server automatically.

Another good application for the AutoLogon feature is for a publicly accessible Windows-based Terminal, such as in a kiosk. You can set up the kiosk WBT to either automatically dial in or connect across a WAN link to a central Terminal Server and log on to it by using the AutoLogon username and password.

Timeout Settings Options

By default, timeout settings inherit their configuration from what is set for the user in User Manager. All timeout settings are set in minutes. The three timeout settings and situations in which they are useful are as follows:

- *Connection*   The connection timeout refers to the maximum amount of time a user can be connected before the session is disconnected or reset. Whether the session is disconnected or reset is determined by the On a Broken or Timed Out Connection option, covered in "On a Broken or Timed Out Connection," later in this chapter. This option is useful for public access terminals in which you want to restrict the amount of time a person can use the terminal.

- *Disconnection*   The disconnection timeout refers to how long a session can remain in a disconnected state before it is reset. This can be a very useful option. Remember, however, that resetting a disconnected session causes users to lose any data that they had in memory. If your users will be working with data locally, such as with a word-processing application, you may not want to set this setting too low. If, instead, users are accessing data remotely, such as through a client/server application, resetting the session will not likely cause problems. Disconnected sessions take up valuable system resources because the system must keep track of the applications that the user left open. In general, it is recommended to set this for between 60 and 240 minutes. If you have a network problem that causes users to become disconnected, this setting gives you time to diagnose the network problem, bring the network back up, and have users reconnect where they left off. At the same time, user sessions that were disconnected by accident and never reconnected are logged off after a reasonable amount of time. If you find that a lot of users are leaving their sessions disconnected or if user applications are not affected adversely by being reset, you might want to decrease this value.

- *Idle* This is another useful parameter. Idle timeout is the number of minutes of inactivity before a session is either disconnected or reset. The Idle option is very useful for conserving both network bandwidth and server resources. Suppose you are limited in your WAN bandwidth and you find that many users at remote sites log on to your server and leave their session active most of the day with only a few bursts of activity. You might want to set the Idle timeout for these users or for these connections. In this way, their sessions would be disconnected or reset when they are not using the Terminal Server, freeing up valuable bandwidth for other users.

To understand the important differences between being disconnected and being reset, see "On a Broken or Timed Out Connection," later in this chapter.

Security Options

Encryption is enabled by default with both RDP and ICA connections. With RDP connections, three levels of encryption security are available: Low, Medium, and High. RDP encryption security is initially set to Low, which is adequate for most internal security needs. Use the Medium or High setting in situations in which the extra processing time taken by encrypting packets is warranted to reduce the security risk. Here are the different RDP encryption levels and what they do:

- *Low* All data from client to server is encrypted using a 40-bit key. All encryption is done using the RC4 encryption algorithm.

- *Medium* Data both from client to server and from server to client is encrypted using a 40-bit key.

- *High* Data going both ways is encrypted using a 128-bit key (40-bit key for exported versions of Terminal Server).

ICA clients have two security settings available: None and Basic. By default, ICA clients are set to Basic, which applies a simple encryption algorithm to ICA connection data. You can save processing power by setting ICA to None, instead. Beware, however, that this is an unsecure setup and should be used only on a secure network on which server processing power is at a premium.

Citrix sells an add-on security product for MetaFrame that offers much greater security and encryption than the Basic security setting, called SecureICA. Using SecureICA your client and server data can be encrypted by using a 40-bit, 56-bit, or 128-bit key with the RSA's RC5 encryption algorithm. This option is covered in more detail in Chapter 4, "Terminal Server and MetaFrame."

Use Default NT Authentication Option

With both NT and Terminal Server, a developer can replace the default logon prompt with a custom logon to provide additional logon features. The Use Default NT Authentication option in the Security section forces clients to use NT's default GINA (`msgina.dll`) or logon program.

A malicious developer could write a logon screen that looks like the standard Microsoft logon but that secretly captures users' passwords to a log file. By checking the Use Default NT Authentication option, you can help prevent security breaches like this.

Initial Program Option

The Initial Program option defines the command line and working directory for an application that will be run after users attach to this connection and log on. By default, the Initial Program is inherited from either the client-level or the user-level settings.

Setting the Initial Program option at a connection level is a good option for environments in which all users need to run only a single application. Be aware, however, that this option also forces administrators who attach using this connection to run that application.

One good use for this option is for asynchronous connections. Suppose you were to set up a bank of modems with an asynchronous connection for each modem that has the Initial Program option set. Any user dialing into this modem bank would be able to run only the application you set. This improves server security by providing remote users access to a single application versus providing them access to an entire Windows desktop.

Real-World Tip: Public Key Encryption

Citrix has an excellent online article describing the basics of public key encryption and how it is used by SecureICA. The address for the article is as follows:

http://www.citrix.com/support/solution/sol00044.htm

You can also go to RSA's Web site at www.rsa.com for more detailed information on RSA's RC5 encyrption.

MetaFrame

Only Run Published Applications (MetaFrame Only)

The Only Run Published Applications option applies only to ICA clients. With MetaFrame, applications can be published using the Application Configuration tool. If you want to force users to use just these published applications, then check this box. More information on application publishing is available in Chapter 15, "Terminal Server and NetWare."

Miscellaneous Advanced Options

The following subsections describe the remaining miscellaneous options that are available in the Advanced Connection Settings window.

User Profile Overrides

A User Profile Override such as the Disable Wallpaper option is recommended for any Terminal Server connection. Graphically complex wallpapers can eat up large amounts of bandwidth when being sent across the wire to clients. It is a good idea to prevent your clients from using wallpaper for this reason.

On a Broken or Timed Out Connection

When a connection is broken or has timed out, Terminal Server can be set to either disconnect it or reset it. The On a Broken or Timed Out Connection option controls whether the connection is severed or reset. It is important to understand the difference between the two choices:

- *Disconnect*   When a session is disconnected, all of the applications remain open. Depending on how reconnection is set, when the user logs back on, he can reconnect to his session just as he left it. Suppose a user was working on a spreadsheet in Excel when his session was disconnected. When he logs back on, he finds himself right back in the spreadsheet where he left off. This is a great option for unreliable connections such as modems. The disadvantage is that the open connection left on the server after a disconnect occupies significant processing and memory resources. It is recommended to use this option along with setting a disconnection timeout. This recommendation works well for most situations.

- *Reset*   When a session is reset, the applications are all closed without saving their data. This can result in corrupted files and lost data. Use this option only if user applications are used just for viewing data and not for changing it.

Reconnect Sessions Disconnected

When a session is disconnected, you have two choices for reestablishing the connection. You can allow a disconnected user to reconnect his session from any client (the default), or you can require a disconnected user to connect from the original client only:

- *From Any Client*   When you select this option, the next time a disconnected user logs on from any client, he will return to his disconnected session.
- *This Connection Only*   If you select this option, then the only way a user can return to a disconnected session is by logging on again at the station from which the connection was lost. This option is rarely used and it is recommended to leave it at its default.

Shadowing (MetaFrame Only)

MetaFrame

Shadowing is one of the most useful administration tools, but is available only with ICA clients. Shadowing allows an administrator to remotely control the desktop of anyone logged on to the server. It is important to note that shadowing can be done only from one Terminal Server session to another. You cannot shadow a Terminal Server session if you are logged on to the server console, unless you run the ICA client at the console.

Shadowing is great for quick user assistance. If a user calls you up to complain of trouble doing something in an application, you can "shadow" his or her session.

The Shadowing option in this window allows you to control whether Shadowing is enabled, whether you can control the cursor and keyboard of the user when shadowing them (Input ON), and whether the user is notified when you try to shadow them (Notify ON). Because this is a connection-level option, these settings apply to all users who attach using this connection. Although by default these options are controlled at a user level (select inherit user config), controlling them at a connection level is generally easier.

Client Settings (MetaFrame Only)

MetaFrame

With MetaFrame you have some additional options available that you can set at a connection level. To view these options, click the Client Settings button in the New Connection dialog box. This brings up the Client Settings dialog box, shown in Figure 6.7. Client settings regulate how the client's local resources, such as hard drives and printers, are accessed in Terminal Server. Automatically incorporating a client's local devices into a Terminal Server session is supported only with the ICA protocol. Although you can access a user's local devices from an RDP session, that user must share them on the network first. The following sections cover the different options you have available.

Connection Settings

Connection settings control whether the client's local drives and printers are automatically added to their Windows Terminal desktop when they log on:

Figure 6.7   Client Settings window.

- *Connect Client Drives at Logon*   Makes the client's local drives available in the Windows Terminal session. For example, when the user opens up Explorer, she sees her local drives along with all the Terminal Server mappings and local drives.

- *Connect Client Printers at Logon*   Makes the client's local Windows-based printers available to applications running in the Terminal Server session. This option is very useful if the user wants to be able to print to their local printer from an application running on Terminal Server.

- *Default to Main Client Printer*   Changes the default printer for the client's Terminal Server session to the user's local default printer.

Figure 6.8 shows basically how this redirection works. When a client tries to print a document to one of their local printers defined within their Terminal Server session, Terminal Server redirects this print job across the network to the client's printer.

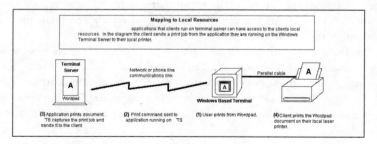

Figure 6.8   Sending data to a client's local resources.

Client Mapping Overrides

By default, with the ICA protocol all local resources are mapped or available from the Terminal Server session. From the Client Mapping Overrides section, you can disable the mapping of a local resource.

Suppose you want to copy a file from a drive on the Terminal Server to your local drive. With client drive mapping, this is easy to do. Your local drives appear in Terminal Server as if they were part of the Terminal Server drive set. The following options are available with client drive mapping:

- *Disable Client Drive Mapping*   Disables the ability for Terminal Server to map drives to the client's local drives.
- *Disable Windows Client Printer Mapping*   Disables the ability for Terminal Server to give Windows applications access to the client's local Windows printers.
- *Disable Client LPT Port Mapping*   Disables the ability for Terminal Server to give applications, such as DOS applications, access to the client's LPT ports.
- *Disable Client COM Port Mapping*   Disables the ability for applications running on Terminal Server to obtain access to the client's local COM ports.
- *Disable Client Clipboard Mapping*   Disables the ability for clients to transfer local data to and from Terminal Server applications by using their clipboards.
- *Disable Client Audio Mapping*   Disables the ability for Terminal Server to play sounds through the client's audio system.

MetaFrame

ICA Settings (MetaFrame Only)

The final option available in the New Connection dialog box for ICA connections is the ICA Settings button. When you click this button, the ICA Settings dialog box opens, which contains only one setting: Client Audio Quality.

Recall that one of the features of ICA connections is the ability to receive audio at the client from audio-enabled applications running off the Terminal Server. Perhaps you want to run an application at the server that records and plays user's voice mail. Using the ICA client, users can play their voice mail off the Terminal Server and hear the messages at their terminals.

For this feature to work, the audio must be packaged and sent across the wire. With the Client Audio Quality option, you can control how much bandwidth this will take. The Audio Quality option basically controls the level of compression and the sampling rate of the audio. By default, this option is set to Low quality. Giving your clients the ability to use audio is not recommended unless they are attaching to Terminal Server across a LAN.

Connection Permissions

Connection permissions can apply for both RDP and ICA connections. Terminal Server gives you a large amount of control over the security of your connections. TS allows you to control the connection permissions that are granted to different users and groups, by connection.

To see how these permissions are controlled, from the main screen of the TS Connection Configuration Tool, highlight one of the connection entries and then select Permissions from the Security menu. The Connection Permissions dialog box, shown in Figure 6.9, appears. From here you can see the default permissions set up when you install Terminal Server.

In the Connection Permissions window, select Special Access from the drop-down box next to Type of Access. The Special Access dialog box appears. The Special Access dialog box lists all the permissions that can be applied to either users or groups. The following is a description of these permissions:

- *Query Information*   Allows clients to query information about their settings with the Connection Configuration Tool.

- *Set Information*   Allows clients to set various options using the Connection Configuration Tool.

- *Reset*   Allows clients to reset other sessions.

- *Shadow*   Allows clients to shadow other clients.

- *Logon*   Gives clients the ability to log on to the server. This option is useful for restricting which groups can or cannot log on to Terminal Server.

- *Logoff*   Gives clients the ability to log off another session.

- *Message*   Allows the selected users or groups to send messages to other users.

- *Connect*   Allows the clients the ability to reconnect to a disconnected session.

- *Disconnect*   Allows clients to disconnect their sessions.

- *Delete*   Allows clients to delete connections using the Connection Configuration Tool.

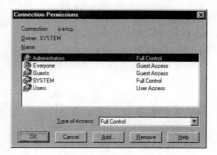

Figure 6.9   Connection Permissions window.

The default user permissions are adequate for most needs. Realize, however, that the default permissions allow everyone in the domain to log on to your Terminal Server. If you have a large domain or you want to control who can access the Terminal Server, the following process is recommended:

1. From the main screen of the Terminal Server Connection Configuration Tool, highlight the connection whose permissions you want to modify.

2. Select Permissions from the Security menu on the main screen.

3. In the Connection Permissions dialog box, remove the Everyone, Guests, and Users groups from the access list.

4. Create a Terminal Server Users group in the domain by using User Manager for Domains (just as you normally would under NT Server 4.0), and add the users who should have access to the connection to this group.

5. Add the Terminal Server Users group in the Connection Permissions dialog box, granting them User Access.

After you create new users who you want to use the Terminal Server, make sure you make them members of the Terminal Server Users group. If you want to further restrict access, you could also make a Terminal Server Administrator group and allow only that group and System to have Full Control to every connection.

7

Creating Users and Groups in Terminal Server

FOR THOSE WHO ARE ALREADY FAMILIAR with the creation of users and groups in a domain with Windows NT Server 4.0, you will find that the basics of user and group creation have not changed with Terminal Server. Users and groups are created in Terminal Server using the User Manager for Domains. User account and group information still reside at the domain's primary and backup domain controllers (PDC or BDC).

However, Terminal Server has several additional per-user properties, such as initial program, client drive mappings, and timeouts. These properties can be set only by using Terminal Server's User Manager for Domains. Several other user properties in User Manager also have special purposes with Terminal Server or may not act the same as you might be used to with Windows NT Server 4.0.

This chapter starts with a basic discussion of users and groups on Terminal Server. Next, the focus turns to the importance of creating a naming policy for your users and groups to make their administration easier. The chapter ends by showing you how to create users and groups in Terminal Server and by describing all the user properties that you can set.

Terminal Server Users and Groups

Every person who needs to access Terminal Server must have a user account on the domain that Terminal Server is a part of (see the following Author's Note). The username and password for a user's account are what he uses to log on to the Terminal

Server. Besides username and password, each Terminal Server user has certain other settable properties that are controlled with the User Manager for Domains:

- *Group membership*   The local and global groups the user is a member of.
- *Terminal Server per-user configuration settings*   Includes initial program, client drive mappings, and timeouts.
- *User environment profile settings*   Includes user home directory, Terminal Server home directory, and profile path.
- *Logon hours*   Hours during which the user is allowed to log on to Terminal Server.
- *Logon workstation*   The workstations that the user can log on to the domain from.
- *Account information*   Information such as the expiration date of the user account.
- *Dialin information*   Whether or not user has been granted dialin access through the Remote Access Server (RAS).

Each of these user properties is covered in detail later in this chapter.

Access to most domain resources, including files and printers, can be granted to particular users. You can, for example, grant a particular user full access to one or more directories on your Terminal Server. The username and password you used to first log on to Terminal Server are, thus, like keys to the locks placed on your domain's resources.

Terminal Server Groups

Each user can be made a member of one or more groups. Groups are the best means to provide access for or identify categories of users. Like users, groups can be granted access to your domain's resources. Granting access to the resources using groups is generally more efficient and more easily tracked than granting access to individual users. Imagine having to grant ten users' access to five different directories. For each of the five resources, you would have to individually select and grant access for each of the ten users. This would take at least fifty steps. However, by adding the ten users to a group, you only have to select the group and add the group once to the access list for each of the five resources. If in the future you need to revoke a user's access or grant access to a new user, you can simply delete or add that user from or to the group.

Group by Function or by Resource

The best way to decide what groups you should create depends on both the users' job functions and the resources that are available on your domain. One effective method of creating groups with Terminal Server is to create groups for resources and job functions. As you will see in the next section, "Local and Global Groups," this method works well with the concept of local groups and global groups.

Author's Note: Assumptions

This chapter assumes that your Terminal Server is a member of a domain. If your Terminal Server is a stand-alone server, most of the discussion in this chapter will still apply, with the exception of global groups, which do not exist on stand-alone servers.

A resource group is used to control access to a particular resource. Suppose you have a particular application called Widgets on your Terminal Server to which you want to grant access. To create a resource group, you would create a group called Widgets and grant only the Widgets group and the administrator group access to the application's directories. Other examples of resource groups are a group that controls access to a particular printer and a group that enables logon to a particular Terminal Server.

Job function groups can often be taken directly from your company's organizational chart. Which departments you decide to make into job function groups depends on whether all members of a department need the same access to a particular set of domain resources. Consider an accounting department whose members all need access to three printers, an online banking application, and a shared directory. You could create an accounting job function group, add the members of the accounting department to that group, and then grant that group access to these resources.

Local and Global Groups

In a domain, there are two types of groups that can be created using User Manager for Domains: local groups and global groups.

- Local groups are server specific. Each server has its own set of local groups. Local groups are used for assigning rights to local resources. Local groups can contain either users or global groups.

- Global groups are part of the domain and are global in nature. You can administer global group membership from any server by using the User Manager for Domains because there is only a single set of global groups for a domain. Global groups can contain only domain users; they cannot contain other groups.

In general, your local groups should be your resource groups. Because local groups are defined locally on a particular server, it makes sense to create local groups that control access to that server's resources.

Local groups can contain users and global groups from both the current domain and any trusted domain. Local groups can thus be used to consolidate access rights across trusted domains to the resources on those domains.

Global groups are best used as job function groups. To make a global group job specific, add it to all the local groups that provide access to the resources that are required for a particular job. Suppose you have a group of domain users that must access a printer on your Terminal Server for their jobs. To grant access to that printer you would take these steps:

1. Create a local group and grant it access to the printer.

2. Add the global group to the local group.

3. Add the users to the global group.

Figure 7.1 provides further illustration of how local and global groups are best used in a domain to control access to resources.

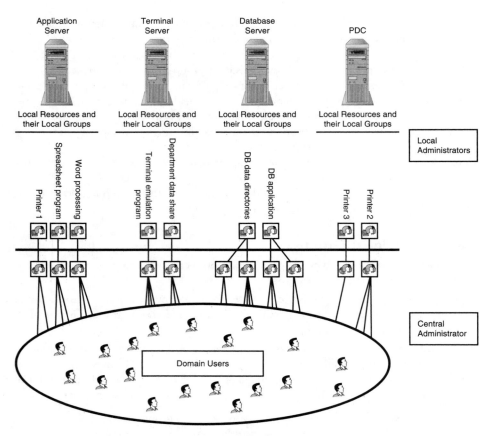

Figure 7.1   Using local groups and global groups in the domain.

Creating a Naming Policy

Having a naming policy for your users and groups makes administration significantly easier. Because the User Manager for Domains lists all the groups and users together, in large domains it is easy for them to become "lost in the list." By establishing and adhering to a naming policy, it is much easier to keep track of them because their names are organized in an understandable fashion. Even in smaller domains, the purpose of every user and group can be difficult to keep track of if a naming policy is not followed. In the following sections, you learn some techniques for naming users and groups in your domain.

Naming Users

When you create a user, you first need to enter the username, full name, and description in the New User dialog box. How you assign these values and what conventions you follow will have a great effect on the ease of future administration of your domain and Terminal Server. The following sections introduce some tips to follow when assigning these values.

Usernames

Table 7.1 contains some basic username policies that you can adopt for your network. In general, try to avoid the following when creating usernames:

- *Creating usernames by using different techniques*   This can quickly lead to confusion.

- *Letting users assign their own usernames*   This again can lead to confusion because it is not likely the users will create usernames in a consistent manner.

- *Using spaces between first and last names*   This is a common policy, but it can cause difficulties when setting up an email system. You must make aliases for the usernames because spaces are not allowed in Internet email addresses. It is best to plan for the future by using Internet-compatible usernames.

- *Using just first names or last names*   You will quickly run into issues with duplicate usernames if you adopt this policy.

Full Name

In general, when you create usernames, it is best to use reverse order for the full name. In other words, if your username policy is first name + period + last name, then your full name policy should be last name first. The reason for this is a little tricky. Under the View menu in User Manager, you can select to view either by Username, which is default, or by Full Name. By using reverse order for the full name, you can sort by either first name or last name by choosing either sort by Username or by Full Name.

Table 7.1   **Basic Username Policies**

Policy Type	Description
First Initial, Last Name (JDOE)	Probably the most common, this policy works well because the names are short and tend to be unique. If there are duplicate names, add the people's middle initials to differentiate the policy names.
First Name, Last Initial (JOHND)	Also a very common policy, but is less likely to generate unique names on large networks. For small networks, it is good because first names are generally easier to remember and spell.
First Name, period, Last Name (JOHN.DOE)	This technique works well for both large and small companies. It is easy to remember. The disadvantage is that usernames are longer and cannot be used for directory names in some cases.
Hash Codes (JD6771)	In corporations whose security is critical, such as financial or government institutions, often a cryptic hash code is generated for users. For example, [the user's initials]+[the user number].

Another suggestion is to put an @ or some other symbol at the start of the full name for special accounts, such as service and test accounts. In this way, when you sort by full name you can easily differentiate between normal users and special purpose users. This technique works well for large networks where service accounts can get lost easily. See Figure 7.2 for an example of how this works.

Description

For the user Description, many people include the department that the user is a member of. For service and system accounts, however, a description of the purpose of the account is normally more useful.

Naming Groups

As with users, it is a good idea to come up with a naming policy for your groups:

- *Local Groups : [Server Name]_[Resource Name]*   Placing the server name in front keeps the local groups, which represent access to resources, together in the group list. You can also put a special character, such as an @ sign, in front to keep all local groups together. Refrain from putting spaces in your group names. The absence of spaces makes it easier to use the names with command line utilities.

- *Global Groups : [Domain Name]_[Server Name]_[Resource Name]*   The [Server Name]_[Resource Name] should match that of the local group that this global group is a part of. Using the [Domain Name] in front keeps all global resource groups for the domain together in the list.

Group descriptions are also very important for keeping track of your groups' intended purposes.

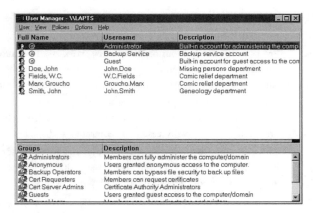

Figure 7.2   Users sorted by full name rather than by username.

Creating Users

The following sections cover the tool you will be using to create your Terminal Server users and groups: the User Manager for Domains. Next, you will learn how to create a Terminal Server user by using this tool. Each of the various user properties you can set will then be covered in detail.

Terminal Server's User Manager for Domains

For those who are not familiar with Terminal Server's User Manager for Domains, this tool is used to do the following:

- Create and delete users and groups
- Modify user properties, including identification, password, group membership, profiles, hours of logon, station restrictions, and account expiration
- Modify system-wide user account polices
- Set up auditing
- Set up user and group rights policies

Terminal Server's User Manager for Domains is nearly identical to the one included with NT Server 4.0. The users that you create from Terminal Server are normal domain users and their information is stored in the domain database on the PDC. Creating users from Terminal Server does not mean that they can log on only to Terminal Server, however. The users you create can access the domain from any workstation or server that is a member of the domain. However, Terminal Server's User Manager for Domains (TS User Manager for short) allows you to set certain Terminal Server-specific user properties that cannot be set from anywhere else. These include the following:

- *Config settings*   Terminal Server has an additional group of settings called the config settings. These include many per-user settings that are related to some of the per-connection settings discussed in Chapter 6, "Creating the Connections," such as client device mappings, initial program, and timeouts.
- *Terminal Server home directory*   Under profile settings, the TS User Manager has an additional field for you to define a home directory that is used only when logging on to Terminal Server.
- *Terminal Server profile path*   You can also define a profile path which is only used when logging onto Terminal Server. In this way, your workstation's profile and TS profile are kept separate.

Author's Note: Managing TS Users

With the exception of the Terminal Server–specific properties, you can still manage Terminal Server (TS) users and groups from NT Server 4.0's User Manager for Domains. Installing Terminal Server on your domain simply adds additional Terminal Server–specific properties to your current domain user database that can be controlled from the TS User Manager. It does not change your user's prior settings.

You will find Terminal Server's User Manager for Domains in the Administrative Tools folder by selecting Properties from the Start menu. Figure 7.3 shows the main window of the TS User Manager. If you are familiar with the User Manager for Domains that is included with NT Server 4.0, you will notice that the options available at the main window are identical.

The first difference that you are likely to see between the TS User Manager and that included with NT Server 4.0 is in the User Properties window. You can get to the User Properties window for any user by double-clicking on that user from the main window of the TS User Manager. Figure 7.4 shows the User Properties window for a Terminal Server user. Notice the addition of a Config settings button in the User Properties window; this button does not exist in NT Server 4.0's User Manager for Domains. When you click the Config button, a dialog box listing some Terminal Server specific settings appears. Additional Terminal Server specific settings can be seen by clicking on the Profiles button in the User Properties window. In the Profiles dialog box you will see such additional settings as the Terminal Server Home Directory and Profile Path.

Creating a User

The following is a basic overview of the steps necessary to create a user using the TS User Manager. Following this overview is a discussion of each group of user properties that you can set in detail. You will learn what they are for and how to set them.

To create a new user, you must do the following:

1. Open the User Manager for Domains from the Terminal Server (in the Start menu, select Programs | Administrative Tools | User Manager for Domains).

2. Select New User from the User menu to create a new user. The New User dialog box appears.

3. Fill in the Username, Full Name, Description, and Password. For ease of administration, it is important that you follow a naming policy when setting these properties, as was discussed previously in this chapter.

4. Check any of the boxes which are appropriate, such as the User Must Change Password at Next Logon box.

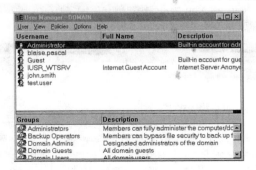

Figure 7.3 User Manager for Domains window.

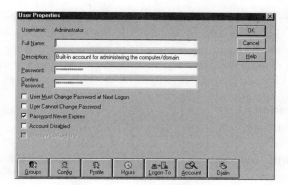

Figure 7.4   User Properties window.

5. Set the properties associated with a particular property, such as the Groups, Config, and Profiles, by clicking the corresponding buttons, filling in the properties in the dialog box that appears and clicking OK. These properties will be discussed in detail in the following sections.

6. Select Add to add the new user to the user list.

The user is now created in the domain's user database at the PDC. The user can log on to any Terminal Server or Windows workstation that is a member of that domain using the username and password that you have set for her.

Group Membership

The Group Memberships dialog box is the first of the properties dialog boxes that can be reached by clicking the buttons at the bottom of the New User window. To get to the Group Memberships dialog box, click the Groups button in the New User window. In the Group Memberships dialog box, shown in Figure 7.5, you can make the user a member of one or more local or global groups by highlighting the groups one at a time and clicking Add.

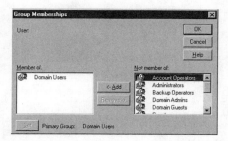

Figure 7.5   Group Memberships window.

Note the difference between the local group and global group icons shown in Figure 7.5. The local group icon shows a group of people next to a computer, whereas the global group shows the group next to a globe. As discussed at the beginning of this chapter, domain users should normally be made members of global groups rather than local groups. In contrast, local groups should be used to control local resources.

User Configuration

To set the user's User Configuration properties, click the Config button in the New User window. The User Configuration dialog box, shown in Figure 7.6, contains many Terminal Server per-user settings such as timeouts, initial program, and client devices. You will notice from the discussion of connection settings in Chapter 6 that many of these options can also be set per-connection. By default, connections will inherit whatever you set per-user. However, if you change the setting at the connection, it overrides what is set for the users.

Consider the initial program setting. To set the Initial Program, uncheck Inherit Client Config and enter the Command Line and Working Directory of the program you want the user to run. The next time the user logs on, Terminal Server takes the user directly to this application rather than to a Terminal Server desktop. Now if you set an initial program on the connection the user is logging onto the server with, as shown in Chapter 6, this setting overrides the initial program setting that you set per-user.

Most of the settings shown in the User Configuration window are discussed in detail in Chapter 6. Refer to that chapter for further information about these settings.

One additional setting that was not covered in Chapter 6 is the NetWare setting, which is intended for NetWare environments. It allows Terminal Server to synchronize your Terminal Server password with your NetWare password. For more details about this setting, see Chapter 15, "Terminal Server and NetWare."

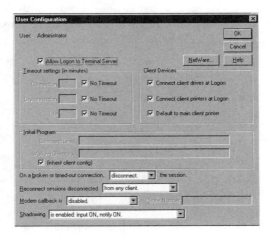

Figure 7.6   User Configuration window.

User Environment Profile

The User Environment Profile window, shown in Figure 7.7, can be accessed by clicking the Profile button in the New User dialog box. In this window, you will find the
following settings:

- *User Profiles*   In this area you will find fields in which to set the Terminal Server
  profile path, standard profile paths, and logon script filename. The profile path is
  mainly used to store the user's desktop settings and the user Registry settings.
  The logon script is a batch file that is run when the user first logs on.

- *Home Directory*   In this area you can set the standard home directory to either the
  user's local drive (Local Path) or to a UNC path (Connect) on the network.
  Home directories are normally used to store user's personal files. As you will learn
  shortly, home directories have additional special purposes with Terminal Server.

- *Terminal Server Home Directory*   This home directory is used only when the user
  logs on to the domain from the Terminal Server.

- *Map Root*   The ability to map root a home directory to a NetWare server is
  important for businesses whose primary network servers are NetWare.

Because of the special importance of the user profile and home directory settings
with Terminal Server, we will be discussing these settings in detail in the following
sections.

Home Directories

Under NT Server 4.0, home directories are used by some programs, such as Notepad,
as the default location for retrieving and saving user data files. With Terminal Server,
home directories are also used for storing application-specific settings files, such as INI
files, for each user. In this way, each user can have individual application settings in
Terminal Server's multiuser environment.

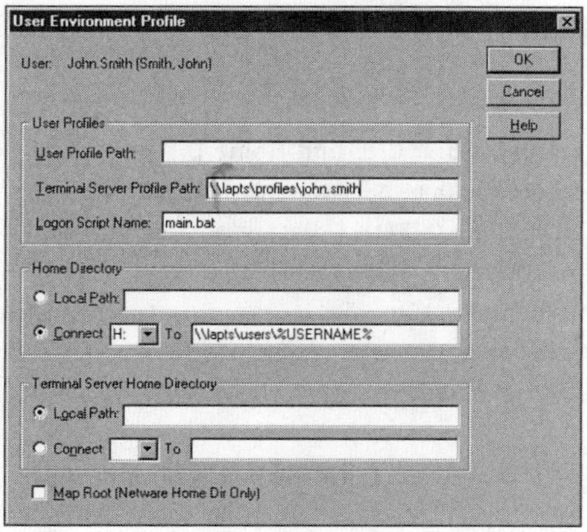

Figure 7.7   User Environment Profile window.

Notice in Figure 7.7 that there are two types of home directories you can set: the standard Home Directory and the Terminal Server Home Directory. Which one your home directory is set to depends on where you log on to the domain from. By default, your home directory is set by Terminal Server to C:\WTSRV\Profiles\ [username]. By setting the Terminal Server home directory path, you can change this default location to either a local path or a UNC path on the network. Because this is the Terminal Server home directory path, it only applies when you log on to the domain from Terminal Server. If you log on directly to a domain from a workstation, your home directory is set to the standard Home Directory path instead.

When you first add a user to the domain from Terminal Server, Terminal Server automatically creates a \Windows and a \Windows\system directory inside the user's home directory. When applications query for the path of the Windows or system directories, Terminal Server returns the user's window or system directory. In this way, any settings files that the application keeps in these directories are kept user-specific.

Within each type of home directory, you can specify one of two paths: either a local path or a drive letter connected to a UNC path. Local paths are useful with Terminal Server if your user only logs on to Terminal Server and does not log on to any other machine in the domain. Because users log on to Terminal Server as if they were locally logging on, the path refers to the local hard drive of the Terminal Server. For example, if you set the Local Path to C:\users\[username], when the user logs on to the domain from Terminal Server, his home directory is set to C:\user\ [username] on the C: drive of the Terminal Server. However, if he tries to log on to the domain from a workstation, such as an NT workstation, his home directory path is mapped to the local C: drive of that workstation.

Entering a UNC path next to Connect is a better option if your users want to keep their home directories in the same location no matter where they log on to the domain from. To set up the home directory using a UNC path, you must first share your user directory on the network. Next, enter the UNC path \\server name] \[user directory share name] for the Connect path and select a drive letter to connect it to. Now when the user logs on to the domain from Terminal Server or from any workstation, his home directory path is set to the UNC path you entered.

> **Note for WinFrame Administrators: Creating Home Directories**
> With WinFrame, home directories had to be defined for each user. If you did not define them, a user's home directory was set to C:\USERS\DEFAULT. This would cause problems in the WinFrame multi-user environment because user-specific application files, such as INI files, were stored for all users in one location. However, with Terminal Server, home directories are created automatically under C:\WTSRV\Profiles\[username] without having to fill in anything in the home directory field.

Map Root Setting

The Map Root setting is useful if you are in a NetWare environment. With Terminal Server, there is no such thing as map root. If you enter \\[Server]\[Share]\[User Directory] in the Connect field when setting up the user's home directory, the root of the home directory drive is always mapped to the root of the share rather than the root of the user directory. If, instead, you are connecting your home directory to a NetWare server (\\[NetWare Server Name]\[Volume Name]\[NetWare User Directory]\) you can map the drive letter to the root of the NetWare user directory by checking this setting.

Profile Settings

The next settings we need to discuss are profiles. If you are familiar with WinFrame, take note, for there have been some changes to profiles and what they can do. Take a look at the section on profiles in Chapter 12, "Administering the Desktop and Server," for more details about the different types of profiles and how to use them.

Your profile includes your user Registry settings (ntuser.dat Registry file), your Start menu programs, and shortcuts to your most recently used documents. By default, your profiles are stored under the C:\WTSRV\PROFILES\[username] directory. Because your username is part of the path, you have your own settings.

The default setting, leaving both profile paths blank, is adequate for most situations. From whatever location you log on into Terminal Server you get your desktop. One reason you would want to change the setting is if you want a roaming profile. *Roaming profiles* allow you to maintain your profile in a central location so that when you log on from any workstation, you receive the same desktop and user settings. To set up a roaming profile, follow these steps:

1. Share a directory on your server as PROFILES, where you want the user profile information to be centrally kept.

2. Enter \\Server Name]\PROFILES\%USERNAME% for either the User or Terminal Server Profile Path and then add the user.

Like the Terminal Server home directory, the Terminal Server profile path is used only when the user logs on to a Terminal Server. By setting both a Terminal Server and User Profile Path in different locations you can keep these two desktops separate for your users.

> **Real-World Tip: The %USERNAME% Variable**
>
> Notice the use of the %USERNAME% variable in Figure 7.7. Terminal Server substitutes the username of the user you are creating for this variable. When you add this user, Terminal Server automatically creates the home directory, using the user's name, if that directory does not already exist. This is a very convenient way to set up user home directories.

Logon Script Name Setting

Logon scripts are batch files, REXX command files (.CMD), or executables that are run when your user first logs on to the domain. Logon scripts are normally used for such things as setting environment variables, mapping drive letters, and connecting LPT ports to printers. By assigning a single logon script to several users you can easily change the drive and printer mappings for all the users simultaneously by changing just the logon script. This is more efficient than having to change the mappings for each user one by one.

Logon scripts are run by default from the \WINNT\SYSTEM32\REPL\IMPORT\SCRIPTS directory of the server with which you authenticated. Because you can authenticate with either a PDC or BDC, it is important that the logon script be copied to this directory on all domain controllers in your domain.

To set up user logon scripts you need to do the following:

1. Enter the name of the logon script batch file, command file, or executable for the user in the Logon Script Name field shown in Figure 7.7.

2. Fill in the rest of the settings for the user and then add them to the domain.

3. Create and copy the logon script to the \WINNT\SYSTEM32\REPL\IMPORT\SCRIPTS directory of the domain's PDC.

4. Copy the logon script to the same directory on all of the domain's BCDs.

Now, no matter whether users authenticate with the domain's PDC or a BDC, they run the same script.

Replicating the Logon Script

For those who want to automate this process, the logon script can be replicated by using the NT Directory Replicate service. To set this service up, follow these steps:

1. From the console of your domain's PDC, go to Start | Settings | Control Panel | Server, and click on the Replication button.

2. From the Directory Replication window, select Export Directories. The export directory is set by default to C:\WINNT\SYSTEM32\REPL\EXPORT\SCRIPTS. Enter the directory that contains the user logon scripts that you want to export.

3. Click the Add button under the To window, add all of your domain's BCDs to the list, and then click OK to start the service.

4. From the console of each of your domain's BCDs, go to the Directory Replication window, select Import Directories and click OK. The import directory is set to C:\WINNT\SYSTEM32\REPL\IMPORT\SCRIPTS by default.

5. Click the Add button under the From window and add your domain's PDC to the list then click OK to start the service.

6. Go to Control Panel | Services on all the servers and make sure the Directory Replicator service is started.

7. To have the service start up automatically, highlight the Directory Replicator service, click the Startup button, and select Automatic for the Startup Type.

Terminal Server's USRLOGON.CMD *Login Script*

With Windows NT Server 4.0, the logon script that you defined in the Logon Script Name field shown in Figure 7.7 was the only logon script that was run for the user. However, with Terminal Server, a C:\WTSRV\SYSTEM32\USRLOGON.CMD logon script command file is run for every user who logs on, in addition to the individual logon script you defined for the user. This logon script is used for running the Terminal Server Application Compatibility Scripts. These scripts are important for certain applications to run properly on Terminal Server. Because the USRLOGON.CMD file is run for every Terminal Server user, you may choose to modify this file instead of creating individual user logon scripts. See Chapter 8, "Using Logon Scripts," for more detail on this logon script and the Application Compatibility Scripts.

Logon Hours

You can reach the Logon Hours window shown in Figure 7.8 by clicking Hours in the New User window when creating a new user. By default, your Terminal Server users can log on at any time. If you do weekly maintenance on your servers or nightly backup, you may want to restrict the hours during which users can log on to the domain. In Figure 7.8, user John.Smith has been restricted from logon on weekends and between midnight and 6:00 in the morning. Unfortunately, with Terminal Server this does not force your users to log off at this time; instead, it prevents users from logging back on during the specified time span after they've logged off. If they leave their terminals on, however, they can still use them during the restricted times.

To set a user's logon hours, click and drag your mouse cursor over the hours you want to modify. After the hours are highlighted, click either the Allow or Disallow button in order to allow logon or prevent logons during that time.

Logon Workstations

To get to the Logon Workstations window, click the Logon To button from the New User window. From the Logon Workstation window you can enter the local workstation name of all of the workstations that the user is allowed to log on to the domain from.

Author's Note: Forcibly Disconnect Remote Users

Experienced administrators may recall the Forcibly Disconnect Remote Users when Logon Hours Expire setting in the Account Policy window (in User Manager, select Policies|Account). Because this option applies to remote users only and Terminal Server users are actually logging on locally, this setting does not apply for users running a Terminal Server session.

Real-World Tip: Idle Timeout

If users are leaving their systems logged on overnight, unattended, you can set an Idle timeout per-connection, as shown in Chapter 6. You can also set the Idle timeout per-user in the User Configuration dialog box discussed previously in this chapter. Setting an Idle timeout of 120 minutes reduces the risk that users' time will run out during the workday. Instead, their sessions are logged off two hours after they leave. Remember that if you set the session for Disconnect rather than Reset, Terminal Server keeps open whatever files users had open on the screen.

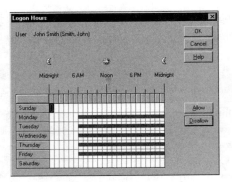

Figure 7.8 Logon Hours window.

This setting can be useful, but with Terminal Server it might not work the way you would expect. When you use this option with Windows NT Server 4.0, you can prevent a user from logging on from any workstation except the ones that you put in the list. With Terminal Server, however, your actual workstation is the server itself. There is no such thing as a local workstation name. You cannot restrict different workstations on your network from being able to attempt to log on to the Terminal Server.

In light of this information, this option might seem useless for users who only log on to Terminal Server. However, you might find the following tips to be of use:

- First, fill in the computer name of the Terminal Server. Users can log on to these workstations, as shown in Figure 7.9. This forces users to access the domain only through the Terminal Server listed. This prevents users from logging on to the domain and mapping drives to the server using their local workstations.

- The second use for restricting logon workstations with Terminal Server is to restrict which Terminal Servers a user can use. Suppose you have three Terminal Servers on your network. If you specify which server your users can log on to in the Logon Workstations window, they receive an error message if they try to log on to any other server.

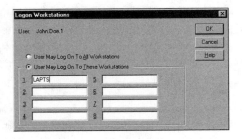

Figure 7.9 Logon Workstations window.

If you want to further restrict who can or cannot access the Terminal Server, turn to Chapter 6 for instructions on setting logon permissions by using the Connection Configuration tool.

Account Expiration and Type

When you click the Account button in the New User dialog box, the Account Information dialog box appears. In this dialog box, you can define the day that an account expires and whether the account is local or global. One good use of the expiration feature is for billable accounts or public accounts. You can set these accounts to expire at a given day.

By default, domain user accounts are global. A global user can be identified in the User Manager window by the little user icon to the left of the username. Global users can be assigned access to resources in trusting domains.

The other type of user is the local user. A local user can be identified by the little user icon with a computer next to it to the left of the username. Local users do not refer to the users that are in the Terminal Server's local user database. In this context, "local users" refers to users who can only access resources that are part of their local domain. These users cannot access resources in trusting domains.

Dialin Permissions and Callback

To access the Dialin Permissions Window, click the Dialin button in the New User dialog box. This window allows you to control whether or not a user has permission to dial in and whether there will be a callback security check (see Figure 7.10). Notice that dialin permission is not granted by default. This dialin permission setting only applies to RAS dialin capability and does not affect direct dialin through MetaFrame. It is a common mistake to forget to grant a remote RAS user dialin access when his account is first set up.

There are two types of callback: Set By Caller and Preset. As with dialin permission, these settings affect only users dialing in using RAS. If you select Set By Caller, when your user first connects to the RAS server, she is prompted for a number to be called back on. The RAS server then calls back that number and establishes a connection with the user.

With a Preset callback, the system calls back a preset number instead of prompting the user for a number.

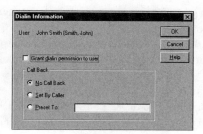

Figure 7.10   Dialin Information window.

You can control the callback and dialin permission settings in either of two locations: You can use either User Manager or the Remote Access Admin program.

For more information about Remote Access Services and how to set them up, see Chapter 14, "Terminal Server and Remote Access."

Changing Multiple Users Simultaneously

Many times you want to make the same changes to multiple users at the same time. Rather than going to each user individually and making the same change, you can use one of several special selection techniques with User Manager. First, select the users whose properties you want to modify by doing the following:

- *Selecting a range of users*   From the main User Manager window, click and drag the selection bar across all of the users you want to select. Alternatively, you can highlight the user at the top of the list. Scroll down to the bottom of the list and Shift+click. This highlights the entire range from the top entry you highlighted to the bottom.

- *Selecting specific users*   Ctrl+click on each user you want to select or deselect.

- *Highlighting groups of users*   In the User Manager window, select Select Users from the Users menu. From the Select Users dialog box that appears, select each group you want highlighted and then click Select. All the members of the groups are highlighted in the user list.

After the users whose properties you want to modify have been highlighted, press Enter or select Properties from the Users menu. The User Properties dialog box shown in Figure 7.11 appears. Notice that all of the users you selected are listed in the top window.

The following are some common situations in which you might want to apply settings to multiple users simultaneously:

- *Creating groups and defining their settings*   If you want to create a group and then change a particular setting such as dialin access for the entire group, this is the best way to do it. Simply highlight all the new members and go into their properties. Select Groups and add them to the `DIALIN_ACCESS` group that you created. Go into Dialin, grant them dialin permission and set up callback if needed.

- *Creating home directories and setting up profiles and login scripts*   After you have created all of the Terminal Server users, you can assign them all unique home directories and profile paths in one shot. Select the users whose properties you want to change and fill in `\\[Server Name]\[Share Name]\%USERNAME%` for the users' Profile Paths and Home Directories. All the home directories for all the users are created simultaneously under the share, each under a directory named after a given user! Also use this technique to fill in the logon script that your users will use.

> **Real-World Tip: `TS_USERS` Group**
>
> If you have a large domain, it is very handy to make a TS_USERS group and keep all of your Terminal Server users in it. If you need to apply a change to just the Terminal Server users, you can use this technique to select just the members of the TS_USERS group.

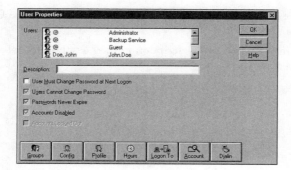

Figure 7.11 Changing settings for multiple users.

■ *Hours of Logon and Config settings* This technique is very useful for setting hours of logon and config settings. Setting either of these on an individual basis can be very tedious. Select all the users to whom you want to give the same hours of logon and config settings. Change these settings and then save them.

It is also a good idea to create a group that contains all the users with the same level of settings, such as TSUSERS or TSADMIN. If you want to change their settings, such as logon hours, just use the group select technique to select them all.

Creating Groups

Now that you know how to create a user and what all the user properties are, it is time to learn how to create groups. Like users, groups are created using the User Manager for Domains. As explained at the beginning of the chapter, there are two types of groups that can be created: local groups and global groups. When creating groups, remember the following points:

■ Group names cannot be changed after they are created, but their descriptions can be.

■ Group names can be up to 20 characters long and can contain all but the following characters:
" / \ [ ] : ; | = + , ★ ? < >

■ Group names are not case sensitive, but they are case aware.

■ Groups are always listed in alphabetical order in User Manager.

■ Global groups can only contain domain users. Local groups can contain both domain users and global groups.

Follow these steps to create a group using User Manager for Domains:

1. Open the User Manager for Domains (in the Start menu, select Programs, Administrative Tools, and User Manager for Domains) and highlight the user or users that you want to make members of the new group.

2. Select either New Global Group or New Local Group from the User menu at the main window.

3. Enter the Group Name and Description in the New Local/Global Group window, and then click OK.

8

Using Logon Scripts

WITH TERMINAL SERVER, LOGON SCRIPTS should be considered a necessity. *Logon scripts* provide the administrator with centralized control over application and data locations. Control is centralized by defining drive mappings in the logon script instead of individually per user. Logon scripts also provide a means to make changes or to control settings for a particular group of users. Logon scripts can also be a means of application installation, automated updates, and automated cleanup. This chapter covers how logon scripts work, how to create them, and how best to apply them. We'll also cover Microsoft's application compatibility scripts, what they're for, how they work, and how to use them.

Terminal Server's *USRLOGON.CMD* Logon Script

Unlike NT Server, Terminal Server includes a logon script that's run every time users log on to the server. This logon script is the USRLOGON.CMD file, located in the C:\WTSRV\SYSTEM32 directory of the Terminal Server the user is logging on to. This logon script is run before any other logon scripts—such as a user logon script or a Novell logon script—that have been configured for the user. The USRLOGON.CMD file has two primary purposes:

- It maps a predefined drive letter to the root of the user's home directory. You'll learn how to define which drive letter it maps in "Setting Up a Home Directory," later in this chapter.

- It runs the application compatibility scripts. These scripts are written for particular applications in order to make the applications run correctly in a multiuser environment.

The inclusion of the USRLOGON.CMD logon script with Terminal Server by Microsoft indicates how important logon scripts are with Terminal Server. You'll learn how this script works in detail in "Application Compatibility Scripts," later in this chapter.

When creating your own logon scripts, you have three choices, depending on your needs and your environment:

- You can add logon script commands to the top of USRLOGON.CMD on all your Terminal Servers. The commands you add will be run for all Terminal Server users who log on to these Terminal Servers. This is the quickest and generally the best way to add logon script commands that are intended only for Terminal Server users.

- You can create user logon scripts and assign them to each user. These scripts will be run by the users whether they log on to the domain from a workstation or through a Terminal Server session. You'll learn how to set up user logon scripts in the next section, "How User Logon Scripts Work."

- In NetWare environments, you can choose to have your NetWare logon scripts processed for users. This is a good option for shops that are primarily NetWare. For more information on enabling NetWare logon scripts, see Chapter 15, "Terminal Server and NetWare."

How User Logon Scripts Work

When a user logs on to a domain, the PDC or BDC that authenticated the user checks to see if the user has a logon script assigned in User Manager and runs it. Logon scripts can be either batch files (.bat or .cmd) or executables (.exe or .com). They are run from the following directory on the NT server that authenticated the user:

```
C:\WINNT\SYSTEM32\REPL\IMPORT\SCRIPTS
```

Author's Note: The USRLOGON.CMD **Logon Script**
The user logon script or NetWare logon script will still be run after the Terminal Server USRLOGON.CMD logon script, if the user logs on to the domain through a Terminal Server session. Make sure the commands you put in either the user or NetWare logon script do not conflict with the commands in the USRLOGON.CMD.

For more information on how to set up user logon scripts and replicate them to your PDC and BDCs, see "Logon Script Name Setting" in Chapter 7, "Creating Users and Groups in Terminal Server."

Creating Logon Batch Files

Several languages are readily available with which you can create logon scripts, so the choice is up to you. In general, the simplest and easiest choice is to use DOS batch file language. This section covers how to create logon scripts using DOS batch file language. You'll also learn about several command-line utilities, available in the NT Server 4.0 Resource Kit, that will bring some of the power of scripting languages such as Perl to your batch files.

For those who want to use a more powerful scripting language, the NT Server 4.0 Resource Kit contains software and instructions for three different scripting languages: Perl, REXX, and kixtart. All three are very powerful scripting languages that allow you to do everything from making execution decisions based on groups to modifying the Registry. However, you'll find that many of the capabilities of these more powerful scripting languages can also be done with batch files if you use the correct utilities. The "Useful Third-Party Utilities for Logon Scripts" section introduces you to some of these utilities later in the chapter.

Logon Script Variables

Let's start with the variables you can use in your batch files. Several system environment variables are very useful in logon batch files. To see the values of these variables, type the command **SET** at the DOS prompt. The variables are as follows:

- **%COMPUTERNAME%** This variable resolves to the computer name of the Terminal Server the user logged on to.

- **%COMSPEC%** The path and filename of the command-line processor. This normally resolves to \WTSRV\SYSTEM32\CMD.EXE.

- **%HOMEDRIVE%** and **%HOMEPATH%** Together, these two variables resolve to the user's home drive and path. These are very important variables, as you'll see later in this section.

- **%PATH%** The system path is a semicolon-delimited list of the paths searched in for executables. The PATH variable plays an important role with many programs.

Author's Note: NT Server 4.0 Resource Kit

The NT Server 4.0 Resource Kit is available for purchase from Microsoft. The utilities included in this kit are intended for use on NT servers. Be sure to test them thoroughly before implementing them on Terminal Server.

■ **%SYSTEMDRIVE%** This is the drive letter that contains the Terminal Server files. Normally, this drive letter is C, but if you select drive letter remapping in MetaFrame, the system drive will be M. Checking the setting of this variable is a good way to tell if the system drive letter has been remapped.

■ **%SYSTEMROOT%** System root is the drive letter and path of the root of the system. This normally resolves to `C:\WTSRV`.

■ **%TEMP%** and **%TMP%** Both resolve to the system-assigned temporary file directory.

■ **%USERDOMAIN%** The domain the user logged on to.

■ **%USERNAME%** The current user's logon name. For NetWare administrators who are used to the `WHOAMI` command, you can simply type `SET` and look at this variable to determine the currently logged-on user. This is a very important variable for making logon script decisions based on username.

■ **%USERPROFILE%** The path to the user's profile directory. This is a very important path with Terminal Server. The profile directory contains the user's Registry settings, desktop, Start menu, and other personal folders.

■ **%WINDIR%** The drive letter and path to the system directory (normally `C:\WTSRV`). This is the same as the `%SYSTEMROOT%` variable. `%WINDIR%` will also resolve to the Windows directory on a Windows 95 workstation.

■ **%WINSTATIONNAME%** The name of the connection shown in the Terminal Server Connection Configuration Tool that the user is using. If the user is at the console, the value will be `Console`. This is a useful way of making logon decisions based on whether the user is at the console or is remote.

Notice that all the variables are surrounded with percentage signs (%). The percentage signs are necessary to tell the batch file language to replace the variable name with its value. The batch file that follows shows how to make use of the variables. Note how the values of the variables are substituted for the variable names when the variable names are enclosed in percentage signs:

```
DISPLAY.BAT:
@echo off
echo Welcome %username% to Terminal Server
echo Winstation : %winstationname%
echo Home drive : %homedrive%%homepath%
echo Profile    : %userprofile%
echo Temp dir   : %temp%
```

Running DISPLAY.BAT:

```
C:\BAT> DISPLAY
Welcome Administrator to Terminal Server
Winstation : Console
Home Drive : Z:\administrator
Profile    : C:\WTSRV\Profiles\ADMINI~1
Temp dir   : C:\TEMP\6
C:\BAT>
```

Note in the example the use of the ECHO command. We'll be going over the use of the ECHO command in the "*ECHO*" section, later in the chapter. Also note that although we'll be referring to commands such as ECHO in uppercase in the text, both variables and commands are not case sensitive in batch files.

Batch File Commands

The batch file language is very simple. The real power of batch files comes from all the useful utilities you can run from them. After you learn the basic batch file commands in this section, see the "Using Terminal Server Utilities in Logon Scripts" and the "Useful Third-Party Utilities for Logon Scripts" sections for examples of what you can do from batch files using command-line utilities.

CALL

Syntax:

```
CALL [drive:][path]batch-filename
```

Use the CALL command to call other batch files from the parent batch file. Within logon scripts, this can be useful for encapsulating different types of logon scripts. For example, you could have a MAIN.BAT logon batch file that every user runs. The MAIN.BAT file could be set to call WTS_USER.BAT if the user is logging on to a Terminal Server or DOMAIN.BAT if the user is logging onto the domain from a standard workstation. We'll go over how to detect this in the "Checking Whether a User Has Logged on to the Domain from Terminal Server" section, later in the chapter. In the following example, the MESSAGE.BAT file is called from the MAIN.BAT batch file using the CALL command. Once MESSAGE.BAT has completed, control is returned to MAIN.BAT, and the current date is shown using the Date /T command.

```
MAIN.BAT:
@echo off
echo Welcome to Terminal Server
echo.
call MESSAGE.BAT
echo.
Date /T

MESSAGE.BAT:
Echo The system will be down for maintenance this afternoon
Echo after 5:00 pm.

Running MAIN.BAT:
C:\BAT> MAIN
Welcome to Terminal Server
The system will be down for maintenance this afternoon
After 5:00 pm.
Thu 6/25/1998
C:\BAT>
```

Note how the MAIN batch file calls the MESSAGE batch file, which displays the The system will be down for maintenance this afternoon message. Once MESSAGE.BAT is finished, control returns back to MAIN.BAT, where the date is displayed.

ECHO

Syntax:

```
[@]ECHO [on¦off] or ECHO message or ECHO.
```

By default, when you run a batch file, it will echo all the commands to the screen as they are being run. This is normally not desired. To disable this feature, put the @ECHO off command at the top of your batch file. The at sign (@) prevents the ECHO off command itself from being displayed.

To display a message to the screen, use the ECHO *message* command. The message can be any combination of text or variables. If you use a variable, make sure to enclose it in percentage signs. To print a blank line to the screen, use the ECHO. command. The following ECHOTST.BAT batch file shows you how to use all three techniques.

```
ECHOTST.BAT:
@echo off
echo You logged on from the %USERDOMAIN% domain
echo.
```

```
Running ECHOTST.BAT:
C:\BAT> ECHOTST
You logged on from the ACME_CORP domain

C:\BAT>
```

GOTO

Syntax:
```
GOTO label
        :label
```

The GOTO command will go to the :label section in the batch file and continue execution. The GOTO command is often used in combination with the IF command, as shown in the following example:

```
If exist h:\windows\app.cfg goto :end
Copy %windir%\app.cfg h:\windows
:end
```

This batch file checks whether the user has a particular application configuration file (APP.CFG) under his or her home directory (h:\windows); if not, the batch file copies the application configuration file there. If the user already has the file, it goes to the :end section, where the batch is finished.

IF

Syntax:

```
IF [not] errorlevel number command
        IF [not] string1 == string2 command
        IF [not] exist filename command
```

Of all the commands, the `IF` command is probably the most useful. With the `IF` command, you can conditionally execute parts of the logon script. As you'll see in "Checking Whether a User Is a Member of a Group," later in this chapter, you can use the `IF` command to check whether a user is part of a particular group and then perform actions for that group. A description of the `IF` commands listed above follows:

- The `IF [not] errorlevel` *number command* command allows the batch file to interact with utilities that return error levels. For example, the `IFMEMBER [group]` utility, included in the NT Server 4.0 Resource Kit, returns error level one (1) if the current user is a member of the group.

- With the `IF [not]` *string1* == *string2 command* command, you can control execution based on a variable or string. This is very useful for controlling execution based on the system variables outlined previously.

- The `IF [not] exist` *filename command* command will check whether a file exists and execute the command if it does. You can use this effectively for testing the presence of certain marker files and for checking which operating system the user is attaching with.

You'll see many examples using the `IF` command later in the chapter.

PAUSE and *REM*

Syntax:

```
PAUSE or PAUSE > nul
        REM message
```

The final two commands are `PAUSE` and `REM`. The `PAUSE` command will stop the batch file, display the `Press any key to continue.` message and wait for the user to press a key. If you do not want the default message to be displayed, use the `PAUSE > nul` command. `PAUSE > nul` will still pause for user input but will not display anything.

The `REM` command is simply used for comments in a batch file:

```
REM Demonstration of the pause and rem commands
Echo After you read this press a key
Pause > nul
```

Using Terminal Server Utilities in Logon Scripts

Many command-line utilities come with Terminal Server that you might know about. This section covers the ones that are most useful in batch file lots of examples of how to use these commands in useful ways in your bat

If you're interested in seeing all the parameters available for a particular command, type **[command] /?** on the command line.

Setting Up Home Directory Drive Letters

The substitute (SUBST) command is the only way to map-root a drive with NT. When it comes to getting applications to run correctly, the SUBST command is very important. Every Terminal Server logon script should have a substitute command to define a home directory drive letter. A map-rooted drive letter for the temporary directory or profile directory is also useful for many situations. Here's how to use the SUBST command to map the letter H to the root of a user's home directory:

```
SUBST H: %HOMEDRIVE%%HOMEPATH%
```

Setting Up Temporary Directories for Applications

If two users are using the same program and they're sharing the same temporary directory, it's likely that the programs will conflict. To resolve this problem, Terminal Server was designed to assign a unique temporary directory for every user. When users log on to the system, they're assigned a numbered directory under C:\TEMP (for example, C:\TEMP\3). The system automatically removes the Everyone group from the access control list (ACL) for this directory and gives Full Control only to the user, administrators, and system. In this way, not only are the user's temporary directories kept separate from one another, but also the privacy of the user's temporary files is protected. After the user logs off, the entire directory is deleted.

If you have a program that needs a location in which to put its temporary files, map a drive letter in the logon script to the root of the temporary directory by adding the following command to the script:

```
SUBST T: %TEMP%
```

Next, set the program to use the T drive as the location to store its temporary files.

Because the %TEMP% directory changes every time a user logs on, this is the only way to keep the %TEMP% directory drive location constant.

Real-World Tip: SUBST Command and Local Paths

One caveat about the SUBST command: It only works for local paths. If you substitute a drive letter for a network path, such as SUBST H: \\[*server name*]\[*share name*], you'll get an error message. In order to map-root to a home directory, that home directory must be on the local server. This is not a problem for a single server, but if you're doing load balancing across two or more servers, you'll want to keep the home directories in the same location. One method to get around this limitation is to put your home directories on a NetWare server and check the Map Root box in the User Environment Profile window in User Manager. To get to this window, double-click the user's name in User Manager and click the Profile button.

Setting Up Drive Letters and Redirecting LPT1

Oftentimes with Terminal Server, administrators manually connect the drives for the users using Explorer and set them to reconnect upon logon. This works fine until either the server name changes or the data is moved. If this has to be done and you have several hundred users, you have a lot of work to do. The better way to handle drive mappings is to map them centrally with a logon script. Not only does a logon script give you tighter control of your drive mappings, but it makes moving data directories a breeze. You can also use the logon script to redirect your LPT ports to a network printer. This is very handy for DOS programs running on Terminal Server, because Microsoft's Terminal Server does not automatically redirect ports.

The following command connects the P drive to the APPS share on `ACME_PDC`:

```
NET USE P: \\ACME_PDC\APPS
```

It's recommended that you assign a single drive letter, if possible, to your main applications directory. By keeping the application drive letter the same for all users, migrations are made much easier.

The following command maps the LPT1 port to the ACCT_HPLJ4 printer:

```
NET USE LPT1:  \\ACME_BDC\ACCT_HPLJ4
```

A print job sent by a DOS application running on Terminal Server to the LPT1 port will be redirected to `\\ACME_BDC\ACCT_HPLJ4` = `printer` on the network.

Checking Whether a User Has Logged On to the Domain from Terminal Server

User logon scripts are run from wherever the user logs on to the domain. This presents a problem if the user normally logs on to the domain from a workstation and then logs on again through a Terminal Server session, because the user will run the same logon script twice. In order for the user logon script to be effective, it needs to be able to determine whether the user is logging on from a workstation or from a Terminal Server session. The trick to doing this is simple. Use the `IF EXIST` *filename command* command to determine whether the current machine has any Terminal Server–specific files on it:

```
IF EXIST %WINDIR%\SYSTEM32\CHGUSR.EXE GOTO WTS_LOGON
```

This simple command checks whether the `CHGUSR.EXE` command exists in the current Windows directory. If so, it goes to the `:WTS_LOGON` label in the script and continues execution. Because the `CHGUSR.EXE` command is unique to Terminal Server, if users are logging on to the domain from their workstations, this file will not exist. Put the commands that should only be run if the user is logging on to Terminal Server into the `:WTS_LOGON` section.

Changing Directory and File Permissions

`CACLS.EXE` is a command-line utility included with Terminal Server that allows you to change the access control list (ACL) for files and directories on NTFS partitions.

This can be very beneficial for distributing security changes to users' home directories while they log on. Sometimes you may need to make the same change to a particular directory in everyone's home directory. Using CACLS, you can easily do this. To view the current access control list of a directory, type **CACLS [*directory*]** at the command prompt, as follows:

```
CACLS H:\APP1
```

This command reports the current access control list of the H:\APP1 directory.

To remove the Everyone group (/R Everyone) from the ACL list of the H:\APP1 directory as well as all files and subdirectories below it, either type the following at the command prompt or add the line to your logon script:

```
CACLS H:\APP1 /E /R EVERYONE /T
```

The /E option is important to use with CACLS. /E means that the access control list will be edited, not replaced. If you do not use /E, the old ACL will be deleted. Also, the /T option means to apply the ACL change to all subdirectories.

The following line grants the user (/P %USERNAME%:R) read-only access to the APP1 directory and subdirectories:

```
CACLS H:\APP1 /E /P %USERNAME%:R /T
```

Note that with the CACLS command, you can only add or remove global groups and users who are part of the domain to the file system's ACLs.

Logging Off After the Logon Script Completes

Use the LOGOFF utility to log off the user after he or she completes a task. For example, you can set up a logon script to run a particular application and then log the user off after it is finished by typing **LOGOFF**.

Displaying a Message to the Users as They Log On

MSG is a very useful command for sending a message to the users as they log on to the system. The message appears as a little dialog box with an OK button. For example, the following line displays the message to the current user for five seconds (/TIME:5). At the end of five seconds, the dialog box disappears:

```
MSG %USERNAME% /TIME:5 Remember the system will be down this weekend.
```

Changing the Registry

Generally, you should not have to change the Registry as users log on to the server. Policies, which are covered in detail in Chapter 12, "Administering the Desktop and Server," provide a much easier and more useful means to do this. If you do have an application-specific reason for changing the Registry, you can use an excellent utility included with Terminal Server called REGINI. You can use REGINI to apply the Registry changes that you define in a .KEY file. For more information on how to set this up,

type **REGINI** **/?.** You can also look under `C:\%systemroot%\Application`
`Compatibility Scripts` for examples of how REGINI can be used to enhance application compatibility.

Useful Third-Party Utilities for Logon Scripts

You'll find a ton of useful third-party logon script utilities in the NT Server 4.0
Resource Kit, available for purchase from Microsoft. Also, numerous batch file utilities
are available on public shareware sites. This section covers some of the most useful
utilities included with the NT 4.0 Resource Kit that come in handy in batch files. Be
sure to test these utilities in your environment first before putting them into production. These utilities were originally designed for use with NT Server, not Terminal
Server.

Checking Whether a User Is a Member of a Group

What if you want to connect certain drive letters and make certain changes to the
environment for members of a particular group? With Terminal Server, you'll need the
IFMEMBER utility included in the NT Server 4.0 Resource Kit. This utility can check
whether the user is a member of a particular local or domain group. The following
example shows how to use the IFMEMBER utility in your logon script:

```
IFMEMBER "\DOMAIN\APP_USERS"
        IF ERRORLEVEL 1 GOTO NOT_APP1_USER
        NET USE P: \\ACME_PDC\APP
        :NOT_APP1_USER
```

If the user is a member of the domain's APP_USERS group, his or her P drive is
mapped to `\\ACME_PDC\APP`. Note how the IF ERRORLEVEL statement is used. IFMEMBER
will return an error level of 1 if the user is *not* a member of the group. For a list of all
groups that the user is a member of, type **IFMEMBER** **/L.** This is also a good way to
check the format you'll need for the group name.

Prompting Users for a Response

If you want to prompt users to make a choice and then make execution decisions
based on those choices, CHOICE is the utility you need. (CHOICE is the same as the utility of the same name included with DOS 6.x and later.) For example, look at the following script:

```
ECHO Do you want to continue?
        CHOICE /c:y,n,m Yes, No or Maybe.
        IF ERRORLEVEL 3 GOTO MAYBE
        IF ERRORLEVEL 2 GOTO NO
        IF ERRORLEVEL 1 GOTO YES
```

Note that the error levels are in descending order. This is necessary in order for the
script to work properly. This short script asks the users whether they want to continue

and then goes to the appropriate label to continue execution. The /T:[*Choice*],[*Time in seconds*] parameter can be added at the end of the CHOICE command line to automatically make the [*Choice*] after [*Time in seconds*] seconds.

Setting Environment Variables

Oftentimes programs, especially DOS programs, rely on the settings of certain environment variables. If you want to set these variables in the logon script, you need to use SETX, which is included in the NT Server 4.0 Resource Kit. SETX can make changes to either the system environment variables or the user's environment variables. For example, the following line sets the APP1_TMP user environment variable to T:\ in the current user's Registry:

```
SETX APP1_TMP T:\
```

To set a system environment variable, use the -m command line option, as follows:

```
SETX ALL_CAN_SEE "Everyone can see this variable" -m
```

You may be wondering why you should use the SETX command instead of the regular SET command to take care of setting the environment. The answer lies in how environment variables work with Windows NT. Windows NT has three types of environment variables: system, user, and temporary. Type **SET** at the command line to display the environment variables that are currently set on the system. You'll see all three types of variables together in the list in alphabetical order.

The system environment variables affect all users on the system and are stored in HKEY_LOCAL_MACHINE. Use the SETX *Variable name-Setting* -m command to set your system environment variables. System environment variables include the path statement from the autoexec.bat file (which is read during system startup), the system directory, number of processors, processor type, and more. To see your current system environment variables, go to the Control Panel, select System, and click the Environment tab. Under the Environment tab, you'll see two small windows; your system environment variables are listed in the System Variables window. All users on the system will be able to see these variables by typing **SET** at the command prompt.

User environment variables are unique to a particular user and are stored in the user's HKEY_LOCAL_USERS file. To see the current user's environment variables, go to Control Panel, select System, and then click the Environment tab. The current user's environment variables are listed in the User Variables window under the Environment tab. When you add a user environment variable to this list using the SETX *Variable name-Setting* command, every time the user logs on, he or she will be able to see the variable you set by typing the **SET** command from DOS.

The last type of environment variable is temporary. Temporary environment variables are the ones that either you or your programs set from the command line using the regular SET *Variable name-Setting* command that's included with Terminal Server, not the SETX command. Once you exit from the command line, the temporary variable is erased.

If you use the SET command in your logon scripts, when the logon script is finished, the variables are erased. That's why you need to use SETX to change user and system environment variables.

Changing Users' Paths

Many applications require particular search paths to be included in the PATH variable in order to run. You can use the PATHMAN utility to add paths both to the system and to the user's PATH statements:

```
pathman /au h:\tools;h:\temp
```

This example adds the h:\tools and h:\temp directories to the users' search paths. Full instructions on using PATHMAN are included in the NT Server 4.0 Resource Kit.

Pausing for a Length of Time

Sometimes you want to display a message for users, but you don't want to force them to type a key. For this need, you should use the TIMEOUT command:

```
TIMEOUT 5
```

In this example, the system waits five seconds and then continues batch file execution. If the user presses a key during this time, the system will continue execution immediately.

Application Compatibility Scripts

Included with Terminal Server are several application compatibility scripts written by Microsoft. These scripts were written to take care of some of the compatibility problems Microsoft found with applications during testing. The scripts are all located in the C:\WTSRV\Application Compatibility Scripts directory and its subdirectories, as follows:

- C:\WTSRV\Application Compatibility Scripts Contains several special utilities written by Microsoft that are used in the application compatibility scripts. Also contains more general-purpose scripts, such as CHKROOT.CMD, which are covered in the following section.

- C:\WTSRV\Application Compatibility Scripts\Install Contains installation scripts for particular applications that are to be run after those applications are installed.

- C:\WTSRV\Application Compatibility Scripts\Logon Contains scripts for particular applications that should be run in the logon script. These scripts normally make changes to individual users' Registry and profiles in order for the applications to run properly in a multiuser environment.

- C:\WTSRV\Application Compatibility Scripts\Uninstall Contains uninstall scripts for the application's compatibility scripts.

In general, when setting up application compatibility scripts, you should follow a particular order. Each of these steps will be covered in detail in the following sections:

1. Set up your home directory using Microsoft's `CHKROOT.CMD` file.

2. Install the application according to the guidelines provided in Chapter 10, "Installing Applications on Terminal Server."

3. Run the appropriate application compatibility install script from the `C:\WTSRV\Application Compatibility Scripts\Install` directory.

4. If you ever uninstall the application in the future, be sure to run the appropriate uninstall script from the `C:\WTSRV\Application Compatibility Scripts\Uninstall` directory, if it exists for your application.

Setting Up a Home Directory

Many of the application compatibility scripts require that you have a home directory set up before they will work. You need to follow a special procedure when setting up your home directories to work with the application compatibility scripts:

1. Set up a home directory for users in User Manager by double-clicking the user's name, clicking Profile, and filling in the Home Directory path. You can use either the Local Path setting if the home directories will be on the local hard drive of the Terminal Server or the Connect to Path setting if the home directories will be off a share on the network. For more detailed instructions, see Chapter 7.

2. Run the `CHKROOT.CMD` file from the `C:\WTSRV\Application Compatibility Scripts` directory to check whether you've already defined a home directory drive letter. If not, it will create a `ROOTDRV2.CMD` command file that you must edit in Notepad. In the Notepad window, fill in the drive letter you want as the root of your home directory next to the `Set RootDrive=` statement; then select Save from the File menu to save the new `ROOTDRV2.CMD` file.

> **Author's Note: The Home Directory Drive Letter**
> Some of the application compatibility scripts will make changes to the Registry based on this home directory drive letter. Make sure this drive letter is not being used for anything else on your system. If you decide to change the home directory drive letter later, you must rerun all your application compatibility install scripts so that they can reapply these Registry changes.

The ROOTDRV2.CMD file is an important command file. Once this command file has been set up, all the application compatibility scripts will be able to use the RootDrive variable to make application-specific changes based on the user's home directory. Also, when you log on, the USRLOGON.CMD file will map the home directory drive letter that you defined in ROOTDRV2.CMD to the root of the user's home directory.

Running the Install Scripts

After you've set up the user's home directory and installed the application, it's time to run the install scripts. In the C:\WTSRV\Application Compatibility Scripts\Install directory, you'll find scripts for all the following applications:

- Corel Office 7 and Corel Office 8 (coffice7.cmd and coffice8.cmd)
- Diskeeper 2.0 (diskpr20.cmd)
- Dr. Watson (drwatson.cmd)
- Microsoft Excel 97 and Word 97 (excel97.cmd and word97.cmd)
- Microsoft Internet Explorer 3.x and 4.x (msie30.cmd and msie40.cmd)
- Microsoft Project 95 and 98 (msproj95.cmd and msproj98.cmd)
- Microsoft SNA Server 3.0 (mssna30.cmd)
- Netscape Communicator 4.0 and Navigator 3.0 (netcom40.cmd and netnav30.cmd)
- ODBC drivers (odbc.cmd)
- Microsoft SNA Server 4.0 and Client (sna40srv.cmd and sna40cli.cmd)
- Lotus Smart Suite 97 (ssuite97.cmd)
- Windows Messaging (winmsg.cmd)

These scripts should be run right after you install the application for the first time. To run a script, simply execute the appropriate .CMD file for the application you just installed. Before you run the .CMD file, you should open it up with a text editor and get an idea of how it works. Many of the scripts assume that you've installed the application in the default installation directory on your system drive. If you installed it in any other directory, you'll need to change the directories referenced in the .CMD file.

> **Author's Note: Configuring Applications**
>
> Just because an application you installed on Terminal Server is not on this list does not mean that the application does not have to be configured to run correctly in a multiuser environment. For more information on how to configure your applications to run correctly in a multiuser environment, see Chapter 10. Some administrators even create their own application compatibility scripts written for their particular applications.

Application Compatibility Logon Scripts

You'll find that most of the application compatibility install scripts make changes to
the application's Registry entries or install directories so that the application runs correctly in a multiuser environment. If changes need to be made to each user's directories or Registry entries, the application compatibility install scripts will set up a special
logon script to run when users log on. These logon scripts are located under
`C:\WTSRV\Application Compatibility Scripts\Logon`. When you run the install
script for an application that uses one of these logon scripts, the install script will
append a statement to the end of either the `C:\WTSRV\SYSTEM32\USRLOGN1.CMD` file or
the `C:\WTSRV\SYSTEM32\USRLOGN2.CMD` file. This statement will call the application-
specific logon script for the application you just installed. As you'll see in the next section, the `USRLOGN1.CMD` and `USRLOGN2.CMD` files are run from the `USRLOGON.CMD` file
every time someone logs on to the Terminal Server.

How the *USRLOGON.CMD* Works

The `USRLOGON.CMD` file, located in the `C:\WTSRV\SYSTEM32` directory, contains many
statements that are essential for the application compatibility scripts to run properly.
The `USRLOGON.CMD` file is the system logon script for Terminal Server and is run by
everyone who logs on to your Terminal Server. Because it's a `.CMD` file, it supports the
REXX language. REXX is an extension to the batch file language, so you can still use
all the batch file commands just covered. Take a look at the default `USRLOGON.CMD` file
to see what it does:

```
@Echo Off
Rem
Rem This is for those scripts that don't need the RootDrive.
Rem
If Not Exist "%SystemRoot%\System32\Usrlogn1.cmd" Goto cont0
Cd /d "%SystemRoot%\Application Compatibility Scripts\Logon"
Call "%SystemRoot%\System32\Usrlogn1.cmd"

:cont0
Rem
Rem Determine the user's home directory drive letter. If this isn't
Rem set, exit.
Rem
Cd /d %SystemRoot%\"Application Compatibility Scripts"
Call RootDrv.Cmd
If "A%RootDrive%A" == "AA" End.Cmd
Rem
Rem Map the User's Home Directory to a Drive Letter
Rem
Net Use %RootDrive% /D >NUL: 2>&1
Subst %RootDrive% /d >NUL: 2>&1
```

```
Subst %RootDrive% %HomeDrive%%HomePath%
Rem
Rem Invoke each Application Script. Application Scripts are automatically
Rem added to UsrLogn2.Cmd when the Installation script is run.
Rem
If Not Exist %SystemRoot%\System32\UsrLogn2.Cmd Goto Cont1
Cd Logon
Call %SystemRoot%\System32\UsrLogn2.Cmd

:Cont1
```

The USRLOGON.CMD logon script first runs the USRLOGN1.CMD file, if it exists, from the C:\WTSRV\SYSTEM32 directory (%SYSTEMROOT%\SYSTEM32) on the Terminal Server. Recall that the USRLOGN1.CMD and USRLOGN2.CMD files will contain statements to run the application compatibility logon scripts for all applications you've installed that need them.

Next, the USRLOGON.CMD file checks whether you have set up the user home directory by calling ROOTDRV.CMD. This command file will check whether ROOTDRV2.CMD exists and then run it. If the home directory has not been set up, the logon script will exit. If the logon script has been set up, USRLOGON.CMD maps the home directory drive letter to the root of the home directory. USLOGON.CMD then calls USRLOGN2.CMD, if it exists, and runs any application-specific logon scripts that it calls. For more information on how to set up the user home directory, see "Setting Up a Home Directory," earlier in this chapter.

Installing Clients

9

$\mathbf{S}$O FAR, WE HAVE DISCUSSED CREATING connections for the clients and setting up the user accounts that they will log on with. Now it is time to set up the client software so that users can connect to Terminal Server. In this chapter, we will go over how to install and use both the Microsoft Terminal Server clients and the MetaFrame ICA clients.

Microsoft Terminal Server Clients

Out of the box, Terminal Server has clients for most versions of the Windows operating system. The Microsoft Terminal Server client uses the RDP protocol to communicate with the server. Because RDP runs only on top of TCP/IP, you need to have that protocol set up on your clients before installing Terminal Server. In this section we will consider the different Microsoft Terminal Server clients that are available, what their minimum hardware requirements are, and how to install and use them.

Microsoft Terminal Server Client Hardware Requirements

One of the main advantages of Terminal Server is that the clients do not need to have a lot of processing power. This makes it very easy to integrate Terminal Server into networks that still consist of a lot of legacy PCs and equipment. You can run a Microsoft Terminal Server client on as little as a 386 PC with 8MB of RAM running Windows for Workgroups.

If your company is like most, you probably have a stack of 386 or 486 legacy computers in a back closet somewhere. If you are on a tight budget, dusting off these old machines and putting them to use might be well worth it. An old 386 or 486 running today's 32-bit Windows applications can be set up to use the power of your Terminal Server in little time.

Of course, for companies with a larger budget, Windows-based Terminals (WBT) are a good alternative. They are less expensive than new PCs, are very easy to install and configure, and normally come preloaded with either the Microsoft or Citrix client.

Another option is to run the Terminal Server client on the desktops of your existing PCs, just as if it were another application.

Whichever way you decide to do it, remember that the Microsoft Terminal Server client will run only on the following Windows operating systems:

- Windows 95/98
- Windows NT 3.51/4.0
- Windows for Workgroups 3.11
- Windows CE (OEM only)

Table 9.1 covers the minimum hardware requirements for the Microsoft Terminal Server clients and which Microsoft Terminal Server client (TS Client) you need for each operating system.

Table 9.1 **Terminal Server Client's Minimum Requirements**

Operating System	Processor	RAM	Hard Drive Space	TS Client
Windows 3.11	386	8MB	4MB	16-bit
Windows 95/98	386	16MB	4MB	32-bit
Windows NT	486	16MB	4MB	32-bit
Windows CE	N/A★	N/A★	N/A★	OEM★

★ *CE clients available only from OEMs for WBTs.*

Remember that these requirements are minimums. If you don't find that they provide acceptable performance, you may need to increase the amount of RAM or processing speed.

Even so, notice how meager the requirements are. The Microsoft Terminal Server client has to have only enough processing power to receive, process, and send screen updates and user interface commands. The real processing power occurs at the server; the clients are merely a window to applications running with the performance and power of your Terminal Server. As you will see in a little while, the "thinness" of the clients makes them incredibly simple and quick to install.

Installing the 32-bit Microsoft Terminal Server Client

The Terminal Server CD comes with two clients—a 16-bit and 32-bit version. The 16-bit client is located in the `D:\CLIENTS\TSCLIENT\WIN16\[Processor]` directory and the 32-bit client is located in the `D:\CLIENTS\TSCLIENT\WIN32\` `[Processor]` directory; `[Processor]` is either I386 (Intel) or ALPHA (DEC Alpha).

The 32-bit Terminal Server client is designed for the 32-bit Windows operating systems: Windows 95, Windows 98, and Windows NT Server or Workstation. In the 32-bit client directory you will find two additional directories, `NET` and `DISK`. The purposes of these directories are as follows:

- The `NET` directory is designed for a network install. If you want to install your clients from a network installation point, copy these files to a directory on your network and give your clients access to them.
- The `DISK` directory contains files to be copied to a floppy disk for installation. Because it is such a thin client, the 32-bit Terminal Server files will all fit on a single formatted 3 1/2-inch high-density disk.

The instructions for installing the TS client are as follows:

1. Prepare the Windows 95/98/NT workstation for the install by loading and binding TCP/IP to the network adapter. Because Microsoft's Terminal Server client uses RDP, it works only with TCP/IP.

2. Check your connectivity with the Terminal Server by pinging either the hostname or IP address of the Terminal Server. If it responds, your network connectivity is good and TCP/IP has been set up correctly. If not, check your cabling, ensure that you have a link light on your network card, and try pinging other devices on your network, such as your default gateway, to help isolate the problem.

Author's Note: The Alpha Processor

Microsoft's Terminal Server client is the only client that will run on NT workstations or servers that use the Alpha processor. The MetaFrame ICA clients support only Intel processors.

Author's Note: Name Resolution

Whether you ping the IP address or the hostname depends on whether name resolution has been set up on your network. Although working with names is more convenient than working with IP addresses, it is not necessary to have name resolution established to connect to Terminal Server with a Terminal Server client. You simply enter the IP address of the Terminal Server at the client to connect.

If name resolution (WINS or DNS) has been established, you should be able to ping the computer name of the Terminal Server; it should resolve the IP address and return the ping. If your name resolution is not working, make sure you have logged on to the domain. On a Windows 95 station, it is possible to click Cancel at the logon prompt and not log on. If you don't log on, you will not be able to resolve names. Also, make sure the WINS or DNS entries are correct in the workstation's Network control panel.

3. Run SETUP.EXE from the D:\CLIENTS\TSCLIENT\WIN32\[Processor]\NET direc-
tory. If installing from a floppy, first copy the D:\CLIENTS\TSCLIENT\WIN32\
[Processor]\DISK1 directory to the disk and run SETUP.EXE from it. The
defaults will work fine for most situations. There is little to decide other than
the location in which the client files will be installed. The client, by default, is
installed in the C:\PROGRAM FILES\TERMINAL SERVER CLIENT directory.

After the install program is finished, you will see several shortcuts to new applica-
tions listed inside the Terminal Server client folder located at Start menu, Programs.
The Terminal Server client is the main application you will use for connecting to your
Terminal Server. The Client Connection Manager lets you set up automated connec-
tions with predefined options such as auto logon and initial program. The use of both
applications will be discussed shortly.

Automating the 32-bit Terminal Server Client Install

By using the quiet (/Q) command-line option, you can completely automate the install
of your Microsoft Terminal Server client. The following is a list of the command-line
options you can use when running the 32-bit client's SETUP.EXE from the command
prompt:

- /Q   Installs the 32-bit client with default options and displays the exit prompt
when finished.

- /Q1   Suppresses the exit prompt at the end of the installation. The user will still
see the file install "blue bar."

- /QT   Suppresses all user interaction and screens; the installation will run in the
background without the user knowing it.

Using these command-line options, you can easily set up scripts (with Microsoft's
SMS or NetWare's NAL, for example) that will roll out the 32-bit Terminal Server
clients for you automatically.

> **Real-World Tip: Using the Terminal Server Client Creator Tool**
>
> Terminal Server comes with a Terminal Server Client Creator Tool that you can use to easily create client
> disks for all versions of the Microsoft Terminal Server client. The following instructions illustrate this
> process:
>
> 1. Open the Terminal Server Client Creator located in the Start menu | Programs | Administrative
> Tools folder.
>
> 2. In the Make Installation Disk Set window, highlight the client you want to create disks for.
>
> 3. Select the Destination Drive and whether you want to Format Disks.
>
> 4. Insert the first client floppy into the drive you selected and click OK.
>
> The program copies all necessary client installation files to the disk and prompts for more disks if
> needed.

Installing the 16-bit Microsoft Terminal Server Client

Many companies have Windows for Workgroups (WFW) stations on their network or have a significant number of WFW licenses. Using the 16-bit Microsoft Terminal Server client, your WFW stations can run today's 32-bit applications with ease. Remember that you need Windows for Workgroups, not Windows 3.1. Windows for Workgroups includes the capability to attach to Microsoft networks and can run the TCP/IP protocol. If you need a Terminal Server client for Windows 3.1, you need to purchase the MetaFrame add-on from Citrix.

The 16-bit client is located on the Terminal Server CD under `D:\CLIENTS\TSCLIENT\WIN16\I386`. A disk image (DISK1, DISK2, and DISK3) and a network image subdirectory (`NET`) exist in this directory. As with the 32-bit client, the `NET` directory is for network or CD-based installs, and the disk image directories can be copied to individual floppies for a floppy-based install.

Installing the WFW TCP/IP Stack

Because Microsoft's Terminal Server client for WFW uses RDP, you must first have TCP/IP installed in WFW. Several different TCP/IP stacks are available for WFW. It is recommended that you stay with the Microsoft TCP/IP stack that is available on the Terminal Server CD; it is included on the Terminal Server CD and is fully supported by Microsoft.

The instructions for installing TCP/IP on WFW are as follows:

1. From the WFW workstation, install Microsoft Networking by running Network Setup from the Network program group in the Program Manager.

2. Make sure Microsoft Windows Network is listed to the left of the Network button in the Network Setup window. If not, click Networks, select it from the list, and add it.

3. Install your network adapter and the TCP/IP adapter by clicking Drivers from the Network Setup window, selecting your network adapter from the list, and adding it. If you don't have one of the network adapters in the list, you will need the NDIS driver for WFW from your network adapter manufacturer.

4. After you have installed the network adapter, select Protocol from the Network Setup window. Because the TCP/IP protocol is not included with the base set of WFW files, you will need to click the Unlisted Protocol button and enter the directory where the TCP/IP protocol install files are located.

> **Real-World Tip: WFW Install Files**
> You need either the original WFW floppy disks or a network image of the WFW install files to add network drivers and client software to WFW. If you still have a copy of the Windows NT 3.51 server CD, you will find a network image of the WFW install files in the `CLIENTS` directory. You will, of course, still need a license for WFW.

5. After you have installed the Microsoft client, network adapter, and TCP/IP protocol, return to the main Network Setup screen. It should look similar to Figure 9.1. Click OK to bind the protocols and complete the installation.

6. Exit and reboot to complete the installation and start the networking components.

7. Test connectivity to Terminal Server by pinging either its IP address or name from the DOS command prompt.

At this point, you are halfway to connecting your WFW workstation to Terminal Server. You have installed and bound the TCP/IP protocol to WFW and established that you can communicate with Terminal Server. Now it is time to finish the second half of the installation.

Adding the WFW Workstation to the Domain

Now it is time to add your WFW workstation to the domain. This is not necessary for connecting to Terminal Server; however, by adding it to the domain you can use the Terminal Server name instead of having to type in the IP address when establishing the connection.

The instructions for adding a WFW workstation to the domain are as follows:

1. Open the Control Panel from the Main group in Program Manager, and then select Network.

2. In the Microsoft Windows Network window, enter the computer and workgroup names. Note that the workgroup name should be the same as the domain name of your Terminal Server.

3. Click the Startup button in the Microsoft Windows Network window. In the Startup Settings window that appears, select Log On to a Windows NT...Domain and enter the domain name again.

4. Exit by clicking OK twice. Exit from WFW and restart your computer.

5. When WFW restarts, it will prompt you for a username and password to log on to the domain. Enter the username and password.

Installing the WFW Client

Up to this point we have been setting up the networking components that the Terminal Server client needs; now it is time to install the client itself. Run SETUP.EXE from the D:\CLIENTS\TSCLIENT\WIN16\I386\NETSETUP directory. You can also run it from Disk1, if you have created the client floppy disks.

> **Author's Note: TCP/IP for WFW**
>
> The TCP/IP protocol for WFW is available in D:\CLIENTS\TCP32WFW\NETSETUP on the Terminal Server CD. There is also a disk image directory (DISK) in the TCP32WFW directory that you can copy to a floppy disk (if you want to install from a floppy instead of the CD-ROM).

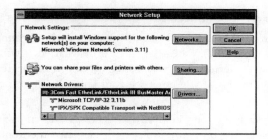

Figure 9.1 Required network components for a machine with a 3COM fast Etherlink card.

There are not many options during the installation other than the directory that the client will be installed into (C:\TSC, by default). The client installation will create a TS Client group in Program Manager. Inside this group you will find icons for the following applications:

- *TS client*   The main Terminal Server client
- *TS Connection Manager*   Allows you to create automated connections for connecting to Terminal Server

Both of these programs will be covered later in the chapter.

Automating the 16–bit Client Install

As with the 32-bit Terminal Server client, you can use the quiet (/Q) command-line option to automate the install of the 16-bit Microsoft Terminal Server client. The following is a list of the command-line options you can use when running the 16-bit client's SETUP.EXE from the command prompt:

- /Q   Installs the 32-bit client with default options and displays the exit prompt when finished.
- /Q1   Suppresses the exit prompt at the end of the installation. The user will still see the file install "blue bar."

Using these options is practical if you already have WFW stations on your network that are currently using TCP/IP to connect to the domain. If your WFW stations do not have TCP/IP installed, you will still have to go out to the workstations and install it for them to be able to connect to Terminal Server.

Running the Microsoft Terminal Server Client

This section covers how to run and use the 32-bit version of the client. Because the 32-bit and 16-bit clients are so similar, you can apply what you learn here to the 16-bit client as well.

Selecting the Server to Connect To

When you first run the Microsoft Terminal Server client, the Terminal Server Client screen appears (see Figure 9.2). When the client is first started, it will browse the network to find all of your Terminal Servers. To log on to one of the Terminal Servers, simply select it from the list. If you don't see your server listed, you can try two other techniques:

- Enter the server name for your Terminal Server, as shown in Figure 9.2. You should be able to log on if you can ping the server name from the command prompt.
- Enter the IP address of your Terminal Server. If you are still having problems connecting, try pinging the server and checking your network connection. If you can ping the server, you should be able to connect.

Setting Screen Resolution

Next, you need to select your screen resolution, which can be a little bit tricky. With Microsoft's Terminal Server client, you need to manually select the correct size. If you want to automate screen size selection, you can create a connection using the Terminal Server Connection Configuration Tool, which you will learn how to use later in this chapter.

Microsoft's Terminal Server client supports three different screen resolutions:

- Standard VGA 640×480
- Super VGA 800×600
- Super VGA 1024×768

When you first start the Microsoft Terminal Server client, you will be given a choice of resolution in the drop-down list next to Resolution. The highest resolution available is the highest one that will work with your current desktop screen resolution. For example, if you are in 800×600, you will see choices for only 640×480 and 800×600.

Figure 9.2 Microsoft Terminal Server client.

If you want the Terminal Server session to take up the entire desktop, choose your current desktop resolution setting. If you want the Terminal Server session to run in a smaller window, choose a lower resolution.

Logging On

After you have chosen the Terminal Server you want to log on to and the correct screen resolution, click the Connect button to connect to the server. After you have connected successfully, you will see the Logon Information screen shown in Figure 9.3.

At the Logon Information screen enter your username and password. If the correct domain has not already been selected, select it from the domain list. Remember that your username is not case sensitive, but your password is.

As you log on for the first time, Terminal Server will create your profile from a copy of the default profile. Chapter 12, "Administering the Desktop and Server," will cover profiles and users' desktop settings in detail.

Microsoft Terminal Server Client Shortcut Keys

The Microsoft Terminal Server client acts just like any another application running on your desktop; you can minimize the window and work on other applications while the client runs in the background. When the Terminal Server window is active, several shortcut keys will affect your Terminal Server desktop. The following is a list of the available shortcut keys:

- *Alt+Home*   Displays the Start menu on the Terminal Server desktop.
- *Alt+Ins*   Switches running tasks.
- *Alt+PgUp/PgDn*   Brings up a small window with icons representing the running applications and lets you switch between them. This is equivalent to the Alt+Tab hotkey used with Windows NT.

Figure 9.3 Terminal Server Logon Information screen.

- *Ctrl+Alt-End*   Displays the Windows NT Security dialog box. From the Security dialog box, you can change your password, launch Task Manager, log off, and more.

- *Ctrl+Alt+Break*   Switches the Terminal Server client between full-screen and window mode. In window mode you can adjust the window size or minimize it.

Changing Passwords, Logging Off, and Disconnecting

In the Windows NT Security dialog box shown in Figure 9.4, you have several important options available, such as the ability to change passwords, log off of the system, or disconnect. With NT Workstation 4.0, you would normally press Ctrl+Alt+Del to get to the Windows NT Security dialog box. However, because Ctrl+Alt+Del is used for special purposes by the Windows operating system that your client is running on top of, you cannot use it to access the Windows NT Security window of the client.

Instead, there are two other ways to access the Security window. The first way is by using the Ctrl+Alt+End shortcut, as shown in the previous section. The second way is by selecting Windows NT Security from the Start menu.

After you have reached the Windows NT Security dialog box, your options are as follows:

- *Change Password*   This is quickest way to change your password and the way you should show users. When you change the password from the Windows NT Security dialog box, you will also be prompted to change the passwords for the other systems you are currently logged on to. For example, if you are logged on to a NetWare server inside a Terminal Server session, you will be prompted to change both your Terminal Server and NetWare passwords.

- *Lock Workstation*   To prevent unauthorized access to your Terminal Server session while you are away, you can lock the workstation by clicking the Lock Workstation button from the Security dialog box before you leave. To unlock the screen and return to your desktop, you need to either enter your username and password or that of a member of the Administrator group.

Figure 9.4 The Windows NT Security window.

- *Task Manager*   You can use the Task Manager to either view or end currently running applications or processes. Nonadministrators have access only to their own applications and processes, whereas administrators can view or end any application or process running on Terminal Server. The Ctrl+Alt+End key sequence is very useful. Suppose you have a process or application that has seemingly locked up your session. By pressing Ctrl+Alt+End and selecting the Task Manager, you can end the troublesome application and continue working.

- *Logoff*   This allows you to log off the system. You can also log off by selecting Logoff from the Start menu. Logging off will close all running applications and end your session on the server.

- *Shut Down*   If you are a member of the Administrator group, you will see the Shut Down button in the Windows NT Security dialog box, as shown in Figure 9.4. By clicking the Shut Down button, you are shutting down the entire server. Beware that this command will forcefully log off all users. If users have applications open, they will lose what they are working on.

- *Disconnect*   If you are not part of the Administrators group, you will see the Disconnect button instead of the Shut Down button shown in Figure 9.4. By clicking the Disconnect button, you will be disconnected from your session running on the Terminal Server. Disconnecting from the server allows you to exit the server yet still keep your applications open and running. The next time you connect you will be returned to your old desktop just as you had left it, with all your applications and documents still open.

The Client Connection Manager

So far, you have been using just the Terminal Server client to connect to your Terminal Server. The client requires that you perform several steps to attach to your server and run an application. When you are familiar with what it takes to log on to the server, you will probably want to use the Client Connection Manager instead.

The Client Connection Manager allows you to define connections and create shortcuts, which automate the process of logging on and running applications on your server. For example, with Client Connection Manager you can create an icon on a user's desktop that automatically logs on to the Terminal Server in full-screen mode and runs Microsoft Word.

Real-World Tip: Shutting Down the Server

Although the server is normally shut down from the console, you can also open a remote Terminal Server session and shut the server down. This can be useful for remotely restarting the server. Be sure to select Shutdown and Restart and not just Shutdown; otherwise you will need to go to the server console to bring the server back up.

The following instructions explain how to set up a connection to your server or to an application running on it, and how to create a shortcut to it:

1. Open the Client Connection Manager from the TS Client group for the 16-bit client; or from Start menu | Programs | Terminal Server Client folder for the 32-bit client.

2. In the Client Connection Manager main window, select New Connection from the File menu to create a new connection.

3. Fill in the Description for the connection and the Server name, and then click Next. You can substitute the IP address of the server for the server name if you want to.

4. If you want the connection to automatically log on to Terminal Server, select Automatic Logon and enter the username, password, and domain name for the user account to log on with, and then click Next.

5. Select the screen size you want for the Terminal Server session. Select Full Screen to have the connection automatically start at full-screen resolution. Select Low Speed Connection for additional compression for this connection. When you are finished, click Next.

6. If you want Terminal Server to launch an initial program after the user logs on, select Program File Name, enter the name of the program executable, and enter the working directory for the program. When you are finished, click Next.

7. If you want to change the connection icon, click Change Icon and select the icon from the browse window. Select from the drop-down list the Program Group that the icon will be placed in, and then click Next.

8. Click Finish to create the connection.

After your connection has been set up, it will be listed in the Client Connection Manager main window, as shown in Figure 9.5. You can start the new connection by double-clicking it.

If you want to create a shortcut for the connection on the user's desktop, right-click on the connection icon in the Client Connection Manager window (see Figure 9.5), and select Create Shortcut on Desktop.

> **Real-World Tip: Disconnecting**
>
> One situation in which the disconnect feature is useful is when you move from one terminal to another. You can disconnect from your old terminal and log on to the new one to recover your original desktop. Disconnecting is also useful for running long processes. You can start a particular process, disconnect from the server, do something else, and then reconnect periodically to check on the status.
>
> It is important to remember, though, that disconnecting uses resources on your server. Your session and all the applications you had open will remain open on the server after you disconnect, taking up memory and processing power. For more information on how to best control the ability to disconnect from your server, refer to Chapter 6, "Creating the Connections."

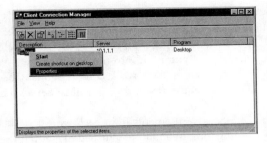

Figure 9.5 Creating a shortcut to a connection.

Accessing Local Resources from a Microsoft Client Session

If you need to access your local hard drives or printers from a Microsoft Terminal Server client session, you will need to share them first. If they are shared, you will be able to establish a connection to them from within your Terminal Server session. The following are some commonly used methods of establishing this connection:

- Browse for your workstation in Network Neighborhood and connect to either your workstation's shared directories or printers.

- Use the NET USE [Drive letter]: \\[Workstation name]\[Share name] command from the command prompt to connect a drive letter to your workstation share.

- Use the NET USE LPT[n]: \\[Workstation name]\[Printer name] command from the command prompt to connect the LPT port on Terminal Server to your local printer.

Real-World Tip: Connect a Drive Letter to Your Workstation

If you cannot see your workstation in any browse list, you may be able to connect a drive letter to it by using one of the following techniques:

- NET USE [Drive]: \\[IP Address of workstation]\[Share name]

- Copy the C:\WTSRV\SYSTEM32\DRIVERS\ETC\LMHOST.SAM file to .\LMHOSTS, add an entry to the bottom of the file with your workstation's name and IP address, and save it. Try connecting a drive letter to the workstation using the NET USE command.

If you still have problems, try connecting a drive letter to the share on your workstation from the workstation itself. If this doesn't work, it is likely that sharing is set up incorrectly or there is a syntax problem.

Setting up workstation shares from several workstations on your network can quickly lead to administrative problems, so you need to do this only in moderation. By allowing users to share their hard drives and printers, you are basically decentralizing your control of the network and putting it into the hands of users who may be untrained in network administration. Each workstation essentially becomes its own file and print server on a peer-to-peer network with Terminal Server. This increases the number of servers you have to manage.

The file and print service advertisements from each workstation also can take up considerable network bandwidth. In addition, you will likely find users who grant full access to their critical data without realizing the security risks of doing so on a network.

If you need seamless and controllable access for users' local resources, your best bet is to purchase the MetaFrame add-on and use ICA clients. See the ICA client section that follows for a more detailed explanation of the differences between the two clients.

Citrix MetaFrame ICA Client

The Citrix ICA client has more features and supports many more platforms than the Microsoft Terminal Server client does. The essential difference is the advanced capabilities of the ICA protocol. Unlike the Terminal Server client's RDP protocol, which works only with TCP/IP, ICA can work with IPX/SPX, NetBEUI, and TCP/IP.

The following is a list of the many operating systems or platforms that the ICA client has been written for:

- *Windows NT and 95/98 (32-bit ICA client)*
- *Windows 3.1 and 3.11 (16-bit ICA client)*
- *DOS*   With the DOS ICA client you can access your server with as little as a 286!
- *Java and ActiveX*   These Web browser-based clients allow you to run Windows applications from a Web site. Java clients are available that can be run from any Java Virtual Machine that supports either JDK 1.0 or 1.1.
- *UNIX platforms*   Versions of the client are available for most popular UNIX platforms, including IBM, HP/UX, Solaris, SunOS, DEC, and SGI.
- *Macintosh*   With this client you can run 32-bit Windows applications on a Macintosh.

Note for WinFrame Administrators: Updating the ICA Client

For those who are currently have several WinFrame users on the network, users' old ICA clients will be automatically upgraded to the latest version when they log on to your MetaFrame server. The new version of the ICA client is compatible with both Terminal Server and WinFrame. Most importantly, all the users' old client settings will be migrated to the new version automatically.

The following sections cover the installation and use of the 32-bit, 16-bit, and DOS ICA clients. The remaining clients will be covered in Part III, "Real-World Terminal Server and MetaFrame Solutions," of this book.

Choosing and Installing the Network Protocol

If you are connecting to MetaFrame across a network, you should make sure the correct protocol is loaded and functional before you begin installing the ICA client. If you will be connecting remotely by using a modem or RAS, see Chapter 15, "Terminal Server and NetWare," for instructions on how to set up the connection correctly.

Because the ICA client supports more protocols than the Microsoft Terminal Server client does, you have a lot of choices to make in terms of which protocol is best for your clients. The following is a list of all the network protocols currently supported by the 32-bit, 16-bit, and DOS ICA clients:

- TCP/IP (the ICA client actually uses just TCP for the establishing the connection)
- IPX or SPX
- NetBIOS (over NetBEUI)

Your choice of protocol depends mainly on your network and your clients. Most often the best protocol to use will be TCP/IP. TCP/IP is routable and is thus an excellent choice for both large and small networks. Most routers support TCP/IP out of the box, making WAN connections relatively easy. TCP is also the most widely supported protocol across the various Terminal Server clients. It is the only protocol supported by the Macintosh, Microsoft RDP, UNIX, and Web clients.

If you have a network that mainly has Novell NetWare servers running IPX/SPX, and if most of your clients already have IPX/SPX loaded, it may be better for you to stick with the IPX/SPX protocol set for your ICA clients. This is the case especially if you intend to install the ICA client on your DOS or Windows 3.x workstations that already have the IPX/SPX protocol stack set up. Whereas it is relatively easy to add new protocols to Windows 95/NT, adding new protocols to DOS or Windows 3.x clients can be tedious. Like TCP, IPX/SPX is routable.

> **Real-World Tip: SPX versus IPX**
>
> Citrix gives you the choice of either running IPX or SPX to communicate with the client. IPX is a connectionless protocol and has less overhead than SPX. In general, IPX is a better choice. If you are having problems maintaining a solid connection across your network with IPX, however, or if you would rather have a connection-oriented protocol, choose SPX instead.

Terminal Server includes an IP stack for DOS and Windows 3.1. All you have to do is use the Network Client Administrator utility to create a network startup boot disk for these environments and you'll get a disk with the necessary software to connect to an NT server. By transferring the information to the local hard drive and changing various configuration files to reflect the new location, you can have a DOS or Windows-based computer running the Microsoft IP stack. A long, drawn-out discussion of this topic here isn't necessary; however, this method works and is free.

NetBIOS is the simplest of the protocol choices. NetBIOS can run on top of other protocol transports, such as TCP/IP and IPX/SPX; however, with the Citrix ICA clients, NetBIOS runs only on top of NetBEUI. NetBIOS over NetBEUI has very little overhead, in part because NetBEUI is not routable. Because of the simplicity and low overhead of NetBIOS, you may find that it has a slight performance advantage over the other protocols. NetBIOS over NetBEUI can be a good choice on small networks, test networks, or on other networks where the inability to route the NetBEUI protocol is not an issue.

Installing the Protocols

This section explains how to set up the protocol stack for the Windows 32-bit, Windows 16-bit, and DOS ICA clients. For those who will be connecting remotely to the server by using modems, see Chapter 14, "Terminal Server and Remote Access." Also, there is a lot of good, detailed information on connecting to the servers using IPX/SPX in Chapter 15.

32-bit Windows Protocol Setup

No matter what protocol you will be using to connect to the server, the steps to setting it up are very simple with Windows 32-bit platforms.

To bind a new protocol to an existing network adapter in Windows 95, follow these steps:

1. Go to Start menu | Settings | Control Panel and select Network.

2. Click Add from the Network window.

3. Double-click Protocol from the Select Network Component Type window.

> **Author's Note: Support from Citrix**
>
> Microsoft's protocols have been thoroughly tested by Citrix and are fully supported. Many third-party protocols will work with the ICA client; however, if you run into connectivity problems and need technical assistance, Citrix may insist that you use the Microsoft version of the protocol for them to help you isolate the problem.
>
> Because of the close relationship between Citrix and Novell, and because of the many Citrix customers who are already running Novell's clients, you will also likely find good support from Citrix when using Novell's protocol stacks.

4. From the Select Network Protocol screen that appears, highlight Microsoft under Manufacturers.

5. Select TCP/IP, IPX/SPX, or NetBEUI—depending on how you want to connect with your MetaFrame server—from the list shown in Figure 9.6, and then click OK.

6. Click OK at the Network window. The protocol will now be bound to your existing network adapters.

   After the protocol files are installed, you will be prompted to restart your computer.

7. Select Yes to restart the computer and to finish binding the protocol to your network adapter.

To bind a new protocol to an existing network adapter in Windows NT 4.0, follow these steps:

1. In the Start Menu, select Settings | Control Panel and then select Network.

2. Click the Protocols tab.

3. Click Add from the Protocols tab window. You will be given a list of the available protocols from Microsoft, as shown in Figure 9.7.

4. Select the protocol you will be using and click OK. For MetaFrame, the only possible choices are NetBEUI, NWLink IPX/SPX, and TCP/IP.

   The protocol files are now installed on your system. When finished you will be prompted to restart the computer.

5. Click Yes to restart the computer and finish binding the protocol.

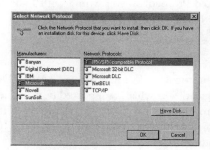

Figure 9.6 Selecting the protocol.

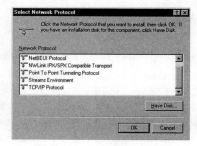

Figure 9.7 Choosing protocols for NT 4.

16-bit Windows and DOS Protocol Setup

With Windows for Workgroups, setting up the network stack is relatively simple because networking ability is built into the operating system. With Windows 3.1 and DOS, installing a protocol stack can be much more challenging.

Windows 3.1 and DOS do not have native network stacks. Thus, you have two choices when installing the network stacks for running the ICA client on these operating systems:

- Use the Microsoft DOS-based clients and protocol stacks provided on the Terminal Server CD-ROM.
- Use a third-party, DOS-based protocol stack.

Your choice will mainly depend on which protocol stacks you already have in place on your network. You will likely find that the Microsoft protocol stacks are supported better, simply because they are included with Terminal Server and they are what most administrators use. However, many third-party protocol stacks will work without problems with the Citrix ICA client. No matter which protocol stack you choose, you should test it thoroughly before implementing on all your ICA clients.

Windows for Workgroups

With Windows for Workgroups, support for both IPX and NetBEUI protocols is included; however, TCP/IP is not. To get TCP/IP you need to install it from the Terminal Server CD-ROM (you can find it in the `D:\CLIENTS\TCP32WFW` directory). The network driver and protocol software are installed through the Network Setup program. For further instructions, refer to the "Installing the 16-bit Microsoft Terminal Server Client" section earlier in this chapter.

The steps for installing the NetBEUI and IPX protocols are similar to the steps for installing TCP/IP. Instead of selecting Unlisted Protocol, as you would with TCP/IP, simply select either NWLink IPX/SPX or NetBEUI from the protocol list when adding the protocol.

Windows 3.1 and DOS Protocol Stacks

You have several choices when it comes to protocol stacks for Windows 3.1 and DOS. Which protocol stack you choose depends greatly on what is supported by your network adapter manufacturer and also what protocol stacks, if any, you already have in place. If you already have a protocol stack in place, the choice is simple: Load the ICA client and thoroughly test it with the current protocol stack.

> **Author's Note: Remote-Node Access**
>
> One interesting note is that WFW includes a simple RAS client for remote connectivity that supports only NetBEUI connections. If you already use this client for remote-node access, you can run the MetaFrame client over this connection.

If you are unable to get the ICA client to connect using your current protocol stack, or if you need to install a protocol stack from scratch, there are two common protocol stack choices: Microsoft's and Novell's protocol stacks for DOS. Both of these are available for free.

Because installing and configuring a protocol stack in DOS can be tricky and support is limited, you may want to choose either the one you have the most experience with or the one that is the most prevalent on your network. You should also check with the manufacturer of your network adapter to ensure that the appropriate DOS drivers are available for the protocol stack you choose. Whereas most network adapter manufacturers have DOS drivers for both Microsoft and Novell protocol stacks, some manufacturers have support for only one or the other.

There are two DOS clients available from Microsoft: Microsoft Client for DOS and the LAN Manager Client for DOS. Both clients are included on the Terminal Server CD-ROM, and both support IPX/SPX, NetBEUI, and TCP/IP. You can find the install files for Microsoft Client for DOS v3.0 on the Terminal Server CD in `D:\CLIENTS\MSCLIENT` and the install files for the LAN Manager client in `D:\CLIENTS\LANMAN`. Both clients come with a limited set of supported network adapters.

To work with other types of adapters you will need to obtain the appropriate DOS driver from your network adapter manufacturer. Because the drivers needed for the Microsoft client are different than those needed for the LAN Manager client, check with your network adapter manufacturer to see which client it supports.

Novell has two DOS clients available: the 16-bit VLM client and the 32-bit client for DOS. With the correct drivers, both of these clients can support either IPX/SPX or TCP/IP. The 16-bit VLM client is no longer readily available from Novell. If you have this client already installed on your network, you should have no problems making it work with Citrix. If you will be installing the 32-bit client for NetWare, you can download it from `support.novell.com`. Drivers for a large number of network adapters are already included with this client.

If you will be using TCP/IP with Windows 3.1, you need to make sure the protocol stack you choose is WinSock-compliant. One of the best TCP/IP stacks to use is the LAN Manager client for DOS that is included on the Terminal Server CD-ROM. When you install LAN Manager, it is best to select basic support, instead of enhanced, because it uses less memory. Also, make sure you enter the hostname under the advanced settings and that you choose to have WinSock installed. After you have installed the client and restarted you PC, try pinging the server.

Another option for TCP/IP is to obtain a third-party, WinSock-compliant protocol, such as Trumpet's WinSock. The configuration is a little complicated, but you can make it work with Windows 3.1. Trumpet WinSock is available at `www.trumpet.com.au`.

The ICA client for DOS supports the following TCP/IP stacks:

- FTP Software's DOS TCP/IP stack
- Novell LAN Workplace
- Microsoft's client for DOS or the LAN Manager client

JSB also makes TCP/IP drivers that allow the ICA client for DOS to work with several more third-party TCP/IP stacks. Out of all of these choices, you are still probably best off using the LAN Manager protocol stack included on the Terminal Server CD-ROM. It is simple, it works, and it is free!

Installing the MetaFrame 32-bit ICA Client

Now that the protocol has been installed, it is time to install the clients. The first thing you need to do when installing the client is to get access to the installation files. The 32-bit ICA client install files are located on the MetaFrame CD-ROM in the D:\ICACLIENT\ICA32 directory.

There are two disk image directories there that can be copied to formatted 3 1/2-inch high-density floppy disks for a floppy-based install. For a network-based install you can copy these directories to your network and run the setup program from the DISK1 directory. Another way to access the install files is to share the MetaFrame CD-ROM from a workstation or server; in this way you will be able to access it from the client stations.

The following instructions cover the basics of installing the 32-bit client:

1. Run SETUP.EXE from the D:\ICACLIENT\ICA32\DISK1 directory on the CD or from disk 1 of the floppy disk installation set.

Real-World Tip: Client Creator Tool

Citrix has included a Client Creator tool for creating the floppy disks for client installs. To use it, perform the following steps:

1. Open the ICA Client Creator tool located in the Start menu | Programs | MetaFrame Tools folder.

2. In the Make Installation Disk Set window, highlight the client you wish to create disks for.

3. Select the Destination Drive and whether you want to Format Disks.

4. Insert the first client floppy in the Destination Drive you selected and click OK.

The program copies all necessary client installation files to the floppy or floppies.

2. Like the Microsoft client, the installation of the ICA client is very simple. Follow the onscreen instructions for installing the client. By default, it installs in `C:\Program Files\Citrix\ICA Client` directory. At the ICA Client Name screen, you will be prompted for your client name. By default, it chooses your computer name. This should be adequate for most situations. This name needs to be unique and keeps track of this connection at the server.

After the client files are copied to your computer, the installation program will create shortcuts for the client in the Citrix ICA Client folder in the Start menu | Programs folder. The client is referred to as the Remote Applications Manager by Citrix.

As with the Microsoft Terminal Server client, there is not much involved in the install. The trickiest part of the installation is generally getting the client networked properly, which should already have been done.

Installing the MetaFrame ICA Client for Windows 3.1/3.11

You can find the 16-bit client on the MetaFrame CD in `D:\ICACLIENT\ICA16`. As with the 32-bit client, you will find two disk images under this directory. These can be copied to a location on your network or to two formatted high-density floppy disks. The simple installation of the client itself can be done as follows:

1. Run `SETUP.EXE` from the `D:\ICACLIENT\ICA16\DISK1` directory or from disk 1 of the installation floppies you created.

2. Follow the onscreen instructions. The client installs into the `C:\ICA16` directory by default.

3. When you are prompted for a connection name, enter something that is unique. Each client connecting to your server needs to have a different connection name for MetaFrame to be able to keep track of the connections properly.

The install program will copy the client files to your computer and create an icon for the Remote Applications Manager. The Remote Applications Manager is the main ICA client administration tool.

Installing the MetaFrame DOS Client

The DOS client is located in the `D:\ICACLIENT\ICADOS` directory on the MetaFrame CD-ROM. Of all the clients, the DOS client is one of the smallest. Here are the steps you need to install it:

1. Run `INSTALL.EXE` from the `D:\ICACLIENT\ICADOS` directory.

2. At the prompt asking you where you want the client installed, either press Enter to accept the default directory of `C:\WFCLIENT`, or enter the install path you want.

   The program copies all the necessary files to this directory, and any settings that currently exist are migrated to the new client.

3. Run `WFCLIENT.EXE` from `C:\WFCLIENT` to start the client.

Connecting to the MetaFrame Server

The steps for connecting to the MetaFrame server are similar for all the ICA clients. The Windows ICA clients use an application called the Remote Applications Manager to manage connections to the server. The DOS client uses a text-based version of this application.

Many of the per-client settings covered in this section can also be set as per-connection or per-user. In general, anything that is set per-connection or per-user will override what is set up per-client. For information on how per-connection, per-user and per-client settings relate, refer to Chapter 6.

The following examples show how to set up a connection using the 32-bit ICA client:

1. Run the Remote Applications Manager from the Start menu by selecting Programs | Citrix ICA Client folder.

2. At the Add a new Remote Application dialog box, select Network and click Next.

3. Enter the name for this connection, and then select your protocol. The window below the protocol selection will probably be blank.

4. (Server connection only) Select the Citrix server that you want to attach to by clicking the down arrow next to the Server field. The client will begin broadcasting on the network to get the nearest Citrix server. A list of the Citrix servers on the network that respond will appear. Highlight the server you want and click Next.

Real-World Tip: Entering the Server Address Directly

If you don't see your server listed, you can enter the address of the server directly. If you are using TCP/IP, enter the TCP/IP address of the server. If you are using IPX/SPX, enter the network:node address (for example, 101:0877789f4509). You can determine the network address and node address by using the `IPXROUTE CONFIG` command on your Terminal Server console. Remember that the network number is unique not only for a segment, but also for a frame type. Make sure your client and the server are using the same IPX/SPX frame type. For NetBIOS over NetBEUI, your only choice is to enter the server name.

5. (Published application connection only) If you will be connecting to a published application instead of a Citrix server, select the Published Application radio button. Either enter the name of the published application or click the down arrow in the field under Published Application to view the applications that have been published on the network. When you are finished, click Next.

   The next window will appear only if you selected a published application. From this window select whether you want to View the Published Application in a Remote Desktop Window or in a Seamless Window, and then click Next.

6. Select whether you have a fast network connection or a low bandwidth connection and click Next. This will optimize your connection settings for your speed.

7. If you want to have this connection automatically log on to the Citrix server, enter the username, password, and domain for logon and click Next.

8. At the next screen click on Enable Sound if you want to be able to hear sounds on your local speakers from applications running on MetaFrame. Also, click the change button if you want to change the selected resolution or number of colors. When you are finished, click Next.

9. If you want to launch an initial program when you first log on, enter the application name and the working directory and click Next.

10. If you want to change the icon for the Remote Applications Manager or change the group (folder) it is installed in, click Change Icon or Select Program Group. When you are finished, click Next.

11. Click Finish to create the connection.

After you create the connection, your entry will appear in the list in Remote Applications Manager. Double-clicking on the entry will launch the connection.

Differences Between MetaFrame's and Microsoft's Clients

After you have launched the connection that you just created and opened a session on Terminal Server, there may seem to be little difference between the ICA client and the Terminal Server client. For the most part this is true; however, there are important differences between the two clients. In this section, we will discuss the main ones.

Real-World Tip: Controlling the Desktop

Setting up an initial program is good way to tighten the control of the desktop. If you set it up to launch a particular application, that is the only application the user will be able to run. As soon as the user exits from the application, the session will close. The initial program can also be set per-user or per-connection. These settings will override the per-client setting created here.

Hotkeys

The hotkeys or shortcut keys used in the MetaFrame client are different than the keys used by the Microsoft Terminal Server client. Figure 9.8 shows the default hotkeys for the MetaFrame client. As you can see, you can easily redefine the keys as you need them. One of the most useful shortcuts to teach users is Ctrl+F1. This is equivalent to the Ctrl+Alt+End keystroke with Microsoft's client. Ctrl+F1 brings you to the Windows NT Security window, where you can change your password, log off, or disconnect.

Access to Local Hard Drives

It is easier to access your local resources with MetaFrame's ICA client. By default, when you log on, your local drives will become part of your Terminal Server desktop. With the Microsoft Terminal Server client, you need to first share your local drives and then connect to them in Terminal Server to access them.

Note the Client Network shown in Figure 9.9. The Client Network represents your local resources. This is how automatic mapping to your local drives works. When you log on with the ICA client, Terminal Server connects a drive to each of the \\CLIENT\[drive letter]: shares. You can also manually connect a drive letter to your local drives by using \\CLIENT\[drive letter]: UNC.

Access to Local Windows Printers

Along with drive letters, printers are also automatically mapped. The names of your Windows printers become [Client Computer Name]#[Printer Name] in Terminal Server when you log on. Your printers are simply added to the printers that are already defined on the Terminal Server. If you want to print to your local printer, you simply need to select [Computer Name]#[Printer Name] from the printer list in any application. Also, the default printer becomes whatever your default printer was.

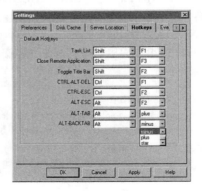

Figure 9.8 MetaFrame's default hotkeys.

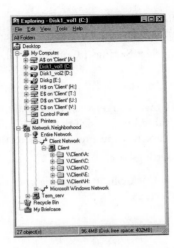

Figure 9.9 Local (Client) Drive Mappings with the Server Drive at C:.

Access to Local Printers Using LPT ports

The LPT ports in your Terminal Server session are remapped to your local LPT ports when you use the ICA client. What this means is that if you are using a DOS application running on the Terminal Server, when you print from the application to LPT1, the print job actually gets sent across the network to your local LPT1 port. This works great for many DOS applications, but be careful about the bandwidth being used. Every print job printed to an LPT port has to travel across the network back to the client.

Mapping to Other Local Resources

In addition to automatically mapping your local hard drives and printers, your local clipboard and audio capabilities are integrated with the Terminal Server desktop when you use the ICA client. What this means is that you can copy something to the clipboard in a Terminal Server session and then paste it into one of your local applications. The audio feature means that applications running on Terminal Server can play sounds on your workstation's speakers.

Running DOS Applications Full-Screen

You may be surprised to discover that you cannot run DOS applications full-screen with any of the Windows-based clients. The only client that can run DOS applications full-screen is the MetaFrame DOS client. If you need this capability, you need to either set up users with this client or adjust the font size of your DOS application window so that it mimics full-screen size. The following steps explain this procedure:

1. Go to the Start menu, select Settings | Control Panel, and double-click on the MS-DOS Console icon.

2. Click the Font tab.

3. Select the font and size that is larger than the default and appropriate for your screen resolution. You should pick a size that makes the DOS window near full-screen size. You might have to experiment a little to find the best setting.

4. Click OK to save the settings.

The next time you run a DOS application from a command window, it will use the new font and size you selected.

10

Installing Applications on Terminal Server

WITHOUT APPLICATIONS TO DISTRIBUTE TO your users, Terminal Server isn't of much use. Installing applications and getting them to work correctly can be one of the most challenging aspects of Terminal Server administration. Although most properly written applications will run without a problem, you might need to tweak some applications for all of their features to run correctly in Terminal Server's multiuser environment. This chapter goes into detail on what it takes to get your applications up and running on Terminal Server.

Preparing to Run Applications with Terminal Server

Installing and running applications on Terminal Server may seem deceptively similar to installing and running them on NT Workstation or Windows 95, but there are some key differences. The key to running applications successfully on Terminal Server is understanding the concept of *application competition*. Applications running on the Terminal Server compete with other applications and users for limited system resources. This means that if one application is taking more than its share of resources, this inequity will quickly start affecting all applications being run by all users on the system.

Unlike running an application on a standard PC, many instances of the same application can be run simultaneously by many remote users. This is where many application problems occur. How your application keeps track of the environment for each remote user is very important. In order for your installation to be successful, you need to have applications that will work together well on the same system as well as applications that can run multiple instances but still keep their users' environment settings separate.

In the following sections, we'll first go over the top ten guidelines for running applications on Terminal Server. Before you install any applications, make sure you read and heed these guidelines. Remember that application installation can be very different under Terminal Server. Not following the guidelines can lead to many problems, even for a seemingly basic installation.

After briefly going over each of the basic guidelines, we'll start breaking down the most important ones in detail. This is where you'll gain an understanding of some of the underlying mechanics of Terminal Server application execution.

Top Ten Tips for Installing and Running Applications on Terminal Server

The following tips go over some of the key points regarding application installation on Terminal Server:

1. *The application needs to be NT compatible*   Of all the guidelines, this is one of the most important. If your application will not run on an NT Workstation 4.0, it will not run on Terminal Server. Always purchase the NT-compatible version of an application, if available.

2. *Use 32-bit applications for the best performance*   It's important to remember that if you're running DOS or Windows 16-bit applications, they can suffer up to a 25 percent drop in performance. This is due, in part, to the 16-bit-to-32-bit API translation that needs to occur in order for these applications to run. This 16-bit translation is handled by the Virtual DOS Machine (VDM). Because each session must load its own VDM, VDMs can take up a significant amount of memory. DOS applications that use polling can also further decrease performance (for example, keyboard polling).

3. *Each user needs to have a drive letter mapped to the root of a personal directory for storing user-specific application information*   One of the most common problems that occurs when installing applications is making the mistake of not giving users a place to store user-specific application information or not mapping a drive letter to the root of this directory. Terminal Server helps handle this need by automatically creating a user home directory under `C:\WTSRV\PROFILES\[USERNAME]`. In this home directory, Terminal Server places a Windows directory for holding

user-specific application information, such as INI files. As an administrator, you need to make sure a drive letter is map-rooted to this directory in the logon script, as shown in Chapter 8, "Using Logon Scripts." You can then use this drive letter for user-specific application settings.

4. *Standardize on a home directory drive letter*   This makes it much easier to resolve application problems in a multiuser environment. If an application needs to store user-specific data, point it to the user's home directory. Because the drive letter is the same for all users, this will always be a unique location for each user using the application.

    The home directory should also be mapped to the root of the user directory using the SUBST command in the logon script, as shown in Chapter 8.

5. *Always install Windows 16-bit and 32-bit applications in user global mode*   This key difference in installing applications on Terminal Server is probably one of the most difficult to understand. The user global mode can either be entered with the CHANGE USER /INSTALL command or by installing the application through the Add/Remove Programs Wizard in the Control Panel. In this mode, any changes to the INI files and Registry and any DLL files or files copied to the Windows directory are redirected by the operating system and kept track of at a central location. When the user opens the application for the first time, these changes are propagated to their own home directory and Registry settings. If this does not seem to make much sense, just remember that the operating system needs a way to keep applications separate; user global mode is one way that Terminal Server does it.

6. *Run applications locally when practical*   Applications can be run off of remote servers, but for the best performance, try to run them locally instead. On the other hand, beware of running processor-intensive applications locally, such as Back Office products. If you need to give your users access to a client/server–style application, run the client piece locally and the server piece on another server so that its processing does not deteriorate the performance of Terminal Server.

    Create an APPS directory on your server, map an application drive letter to the root of it, and install your applications in it using the application drive letter. Whether you decide to run your applications locally or remotely, always install and run them from the same drive letter. If you're running the applications locally, use the SUBST command in the logon script to map your application drive letter to the root of the local application directory (for example, SUBST S: C:\APPS). If you're running your applications from a remote server, use the NET USE [application drive letter]: \\[server]\[application share] command in the logon script to map the application drive letter to the root of the application share. Keeping all your apps together under a single APPS directory makes administration easier.

7. *Control access to your applications and their data using local groups and put global groups into the local groups* By default, the Everyone group will have access to everything under your APPS directory. When you install a new application directory, first create a local group for the application's users (for example, SERVER1_OFFICE97_USERS). Install your application into this directory in user global mode, logged in as an administrator. Using NTFS security, remove the Everyone group from the permission list and add the Administrator group and the Local Application group. Create and add the Global Application group (for example, DOMAIN1_OFFICE97_USERS) to the member list of the Local group. With this setup, only administrators and members of the Global Application group will have access to this application. Controlling who has access to what application makes licensing administration easier and gives your server greater security. If you want to know how many users have rights to run the application, simply look at the membership list for the group. For easier administration, you may want to create one Local Application group for the applications that most of your users need access to, instead of creating a separate group for each application.

8. *Use common program groups to distribute applications* If you want to distribute a single application to everyone, first install it in user global mode and then add its icon to a common program group. Icons in the common program groups will be seen by all users in their Start menus. By default, many applications store all their icons in common program groups. To edit the list of icons or to add an icon to a common program group, right-click the Start button and select All Users.

9. *Keep data and applications separate* This is a general guideline that's a good idea for most operating systems. Keeping data and applications separate helps simplify backups, drive storage arrangement, and security. Application programs are generally static, but the user data is generally dynamic. Because user data is changing all the time, it needs to be backed up daily. Applications, on the other hand, may only need to be backed up weekly. Also, in general, user data requires read/write access, and applications require only read access. If a user is given read/write access to a directory that contained both applications and data, he or she can delete or overwrite critical application files. By keeping user data and applications in separate directories, you can more easily address the different backup and security requirements for these two types of information. Also, keeping user data on a separate server works well for load balancing, because users will have access to their data no matter which load-balanced server they're using.

10. *Test, test, test, and then test again* Last, but definitely not least, always test your applications thoroughly before implementing them widely. A good idea is to create two application test users. Make them a member of the same groups as the users who will be using the application. After installing the application as administrator in global mode, logon as the application test user. Check the following:

- Did the INI changes, DLL files, and Registry settings get propagated properly to the home directory and `user.dat` file? If not, you may have forgotten to exit global mode before logging out. Before you install the application, enter user global mode with the `CHANGE USER /INSTALL` command; after it's installed, return to user-specific mode using the `CHANGE USER /EXCECUTE` command.

- Is the icon readily available in the Start menu? If not, you may need to add it to a common group so that the application user can see it. For more ideas on putting icons onto the users' desktops, see Chapter 12, "Administering the Desktop and Server."

- Do all the features of the application work correctly? It's important to test all features thoroughly. Be on the lookout for features that have user-specific settings, such as colors.

  Open up a second connection to the terminal and log on as the second test user. Change as many user-specific settings as you can; then with application test user 1, exit out of the application and enter it again. Do the user-specific settings for test user 2 affect test user 1's settings?

For more information on troubleshooting application problems, see "Troubleshooting Application Problems," toward the end of this chapter.

Using Home Directories to Keep Applications Separate

Home directories are meant to keep user-specific application information separate. In the following sections, you'll learn how this occurs with Terminal Server by walking through a typical installation. In this example, you'll install the applications in user-specific mode, which is the default mode. Normally, you want to install applications in user global mode. In the next section, we'll go over why.

Real-World Tip: Testing Applications

The importance of testing your applications before implementing them cannot be overstressed with Terminal Server. You'll probably find application implementation to be one of the most challenging and sometimes frustrating aspects of Terminal Server administration.

Keep in mind the concept of application competition. If you implement an application that overtaxes your server's resources, it will affect all the users of the system.

One good method of testing your application's use of resources is with a utility called *WinBatch*, which is a Windows macro recorder. With WinBatch, you can simulate user interaction with the applications running on Terminal Server. By setting up several sessions, each running the WinBatch macro to simulate user interaction, you can simulate how your application will behave with multiple users. WinBatch is available at www.winbatch.com. See Chapter 13, "Measuring Performance," for details.

If you want to follow along with the example, pick out a Windows application from your CD-ROM collection. For this example, the 16-bit Visual Basic runtime files are used. These are available from many shareware sites, including www.shareware.com. The filename is vb40016.zip. The focus here is on how Terminal Server acts during an application installation and how home directories are used by Terminal Server to keep application settings separate.

Creating the Home Directory

First, before installing any applications on your server, you need to ensure that your home directories are set up properly. By default, Terminal Server creates home directories for your users under C:\WTSRV\PROFILES\[Username] when they log on for the first time. Terminal Server will also automatically grant only the user, administrator group, and system account access to this directory, and it will create a WINDOWS and WINDOWS\SYSTEM subdirectory. These subdirectories are very important on Terminal Server, because they're where user-specific application files will be kept.

For some, these default settings may not be adequate. You may instead want to put your user home directories on another server. This is especially important to do if your servers are load balanced. In a load-balanced situation, your users may log onto the network using any of the load-balanced servers. No matter which server they log on from, their home directories should remain the same so that their application settings, which are stored in their home directories, also remain the same.

To set up a home directory on another server, you would normally create a USER share on that server. When you create your user, you enter \\[Servername]\USER\%USERNAME% for the path to the user's home directory in the User Profile dialog box, as shown in Chapter 7, "Creating Users and Groups in Terminal Server," in the "Home Directories" section. When you add this user, Terminal Server creates a home directory for the user in the \\[Server name]\USER share, using the user's name (%USERNAME%). For example, if the user's name is JSMITH, Terminal Server would substitute JSMITH for the %USERNAME% variable and create a home directory called JSMITH in the \\[Server name]\USER share. As with the default local home directories, Terminal Server will automatically grant, if possible, only the administrator and the user access to this directory. It will also create the WINDOWS and WINDOWS\SYSTEM subdirectories for user-specific application settings.

The following steps walk you through creating a typical user named John Smith; this user will be referred to throughout the following sections. The default home directory location will be used. Here are the steps involved:

1. Log on as Administrator and run User Manager for Domains from Terminal Server. User Manager for Domains is located in the Administrative Tools folder in the Start menu's Programs folder.

2. Select New User from the User menu at the User Manager main window.

3. In the New User window that appears, fill in **JSMITH** for the username, **John Smith** for the full name, and **Example User** for the description. You can fill in an arbitrary password if you want. When finished, click Add.

4. Log out and log back on as JSMITH.

When you log on to Terminal Server as JSMITH for the first time, Terminal Server does four things automatically. First, it creates a profile directory for JSMITH under `C:\WTSRV\PROFILES` and copies the contents of the `C:\WTSRV\PROFILES\Default User` directory to JSMITH's profile directory. Second, because you did not specify a home directory location when setting up John Smith, TS assigns the default home directory location (`C:\WTSRV\PROFILES\[USERNAME]`) as John Smith's home directory. Third, TS creates the `WINDOWS` and `WINDOWS\SYSTEM` directories under the `C:\WTSRV\PROFILES\JSMITH` directory. Finally, TS removes the default Full Access by the Everyone group from the `JSMITH` directory's access control list and replaces it with Full Access for the user, the local administrator group, and the system account.

You can verify that these steps occurred by taking a look at the `C:\WTSRV\PROFILES` directory to ensure that the `JSMITH` directory was created. Also notice the `WINDOWS` and `WINDOWS\SYSTEM` directories that were created in the `JSMITH` directory. Had you assigned John Smith a home directory when he was created, Terminal Server would have created that home directory and the Windows subdirectories as soon as you had clicked Add. When you logged in as JSMITH, only the profile directory would have been created. The home directory would have remained where you assigned it.

Real-World Tip: Mapping Your Home Directory

Be careful to use a high drive letter so that it won't be overwritten by local drive mappings. When NT logs a user on, it first connects to any static mappings, including what you set for the home directory. Next, it starts a process to run the logon script. At about the same time, MetaFrame starts a process to map the user's local drives to Terminal Server. You can use the NET USE and PAUSE commands in your script to troubleshoot mapping problems.

Another technique is to use a Novell server for your home directories. Because there's a Map Root option in the Config window, this can be a handy technique. NT will automatically map-root the drive you specified in the Terminal Server window to the NetWare Server. You'll need long filenames enabled on the Novell server and bindery context set if you're using 4.x. For more information on integrating with NetWare, see the chapter on it.

For more adventurous souls, Microsoft's new DFS (Distributed File System) technology offers some interesting possibilities when it comes to home directories. For one, it supports map roots! For information on this technology, visit Microsoft's Web site and do a search on DFS. Until this technology is tried and tested thoroughly, though, tread with care.

Mapping a Drive Letter to the Root of the Home Directory

Mapping a drive letter to the root of your users' home directories is a very important step. This drive letter will be referred to as the home directory drive letter. Often, applications need a directory where they can store user settings. When providing the directory path for an application's user settings, use a directory under the home directory drive letter. Although the home directory drive letter is the same for all the users, the location is unique for each user because it points to the user's personal home directory. In this way, you can have several users working in the same application and all of the application's user-specific settings are kept separate. Take, for example, a word-processing application. One of the user-specific settings might be the location of the users' documents. In this example, suppose your home directory drive letter for your users is W. To set up this application to work properly in a multiuser environment, you might enter `W:\DOCS` for the location of the users' documents. When the users log on and use the application, their document directories will be `\DOCS` under their personal home directories; therefore, each user's document directory will be separate.

When choosing a drive letter for the home directory drive letter, you should choose something high in the alphabet so that there's no chance it will conflict with a local drive letter.

For this example, we'll assign W as the home directory drive letter for the server. If set up correctly, this drive letter will automatically be mapped to the root of John Smith's home directory by the `USRLOGON.CMD` logon script when he logs onto the Terminal Server. The easiest way to set up the home directory drive letter with Terminal Server is to use the `CHKROOT.CMD` command file that's part of the application compatibility scripts. The following example shows how to do this (for more information, refer to Chapter 8, where application compatibility scripts are covered in detail):

1. Log on as Administrator and run the `CHKROOT.CMD` command file located in the `C:\WTSRV\Application Compatibility Scripts` directory from the command prompt. It will create a `ROOTDRV2.CMD` command file and bring up Notepad in order for you to edit it.

2. In the Notepad window, fill in `W:` for the root drive for the `SET` command so that the line reads `Set RootDrv=W:`.

3. Select Save from the File menu to save `ROOTDRV2.CMD` to the `C:\WTSRV\Application Compatibility Scripts` directory.

4. Log out and log back on as JSMITH.

Setting the `RootDrv` variable to `W:` and creating the `ROOTDRV2.CMD` file will set the home directory drive letter to W for any user who logs onto this Terminal Server. This is done through the `USRLOGON.CMD` logon script located in `C:\WTSRV\SYSTEM32`. This logon script is run for every user who logs onto Terminal Server, as discussed in Chapter 8. The `USRLOGON.CMD` file will check whether `ROOTDRV2.CMD` exists, and if it does, USRLOGON.CMD will map the RootDrv drive letter (W) defined in this file to the root of the user's home directory. Use the following command:

```
SUBST %RootDrv% %HomeDrive%%HomePath%
```

To check that this occurred for John Smith, open Explorer. You should see a W drive in Explorer that is mapped to the root of John Smith's home directory (C:\WTSRV\PROFILES\JSMITH).

Watching Home Directories in Action

Now that the home directory has been set up properly, it's time to install an application and watch how home directories are used by Terminal Server for storing user-specific information.

Applications can be installed in one of two modes: user global or user specific. Unless you have a specific reason for not doing so, all applications should be installed on Terminal Server in user global mode. The differences between these modes are as follows:

- *User global mode*   This is a special application install mode that helps applications work correctly in a multiuser environment. When an application is installed in user global mode, Terminal Server records what changes the application makes to the user Registry in a special location. When users log on and use the application, these recorded user Registry changes are propagated to the user's Registry. User-specific application files, such as INI files and settings files, are also copied to the Windows directory in the user's home directory. By installing applications in user global mode, you help ensure that user-specific application settings will be kept separate for each user. Applications installed in user global mode only need to be installed once for all your users because the user-specific changes that the application makes will be propagated to each user as the user logs on and runs the applications.

- *User-specific mode*   In user-specific mode, an application is installed for use only by the user who installed it. User Registry changes are *not* recorded centrally; only the user who installed the application will receive the user Registry changes for that application. The application also installs its user-specific files in the user's home directory. Any other user who attempts to run this application will not have access to these files. An application installed in user-specific mode needs to be installed once for every person who needs to use it. This means that if you have 50 users who need access to a new application, you'll need to install the application 50 times, once for each user (if you choose to use user-specific mode).

As you can see, user global mode is a more efficient means of installing applications in a multiuser environment. You'll learn about the differences between these to modes in much more detail in "User Global Mode Versus User-Specific Mode," later in this chapter.

Now it's time to see what we've discussed in action. In the following example, we'll install Outlook 97 in user global mode. We'll then log on as John Smith and watch how Outlook 97's application files are propagated to his home directory.

First, take a look at Figure 10.1, which shows John Smith's home directory before Outlook 97 is installed. Note that the contents of the home directory are directly under the W drive, which is the home directory drive letter. W was mapped to the root of C:\WTSRV\PROFILES\JSMITH by the USRLOGON.CMD logon script when John Smith logged on. The W:\WINDOWS directory, shown in Figure 10.1, contains only two files: the SYSTEM.INI file, which was propagated here from the system directory (C:\WTSRV) when John Smith logged on, and the INIFILE.UPD, a file used by Terminal Server to keep track of INI file updates.

Before you continue, note that this example is intended only to demonstrate how user global mode works. (For the latest installation procedures for Outlook 97 on Terminal Server, always refer to Microsoft's Online Support.) Here are the steps:

1. Log on as Administrator.
2. Change to user global mode by executing the **CHANGE USER /INSTALL** command from the command prompt.
3. Install Microsoft Outlook 97 according to the installation instructions provided by Microsoft. If you do not have Outlook 97 but you still want to follow along, pick out one of your 32-bit apps and install it.
4. Once the installation is finished, switch back to user-specific mode by typing **CHANGE USER /EXECUTE** at the command prompt.
5. Log out and log back on as JSMITH and run Outlook 97. Remember that for some applications, you may have to move their shortcuts to the common folders in order for other users to be able to see the shortcuts.

Figure 10.1   The "before" shot of the user home directory.

While you were installing Outlook 97 in user global mode, several things happened:

- All changes to the `HKEY_CURRENT_USER` Registry were copied under `HKEY_LOCAL_MACHINE\SOFTWARE\Microsoft\WindowsNT\CurrentVersion\TerminalServer\Install\Software`.

- All changes to the `HKEY_LOCAL_MACHINE` Registry were copied under ...`\MACHINE` of the same key.

- When the application requested the location of `%SYSTEM_ROOT%`, it was given the Terminal Server system directory. In other words, any INI files or DLLs were copied to the central system directory.

The next section explores these changes in more depth. For now, however, look under John Smith's home directory. Figure 10.2 shows John Smith's home directory after Outlook 97 was installed by the administrator and then run by John Smith for the first time.

User Global Mode Versus User-Specific Mode

The preceding example works great if you're installing an application for a single user. However, what if you had 50 to 100 users who all needed a new application? How would you install an application so that all users had their own INI files, Registry settings, and DLLs? Well, either you could install the application for each user one by one using user-specific mode, or you could install it once by using user global mode and the user-specific files will be distributed automatically.

Before we go into the technical details of what user global and user-specific modes actually are, we need to discuss the Registry and how it's used in Windows NT. This discussion will be very important for understanding how applications work with Terminal Server, as well as for troubleshooting application problems.

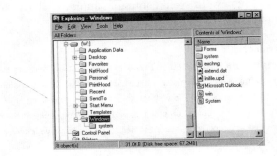

Figure 10.2 The "after" shot: Outlook files are propagated to the user's home directory.

The Registry and Terminal Server

In order to effectively administer Terminal Server, especially on a large scale, you need to gain some intimate knowledge of the inner workings of the Registry. What you really need to understand is how your applications use the Registry.

For those not familiar with the Registry, it's simply a central database for keeping operating system and application settings. Every time you change the wallpaper on your desktop, install a new piece of hardware, or change a setting in a control panel, you're saving your changes in the Registry. The Registry is mainly used by Windows 32-bit applications, although some Windows 16-bit applications are able to write to it.

In order for the information in this section to really sink in, open up the Registry on your Terminal Server using REGEDT32.EXE and follow along.

When you first open the Registry on NT using REGEDT32.EXE, the following five Registry keys pop up:

- *HKEY_LOCAL_MACHINE*   Settings that apply globally.

- *HKEY_CURRENT_USER*   Current user's user-specific settings.

- *HKEY_USERS*   The currently cached user keys, including the .DEFAULT user key. The .DEFAULT user key is also called the *system default profile*. This key controls the settings, such as the wallpaper and colors, you see when you first log onto Terminal Server.

- *HKEY_CURRENT_CONFIG*   Alias to a location in HKEY_LOCAL_MACHINE (hardware profiles).

- *HKEY_CLASSES_ROOT*   Alias to another location in HKEY_LOCAL_MACHINE (file extensions).

Out of these five keys, only two are of importance to you when administering Terminal Server: HKEY_LOCAL_MACHINE and HKEY_CURRENT_USER. The rest of the keys are merely pointers (or *aliases*) to sections of these two main keys. Because they are aliases, they don't contain anything new. To avoid confusion, minimize all the keys except HKEY_LOCAL_MACHINE and HKEY_CURRENT_USER.

> **Author's Note: Warning!**
> Never make any changes to the Registry unless you know exactly what you're doing as well as what effects it will have. Simply browsing the Registry is necessary to gain an understanding of how your applications interact with Terminal Server and will not hurt it. On the other hand, if you need to make changes to the Registry to solve an application problem, make sure you document the changes and test them on a test platform first. Improperly changing the Registry can disable your server, thus requiring a reinstall.

What Is *HKEY_LOCAL_MACHINE?*

HKEY_LOCAL_MACHINE is the most critical system Registry key. This key contains configuration data for the system as a whole. If a setting applies to all the users and not just one, it belongs in HKEY_LOCAL_MACHINE. You'll find information about device drivers, hardware resources, file extensions, network settings such as machine name, and much more. A complete coverage of all the keys in HKEY_LOCAL_MACHINE could fill a book on its own! We'll only be covering the most relevant ones here.

The most important thing to remember about HKEY_LOCAL_MACHINE is that any settings in here affect all your users. If your application stores any settings in HKEY_LOCAL_MACHINE, they will apply for everyone who uses the application. Properly written applications only put global parameters under this key. One of the problems you may encounter with Terminal Server is applications that store user-specific settings under here and not global settings. For example, if you have an application that stores its color scheme in HKEY_LOCAL_MACHINE, every time someone changes his or her colors, it will affect all the users of the application. There are ways to detect and prevent problems like this, however, which we'll cover in a bit.

With Terminal Server, you need to be concerned mainly about the settings under a single key—the SOFTWARE key. Under this key you'll find several subkeys. Here are the most pertinent ones:

- *Classes*   This contains mainly file extensions and their associated applications. For example, when you click a text file in Explorer, it automatically opens Notepad. This is due to the settings under this Registry key. Many new applications will make changes to Classes when they install in order for their extensions to be registered. For example, when you install Excel, it will add a key under Classes for .xls, the extension for Excel spreadsheets. When you double-click an XLS file, it will open up in Excel. Because this is a global key, when new applications extensions are installed under Classes, they are available to all users. Common problems that can occur with Classes are extension conflicts. One common culprit is graphics file extensions. For example, suppose you install automated fax software that registers itself as the default viewer for several graphic formats (GIF, TIFF, PCX) so that users can view and save their incoming faxes in electronic form. A couple of months later you install a Web browser for a couple of users, which also registers itself as a viewer for graphics formats. A day after installing it, you start getting calls from your users saying that their faxes now open up in the browser instead of the fax viewer! The moral of the story: Be careful of which extensions your applications install.

- *Microsoft*   Under this subkey are some of the most important keys. Any Microsoft product, including the operating system itself, will store its global settings under here. Many useful ones can be found under Microsoft\Windows NT\Current Version. As you'll see in a bit, this is where you'll find the main difference between user-specific and user global modes.

- *Secure*   Programs will store settings under here that should only be changed by an administrator.

- *Citrix*   MetaFrame keeps track of some global settings under this subkey.

Backing Up the Registry

You may be wondering in which critical file HKEY_LOCAL_MACHINE is kept. The answer is actually several files. They all reside under C:\WTSRV\SYSTEM32\CONFIG.

With Windows NT Server, it has always been a good idea to back up the Registry before any installation. With Terminal Server, it's even more important. The installation of one poorly written application can affect all your users. By backing up the Registry, you create a back door through which you can get back to a working system.

You can back up the Registry in several different ways. Because the Registry files are open when Terminal Server is running, you cannot use the COPY or XCOPY commands to back up the files. You need a program that's specially written to back it up.

The first and simplest is RDISK.EXE, the Rescue Disk program included with Windows NT. You can run it from the Run command in the Start menu. With this utility, you can either back up the Registry files to another directory (C:\WTSRV\REPAIR) by clicking Update Repair Info or create a floppy disk with the Registry info on it by clicking Create Repair Disk.

The second option is to use a utility called REGBACK.EXE, which is included with the Windows NT Resource Kit. This utility is like XCOPY for the Registry. You can back up the Registry files into any directory you want.

Of course, the safest technique is to only do installs after you've done a full system backup using NT Backup or another backup program. Be aware that many backup programs, such as NT Backup, require you to manually specify that you want to back up the Registry.

When you back up the Registry with any of these techniques, you'll back up or be able to back up both the HKEY_LOCAL_MACHINE and the HKEY_CURRENT_USER Registry files. Be aware that on large installations, the Registry files can become very large (well over 10MB).

Real-World Tip: The .DEFAULT key under HKEY_USERS

The .DEFAULT user key is also called the *system default profile*. This key controls the settings you see when you first log onto Terminal Server. Such things as the wallpaper, screensaver, and colors used for the logon screen can all be found under here.

The settings in the Registry are organized in a hierarchical fashion. For those not familiar with the Registry, browsing through it is a lot like browsing through a file system. Instead of the folders being called *directories*, they are called *keys*. Under the keys are subkeys. Both subkeys and keys can contain values. Values can be anything from strings to binary numbers. These values are used by the operating system and applications to store their settings.

What Is *HKEY_CURRENT_USER?*

`HKEY_CURRENT_USER` contains settings that only apply to the user who is currently logged on. If an application needs to maintain a setting for this user only (such as the location of his or her document's directory or preferred text colors), that setting belongs here. The most important thing to remember about `HKEY_CURRENT_USER` is that it applies to one user, and one user only. If you log out and log back on as a different user, the system will load the `HKEY_CURRENT_USER` key for the new user.

The `HKEY_CURRENT_USER` key is actually stored in the user's profile directory, in a file called `ntuser.dat` (see Figure 10.3). By default, the user profile directories are under `C:\WTSRV\PROFILES`, under the user's name. The `ntuser.dat` file is stored in that user's profile directory. Chapter 12 covers profiles in depth, but for now, you need to be aware that every user has his or her own profile directory to keep track of user-specific information.

Several keys under `HKEY_CURRENT_USER` are of concern to you as a Terminal Server administrator, but, as with `HKEY_LOCAL_MACHINE`, the primary one of concern is the `SOFTWARE` key. The following is a list of the main keys under `HKEY_CURRENT_USER` and what they're for:

- **`AppEvents`**   This one sounds more important than it really is. This key keeps the associations between sounds and Windows events. For example, when Windows starts up and you hear a startup sound, it's because of a value in a subkey here.

- **`Console`**   In this key are the default options for the DOS command console. You can change these settings by going into Control Panel and selecting Console. Remember that these settings affect the current user only.

- **`Control Panel`**   Just about every user-specific setting you can change with Control Panel is under this key, including color scheme, mouse settings, international settings, cursors, accessibility settings, and more.

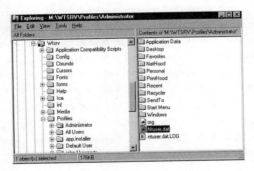

Figure 10.3 The `ntuser.dat` file in the user profile.

- *Environment* Here's where the user's environment variables, such as the PATH variable, are kept. You can control these variables by going into Control Panel and selecting System | Environment. Environment variables can also be set with AUTOEXEC.BAT and AUTOEXEC.NT, as you'll see when we cover integrating DOS applications.

- *Keyboard Layout* This controls which input locales and keyboard layouts are currently loaded. You can control these through Control Panel by selecting Keyboard | Input Locales.

- *Network and UNICODE program groups* The Network key was used to store persistent connections. Neither of these keys is used any longer with Window NT 4.0.

- *Printers* Under this key, you'll find the settings for the user's currently installed printers.

- *Software* Out of all the branches, this is where you'll probably spend most of your time. The Software branch is where your applications keep their user-specific settings. Traditionally, you can find a key by the name of the application's publisher under this branch, which contains all the applications' user-specific settings. Under here, you'll find the Microsoft branch. Under the Microsoft branch are Registry settings for all the Microsoft applications on the server, including the operating system itself.

Real-World Tip: SIDs

You may be wondering what the long number is at the root of your key under HKEY_USERS (remember, HKEY_USERS contains the currently cached user Registries along with the .DEFAULT Registry). The number is your SID, a unique number assigned to your user ID. Just about everything NT does or stores that pertains to your user ID is referenced by SID (your profiles and your user Registry).

There are occasions when it is useful to know what the SID is for you or someone else. One example of this is cloning. There are several cloning utilities on the market which allow you to clone machines' entire hard drives to other machines. This is great for large rollouts. Unfortunately you also duplicate the SIDS, causing havoc on peer-to-peer networks, if two users with the same SID try to access a shared resource. There are SID generators provided by many of these cloning software publishers. Being able to view the SID is one practical way of making sure the SID generators are working.

There are a couple of ways to obtain the SID. First, and most crudely, simply log on as the user and find the user's Registry under HKEY_USERS (it will be under his or her SID). The second way is to use the GETSID utility, available in the NT 4.0 Resource Kit. Basically, you specify the server name and username, and the utility gives you the SID for that user.

Keep in mind that SIDs are unique and do not rely on the username. In other words, if you have to re-create a user who was deleted (such as after a reinstall or recovery), the SID will be different. This means that any setting that referenced the original user's SID will not apply to the new user, even though the username is the same.

■ *Windows 3.1 Migration Status* Keeps track of the INI and GRP conversions. This key is only used if you're doing an upgrade of a Windows 3.x install.

What Is User Global Mode?

You now understand what HKEY_LOCAL_MACHINE is for (global settings) and what HKEY_CURRENT_USER is for (user settings). Now that you understand the importance and function of the Registry, the groundwork has been set to discuss user global mode. User global mode is the main mode in which you should be installing applications on Terminal Server. First, we'll discuss in detail the differences between user-specific and user global modes. We'll end the section with a practical example, by installing Microsoft Outlook 97.

Remember from the discussion of user-specific mode that an application's Registry settings are applied normally (see Figure 10.4). Any files that the application tries to write to the WINDOWS or WINDOWS\SYSTEM32 directories are redirected to the installing user's home directory. After you're finished installing an application, you'll see the application's new DLLs and INI files in your home directory.

In user global mode, applications are installed differently. The first difference between user-specific and user global modes is that the Registry settings that the installation makes are put here:

```
HKEY_LOCAL_MACHINE\Software\Microsoft\Windows NT\Current Version\
Terminal Server\Install
```

All changes that an application makes to HKEY_CURRENT_USER are put here. If the applications make changes to HKEY_LOCAL_MACHINE, they are kept under the MACHINE key, in this location.

The second difference between user-specific and user global modes is that any files written by the application to WINDOWS or WINDOWS\SYSTEM32 are not redirected to the user's home directory.

> ### Note to WinFrame Administrators: Central Registry Collection Key
> For the most part, user global mode and user-specific mode work the same between WinFrame 1.6/1.7 and Terminal Server. However, you should realize that the location of the central Registry collection key has changed from HKEY_LOCAL_MACHINE\Software\Citrix\Install to HKEY_LOCAL_MACHINE\Software\Microsoft\Windows NT\Current Version\Terminal Server\Install. When we get into the discussion on advanced application Registry settings, you'll notice that the central Registry collection key has also moved to ...\Terminal Server instead of ...\Citrix.

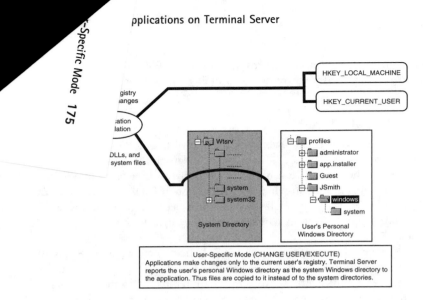

Figure 10.4 How user-specific mode works.

At this point, you might be wondering how you'll get the application to work correctly for all users if all the application system files are put centrally and all the Registry changes are kept in a special location? The answer is through automated Registry and system file distribution. This is the magic by which Terminal Server is able to distribute an application's user-specific files to all its users. When a particular user runs the application, and the application accesses one of its user Registry keys, the entire key is copied to the user's HKEY_CURRENT_USER key. When the application accesses a machine Registry key, it's copied to HKEY_LOCAL_MACHINE. If the application tries to access an INI file or DLL, it's first copied to the user's home directory. In this way, the application's user-specific files and settings are automatically distributed to its users. To reinforce this concept, take a look at Figure 10.5.

With user global mode, application installation is a two-step process:

 1. Enter user global mode by typing the command **CHANGE USER /INSTALL** and install the application. Terminal Server now "collects" all the application's settings and system files. With some applications, which create these files and settings when they are first run, you need to open the application once in user global mode.

 2. After the application is installed, use the command **CHANGE USER /EXECUTE** to return to user-specific mode. This is the normal mode your users need to be in to run the application. In this mode, the settings and system files that were collected will be distributed to your users. When the users run the application and access these files or settings, they are copied to their home directories and Registries.

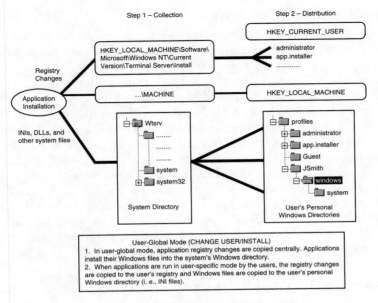

Figure 10.5 How user global mode works.

Troubleshooting Application Problems

As you can see, there's a lot going on under the surface to help applications run correctly in a multiuser environment. Even so, sometimes an application just doesn't want
to run correctly on Terminal Server. The following sections give you the tools and
guidance you need to start troubleshooting application problems.

Real-World Tip: The CHANGE USER **Command**

By default, when you first log onto Terminal Server, you're in execute or user-specific mode. You can
find out which mode you're in by running the CHANGE USER /QUERY command.

When you want to install an application and you switch to user global mode, remember that this command affects every application you run. Always close your applications before changing to user global
mode and installing an application.

When you finish installing the application, you need to switch back to user-specific mode (type
CHANGE USER /EXECUTE). If you stay in user global mode and then run other applications, they will
overwrite the central Registry and INI settings for those applications. This can cause a lot of problems
that might be difficult to troubleshoot.

Application Compatibility Scripts

Both Microsoft and Citrix do extensive application testing to ensure that the major applications on the market will run correctly with Terminal Server. One outcome of this testing is application compatibility scripts.

You'll find the scripts under the `\WTSRV*\Application Compatibility Scripts\install` directory on your Terminal Server. The scripts are combinations of `.cmd` REXX command files and `.key` REGINI Registry change files. In essence, the command files are scripts you can run from the command line. The scripts, for the most part, run the `REGINI.EXE` utility in order to change your application's Registry settings to be compatible with Terminal Server.

You can view the `.cmd` and `.key` files with a standard text editor to see how they work. Before using them, always take a look at what they're intended to do. Many of the scripts use hard-coded drive letters to represent the user's home directory. This is where it's important to have a standard home directory drive letter set up for your users. If the script you need to run has a hard-coded drive letter for the home directory, replace it with your standard drive letter for your home directories.

Troubleshooting DOS Applications

So far, we've mainly been talking about running Windows 32- and Windows 16-bit applications with Citrix. Remember that several limitations are imposed by running DOS applications on Terminal Server. First, running DOS applications decreases overall performance significantly. Second, there limitations on screen size (see the following list). Third, DOS applications can tax the processor and memory significantly if not controlled properly. Even with all these downfalls, you still may have to support a DOS application on Terminal Server. If you're going to run DOS applications, here are several tips that may help you out:

- *Full-screen versus half-screen mode* The most common complaint heard with DOS applications is that they will not run in full-screen mode; instead they only run in a window. If you're using a Windows-based Terminal Server client, you have no choice but to run the DOS application in a window. The only way to make the application run in a full screen is to use MetaFrame's DOS client. The DOS client is simply the Terminal Server client written for DOS.

- *Dual boot to the DOS-based client* If your users have to run Windows, one possibility is to set up the machine for dual boot. When the users need to log onto Terminal Server, they'll need to reboot and run the MetaFrame DOS client.

- *Set an MS-DOS mode icon in Windows 95 for the MetaFrame DOS client* The MS-DOS mode icon is a built-in feature of Windows 95. It allows you to create an icon on the desktop for a DOS application, which will automatically shut down and reboot the desktop into MS-DOS mode before running the application. When the user is done with the application, a quick reboot is executed and the user is brought back into Windows 95. In order to see this in action, first install MetaFrame's DOS client. Create a shortcut on the user's Windows 95 desktop for the `WFCLIENT.EXE` executable. Right-click Properties and select Advanced from the Programs menu. Select MS-DOS Mode and change `autoexec.bat` and `config.sys` to load the network drivers for the MetaFrame DOS client. Now click the icon and check it out. If you did everything correctly, the computer should shut down, restart in MS-DOS mode, and run the MetaFrame DOS client. When you exit from the client, you should return to Windows 95.

■ *Attempt to run the DOS mode client under Windows 95*   You may have success in running MetaFrame's DOS mode client under Windows, especially Windows 95 with IPX/SPX or NetBEUI. Be aware that this option is not supported and has not been thoroughly tested.

■ *Memory overutilization*   If your server slows to a crawl every time your users try running DOS applications, there's a good chance that they are overutilizing memory. Certain DOS applications, in particular FoxPro for DOS, will use up all available server memory by themselves. To check whether this is the problem, run Windows Task Manager (Select WinFrame Security | Task Manager from the Start menu) and go to the Performance tab (see Figure 10.6). Watch the physical memory available and memory utilization as you run your DOS application. If the amount drastically changes, your DOS application is the culprit. You can try adjusting the PIF settings (see the PIF tips later in this list). Also, refer to your application's developers for tips on limiting the amount of memory. With FoxPro for DOS, you can solve this problem by adding `MEMLIMIT=60,4096,6144` to the `CONFIG.FP` file found in the `FOXPROxx` directory.

■ *Processor overutilization*   DOS applications were never designed for a multitasking environment. Many DOS applications will overutilize the processor with idle processes. There are several ways to control this problem. The first and foremost is to use the `DOSKBD` utility. You should use this utility for most every DOS application you run. The `DOSKBD` utility prevents a DOS application from over utilizing the processor by polling constantly for user input. To use the utility, simply add `DOSKBD` to your `\WTSRV\SYSTEM32\AUTOEXEC.NT` file.

This starts `DOSKBD` with the default settings. These settings should be adequate for most situations. Compare the processor utilization of the application, with and without `DOSKBD`, using the Windows Task Manager. If you find you need to further adjust the settings, type **`DOSKBD /?`** for an explanation of the settings available.

You can also try adjusting the idle sensitivity using PIF files. See the entry on PIFs, later in this list.

■ *Blinking cursors and other animations*   If your DOS application uses blinking or spinning cursors or any other type of animation (scrolling banners, for example), make sure you turn them off if possible. These animations will use up tremendous amounts of processing power and network bandwidth in order to handle all the screen updates necessary to display them.

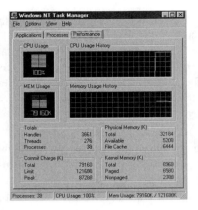

Figure 10.6 Using Windows Task Manager to check memory utilization.

■ *PIF tips* Many WinFrame administrators are used to using PIF files to control their DOS applications. Terminal Server will support old PIF files, but it handles PIF file settings in a different manner than WinFrame. If you have DOS applications that you need to create a PIF for, right-click the application executable in Windows Explorer and select Properties. You'll see several tabs containing many different DOS-related PIF settings. If you change any of these settings and apply them, Windows Explorer will automatically create a PIF file for your application in the current directory. The following settings are the most important:

Program, Windows NT Under here you can define the Autoexec and Config files used by your DOS application. By default, all DOS applications run `CONFIG.NT` and `AUTOEXEC.NT` from the `\WTSRV\SYSTEM32` directory. If you want to define a special Autoexec or Config file to be used by your application, you need to specify it here. You should create a `SCRIPTS` directory under your `USER` share where you keep all of your applications batch files, Autoexec files, and Config files.

Memory There are several settings under here to control the memory environment for your DOS app. You can get a more detailed description of a particular setting by pressing F1 with the setting being highlighted.

Screen, Full Screen If you want to launch your DOS application in full-screen mode, you need to set it here. Remember that full-screen mode only works with the DOS-based MetaFrame client.

Misc, Idle Sensitivity You may be able to use this setting to help with processor utilization problems of your application.

Troubleshooting Windows 16- and 32-bit Application Problems

What if you've followed all the tips, created your users' home directories, installed the application in user global mode, and you're still having problems? Here are some solutions to common problems running Windows 16- and Windows 32-bit applications:

- *Application doesn't run*   If the application doesn't run at all, you need to step back and do a couple of tests. First, try running the application on a Windows NT 4.0 workstation. If it doesn't work on the workstation, it will not work on Terminal Server. Next, try running the application after installing it while in user-specific mode. If it works, you either need to find out what pieces are not being copied with user global mode or install the application in user-specific mode for each user who needs it.

- *Strange behavior, lockups, or "file missing" errors*   Double-check that the user is running the application in user-specific mode and that the home directory is set up correctly. This may seem simple, but this is where a lot of problems occur. Type **CHANGE USER /QUERY** while logged on as the user to ensure that they're in execute or user-specific mode. Next, type **SET** to check the environment setting variables. The HOMEDRIVE and HOMEPATH variables should point to the correct location for the user's home directory. If this is not the case, make sure User Manager is set up with the right location.

- *Application says certain files are missing*   This is a common problem. More often than not it's due to either running the application under Windows NT or files are not being copied over with user global mode. If your application does not use the standard Windows APIs to access the INI or DLL files, it will not work correctly with user global mode installations. To solve this problem, try installing the files in user-specific mode. If it works, you can either install the application for each user in user-specific mode or you can write a script to distribute the missing files. If it doesn't work even in user-specific mode, try running it on a Windows NT 4.0 workstation. If you have the same errors running on a Windows NT 4.0 workstation, contact the software vendor for suggestions on making it work with Windows NT.

- *"Access denied" errors*   Often on new installations, you run into security issues. It's always a good idea to try running the application as an administrator equivalent. This quickly rules out the possibility of file or directory security being the problem with the application.

- *Application requires a temp directory, some type of user-specific storage area, or pathnames for user data files*   This is a very common need and is one of the main reasons why map-rooting home directories is so important. Many times an application keeps this setting in the global key. The dilemma then becomes how to enter a single path that will be unique for all your users. For example, suppose you have an application called Acme-Organizer that has a setting for the directory for the user's organizer files. Unfortunately, the developer put this setting in

HKEY_LOCAL_MACHINE. You need to distribute this application to 50 users, all of whom will need their own location for their Organizer file. How do you do it? Simply specify the location for the Organizer files as [Home drive]:\ORG, where [Home drive] is your standardized user home drive letter. When users log on, [Home drive] will be map-rooted to their personal home directory. Their personal Organizer files will be put under \ORG. You could take this a step further and lock the Organizer data path in the Registry using Registry security (see the previous Real-World Tip). This way, one user would not have the ability to change the setting and thus disable everyone's Organizer.

■ *Users complain that their settings keep changing*   After installing an application in user global mode, log on as one of the users and run the application. Change as many of the user-specific default settings as possible, such as those under a Properties section of the application (text colors, server names, cache parameters). Now log on as another user and run the application. Do you see the default settings or do you see User 1's settings? If you see User 1's settings, the application is storing user-specific settings in HKEY_LOCAL_MACHINE. Remember that HKEY_LOCAL_MACHINE is only for global settings, and HKEY_CURRENT_USER is for user settings. If this is the case, you can warn your users about the problem and request that they not change their settings; you can research where the Registry settings are and use Registry security to prevent users from changing them. Finally, you can contact the software publisher for a solution.

If your application stores its settings in INI files and you're having this problem, check to make sure that the user has his own copy of the INI file in his home directory. If not, make sure you're in user-specific mode and that the home directory settings are correct.

Determining Where Applications Keep Their Settings

Knowing how to find out where applications keep their settings is one of the most important skills to learn with Terminal Server.

The first and simplest tool is the built-in Find command. Find allows you to search the entire hard drive for files that have changed recently. Logically, if you make a change in an application and then do a search for recently changed files, you'll find the file in which the application makes those changes. Here are the steps you need to follow (do this test after hours or when there's little activity):

1. Run the application in question and make a change to a specific setting, such as text color.

2. Select Find|Files or Folders|Date Modified. Select the During the Previous 1 Day setting and select Find Now.

3. Click the Modified column header to sort by date. At the top of the column under the folders will be the most recently changed file.

This trick works best for INI files. You can quickly see which INI files have changed recently because of the application change you made.

If this doesn't work, it's time to break out the big guns. Go to www.sysinternals.com. and download the freeware `REGMON.EXE` utility. This is one of the most powerful and useful tools in the Terminal Server universe. With `REGMON`, you can watch all the Registry changes an application makes while it's running. Very simple, very powerful. Now go into the application and make the same change again and watch the `REGMON` log to see what happens. If the application records the changes in the Registry, you'll see exactly where it puts them.

If you find that the application stores the settings in `HKEY_LOCAL_MACHINE` and not in `HKEY_CURRENT_USER` and you absolutely cannot have your users playing with those settings, you can use Registry security to restrict who is able to change them. This technique may or may not work with your particular application. Before you make any changes to Registry security, make sure you document them centrally and test them thoroughly; otherwise, you'll cause yourself more problems than it's worth. Complete coverage of Registry security is beyond the scope of this book. Refer to either Microsoft's TechNet or one of the many books dedicated to Registry settings.

Note that `REGMON` is also a very useful learning tool, especially during application installation. The next time you install an application, use `REGMON` to monitor the installation to see what changes your application makes to the Registry. Again, tools such as `REGMON` are powerful but are meant for use during low activity or off-peak hours. If you attempt to use `REGMON` on a heavily active server, you'll not only severely limit its performance, but you'll never be able to keep up with all the Registry changes that occur.

Advanced Application Troubleshooting

If you absolutely have to get a particular application to run with Terminal Server and have completely run out of options, there's one more possibility to look into—the `Compatibility` keys. These are a set of three keys you can use to help solve application Registry, INI, and performance problems. We'll get into the performance keys in Chapter 13. For now, let's take a look at the Registry and INI keys. The `Compatibility` keys are located under

```
HKEY_LOCAL_MACHINE\SOFTWARE\Microsoft\WindowsNT\CurrentVersion\
TerminalServer\Compatibility
```

Here they are and here's what they do:

- *Applications*   This key and its subkeys are used for tuning the performance of your applications. This will be covered in more detail in Chapter 13.

- *IniFiles*   This Registry key controls how the INI files located in the system directory are synchronized with the files in the users' home directories. The INI name with a `REG_DWORD` of `x44` means that changes to that INI file will be merged with the user's INI file of the same name. Notice that the `SYSTEM` and

WIN.INI files are, by default, included in this Registry. If, for example, you edit the SYSTEM.INI files using SYSEDIT while in user global mode and then log on as a user, the changes you made to the central SYSTEM.INI file will be merged with the user's SYSTEM.INI file.

- *Registry entries* This Registry key controls how and if the Registry keys under HKEY_LOCAL_MACHINE\SOFTWARE\Microsoft\WindowsNT\CurrentVersion\TerminalServer\Software are synchronized with the user's Registry keys. A value in here with a DWORD of x108 means that that particular key under ...\Software and its subkeys will not be synchronized with the user's keys.

Making the Most of Your Resources

There are many, many troubleshooting resources available to you for resolving application issues. After trying the basics to resolve a problem with an application, try doing a search on Citrix's Web site for implementation tips (www.citrix.com). Citrix maintains an excellent online database of application installation tips. It also has a Solutions Guide available (solg.exe) with specific installation instructions for several major applications. Because the technology for Terminal Server is based closely on Citrix's WinFrame products, many of the tips will directly apply. As the product matures, Microsoft will also become a good online resource for Terminal Server troubleshooting. Of course, if all else fails, the people who will be able to help the best are those who wrote it. The next section brings you up to speed on issues that a developer will need to understand when working with Terminal Server.

TS Applications and the Developer

On some occasions, getting an application to run properly on Terminal Server will require the assistance of the developers. If you're going to develop applications for Terminal Server or you desire a developer-level understanding of what's required, this section is for you. If you can understand how TS is designed, you can understand how it can be fixed.

The following are basic guidelines you need to follow when developing applications for Terminal Server:

- *Applications need to be able to work with Windows NT.* This is by far the most important rule.
- *Applications need to make use of standard Windows API calls.* Terminal Server captures several Windows API calls in order for Windows applications to be able to work correctly in the multiuser environment. Applications that do not adhere to Microsoft's guidelines on writing them to the Windows API might not run well on Terminal Server. If your application uses custom code, especially machine-coded sections for additional speed, it will not run well or run at all on Terminal Server.

One very important point on this topic is how an application makes changes to INI files or the Registry. It needs to do so through the Windows API in order for Terminal Server to keep these changes separate. If one application running on Terminal Server records something in the Registry or an INI file, you do not want this to affect all users of the application.

■ *Applications that write directly to the hardware are not allowed.* Examples of these types of applications are DOS graphics applications and Windows applications that use VxDs. Because they write directly to the hardware and do not work through the Windows APIs, there's no way for Terminal Server to capture these calls. Typical DOS applications that use graphics are desktop publishing, spreadsheets with graphs, graphing programs, and games. Typical windows applications that use VxDs are communication programs that use VxDs for the COM ports, hard drive caching programs, and games. Typically, the DOS and Win16 applications you need to worry about are applications you wouldn't want to run on Terminal Server anyway.

■ *Applications cannot rely on the IP address, MAC address, or network name to identify users.* This rule applies mainly for client/server or terminal applications. In a Terminal Server environment, the MAC address, IP address, and network name are that of the Terminal Server for all users. If, for example, you want to run a mainframe client through a gateway that identified the user by MAC address, you would be able to allow only one user through the gateway. The software needs to be able to support some other means of identifying the user, such as a workstation ID setting, in order to work.

■ *Applications should return control to the OS.* When an application is idle or waiting for a response, it should return control to the OS. Applications that constantly poll the user, have time animations (such as blinking or spinning cursors), or any other constant activity during idle time will slow application performance significantly and tax the processor. If there's any way to turn the animations off, you should do so.

■ *Novell NDS API calls are not supported.* If you have an application that makes Novell NDS API calls, you'll not be able to run it on Terminal Server. One example of this is Novell's Netadmin utility. On the other hand, bindery mode applications, such as SYSCON, are fully supported. If you need to run applications such as these remotely, you need to set up for remote node access, such as with RAS. See Chapters 14, "Terminal Server and Remote Access," and 15, "Terminal Server and NetWare," for more information.

■ *Applications should not store user-specific information in global areas.* This guideline is very important for proper application function. Global settings belong under HKEY_LOCAL_MACHINE. User-specific settings belong under HKEY_CURRENT_USER. Global data files belong in a central directory, and user data files belong in the user's home directory.

- *Stay away from animations or complicated graphics.* Animations and complicated graphics take extra processing power in order to be compressed and sent across the line to the users' terminals. You should use simple graphics. Also, stay away from bitmaps, and use vector graphics when possible.

- *Remember that your application is in resource competition.* If your application uses resources unfairly, it robs resources from the rest of the applications running on the server. Remember that your application is always in competition for the limited resources of the Terminal Server.

Securing the Server

11

IS YOUR SERVER SECURE? This is a tough question to answer because security is more of a process than an attainable goal. Good security requires constant diligence on the part of the network administrator. As you make changes to your server, you need to keep in mind the effects that those changes have on security.

Having a secure system often means both controlling access to information and ensuring that information is accessible. First, if someone can obtain unauthorized access to information from your server, your server is not secure. Second, if someone can disable others from being able to access your server or its resources, your server is not secure. Reliability is directly related to security—if you want a reliable system, you first have to secure it. While reading this chapter, keep in mind these two distinct goals—controlling access and ensuring accessibility. The tips throughout the chapter are geared toward both of these goals.

Terminal Server Security

Terminal Server presents special security problems that you may not be used to if you're coming from a Novell or even an NT server background. Users no longer are accessing your server's resources across a network through a file security barrier; instead, they are at your server working with its files as if they were sitting at the console. Imagine the security problems that could occur if a hundred different users were able to sit at the console of your NT server in your computer room and access its resources, and the resources of the server were not locked down properly! If one user accidentally deletes a critical system file that's not locked down, all users are immediately affected. The use of file share security is no longer a shield, because users have direct access to the server's hard drive itself. For this, and many more reasons, security is a topic that you should take very seriously with Terminal Server.

In the military, information is protected by a "need to know" test. Likewise, with Terminal Server, you as the administrator need to determine a user's or group's "need to access." Ideal security happens when users are given the minimal level of access necessary to perform their jobs. Think of the simplicity of a mainframe terminal when setting up your user's desktops. Give your users icons only for applications they need. If they only need to use one application, then take them directly to it when they log on.

Documenting Your Security

Before going into the details of securing your Terminal Server, the importance of documenting your security must be emphasized. The following are some of the many reasons why documenting your security setup is important:

- *Application troubleshooting* Setting up proper security for your system can quickly become very complex. As you implement more and more security measures, the likelihood increases that a security measure will cause an application problem. Security-related application problems can be very difficult to troubleshoot without meticulous documentation. Your documentation should include what security changes were made, why they were made, when they were made, and who made them.

- *Disaster recovery* You should have enough information in your documentation to be able to re-create your security setup in case of disaster recovery or for setting up a new server. Automating your security setup with documented scripts is also recommended for quick recovery times.

- *Consistency* Consistency is very important for effective security. Often, as an administrator, you'll encounter the same security issues. By documenting the correct security setup for a particular security issue, such as how to secure a particular application, you can re-create the security setup accurately in the future. By having those who work for you refer to the same documentation, you can keep your security approach consistent on all the servers both you and your team manage.

- *Justification* Security often comes at the cost of convenience. Once you've decided on the appropriate level of security for your Terminal Server, documented it, and obtained approval on the documentation, you can use that documentation as justification for the security measures you need to take.

Creating a System Security Manual

While going through the tips in this chapter, you should start a system security manual. Start the security manual with the assessment of threats. Which of your security threats are the most critical? How do you detect breaches in security? How do you recover from security problems?

Next, pick out the tips you think will work well in your environment and then implement them. Then document them in the system security manual. This is the most important part. In this section, list every security measure that has been taken to secure your system.

The tips have been organized into the following categories to make it easier for you to document the ones you want to use in an organized fashion:

- *Physical security*   How is your system physically secured? Who is responsible for what aspects of the physical security?

- *Desktop security*   How are your desktops secured? What policies and profiles have you implemented, and why?

- *File security*   Include changes that were made to the default NTFS security and why. Also, include information on the directories on your server. What is stored under them, and how they are secured (home directories, application directories, data directories, system directories, temporary directories)? Every directory on your server should have a specific purpose and should be locked appropriately. Remember that the users may have direct access to your server's drives.

- *Registry security*   Include what Registry keys were changed or added for security reasons. Also include changes to the default Registry permissions, and why.

- *System security*   What security changes apply to your entire system? What is your password policy? What are your backup and recovery procedures?

- *Monitoring*   What are your regularly scheduled security checks? How is auditing set up on your system?

Security Tips

The tips are broken down by categories, as previously listed. Remember these tips are only a start. As an administrator, you need to decide which of the many tips make the most sense for your environment and apply them. Not all the tips will apply or even make sense for your situation. The final word on security lies with you. Through the continual diligence and careful observation of the network administrator, a network and its servers are kept reliable and secure.

Physical Security

One often-overlooked area of security is the physical security of your server and network. If you want a reliable and secure Terminal Server solution, you need to control the physical security of your server. Good physical security helps prevent both accidental mishaps, such as the pulling of a plug, and malicious attacks, such as vandalism. The following are some commonsense tips on how to ensure good physical security:

- *Locked server room with access cards*   Having a locked server room is self-explanatory. Locking it by using access cards provides an audit trail of who came and left the server room and at what time. With readily available shareware utilities on the market, a potential hacker can retrieve the administrator password in seconds from your servers—all that's required is physical access to your console.

- *Floppy, case, and cabinet locks*   Nothing deters the curious or unwelcome as well as a good lock. Most cabinets are lockable, as well as most computer cases. Giving general floppy drive access to your servers is not recommended. Again, with readily available utilities, administrator passwords can be obtained and NTFS partitions can even be read (from a bootable floppy). In addition, floppies are the most common and easiest way to infect a server with a virus. Some servers allow you to disable booting from floppies, which is a good idea.

- *Uninterruptible power supplies (UPS)*   Power problems are common in many areas of the country. Using a UPS you can protect yourself from many of the types of power problems that can occur. Most UPSs also come with notification software that can be set up to warn you via pager, email, broadcast message, or other means of an impending power failure.

- *High temperature and fire alarms*   Security does not do too much good if your servers melt down. High temperature alarms are an often-overlooked measure. You could toast a marshmallow with the heat that comes off most processors today. Don't make the mistake of thinking air conditioning just happens. Installing a fire suppressant system or having electrically safe (Class C) fire extinguishers readily available in the server room is also a good idea.

- *Fireproof safe for backup tapes and offsite storage*   No matter what natural or unnatural disaster occurs, you should always be able to get back your backup tapes and original install media. By sending your tapes offsite using an offsite data storage service, you have recourse in case of a major disaster.

Desktop Security

Desktop security is perhaps the most important type of security. Remember, with Terminal Server, when you sit at a desktop, it's as though you're sitting at the console of the server itself. Desktops are windows onto your server that can be opened from any location for which you have given access.

The key to good desktop security is simplification. You need to decide exactly what your users need access to, provide them that access, and take away all else. For example, if users only need to run two remote applications, do they need to have the Run program option in their Start menu or access to the command line or any other program icon in the Start menu or desktop except for the icons for those applications?

By default, desktops are riddled with potential security holes. The main tools you can use to control the desktop are policies and profiles. Policies are Registry settings that can restrict what users can do on their desktops. With policies, you can prevent a user from being able to use the Run command or from getting access to the command line, and much more. Profiles contain all of a user's personal settings, such as the programs that are on the user's desktop and in the Start menu. With profiles, you can control which program icons users have and, therefore, which programs they can run. See Chapter 12, "Administering the Desktop and Server," to learn more about both of these features. Here are some general guidelines on desktop security:

- *Simplicity*   The more options users are given, the greater the potential for security problems. Users' desktops should be devoid of any icons or options that they do not have an absolute need to use. Keeping desktops simple also makes them significantly easier to administer.

- *Application security*   The number of applications that your users need access to with Terminal Server is usually very short. With the Application Security tool, you can restrict the applications your users can run. We'll go over the use of this powerful tool in the next section.

- *Running applications directly after logon*   The most secure desktop is one that's bypassed completely. Desktops are merely launching pads for user programs. If users only need remote access to a few applications, it's best to run these applications directly after the user logs onto the system. You can set up a program to execute right after a user logs on by defining the program executable and working directory at the client (in User Manager or for the connection). Once users exit an application, they are logged off the system.

- *Publishing applications*   If you're using MetaFrame, you have the option to publish your applications. This is the best way to provide application access for most systems. Not only can you control who has access to run an application, but you also can make a single application available from multiple servers using load balancing. This greatly increases reliability and performance and is a very secure alternative to providing the user with a desktop.

- *Disable access to the command prompt, Run command, My Computer, Network Neighborhood, and Explorer*   These are all huge security holes that hackers with even a small amount of knowledge can exploit to gain further access to your system. Carefully weigh the potential security problems of giving access to these tools against the inconvenience of not having them available when setting up your users' desktops. All of these can be restricted using the policies shown in Chapter 12. Also, be careful of applications that have backdoors that can access the command prompt; these can also be just as much of a security risk.

Author's Note: Hidden Backdoors

An example of a hidden backdoor can be found in Word 97. A user can run any application he wants from Word 97 by selecting About Microsoft Word from the Help menu, clicking System Info, and selecting Run from the File menu.

- *Add/Remove Programs*   Be careful of what's installed through the Add/Remove Programs dialog box during the initial install of Terminal Server (Start menu | Settings | Control Panel | Add/Remove Programs). Never give your user's access to any program that could needlessly rob your other users of processing power. The main examples of this are games and screen savers. Games should not be installed, and no screen savers should be used except for those that require minimal processor power, such as the blank screen saver or logon screen saver. Animated cursors should also not be installed.

- *User policies*   Access to the Control Panel, Registry (REGEDT32), Run option, Find option, Network Neighborhood, and much more can all be controlled through policies. Use policies to keep the desktop simple and to control what your users have access to. Policies are covered in detail in Chapter 12.

- *Common folder*   Be careful of what's in the common folder, because this contains the icons that will appear in everyone's Start menu. To look at what's in the common folder, select Programs from the Start menu. All the icons and folders below the divider line, as shown in Figure 11.1, are in the common folder. Their folders will have a computer next to them to indicate that they are accessible by all users of this computer. They will appear in everyone's Start menu.

By default, most applications install their icons in the common folder. If the application is only going to be used by a select group of users, you may want to manually add the icon to their personal Start menu folder located in their profile directories. By doing this, the icon will only be accessible by those users. If the application is for general use and you want to put it in the common folder, make sure that only the proper icons are shown. For example, your application may create an Uninstall icon. It would be a good idea to remove this so that your users cannot uninstall the program by accident! Another problem with the common folders is the Administrative Tools folder. The Administrative Tools folder contains applications only an administrator should use. It should be moved to the administrator's personal folder.

To change what's in the common folder, right-click the Start button and select Open All Users. The icons in here are the ones that are in the common folder. You can delete them or move them to other locations, such as the personal folder (select Open from the Start menu), as necessary.

The simplest and perhaps best common folder is made up of the program icons your users need and nothing more. Specific examples of how best to set up your desktop are covered in Chapter 12.

Figure 11.1   Common group icons.

File Security

Setting appropriate file security can be very challenging, especially with Terminal Server. To make sure the correct file security is implemented, you must make the appropriate choices; the first and most important of which is to choose NTFS during installation. The next choices you have to make occur when you install your users' applications. The following are some tips on securing your file system:

- *Choose NTFS during installation, not after*   This is worth saying twice. If you use FAT for your system partition, you have little or no protection from a user wiping out a critical system file. You should choose NTFS for your system partition during installation. Don't plan to convert afterward from FAT to NTFS. During installation, if you choose NTFS, it will apply a default set of security rights (see Table 5.1 in Chapter 5, "Installing Terminal Server and MetaFrame"). These rights are crucial for protecting your critical system files. If you convert to NTFS later using the CONVERT command, these default rights are not applied. If you're already stuck and have chosen FAT, convert it to NTFS and apply the rights covered in Chapter 5.

- *Back up your data daily*   This is a self-explanatory item. Just remember, no matter how much security you have, you still have to trust someone with access to the data. If anyone breaks that trust and loses or destroys a file, the most recent backup may be your only recourse.

- *Choose a reliable storage solution*   One of the most common and reliable storage solutions is using RAID 5. With RAID 5, you can lose an entire drive, and the system will still function. Mirroring or duplexing are also useful alternatives.

Real-World Tip: The "Everyone Has Full Access" Dilemma

By default, when you create a new share or a new directory on your server, the Everyone group has Full Access. For those used to the security systems of other operating systems, this may come as a surprise. What this means is that after you create the new share or directory, you must remove the Everyone group and add whatever groups or users should have access to the access list.

For those who think it should be the other way around, a utility is included with Terminal Server that can help: ACLSET. This is a very powerful utility and needs to be used with great care. ACLSET locks down all your server's hard drives so that only the administrator and system have access to the files. When you type ACLSET on a command line by itself, it will immediately start the lockdown process. After the server drives are locked, you'll need to begin giving appropriate levels of access to the users. The techniques to do so are covered in this chapter.

- *Failure notification*   Make sure you are notified upon failure of any part of your Terminal Server, especially its storage devices. Many systems today offer various types of notification options, such as audible, pager, mail, and SMTP. If you lose one drive in a RAID or mirrored system, you're still okay. If you lose two, prepare for a restore. Performing a test failure of your RAID system during prototyping is also a good idea to ensure that the notification system you set up works properly and that the system can correctly handle a drive failure. Many administrators wisely dedicate a few minutes every morning checking the hardware status of all their servers.

- *Make a separate partition for user data or use a third-party disk quota program*   One problem with Terminal Server security is the lack of a space restriction per user. For this reason, you should make a separate partition for user data. If users are allowed to store data in the same partition as your system files and print queues, when the partition is filled up, users will lose their ability to print. What's more, the system and/or applications could crash. By keeping the data in a separate partition, your users will instead get an out-of-space error when trying to save, but they will otherwise not be affected.

- *Compartmentalize your data and applications*   This goes along with simplification. With a properly organized server, security problems become readily apparent and can be fixed quickly. Always compartmentalize your applications and data. Application directories should be kept together under a single directory. User data from the application should also be kept together in a separate directory or in individual user home directories, as appropriate. In general, users should be given read-only access to the application directories they need and read/write/change access to the user data directories. By treating applications and user data as separate security entities, administration is much easier.

- *Control access through groups*   Using groups is the best way to control file access. Many administrators make local application groups, assign those groups the rights necessary to run a single application, and add global groups to them containing the users who need access to the application. For example, you could create an APP_OFFICE97 local group for users of Office 97. Remove the Everyone group from the access list to the Office 97 directories and give the APP_OFFICE97 group access to the application using the appropriate rights. When you want to give your domain users access to this application, add them to a global DOM1_APP_OFFICE97 group and add that group to the local APP_OFFICE97 group. This makes it easy to control who has access to applications on the Terminal Server.

Real-World Tip: Quota Manager

One of the most popular solutions to the disk quota problem is Quota Manager, written by NTP Software (www.ntpsoftware.com). Quota Manager allows you to restrict the space usage of your users. It has been written for both the Intel and Alpha platforms. Although it's a little on the expensive side, the ease of use and relief from space usage headaches makes Quota Manager well worth the purchase. Because Terminal Server is relatively new on the market, make sure you analyze any NT third-party solution thoroughly in a test environment before implementing it.

- *Periodically review your file security* In the "Monitoring Your Server" section in this chapter, you'll learn how to use the ACLCHECK utility (included with Terminal Server) to keep track of exactly who has access to which files in your system.

- *Audit critical file access* The auditing tools included with Terminal Server are very powerful. You can use them to keep an eye on critical system files and data. You can also use them to record logon and logout times, which are also important. If you ever have a security problem, this will help provide proof of the culprit's actions.

- *Control what can be executed using the read permission* Removing the read permission is one of the simplest ways to prevent users from executing programs they have no reason to execute. Take a look through your system directories for utilities and programs you do not want your users to execute. One particular program you should disable execute access to is REGEDT32.

Registry Security

This is probably one of the most often overlooked areas of security. Many administrators may not realize that the Registry has security at all. Fewer still may recognize how important this security can be. The Registry contains a wealth of information about your system that an intruder can take advantage of. Because many programs are loaded from the Registry with system-level access, the Registry is a common point of access for setting up Trojan horse attacks.

By default, the Everyone group has read access to most of the machine Registry's keys (HKEY_LOCAL_MACHINE), and the Administrator group has full control. This means that only administrators will be able to change Registry entries that affect the hardware, such as which device drivers are loaded at startup.

By default, the Everyone group is additionally granted special access to the majority of the SOFTWARE key, underneath HKEY_LOCAL_MACHINE. The special access granted to Everyone includes the rights to view, create, and delete keys/values. This is a very important security point to realize. If users are given access to REGEDT32, if they can run any program that changes the Registry (REGINI for example), or if they start installing their own software, they have the ability to make changes to the Registry that will affect everyone on the system!

> **Real-World Tip: Log Out Users After Any Security Change**
>
> When a user logs on to the system, the system generates an access token object that contains all the user's security-related information, including which groups he or she is a member of. This access token object is used to validate users whenever they try to access a secured resource.
>
> What this means to an administrator is that if you make security changes, such as removing a user from a group such as Domain Admins, the user will still have Domain Admin rights until the user logs out. The reason is that although you have changed the user's security in the SAM, the user's access token list still has the user as a member of the Domain Admins group. Be careful which groups you make users a member of and always have a user log out after you make changes to his or her security.

If the solution to this problem were as simple as restricting users to read-only access to this key, life would be good. Unfortunately, many applications will not run or run properly unless users have read-write access to at least some of the applications' keys under SOFTWARE. Your job is to figure out which keys are used by an application and how best to secure them.

Understanding Registry Security

To best secure the Registry, you first need to understand it. As a Terminal Server administrator, you should have an excellent understanding of the Registry. This book goes into detail on components of the Registry that directly pertain to Terminal Server. However, full coverage of the Registry is beyond the scope of this book. It may be worthwhile to get a book dedicated specifically to the Windows NT Registry as a reference guide when you need it.

Although you need to understand the Registry to ensure that your server is secure, playing with the wrong parameters in the Registry can crash the system. If you need to test the effects of changes to the Registry or want to discover how your applications interact with it, perform the task on a test server. You could install Terminal Server on your own workstation using one of the many dual-boot techniques. Using third-party software, such as Partition Magic, you can set up a dual-boot Windows 95 (FAT)/Terminal Server (NTFS) workstation, or whatever operating system combination works best for you. It's better not to install Terminal Server on a FAT partition, simply because Terminal Server on NTFS will give you the most accurate idea of how your applications will run.

Even if you test your changes carefully before you implement them, as well as document these changes thoroughly and take every precaution necessary, you should still perform a backup before making any changes. The REGBACK utility, included with the Windows NT Resource Kit, provides an easy way to do this. Just remember that the size of the Registry can be large with Windows Terminal Server. You can also back up the Registry by following these steps:

1. Run the Repair Disk Utility by entering **RDISK.EXE** in the Start menu's Run dialog box.

2. From the Repair Disk Utility window, click Update Repair Info. This will make a copy of the current Registry files, autoexec.nt, config.nt, and setup information in the C:\WTSRV\REPAIR directory on the server.

You can also make a copy of the repair information on floppy disk using this utility by clicking the Create Repair Disk button from the main window.

Some backup programs will also let you back up and restore down to a key level. In general, the following tips will help keep you out of trouble:

- Always fully back up the Registry before any changes.

- Do any planned Registry work after hours during system maintenance time when no one is logged on. Disable logon first and then make sure all users are off.

- If you have to look at the HKEY_KEY_LOCAL_MACHINE key, stay out of the SYSTEM subkey. Manually changing parameters under this key is rarely necessary and can quickly crash the system if you change the wrong ones.

- Document any changes.

General Registry Tips

The following are some general tips on how to secure your Registry:

- *Replace the Everyone group with WTS_USERS*   Everyone means *every user* in the NT domain that Terminal Server is a part of. The Everyone group is used in countless places to provide access to Terminal Server's Registry and file system. In reality, not everyone needs access to your file system and Registry. By replacing the Everyone group with the WTS_USERS group in your system's ACLs, you can increase security significantly.

- *Make sure your backup software is backing up the Registry*   The Registry is not always backed up by default. With many backup programs, you need to specify that the Registry is backed up. Make sure that Registry backup is part of your backup jobs.

- *Carefully restrict user access to application keys under HKEY_LOCAL_MACHINE\SOFTWARE*   The emphasis here is on *carefully*. HKEY_LOCAL_MACHINE\SOFTWARE contains global settings for your applications. If users are allowed to change the application settings under this key, their changes will affect all users of the application. If, on the other hand, you arbitrarily restrict all users to read-only access to the entire SOFTWARE key, no user will be able to log on. Even if you restrict access to read-only on only a single subkey, you may disable an application that needs more access. If you're serious about Registry security, refer to the developers of the applications you need to restrict. Whether your application will work with read-only access to these setting keys needs to be thoroughly tested.

- *Use auditing to tune security*   Auditing can be an excellent tool for helping secure the system. One approach is to lock down the Registry and file system tightly and then enable auditing upon access to the Registry keys and parts of the file system you locked. Then run your applications. If you encounter any errors during their execution because they cannot access certain parts of the Registry or file system, you should be able to see in the audit log which parts they were trying to access. Enable access to these parts and try the application again. Through this process, you can build a picture of your application's Registry and file system access needs.

- *Beware of the Trojan horse attack*   Many areas of the Registry are subject to Trojan horse attacks. For example, if you allow users the right to create keys under the HKEY_LOCAL_MACHINE\SOFTWARE\Classes key, which contains file extension association, they could implant a Trojan horse that would be run the next time the administrator opens up a text file (*.txt). Some good listings of the keys that should be protected can be obtained from the following documents:

- www.microsoft.com/ofc/ntofc.doc
- "Securing Windows NT 4.0 Installation," *Microsoft TechNet*, August 11, 1997.
- www.trustedsystems.com/nsaguide.htm

You can also find information on protecting yourself from Trojan horse and other types of NT security attacks in the sites referenced in the "Monitoring Your Server" section, later in this chapter.

System Security

The tips in this section cover general system-wide security.

Set Up Virus Protection

You can protect your system from viruses in several ways. The first is to schedule periodic virus scans using third-party virus scanning software. The second is to prevent users from copying files to your server. The easiest way to do this is to disable the connection of client drives at logon (MetaFrame only). The instructions to do this are as follows:

1. Run the User Manager for Domains, located in the Administrative Tools folder in Start menu | Programs.
2. Double-click the username of the user whose client drive mapping you want to disable.
3. In the User Properties window, click Config.
4. Uncheck Connect Client Drives at Logon and click OK.

Any way a file can get onto your server is a way a virus can enter. This means you should also consider things such as locking the floppy drive on the server, preventing users from connecting their own drives, and preventing users from downloading files to the server. The third way to protect your system is to enforce proper file security using NTFS.

In general, boot sector viruses cannot infect Terminal Server. The majority of virus problems you'll run into will be with infected files (macro viruses and Trojan horses). On the other hand, if you accidentally leave a floppy disk in the drive while the server is rebooting, it could easily be infected with a boot virus. This is why you should disable booting from the floppy drive (if your system has the capability).

Create an Administrator Account and a Maintenance Account

Use an alphanumeric, 14-character password for the Administrator account and create a separate account for maintenance. The Administrator account is the only account that cannot be locked out by hacking attempts. It is therefore subject to brute-force password guessing attempts. In general, you should choose as secure a password as possible for your Administrator account, lock the password up in a secure location, and then use a separate administrative account for system maintenance. Changing the administrative password periodically is also recommended.

Change the Administrator Name

It's common knowledge that the default administrator account name is Administrator on Terminal Server. With this knowledge, hackers are already halfway on their way to getting into your system. Simply changing the administrator logon name to something less obvious can increase your server's and network's security. Do not use this as a substitute for proper password security, however. Your system's usernames are readily accessible for anyone on your network who has a little knowledge of NetBIOS. Also, be careful of using utilities that change the ACL list; some utilities rely on the administrator name being Administrator (C2CONFIG, for example).

Secure the Local Administrator Account

When you create a standalone server and then add it to a domain, you've allowed two administrative accounts access to your server—the local administrator and the domain administrator. The reason for this is that any NT-based workstation or server has a user database. When you add your server to a domain, you are in essence telling it that you want to use the domain's user database for primary validation and not the local one. The local database remains and will still validate users. All users have to do is select the local computer name from the domain list when they log on and they will be validating against the local user account database.

What this means to an administrator is that the local administrator account should be locked just as tightly as the domain administrator account to protect the server. Always make sure while installing a new standalone server that you choose a secure password for the local Administrator account. Lock this password up in a secure place and disable any other accounts besides Administrator. Do all of this before you add the server to the domain.

Disable Unnecessary Services

Services that run on Terminal Server are often run using the System account. With system-level access, a service can run anything. Terminal Server services, therefore, are another entry point for Trojan horse attacks. One particular service that's often the focus of such attacks is the Schedule service. The Schedule service handles running programs scheduled with the AT command. A potential intruder who gains administrative access can use the AT command to schedule the execution of a rogue program. If you're not using the AT command, this service should be disabled by doing the following:

1. Select Services from the Control Panel.
2. Highlight the Schedule service and click Startup from Service window.
3. Select Disabled for Startup Type and click OK.

Restrict Network Access to TS Using the Connection Configuration Tool

By default, when you install Terminal Server into a domain, all users in the domain can log onto the server. To restrict access to Terminal Server to just your Terminal Server users, do the following:

1. Create a WTS_USERS group in User Manager (see Chapter 7, "Creating Users and Groups in Terminal Server," for specific instructions) and make your Terminal Server users members of the group.

2. Open the Terminal Server Connection Configuration tool, which is located in the Administrative Tools folder in the Start menu.

3. In the Terminal Server Connection Configuration main window, highlight one of the network connections in the list and select Permissions from the Security menu.

4. In the Connection Permissions window that appears, remove the Everyone, Guests, and Users groups from the access list by highlighting each one and clicking Remove.

5. Add the WTS_USERS group and grant it user access by clicking Add.

6. In the Add Users and Groups window that appears, double-click the WTS_USER group to add it to the Add Names window. Make sure the type of access is user access; then click OK.

7. Do this for each type of network connection you've defined.

Restrict Network Access to TS Using User Rights

In general, user rights are adequate by default. To view the default user rights, go into User Manager and select User Rights from the Policies menu. This is where you define which groups and users are given which system rights. With Windows Terminal Server, you may want to change the following rights:

- *Access this computer from the network* Take out the Everyone group and add the WTS_USERS group. This ensures that only WTS_USERS can access the shares of this computer from across the network.

- *Log on locally* Take out the Everyone group and add the WTS_USERS group. This, in effect, prevents anyone from using Windows Terminal Server who is not in the WTS_USERS group. This is similar to restricting who can access the connections.

Real-World Tip: The WTS_USERS Group

Creating a group that contains only Windows Terminal Server users is useful for many security and administrative reasons. One of the best ways to get around the "everyone has full access" problem is simply to replace the Everyone group with the WTS_USERS group and grant appropriate access in the system's various ACLs. This chapter refers to this group frequently. The WTS_USERS name is arbitrary; you may want to choose a name that works better for your network.

Control Dial-In Access

Dial-in access is a big security risk. If you have dial-in access to your server, you may want to increase the level of password security. In addition, you may want to assign special dial-in user account names that are not as accessible as your regular account names. It's a good idea to create a WTS_DIALIN group for your dial-in users. Use file and Registry auditing to carefully monitor the WTS_DIALIN groups activity. Also. be sure to audit logon/logoff times. If you have a MetaFrame server with dial-in async connections, use the Terminal Server Connection Configuration tool permissions, located in the Administrative Tools folder, to restrict anyone who is not a member of this group from being able to dial in. If you're using RAS, make sure that only members of the WTS_DIALIN group have dial-in permission. We'll cover the difference between remote access with MetaFrame async connections versus RAS in detail in Chapter 14, "Terminal Server and Remote Access."

Many security features, such as RAS dial-in permission, are controlled only on a user level instead of a group level. To ensure that only members of the WTS_DIALIN group have the ability to dial in using RAS, follow these steps (be aware that these instructions will disable RAS access for everyone on your domain except the members of the WTS_DIALIN group):

1. Select all the users in the domain in User Manager by first highlighting the top user in the user list and then scrolling down and selecting the last user by pressing Shift while clicking. This will highlight all the users.

2. Press Enter to modify everyone's properties at once.

3. In the User Properties window, click Dialin.

4. Remove the check next to Grant Dialin Permission to User under the Dialin section; click OK to save your changes. Click OK again to return to the User Manager main window.

5. Now select the members of the WTS_DIALIN group by selecting Select Users from the Users menu, highlighting the WTS_DIALIN group, and clicking Select.

6. In the User Properties window, click Dialin.

7. Check the box next to Grant Dialin Permission to User so that WTS_DIALIN members are granted dial-in privilege.

This technique works well for any situation where you want to ensure that only members of a certain group have a particular setting in User Manager. Be aware that with Terminal Server, if you add another person to the WTS_DIALIN group at a later time that person will not automatically be given dial-in access. You will have to manually grant the permission.

Display a Legal Notice

The Terminal Server logon prompt can legally be construed as an invitation to enter the system without proper authorization! Therefore, in order to be able to prosecute potential system hackers, you should display a legal notice when users first log on. The legal notice normally warns the users that they will be held liable for unauthorized access to the system. You may also use the notice to tell your users about important system events, such as regularly scheduled downtimes.

In order to make it so that a legal notice window pops up before users log on, you need to change the following values of type `REG_SZ` under the following key:

- *Key Name* `HKEY_LOCAL_MACHINE\SOFTWARE\Microsoft\Windows NT\Current Version\Winlogon`
- *Value Name (type `REG_SZ`)* `LegalNoticeCaption`
- *Value Name (type `REG_SZ`)* `LegalNoticeText`

As usual, take the appropriate precautions when working with the Registry. The `LegalNoticeCaption` value will become the window title, and the `LegalNoticeText` value will be the text inside of the window, as shown in Figure 11.2.

Don't Display Last User's Logon Name

Because Windows Terminal Server clears the last logon name by default when logging on remotely, this value is not as useful as with NT Workstation. Even so, it will prevent the last logon name from appearing on the system console. This is most useful when you've changed the name of the Administrator. To enable this security feature, add the value `DontDisplayLastUserName` of type `REG_SZ` (select Add Value from the Edit menu) under the previous key and set it to the number 1. Note that both this security feature and the legal notice can also be controlled with policies. We'll go into detail on policies in Chapter 12.

User Account Policies

With user account policies, you can set a password expiration age and a minimum password length, enforce password uniqueness, and even temporarily lock out accounts that fail logon attempts too many times. User account policies are often confused with policies. These are two very different features of Terminal Server. User account policies are controlled from User Manager, whereas policies are controlled from the System Policy Editor. To set user account policies for your system, follow these steps:

1. Open User Manager, located in the Administrative Tools folder in Start menu | Programs.

2. Select Account from the Policies menu.

3. In the dialog box that appears, set the user account policies, as appropriate, for your system (see Figure 11.3).

It's highly recommended that you set the Minimum Password Length field to at least six characters and enable account lockout after five attempts.

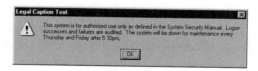

Figure 11.2 Legal caption.

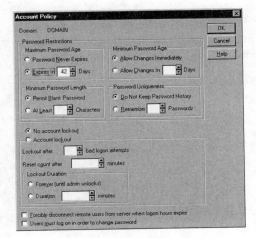

Figure 11.3   User account policies.

Use *PASSFILT.DLL*

If you're installing Terminal Server in a situation where inconvenience at the cost of security is not an issue, you may want to consider enabling *strong password filtering*. Ever since Service Pack 2 with NT, and now with Terminal Server, you can enable strong password filtering with the PASSFILT.DLL file. With strong password filtering enabled, your users will have the following restrictions applied when choosing a password:

- Passwords must be at least six characters in length (this can still be increased with the Password Length setting in User Account Policies).

- Passwords must contain characters that are part of at least three of the following four classes:
    - English uppercase (A, B, C, D...Z)
    - English lowercase (a, b, c, d...z)
    - Numbers: 0–9
    - Nonalphanumeric characters (quotation marks, periods, commas, and so on).

- Passwords cannot contain the user's name or any part of the user's full name.

To enable password filtering, you must make a change under the HKEY_LOCAL_MACHINE\SYSTEM key. Remember from the discussion in Chapter 10, "Installing Applications on Terminal Server," how important this key and its subkeys are. Make sure you create an emergency disk and back up the Registry before you do this. Full instructions on how to enable strong password filtering can be found in Microsoft Knowledge Base article Q151082, available in the online support section of Microsoft's Web site (search for PASSFILT.DLL).

Monitoring Your Server

No environment is secure without ongoing monitoring. The following sections provide some tips on how best to monitor the security of your server.

Use Third-Party Security Tools

As you've undoubtedly ascertained from this extensive list of Terminal Server security tips, security is very complex. Fully understanding the many security risks of Terminal Server and knowing what to do to prevent them can take an extraordinary amount of time. The reality is that most administrators do not have the luxury of time. Several third-party security analyst tools are available that may help you with securing you Terminal Server:

- *Internet Scanner for Windows NT by ISS (www.iss.net)* If you're going to install Internet services on your server and publish applications on the Web, this is a great tool to have.

- *Kane Security Analyst for NT by Intrusion Detection, Inc. (www.intrusion.com)* A comprehensive security analysis tool for your NT servers.

- *DumpACL and DumpEvt by Somarsoft (www.somarsoft.com)* DumpACL is similar to the ACLCHECK utility included with Windows Terminal Server (see the following Real-World Tip). It scans the ACL lists for your entire file system, Registry, printers, and shares and quickly highlights security holes. It's easier to use than ACLCHECK and its output is easier to read. DumpEvt helps you organize and sift through your event log. This is a very useful utility to have if you're heavy into auditing.

- *SuperCACLS by Trusted Systems (www.trustedsystems.com)* A good collection of command-line utilities for automating the administration of ACL lists.

Keep in mind that these applications were originally designed for NT Server, not Terminal Server. Because they haven't been fully tested with Terminal Server, there's no guarantee they'll work properly in a multiuser environment. As always, test new applications in a test environment first before implementing them into production. It's likely that security analyst programs specifically designed for Terminal Server will soon be available, so keep your eyes open for new products like these.

Set Up Logon/Logout Audit Logs

Setting up auditing for logon and logout attempts is strongly recommended. You'll be able to see both successful and failed logon attempts. Make sure you check this log on a regular basis for attempted intrusions. To set up auditing, follow these steps:

1. Open User Manager from the Administrative Tools folder in Start menu | Programs.

2. Select Audit from the Policies menu. The Audit Policy window will appear.

3. Select Audit These Events and check the Success and Failure boxes next to Logon and Logoff; this will audit both successful and failed user logon and logoff attempts. If you want to enable auditing for any other system events, check those boxes as well. Click OK when finished.

4. To check user logon and logoff attempts, open the Event Viewer, which is also located in the Administrative Tools folder, and select Security from the Log menu.

Log off and then log back on to the system. Go into the Event Viewer. You should see record of your logoff and logon in the security log. Try logging off and then logging back on using an incorrect password at least once. When you log on with the correct password and look at the security log, you should also see your failed logon attempt.

By default, the security log will be overwritten after seven days. You can change this and other security log settings from the Log Settings dialog box, located by selecting Log Settings from the Log menu in Event Viewer.

Use the ACLCHECK Utility

To check your file and Registry security, use the ACLCHECK utility included with Terminal Server. This DOS-based utility will scan your server's directories and Registry for instances where access has been granted for users and groups other than the system account or administrators.

The ACLCHECK is one of the simplest and best security monitoring tools. Running ACLCHECK periodically on your directories and Registry highlights security holes immediately. You should also run ACLCHECK after installing applications to ensure that the installation did not create any security problems.

One simple technique is to create a shortcut on your desktop that runs a batch file on the Windows Terminal Server, similar to the following:

```
ACLCHECK M:\ /FILES_ONLY > H:\CHKFIL.TXT
ACLCHECK /REGISTRY_ONLY > H:\CHKREG.TXT
```

Here, "H:" is map-rooted to your administrator home directory on the Windows Terminal Server. Using a common spreadsheet program such as Microsoft Excel, you can import these text files. Once they're in spreadsheet format, you can sort and arrange the data as you wish. This will make it quickly apparent exactly what your users have access to.

Use a Directory Tree-Sizing Utility

One of the more useful shareware utilities to purchase is a good directory tree-sizing program. Quite a few are available, but their basic function is the same. They simply graph out your hard drive, tallying the amount of space used under each directory. This way, you can get a better picture of where the majority of your data is and how fast it's growing.

Real-World Tip: Disk Frontier

One of the best tree-sizing or disk-sizing utilities is Disk Frontier by Choice Computing (www.choicecomp. com). It's simple, small, inexpensive, and elegant. It sums up the directory sizes under any drive or directory you specify using a simple bar graph. In addition to directory sizes, the bar graph also relays information on how much of the directory has been read from or written to within the last 30 days.

Monitor Security Sites on the Internet

We'll close this section with probably the most important security tip of all—use the Internet. Literally hundreds of security-related Web sites, mailing lists, and other sources of information are available on the Internet. The following are a few well-known ones to get you started. It's a good idea to join security mailing lists and periodically browse security-related sites for the most current NT security news. Much of the security-related information for NT available on these sites also applies to Terminal Server:

- *www.microsoft.com/security* The authoritative source on security issues with Microsoft products. Scan this page frequently for the latest news. The page also has excellent links to other security resources on the Net.

- *www.ntsecurity.net* A good compendium of NT security problems and solutions, along with many links to other sites.

- *www.iss.net* Makers of Internet Scanner 5.2 for NT, a highly rated scanning tool. They also have lists of NT security problems, with emphasis on problems that can occur when attaching an NT server to the Internet (publishing applications on the Web). In addition, they have a security-related mailing list that can provide a lot of good information.

12

Administering the Desktop and Server

IN ESSENCE, TERMINAL SERVER'S PRIMARY PURPOSE is to provide the Windows experience to remote desktop systems. For a Terminal Server administrator, desktops are of great importance. For example, you have probably had a user who accidentally deleted, changed, or installed something on a workstation that disabled the user's capability to work. If this happens on Terminal Server, not only is the user unable to work, but the error might bring down other users as well. In this chapter, you learn how to administer and organize users' desktops so that the users have access to what they need, but are prevented from doing things that could cause problems on Terminal Server. You learn how to use the powerful tools that are available to you, such as policies and profiles, which make desktop administration easy. You also learn about the server administration tools that you can use to monitor and manage your desktop sessions.

Desktop Organization

Before you delve into the details of setting up desktops properly, you need to go over the primary goals and purposes of desktop administration and organization. What you decide to put on users' desktops has a direct effect on the reliability, security, and administrative cost of your network. Your decision also affects the productivity of the user. The primary goal of desktop administration is to give the users access to only what they need by removing items on the desktop that are nonessential. The more nonessential items that users have access to, the more you will have to support and the more likely you will have problems with your server.

Take a look at the problems of the disorganized desktop and concentrate on some of the risks that it presents in a multiuser Terminal Server environment. Figure 12.1 shows an example of a disorganized desktop in Terminal Server. Although this desktop may look similar to what you are familiar with on a Windows workstation, the extraneous items on this desktop can lead to serious problems in a multiuser environment. In the later "Profiles" and "Policies" sections, you learn how to fix these problems using powerful administrative tools such as profiles and policies.

Here is what is wrong with this picture shown in Figure 12.1:

- *Access to the Control Panel*   When users have access to the Control Panel, it is possible for them to cause server-wide problems. Although many of the items in Control Panel are usable by administrators only, it is best to restrict user access to Control Panel.

- *Complicated desktop and background*   Remember that users' desktops must be compressed and sent across the wire to them. Wallpaper and patterns should not be used, and desktop shortcuts should be kept to a minimum.

- *Access to common folders*   Note that in the Start menu the user has access to the Administrative Tools common folder. You should evaluate which common folders users do and do not need access to. Remember that common folders— the folders on the lower half of Start menu—are seen by all users on the system.

- *Access to the Run command, Find utility, and MS-DOS prompt*   Access to the command line, Run command, and Find utilities are potential security risks, no matter how secure your system is. In addition, users may be able to install applications by using the Run command.

- *Access to Windows Explorer, My Computer, and Network Neighborhood*   Giving access to these icons opens up your entire Terminal Server and network to user browsing. Although these icons are often handy for administrators, be aware of the security risks of giving this level of access to users.

- *Internet Explorer and Briefcase*   Do users require access to Internet Explorer or the Briefcase? If not, then it is best to remove these shortcuts from their desktops. Browsing the Internet using Internet Explorer from a Terminal Server session can occupy a lot of processor power and network bandwidth. Give access to Internet Explorer to only those users who really need it.

- *Accessories*   On the same note, do users really need access to the accessories? If they have a word processing program already, they should not need Notepad or Wordpad. Do they really need MS Paint? How about Hyperterminal, or the Disk Tools? Having fewer extraneous shortcuts can reduce administrative problems.

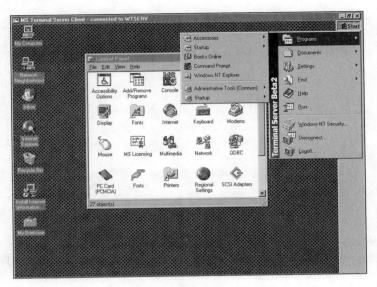

Figure 12.1 The disorganized desktop.

Now that you have gone over the problems of the disorganized desktop, it is time to learn how to organize it. In the following sections, you learn what profiles and policies are, how they work, and how to use them to organize users' desktops effectively.

Profiles

Profiles primarily contain user-specific Registry settings and the shortcuts that make up each user's desktop and Start menu. Each user has his own profile, which, by default, is stored under `C:\WTSRV\PROFILES\[USERNAME]`.

You can break a profile down into two basic components: the user Registry and the user's personal folders. The user Registry is contained in the `ntuser.dat` file located at the root of the user's profile directory (see Figure 12.2).

> **Author's Note: Common and Personal Folders**
>
> It is important to understand the difference between common and personal folders. For those who have worked with WinFrame, common folders and personal folders take the place of what used to be known in WinFrame as common groups and personal groups. In Figure 12.1, the folders that are below the gray line—Administrative Tools and Startup—are common folders and are seen by all Terminal users on the system. The folders above the gray line are part of a user's personal folders, seen only by the current user. Both common folders and personal folders are normally found in the profile directory (`C:\WTSRV\PROFILES`).

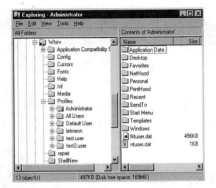

Figure 12.2 The default profile directory.

The `ntuser.dat` file contains the user's `HKEY_CURRENT_USER` hive. Going back to the discussion of the Registry in Chapter 10, "Installing Applications on Terminal Server," recall that the `HKEY_CURRENT_USER` hive contains settings such as the following:

- *User desktop preferences* Wallpaper, colors, patterns
- *Environment and control panel settings* Many of the user environment settings and user-specific Control Panel settings, found in the `HKEY_CURRENT_USER` key
- *Application events* Sound events for certain system actions
- *Software* User-specific software settings for installed software

The second part of a user's profile is the user's personal folders. The personal folders are all located under the root directory of each user's profile, as shown in Figure 12.2. The following is a list of the user's personal folders and their purposes:

- *Application Data* This folder is available to developers so that their programs have a place to store their user-specific application data. For example, Outlook Express uses this directory to store a user's address book by default.
- *Desktop (hidden directory)* This is a very important folder for reducing the amount of clutter on a desktop. All user-specific desktop icons, such as My Briefcase, are stored here.
- *Favorites* This folder is used by Internet Explorer to store a user's favorite URLs.

Real-World Tip: URL Shortcuts

You can distribute common Internet or intranet URLs to all users quickly and easily by copying the URL shortcuts to users' Favorites directories. When a user opens Internet Explorer and selects Favorites, the user sees the URLs that you added.

- *NetHood (hidden directory)*   This is an add-on folder to the Network Neighborhood. You can put shortcuts to servers and other devices on the network in here so that they are added to the user's Network Neighborhood.

- *Personal*   Personal items can be stored here. Some programs, such as Word, default to this directory to store user documents.

- *PrintHood (hidden directory)*   The shortcuts to printers that are defined here are added to the printers that are already defined in the Printer control window.

- *Recent (hidden directory)*   This is a list of the user's most recently used files.

- *SendTo*   This folder contains shortcuts to system devices or programs that can receive data.

- *StartMenu*   The StartMenu folder contains all of the user's personal shortcuts and folders in the Start menu. These shortcuts and folders are the ones shown above the gray line (refer to Figure 12.1).

- *Templates*   This folder contains template files. Some applications, such as Word, may make use of this folder.

- *Windows*   This folder, commonly referred to as the user's personal Windows folder, is unique to Terminal Server. It contains the user's personal application files, such as INI files. By default, Terminal Server creates the user's personal Windows folder under the user's profile directory, unless a home directory is specified for the user in User Manager.

Types of Profiles

There are three types of profiles: local, roaming, and mandatory. Because of the great importance of profiles with Terminal Server, it is important to understand these three types. The following sections describe each type of profile in detail and cover the situations in which each is best used.

Local Profiles

Local profiles are stored locally on the machine the user is working on. By default, when you create users on Terminal Server, their profiles are stored locally on the hard drive of the Terminal Server under `C:\WTSRV\PROFILES\[USERNAME]`. To change the location of a user's local profile, follow these steps:

1. Go into User Manager for Domains, located in the Administrative Tools folder in Start menu | Programs.

2. Double-click on the user whose profile location you want to change.

3. In the User Properties window, click Profile.

4. Fill in either the User Profile Path or Terminal Server Profile path field with the directory on the local hard drive on which you want the user's profile stored (for example, `C:\PROFILES\JSMITH` or `C:\PROFILES\%USERNAME%`). Click OK.

As long as you enter a location on the local hard drive, the profile is considered a local profile.

In a standard Windows NT environment, your local profile is stored on the workstations that you use to log on to the NT server. If you log on to the server from two different workstations, a local profile is created for you on the hard drive of each workstation. Because a profile is created on both workstations, you could have two entirely different desktops with different applications, depending on which machine you log on. This doubles the amount of administration necessary because you now have two individual desktops to deal with.

With Terminal Server, your local profiles "follow" you as long as you log on to the same Terminal Server. Because your local profile resides centrally on Terminal Server, you can get the advantages of a roaming profile (discussed in the following section), even if you are using local profiles!

Roaming Profiles

Whereas local profiles are stored locally on the machine the user is working on, roaming profiles are stored centrally on a share on the network. Because they are stored in a central location rather than locally, they follow, or roam, with you. No matter which workstation you log on to the network from, you receive the same profile. Your color preferences, background wallpaper, desktop icons, personal folders, and user Registry settings are the same no matter where you roam. To create a roaming profile, follow these steps:

1. Create a directory for profiles on a server on your network and share it as PROFILES.

2. Go into User Manager for Domains, located in the Administrative Tools folder in Start menu | Programs, and double-click on the user whose profile location you want to change.

3. In the User Properties window, click Profile.

4. Fill in either the User Profile Path or Terminal Server Profile path to a user directory under the PROFILE share that you created by entering \\WTSRV\PROFILES\[USERNAME]. (You can use the %USERNAME% variable for [USERNAME] if you want.) Click OK.

Figure 12.3 shows how to set up a roaming profile for user John.Smith. Note that it was set up as a Terminal Server Profile Path. This means that John.Smith will retrieve his profile from this path when he logs on to the domain from any Terminal Server. By setting different paths for the Terminal Server profile path and the User Profile path, you can keep users' Terminal Server profiles separate from the profiles they receive when logging on to their workstations.

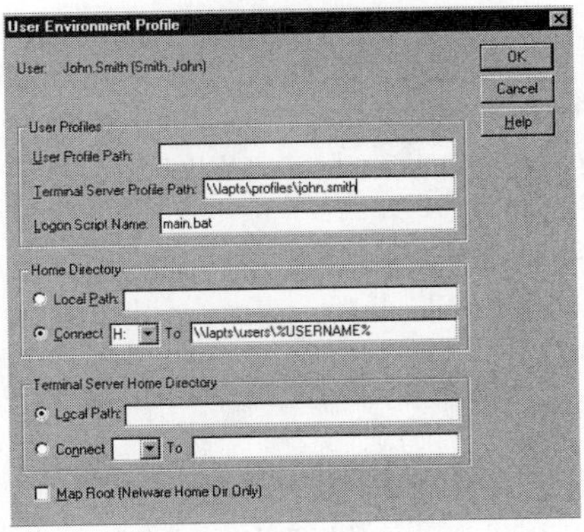

Figure 12.3 Profiles in User Manager.

Be aware how profiles use network bandwidth and space on the local hard drive. A typical profile is between 500KB and 1MB, but can vary considerably depending on the size of your personal folders and the number of Registry entries that you have. If you have roaming profiles set up, when you log on to a server or a workstation that you have not logged on to previously, your profile is downloaded across the network and cached locally on that system's hard drive. The next time you log on to the system, your locally cached profile will be synchronized with your roaming profile. Only the updates will have to travel across the network.

If you have a hundred or more simultaneous users, the locally cached profiles can add up to a lot of space under the system directories. Make sure you always leave enough free space on your system partition for locally cached profiles.

Roaming profiles are very useful for load balancing and other situations in which users may log on to several different Terminal Servers. If you use roaming profiles, users can log on to any Terminal Server they want and still have the same desktop and user Registry settings. You must make sure that you install all the users' applications in the same manner if you want all their applications to work across the different Terminal Servers.

Real-World Tip: Mirror Image

You might find it useful to "mirror image" your load-balanced servers and keep all user profiles, home directories, and other changeable data on a separate central server. You can *mirror image* a server by using an imaging product, such as Ghost, to make an image of the original server. The image program creates mirror servers by restoring the original image to the new server. Because all the applications have been installed the same way, you should not have application problems when logging on to any of your duplicate load-balanced servers. You should be aware of a few things about this technique. First, it does not work if your Terminal Servers are PDCs; mirror imaging is recommended only if your server is a member server on a domain. Second, ensure that SIDs are unique by using a SID conversion utility; the Ghost product comes with a utility that will do this. Third, license information must be reentered and the server name has to be changed on the new server.

Mandatory Profiles

The third type of profile is a *mandatory profile*, which is similar to a mandatory profile under WinFrame. Mandatory profiles allow an administrator to prevent users from making permanent changes to their desktop settings and Registries. To enable mandatory profiles do the following:

1. Rename the `ntuser.dat` file to `ntuser.man` under the user's profile directory.

2. Make the user's entire profile directory read-only. This locks down the Start menu, desktop, and other user settings contained in the personal folders.

Default User and All User Profiles

There are two special-purpose profile directories on a Terminal Server located under `C:\WTSRV\PROFILES`: Default User and All Users:

■ *Default User*   When you log on for the first time, Terminal Server creates your initial profile by copying the Default User profile directory to the your profile directory. Therefore, whatever desktop icons, Start Menu items, and user Registry settings are set for the Default User are set up for you as well.

■ *All Users*   The All Users directory is very important with Terminal Server because it contains the desktop icons and Start Menu items that will be seen by all users who log on to Terminal Server. This is where the common folders are kept.

Using Profiles Effectively

Up to this point you have been concentrating on what profiles are; now it's time to learn how to use them. Profiles are used most effectively for controlling the icons that are on users' desktops and in their Start menus. The following sections present some useful tips on how to use profiles effectively with Terminal Server.

Copying Profiles

Although you can copy profile directories manually from one location to another, Terminal Server enables you to copy a profile and apply security in a single step with the User Profile Copy tool.

> **Author's Note: Lock Down the Registry**
>
> Renaming the `ntuser.dat` file to `ntuser.man` under the user's profile directory locks down the Registry and prevents the user from making permanent changes to its settings. To see the effect of this, try logging on as the user and changing the color of the desktop. Log off and then log back on. Notice that the desktop has returned to its original color.

To use the User Profile Copy tool, follow these steps:

1. Go to the Control Panel (Start menu | Settings | Control Panel) and select System.

2. Click on the User Profiles tab in the System window.

3. In the User Profiles tab, select the profile you want to copy and click Copy To.

4. Browse to the destination directory.

5. Change the Permitted to Use settings to whatever group or user needs access to the profile.

Distributing Identical Desktops

One of the most useful capabilities of profiles is creating "cookie-cutter" desktops for groups of users. In this way you can create a single desktop and then distribute it to all of the users. With Terminal Server, there are several ways to do this, depending on what you need. The following sections describe the most common techniques.

Create a Template Profile

The first technique involves creating a template profile and copying it to new users. If you have a group of users who all need to run the same applications, you can create a template user and then copy the template user's profile to new users' profile directories. To use this method, follow these steps:

1. Create a template user called TS_USER_TEMPLATE in User Manager and point the profile setting to the directory in which you want the template user's profile to be created.

2. Log on as the template user. Now arrange the desktop and user settings the way you want new users to have them and log back out.

3. Log on as an administrator and copy the template user's profile to new users' profile directories.

Modify the Default User Profile

Another way to make cookie cutter desktops is to use the Default User profile. Every new user receives a copy of the Default User profiles when they are first created. By modifying the Default User profile and then creating a group of users, you can effectively distribute the same desktop settings to all of these users. To use this technique, follow these steps:

> **Author's Note: The User Profile Copy Tool**
>
> Although you can copy directories under the profile from one user to another by using a program such as Explorer, if you want to copy the user's Registry settings (ntuser.dat) to another user, you must use the User Profile Copy tool.

1. Log on as a test or template user.

2. Change the desktop the way you want. Copy the user's profile to the Default User directory.

3. Finally, create the new users.

As each new user is created and logs on, he receives the identical desktop. This is a good technique for distributing user-specific Registry settings to your new users. It is always a good idea to back up the Default User profile before changing it, in case you want to return to default settings in the future.

Creating a Mandatory Shared Profile

One disadvantage of the techniques described so far is that although all users receive the same desktop initially, they can still change their desktops. Also, because each user has a copy of the profile, if you want to add an icon to a particular set of users, you must manually add it to all of the users' profile directories.

For the best combination of security and central control, you can create a mandatory shared profile for either all of users or just a subset:

1. Log on as a template user and arrange the desktop as you want it to appear. This is also a good time to apply any policies to the desktop, such as disabling Registry editing tools, Control Panel, and the capability to change the desktop. Policies do not work after the read-only mandatory profile has been set up.

2. After the desktop is the way you want it, log out and then back on as an administrator.

3. In User Manager, select each user whose profile needs to be set the way same by clicking on his username while holding down the Control key. After all of the users are selected, press Enter. (More multiple user selection techniques are shown in Chapter 7, "Creating Users and Groups in Terminal Server.")

4. Click the Profile button in the User Properties window.

5. Change the Terminal Server profile path to the path of the template user's profile directory.

6. Make the template profile directory and all sub-directories read-only and change the `ntuser.dat` to `ntuser.man`.

Now when the users in the group log on, they all receive the same desktop. To add a new icon to their desktops or Start menus, simply add it to the template user's profile. You can simplify administration by creating a template user and user group for each group of users that requires the same desktop settings.

Centralizing Administration with Profiles

Another of the many advantages of profiles is central administration. Following are some simple techniques for centrally controlling users' desktop settings.

- *Clean up the clutter centrally* By putting all your profiles in one directory, you can easily go through the desktops and Start menus of all the users and clean out unnecessary icons.

- *Distribute application icons to all users* By copying icons to the All Users' Start menu or Desktop folder you can distribute applications to all users. The next time she logs on, every user sees the icon you copied there on her Start menu or Desktop. The shortcuts and folders in the All Users' Start menu are displayed below the divider line, under Programs.

- *Make modifications centrally to a user's Registry* By loading the `ntuser.dat` from each user's profile directory into `HKEY_USERS`, you can modify the user Registry settings of all users without leaving your chair. The following section describes this technique.

Centrally Administering the Users' Registries

Often it is useful to view or make changes to a particular user's Registry or to the default user Registry. With the Registry Editor, you can load a particular user's `ntuser.dat` file into the `HKEY_USERS` key and edit it:

1. Run REGEDT32 and open the `HKEY_USER`'s key. Highlight the root key `HKEY_USERS`.

2. Select Load Hive from the Registry menu.

3. Select the `ntuser.dat` file from the user's profile directory—normally `C:\WTSRV\PROFILES\[USERNAME]`. If the user is using roaming profiles, you can find the path to her profile in User Manager by selecting [USERNAME]|Config. Click OK.

4. Enter the user's name as the key name. The hive loads directly under `HKEY_USER` with the key name of the username. You can now edit or view the key. Figure 12.4 shows the `HKEY_USER`'s hive with the Test User's Registry loaded.

5. When you are done editing the key, save it by unloading it. To unload it, highlight the root of the user's key (the user's name) and select Unload Hive from the Registry menu.

Real-World Tip: Applications and Icons

When administering Terminal Server, be careful of applications that place their icons in the All Users' folder. Because many applications do this by default, after you install a new application, you should delete or move any icons that you do not want to distribute to all of the users.

Figure 12.4 Loading the Test.user key into the Registry for editing.

If you try to load a user hive that is currently active (the user is logged on) you receive a warning that you cannot load it. To edit the Registry of an active user, you must know the user's SID. Every active user's Registry key is loaded in HKEY_USER under a SID. To obtain a user's SID, use the GETSID utility included with the NT Resource Kit. Next, look through the hives loaded in HKEY_USER for the user's SID. After the SID is found, you can view and edit it as necessary. Remember that some changes to the Registry do not take effect until the user logs out and back on again.

Policies

Policies are some of the most powerful tools at your disposal for administering users' desktops. Policies are used to control a user's environment and system environment through a specific set of Registry settings. You can control many things, including the following:

- The ability for the user to view the Control Panel, Network Neighborhood, My Computer, Find, and Run buttons
- User's colors and wallpaper
- Drive letters that are available to a user
- The ability to use the Registry Editor
- Whether common program folders are shown

With policies you can lock down a desktop very tightly and provide access only to the applications and settings that users absolutely need to perform their daily work.

How Policies Work

Policies are implemented by using the System Policy Editor included with Terminal Server. With the System Policy Editor, you create a policy file that contains all of the restrictions you want to apply for users. Restrictions can be applied to groups and users. When a user logs on, the system reads the settings in the policy file and applies the restrictions to his Registry.

The policy file that you create with the System Policy Editor should be called
`ntconfig.pol`. This file should reside in the `Netlogon` (`C:\WINNT\SYSTEM32\REPL\`
`IMPORT\SCRIPTS`) directory of your domain controllers. When you log on, Terminal
Server looks in the `Netlogon` directory of the domain controller it is validating against
for the `ntconfig.pol` file. If the file is there, TS applies the settings in that file to its
Registry.

Because the `ntconfig.pol` file is read only during user logon, changes to the file are
not dynamic. In other words, users must log off and log back on again for the new
changes to the `ntconfig.pol` file to take effect.

System Policy Editor and Policy Template Files

The first step in setting up policies on your Terminal Server is to create them using
the System Policy Editor. The System Policy Editor is located in the Administrative
Tools folder in Start menu, Programs. System policies are based on policy template
files; these files end with the .ADM extension. The policy template files are customiz-
able text files that contain instructions for changing various system and user Registry
settings. You can load as many policy template files as you want to have the settings
you need to create your `ntconfig.pol` policy file. Windows NT comes with three
policy template files by default:

- *common.adm*   Contains both machine Registry and user Registry settings that
  can be used with Windows 95 or Windows NT
- *winnt.adm*   Contains Windows NT–specific user and machine settings, such as
  the ability to make customized Windows NT Program folders and logon
  banners
- *windows.adm*   Contains Windows 95–specific user and machine settings

When you first run System Policy Editor, it loads the `winnt.adm` and
`common.adm` policy files by default. These files are located under the `C:\WTSRV\INF`
directory. You can view the files that are loaded by selecting Policy Template from the
Options menu. In the Policy Template Options window (see Figure 12.5) you see all
the currently loaded template files. At this point, you can add or remove template files
as necessary to have the settings you need for users.

Creating Your Own Policies

After you have loaded the policy templates you want, it is time to create the policy
file. Go into the System Policy Editor and select New Policy from the File menu.

Figure 12.5 Loading template files into the Policy Editor.

In the System Policy Editor window, you will see two icons: Default User and Default Computer. The Default User settings are Registry settings that change keys in the user's `HKEY_CURRENT_USER` hive (`ntuser.dat`). The Default Computer settings change keys in the system Registry or `HKEY_LOCAL_MACHINE` of the user. Because all users on Terminal Server share the same machine, any setting changed under Default Computer affects all users on Terminal Server, including the administrator! This is a very important distinction to remember. For the most part, you will want to make changes only to the Default User settings. Always keep in mind the global nature of changes to the Default Computer key.

Creating the policy is fairly simple to do. For this example, double-click on the Default Users icon. In the Default User Properties screen, you see a hierarchical list of all the different policy categories from the loaded policy template files. This is an all-in-one view of all user policies that are available. As you load more policy template files you see additional categories and settings in this list, depending on which template file you add.

Each policy can have one of three settings: checked, unchecked, or grayed out (see Figure 12.6).

Figure 12.6 Checked, unchecked, and grayed out policy settings.

Knowing the difference between these three settings is very important for implementing policies properly. While reading the differences between the three, it is important to remember that policies actually represent specific changes that occur to a key in the Registry during user logon.

- *Checked*   Enforces the policy and applies the necessary change to the Registry as the user logs on
- *Unchecked*   Removes the effects of the policy by resetting the policy Registry key to its default setting
- *Grayed out*   Makes no changes to the policy's Registry key

If the policy presented in Figure 12.6 were implemented, it would work as follows. When the user logs on, the system reads the policy from the `ntconfig.pol` file located in the `NETLOGON` directory of the authenticating controller (`C:\WINDOWS\SYSTEM32\REPL\IMPORT\SCRIPTS`). Because the options Restrict Display of the Control Panel and Remove Taskbar from Settings on Start Menu are checked, the system applies these Registry settings to the appropriate policy keys in the user's Registry. This prevents the user from accessing the Control Panel or Taskbar settings. Next, the system returns the policy key for the Remove Run command from Start Menu policy to its original setting, thus enabling the user to see the Run command. Because the rest of the settings are grayed out, the system skips over them.

It is important to remember that after you have set a policy for a user and that user logs on, that policy is saved in his Registry. The only way to reverse a policy is to clear the policy by unchecking it, and have the user log out and then log back on.

ZAK Policy Template Files

The Zero Administration Kit (ZAK) is a freely available set of administration tools that you can download from Microsoft at the following Web site: `http://www.microsoft.com/windows/zak`.

If you are already familiar with using the ZAK on Window NT, you may be wondering how you can use the Zero Administration Kit with Terminal Server. To answer that question, you should understand what is included with the kit and what it was intended for. The ZAK is a specially designed set of policy files and techniques to simplify the administration of multiple Windows machines. One of the primary needs addressed by the ZAK is application distribution. Using custom scripts and system difference files, the ZAK allows you to distribute applications automatically to machines as they log on to the system. With Terminal Server, the ability to distribute applications is built in. Because the ZAK is designed for use on multiple machines and not for a Terminal Server, you must be careful about implementing some of the techniques included with the kit. One of the most useful pieces of the ZAK that can be used with Terminal Server is the policy template file. The ZAK includes the following policy template files, which you can add to your System Policy Editor:

- *access97.adm*   Access 97–specific user and machine settings such as default database directory and screen settings.

- *ieak.adm*   Internet Explorer–specific user and machine settings such as Proxy server settings and start pages. These are very useful for controlling users' access to their browsers.

- *off97nt4.adm*   Office 97–specific user and machine settings such as default directories and shared tools settings.

- *outlk97.adm*   Outlook 97 user and machine settings that control things such as screen settings and folder locations.

- *query97.adm*   Query 97 user settings.

- *zakwinnt.adm*   Windows NT–specific user settings such as user folder locations and hiding drive letters. The drive letter hiding technique can be very useful in a Terminal Server environment to hide the server's system drives.

With the combination of the default policy files and the ZAK policy files, you can do everything—in terms of desktop administration—that you can do with the ZAK by simply using the System Policy Editor with Terminal Server.

In addition to the policy files, the ZAK comes with several useful utilities that you can incorporate into your Terminal Server logon scripts, such as CON2PRT.EXE, which allows you to connect to Windows Printers through a logon script.

Useful Default Computer Policies

The majority of the most useful policies for Terminal Server are listed under Default User. Even so, there are several policies under Default Computer that you might consider implementing. Remember that with Terminal Server, any policy you implement under Default Computer will affect everyone who logs on to the server.

To set the default computer policies for users, you must first get to the Default Computer window:

1. Double-click on the Default Computer from the main System Policy Editor window.

2. From the Default Computer Properties window, go to the policy setting in the order shown for the bulleted item.

Author's Note: Terminal Server ZAK

Microsoft has also recently come out with a ZAK intended specifically for Terminal Server. This ZAK is freely available from Microsoft's Terminal Server Web site at

http://www.microsoft.com/ntserver/basics/terminalserver.

For example, to get to the Remote Update policy, from the Default User Properties window click Network, then System Policies. You will see the Remote Update Policy check box, underneath System Policies Update. If you put a check mark in the Remote Update Policy check box, then that policy will be in effect for users the next time they log on. If you remove the check mark, then that policy will be "reset" or cleared the next time users log on.

To put a policy into effect you always need to put a check mark in the policy's check box. This policy will be in effect until you remove the check mark from the check box. The following list describes many of the most useful default computer policies:

- *Network, System Policies, Remote Update*   The Remote Update policy controls from what directory the policy file is retrieved. One problem with policies is that they affect everyone in the domain. If your Terminal Server is on the same domain as standard NT or Windows 95 workstations, any policies that you implement also affect those workstations. The reason is that you are required to store the `ntconfig.pol` file in the `NETLOGON` directory of your authenticating servers. If you want a policy that applies only to your Terminal Server, this Remote Update policy key is the answer. By checking this policy and setting Manual Update, you can specify the UNC path to your Terminal Server–specific policy file (`\\[server]\[share]\ [filename]`). To implement the policy, you must save it to `ntconfig.pol` and place it into the `NETLOGON` directory. The next time someone logs on to the Terminal Server, the change is made to the Registry. From then on, the policy file is retrieved by the Terminal Server from the directory you specified. To reset the setting you must set the Update mode back to automatic.

- *Windows NT System, Logon, Logon Banner*   With this policy, you can create a logon banner that users see when they log on to the system. This is a good technique for some types of system notices.

- *Windows NT System, Logon, Run logon scripts synchronously*   By default, logon scripts run as a thread and do not have to finish before your desktop comes up. By setting logon scripts to run synchronously, however, they must finish before any other programs are run. If you have settings in the logon script that your applications require to run, such as drive mappings, it is a good idea to have the logon script finish before any applications can be run.

One problem with using Default Computer policies on a domain is that they affect the computer settings for all computers on the domain. To restrict the changes to just the Terminal Server, in the System Policy Editor select Add Computer from the Edit menu. Select the Terminal Server from the browse list. A computer icon representing the Terminal Server (see Figure 12.7) appears in the System Policy Editor window. You can double-click on this icon and set policies that affect only users of the Terminal Server.

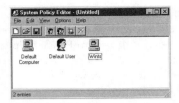

Figure 12.7 Specifying Terminal Server–specific policies.

Types of User Policies

Now that you have learned about some useful computer policies, it is time to discuss user policies. There are three types of user policies that can be implemented: default user, group, and single user.

- Default user policies affect all users on the Window Terminal Server.
- Group policies affect all users in a particular Windows NT global group.
- Single user policies are settings for a specific user on the system.

Group and single user policies are implemented in a similar way to computer-specific policies. To implement a group policy, select Add Group from the Edit menu in the System Policy Editor main window, and select the global group for which you want to set policies. To implement a single user policy, select Add User from the Edit menu in the System Policy Editor main window, and select the user for whom you want to create specific policies. Because group policies are implemented globally, they apply for global groups only.

Because the policies implemented under Default User take effect for every user on the domain, they are a rather blunt administrative tool. The best way to control policies, therefore, is through groups. One of the better ways to do this is through job function groups. Suppose you have ten remote users who need access to corporate email and an accounting application. You could create an ACCT_USERS group that has a group policy assigned to it. In the group policy you could set up several controls on the accounting users' desktops, including a shared read-only directory for program menu items. In this way, all the accounting users would have the same desktop and icons, and the same level of control over their desktops. Distributing new applications to this group would simply be a matter of installing the new application in install mode and putting the icon for the application in their shared program menu item directory.

Implementing User Policies

The following list describes some of the many useful user policies. The listed policies are set in the same manner as described previously for default computer policies. To understand the user policies and how to set them, open the System Policy Editor on your server and follow along. The System Policy Editor is located in the Administrative Tools folder in Start menu | Programs. In the System Policy Editor, click the Default

User icon. In the Default User Properties window that appears, open up the policy settings as shown for each policy covered in the following list:

- *Control Panel, Display, Restrict Display* Checking this policy prevents the user from seeing the Control Panel.

- *Desktop, Wallpaper* This policy restricts the user to a particular wallpaper for the desktop. Because of the extra network bandwidth that could be taken up by transmitting complex desktops to the user, you may want to consider using this policy. This policy is especially useful for remote sites, where network bandwidth is at a premium. A single-color, blank desktop is the easiest to compress and send across the wire.

- *Desktop, Color* This policy restricts the user to a particular color scheme. This is a good policy to implement for public access Windows Terminals, where user color preference is not important.

- *Shell, Restrictions* Under shell restrictions there are several very useful policies for controlling users' desktops. One of the most useful is Hide All Items on the Desktop. By hiding all the items on the desktop, you greatly reduce desktop clutter and force the user to use only the items under the Start menu. This restriction significantly improves network performance because very few graphically complex icons must be transmitted across the wire. Two other recommended restrictive policies are removing the Run command and removing the folders under Settings. With the Run command, users have complete access to any executable or document on any drive that they have read has access to. This can be a potential security problem. With the Run command, users may also attempt to install their own applications.

- *System, Restrictions* Under System, Restrictions, there are two policies: Disable Registry Editing Tools and Run Only Allowed Windows Applications. Disable Registry Editing Tools prevents the user from running the Registry Editor (REGEDT32.EXE), even from the command line. This restriction is highly recommended. The Run Only Allowed Windows Applications tool allows you to enter a list of applications that a user can run. In general, it is easier to control the applications a user can run by disabling the Run command and removing all icons except for the ones a user needs.

- *Windows NT Shell, Custom User Interface, Custom Shell* With Custom Shell, you can make any application the user's default shell. If a user runs only a single application off Terminal Server, this setting may work well for you. The user is taken directly into the application when she logs on, and is logged off when she exits. This prevents the user from doing anything other than running the application she needs. The same restriction can be enabled by setting the Initial Program setting in the user's Config in User Manager to this application. The advantage of using Custom Shell is that your administration is centralized with policies, instead of having to keep track of both User Manager and policy settings for a particular group.

- *Windows NT Shell, Custom Folders* This is one of the most powerful and useful set of policies. With these policies, you can define custom folders that contain the shortcuts you want to appear in the user's Start menu | Programs, on the user's desktop, in the Startup Folder or in the Network Neighborhood. To use this policy to set up the user's program items, make a folder on your Terminal Server that contains the program items you want the group to have. Make the folder read-only. Enter the path to the folder in the policy for the group. When members of the group log on they receive the program folder you just created. If you need to distribute applications to the members of the group in the future, simply add the shortcuts to the group's program folder.

- *Windows NT Shell, Restrictions* There are several useful policies under here for restricting user actions in the NT shell. One of the most useful is the Remove Common Program Group from the Start Menu option. A common security problem with Citrix is applications that leave their icons in the common program group or folder after they are installed. This makes the application available to all users on the server, which often is not desirable. To control the proliferation of common folder icons, it is recommended to disable the ability for users to see common program group icons. Use group policies and custom shared folders to distribute application icons instead.

- *Windows NT System* The Run Logon Scripts Synchronously option is one of the most useful policies under this folder. By setting this option on a user or group level, you have more control than if you set it system wide using the equivalent Default Computer policy.

Top Ten Tips for Setting Up Desktops

Now that you have an understanding of what policies and profiles are and how to implement them, take a look at this summary of the top ten recommended tips on using them to lock down the users' desktops.

1. *Simplify, simplify, simplify* Simplicity is the most important aspect of any well-designed desktop. Put on the desktop only the icons or Start menu items that the user absolutely needs to perform his job. The best approach is to first imagine a blank slate: a Windows NT 4.0 desktop with no icons, a Start button, and no shortcuts in the Start menu. Now think about the icons you need to add for the user to perform his job. This is the desktop design you want.

2. *Deny access to the Run and Find commands, and remove icons from each user's profiles for Explorer and the command prompt* A user who has access to the Run command, Find command, command prompt, and/or Explorer can cause a lot of damage very easily. By using user policies, deny access to these commands if they are not necessary for users to do their work.

3. *Restrict drive and network access* If users absolutely need access to Explorer or the command prompt to perform their jobs, you can still limit the drives they

have access to. To control what is available to users on the network, try setting a policy to Hide the entire network and workgroup contents (under the Shell, Restrictions user policy set). Now create a read-only custom Network Neighborhood folder with shortcuts to the servers that users need access to. Now when they go into Network Neighborhood they see only the servers you defined. If you want to restrict the drive letters users can see, there is actually a Registry setting that will allow you to do this. An example of how to use this setting is included with the Zero Administration Kit in the ZAKWINNT.ADM policy template. With this setting, you can define a 26-bit binary number that controls which drive letters the user can and cannot see.

4. *Create Custom Program folders for each group of users*   Group users by application needs. Create custom read-only folders that contain shortcuts to the applications they need and set a group policy that points the group to this program folder.

5. *Hide desktop icons and have the user use the Start menu to launch applications*   With Terminal Server, users can launch applications either from the desktop or from their Start menu by default. Because you have shortcuts in two places, this adds to the desktop clutter and increases the administrative burden. There are also several desktop icons that are difficult, if not impossible, to remove that you may not want users to have access to. Examples of this are the Internet Explorer, My Computer, Network Neighborhood, and In Box icons. Enable the Hide All Items desktop user policy (under the Shell, Restrictions user policy set). You can completely clean up the desktop, prevent users from going places where they do not belong with My Computer or Network Neighborhood, and make the client run faster because there is less desktop clutter to send across the wire.

6. *Restrict display of the Control Panel*   There's rarely a need for users to access items in the Control Panel. To restrict access, select the Restrict display user policy under Control Panel, Display in the User Policy window.

7. *Disable use of Registry editing*   Remember that even on a secure system, the user necessarily has to have read/write access to several keys in the Registry. Giving the user direct access to tools that can edit or delete these keys, especially the system-wide keys, is a potential security risk. To reduce this risk, check the Disable Registry Editing Tools user policy under System, Restrictions in the User Policy window.

8. *Be careful of common folders*   Unless you specifically restrict their display by checking the Remove Common Groups from Start Menu user policy under Windows NT Shell, Restrictions, the common folder icons can be seen by all users. These icons are actually stored in the All Users' folder under C:\WTSRV\PROFILES. Common folders can be useful in situations in which all users on the system need access to certain applications. By putting the shortcuts to the applications in the All Users folder, you basically have distributed the application to all the users. If you decide to use common folders, you must first

clean out the shortcuts that users do not need access to. One example is the Administrative Tools folder, which can be copied to the administrator's personal folder instead. Other examples are shortcuts to uninstall applications and utilities to which the users do not need access.

9. *Use the custom shell policy to launch an application on startup for single-application users* Making an application the shell is a secure way to run a single applications for users. You will find this user policy under Windows NT Shell, Custom User Interface, Custom Shell in the User Policy window.

10. *Lock user's wallpaper and screen savers* Complicated backgrounds can take up large amounts of network bandwidth to transmit; locking the wallpaper is recommended for Terminal Server users. You will find the user policy that controls desktop wallpaper under Desktop, Wallpaper in the User Policy window. Also, restrict users to blank-screen screen savers by deleting all other screen savers (.SCR files) in the C:\WTSRV directory.

Terminal Server and MetaFrame Administration Tools

So far, you have learned about all the different ways to set up and manage users' desktops. Now it is time to cover how to manage users after they have opened a session with Terminal Server, logged on, and received the desktops you set up. The primary administrative tool you use to administer users' sessions is either the Terminal Server Administration tool, or, if you have MetaFrame, the MetaFrame Administration tool. The Terminal Server Administration tool is located in the Administrative Tools folder in Start menu, Programs. The MetaFrame Server Administration tool is installed with MetaFrame; it is located in the MetaFrame Tools folder in Start menu | Programs. If you run both tools and compare them you immediately notice how similar they are in both function and appearance. The main difference between the two is that the MetaFrame tool provides the additional ability to administer Published Applications. With both tools, you can do the following:

- View session information on a user, server, domain, and entire network level
- Reset, disconnect, or send messages to sessions
- Get network status information on a session

The following sections go over each of these capabilities, what they are, and how to make the best use of them.

Viewing Session Information

With the Terminal Server and MetaFrame Administration tools, you can view copious amounts of information on the status of your Terminal Server network.

You can view information on several levels. To view information at any level, simply highlight the device or group of devices on the left and choose the information tab you want to see on the right.

The following instructions apply for both the Terminal Server Administration tool and the MetaFrame Administration tool. You can view the same basic information on your servers with both tools.

All Listed Servers and Domain Information

If you highlight either All Listed Servers or one of the domains listed in the left pane of the Terminal Server Administration window, the Servers, Users, Processes, Sessions and Licenses tabs appear in the right pane. By clicking these tabs, you can view the following information for All Listed Servers or the domain you selected:

- *Servers* Under the server tab is a list of the Terminal Servers. You will find the IP address, IPX address, and number of users connected to the server.

- *Users* By clicking the Users tab, you will see a list of all users, either for All Listed Servers or for the domain. The most useful functions in this list are the options that appear when you right-click on a user's name, such as Reset, Disconnect, and Send Message. See the next section for more information.

- *Sessions* This tab lists both the current active and inactive sessions on your Terminal Servers.

- *Processes* This tab lists all running processes on your servers. By right-clicking any of the processes, you can terminate the process.

- *Licenses* The Licenses tab shows the total licenses and how many are in use on your servers.

Server Information

If you highlight a single server in the left pane of the Terminal Server Administration tool window, the Users, Sessions, Processes, and Information tabs appear in the right pane. The information under the Users, Sessions, and Processes tabs is the same as described under "All Listed Servers and Domain Information," except that the information applies only to the server you selected.

Under the Information tab, which can be seen only when viewing server information, you see the current Service Pack and a list of all current hotfixes on the system.

Session Information

When you select an active session in the left pane of the Terminal Server Administration tool window, the Processes and Information tabs appear in the right pane. If the session is an ICA session, you see two additional tabs: Modules and Cache. The following list describes the information you can find under each tab:

- *Processes*   Lists the current processes in the session you selected. You can terminate any process by right-clicking on it and selecting Terminate.
- *Information*   Shows the session client's name, address, video information, encryption level, and more.
- *Modules*   Shows the versions of the modules being used by the client.
- *Cache*   Shows Bitmap Cache and Client Cache information for the ICA client.

Resetting, Disconnecting, and Sending Messages

When you right-click any session icon in the left pane of the Terminal Server Administrator window, you receive a list of actions that you can perform. For most active sessions you can choose to reset, disconnect, or send a message to the session. Remember that if you reset the session the user loses what she was working on. If you instead disconnect the session, the user is able to log on again at a later time and return to the desktop as she left it. You can also send messages to the session.

Network Status Information

Sometimes, especially when benchmarking or testing the network, it is useful to retrieve the network status information for a particular session. To retrieve this information, simply right-click on an active session listed in the left pane of the Terminal Server Administration tool and select Status. You see the Status of LogonID window, as shown in Figure 12.8. With this information and a stopwatch, you can make a rough guess of how much network bandwidth this session is actually taking up.

Shadowing Session (MetaFrame Only)

The ability to shadow accounts is one of the most useful administration features of MetaFrame. When you shadow another account, you remote control it. You are able to see what is on the user's desktop and interact with it by using the mouse and keyboard. This is a great feature for customer support. If a user calls in with a problem, you can shadow his session and walk him through a solution without leaving your desk.

> **Real-World Tip: Send Messages to Multiple Users**
>
> You can reset, disconnect, or send messages to users or sessions by selecting the server on the left pane and clicking the Users tab on the right. When you right-click one of the users listed on the left, you are given the choice to reset, disconnect, or send a message to the user.
>
> One of the more useful things you can do is to send messages to multiple users simultaneously. Press Ctrl or Shift as you click and highlight all of the active users you want to send a message to. Right-click on the group and select Send Message.

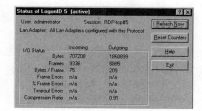

Figure 12.8   Network status information.

There are two rules that must be followed when shadowing accounts. First, you can shadow accounts only if you are logged to Terminal Server from an ICA client. If you are logged on to the console, you cannot shadow another account unless you first run the ICA client from the console. Second, you can shadow ICA connections only.

By default, the user you are attempting to shadow is notified that you wish to shadow his session. The notification can be turned off on a per-user basis, as described here:

1. Open User Manager from the Administrative Tools folder in Start menu | Programs.

2. Double-click on the user's name whose shadowing properties you want to change.

3. Click Config in the User Properties window that appears.

4. Click the down arrow next to Shadowing and select whether Shadowing and Notification should be enabled from choices in the drop-down list.

The Shadow Taskbar

MetaFrame comes with a special-purpose shadowing tool called the Shadow Taskbar, located in the MetaFrame Tools folder in Start menu | Programs. The first time you run the Shadow Taskbar, it installs the ICA client on the console. This is necessary to be able to shadow other sessions from the console. When you run the taskbar, again it prompts you to log on to Terminal Server using the ICA client. After you log on, the Shadow Taskbar appears at the top of the screen. If you click the Shadow button, it takes you to the Shadow Session screen where you can select all of the users you want to shadow from the console.

Measuring Performance

13

THE LAST THING AN ADMINISTRATOR wants to hear after a deployment of Terminal Server is that it's too slow. Many things can be done to improve the performance of a Terminal Server system. Trying to improve the performance after the system is already deployed, however, is not the best time to do it. The first and most important thing you can do is proper performance testing of the system before deployment occurs. This chapter covers how to set up good performance tests, the top ten performance tips for Terminal Server, and some of the tools, such as Performance Monitor, that are available to both measure performance and prevent future performance problems from occurring.

Performance Testing

Planning and prototyping are critical for successful Terminal Server deployment. As part of planning and prototyping, you need to first determine what problems, if any, your application may have with Terminal Server. Guidelines for the installation of applications are covered in Chapter 10, "Installing Applications on Terminal Server."

After the application has been installed and any issues worked out, you need to test for acceptable performance. You can use several different methods to do this. This section covers two different methods: scaling and user simulation using scripting.

Understanding the Application

The first step with any prototyping is gaining an understanding of the application being tested. The best way to do this is often to just sit down with the people who use the application the most and have them show you what they do. What you're looking for are commonly used features of the applications, particularly features that take up significant processing time or memory on Terminal Server. Out of this training, you need to gain enough of an understanding of the application that you'll be able to accurately simulate day-to-day operations and find out which uses of the application will cause the most use of resources on the server. If you're learning the application on an NT workstation, you can open the Task Manager and watch processor utilization while going through different procedures in the application. While learning the application, keep a watchful eye out for the following:

- *Procedures that change large sections of the screen rapidly*   Remember that every time the screen changes, the change needs to be sent across the wire. If large sections of the screen change rapidly during certain procedures, be sure to include these procedures in your stress testing.

- *Animations*   Be especially careful of animated graphics or cursors. By themselves, they take up large amounts of bandwidth. Before doing any testing or prototyping, find out if these animations can be disabled.

- *Report printing or querying*   Printing or viewing reports can take up significant processor and network time. Try to get an idea of how frequent various reports are accessed. Check with the user whether there are reports you can use in your stress testing.

- *Calculations*   Any procedure that requires a significant amount of calculation will require a significant amount of processing. Examples of this are frequent spreadsheet calculations, database reports with calculations, multimedia applications, and accounting reports.

- *Heavy use of memory*   If the program is displaying a large amount of data on the screen without much hard drive access, it's likely using up a large amount of memory. Using Task Manager, you can watch how much memory the program is using up while you try various procedures. Some examples of large memory use are viewing large reports, queries, or tables; loading large spreadsheets or documents; and using programs that cache drive access.

Remember that many of the programs you may want to run on Terminal Server are client/server applications. Because most of the processing in a client/server application is done at the server, you need to mainly be concerned about how rapidly the screen will be changing at the client during typical use.

As you can probably tell, application simulation is more an art than a science. The goal of the performance-testing process is to discover any potential performance problems before the application is implemented on Terminal Server.

Simulating User Interaction Using Task Sheets

Once you understand how users interact with the application, you'll need to find a way to accurately simulate typical user interaction for performance testing. Setting up this simulation can be one of the most time-consuming parts of performance testing. The first step in doing this is to generate a simulation task sheet.

While you're learning the application, you need to keep detailed notes of the most common procedures. Out of this learning process, you need to create a task sheet. A *task sheet* is a list of typical user jobs that are regularly performed with the application. The idea is to generate a task sheet that will be used during simulation. Include sample data and reports that can be used during the simulation. Try to make a task sheet that's circular in nature. For example, if the application is a hospital patient database application and the typical user is a data entry person, you might generate the following task sheet:

1. Create a client record for user Jane Doe with the following information:

    First Name: Jane

    Last Name: Doe

    Address: 123 N Highway One, Boston, MA

    Phone: 343-888-1212.

2. Enter in the following sample health insurance information:

    [Sample insurance info]

3. Create an appointment for the patient on date [sample appointment date].

4. Print out a report of all patient appointments for that date.

5. Enter the following billing information for that appointment:

    [Sample billing info for procedures performed]

6. Generate a billing report for the day.

7. Delete the billing record, patient record, and appointment information.

Notice how the process is circular in nature. In other words, these tasks can all be repeated because the sample information that's created is deleted at the end.

Depending on the size of the implementation and the nature of the application (or applications), you may want to create additional task sheets to simulate different types of use. The idea again is to simulate what will be typical use when the server is in production.

Implementing Task Sheets Using WinBatch Scripts

Now that you know what you're going to implement and have the steps for implementation, it's time to do it. You have several ways you can perform the actual simulation. The first is to have either your coworkers or the end users run through the scripts while you watch the performance data. This works well for simple testing of the data, but repeating the tests and trying to get consistent results can be an ordeal.

The best way to implement the task sheets is to write a script that simulates user interaction. This section shows you one of many ways to do this by demonstrating a popular Windows scripting language called *WinBatch*.

WinBatch is a shareware Windows scripting language and macro creator program, by Wilson Windowware. It's available for trial download and purchase from www.windowware.com. WinBatch will work with both 16-bit and 32-bit versions of Windows. What WinBatch does is allow you to record a series of keystrokes in Windows into a macro file. You can then play this macro file to simulate user keyboard interaction. Although WinBatch is primarily designed for automating repetitive Windows tasks, it works well for simulation.

Installing WinBatch

Installing and setting up the program is easy. Simply download it and run SETUP.EXE on the workstation. Although you can install the program on the workstation or on the Terminal Server, it's important that you install it on the workstation. The reason is that you want to simulate keystrokes coming from the workstation across the network for true performance testing. If you install it on the server, instead, then even though your keystrokes will be recorded from across the network, when the macro plays, it will send the keystrokes locally to the application. This will affect your network bandwidth results. The other reason to install SETUP.EXE on the workstation is that the server should not have to process the macro language, only the keystrokes.

Setting Up the Client

Once WinBatch is installed, log on to the Terminal Server with your client of choice. Remember that many decisions you make on the client side will affect your performance results. Make sure you keep track of how the clients are set up for each test you perform. All the following settings will affect the results:

- Choice of Terminal Server protocol (either ICA or RDP)
- Choice of network protocol if using ICA (either IPX, SPX, TCP/IP, or NetBEUI)
- Choice of video resolution and colors
- Whether compression is enabled or disabled
- Level of encryption

Using the performance tests, you can determine which combination of these settings will work best for you on the client side.

> **Author's Note: Visual Test**
>
> Although WinBatch was chosen for this example, you should note that several other user simulation products are available on the market. One popular and often used one is Microsoft's Visual Test. Although the scripting language and procedures are different with Visual Test, the basic ideas covered in this section are the same.

Recording and Viewing the Macro

Once you're logged on, bring up the application you'll be testing, and then follow these steps:

1. To begin recording the macro, run the WinMacro program from the WinBatch folder you just installed on the client.

2. Right-click the WinMacro icon in the task bar and select Begin Recording.

3. Enter the macro filename with an extension of .WBM and press Enter.

From here on, all of your keystrokes will be recorded. It's important to remember that only keystrokes will be recorded. Mouse movements will not be recorded in the batch file.

Using the task sheet you created earlier, go through the steps you want to record. You'll need to use the keyboard to get around because mouse movements are not recorded. The timing of your keystrokes is not recorded, just the keystrokes themselves. Once you're done with the tasks, right-click the flashing WinMacro icon and end the recording of the macro.

Now let's look at what was recorded. You'll find the macro under the C:\PROGRAM FILES\WINBATCH\WINMACRO directory. WinBatch translates your keystrokes into Wilson Windowware's Window Interface Language (WIL). Because these are all text commands, you can edit the macro file with any standard text editor, such as Notepad.

For this example, we recorded a simple WinBatch macro using WordPad running on Terminal Server. While recording the macro, we entered a short line of text, highlighted the text (Shift+up arrow) and then deleted it. Here's the resulting macro:

```
SendKey(`The{SPACE}quick{SPACE}brown{SPACE}fox{SPACE}jumped{SPACE}over`)
SendKey(`{SPACE}the{SPACE}lazy{SPACE}dog.+{UP}{DELETE}`)
```

The SendKey command simply sends keystrokes to whatever window is currently open on the desktop. Even though hundreds of macro language commands are available in the Window Interface Language, you'll probably need to know only a handful in order to do performance testing.

User Interaction and Usage Delays

The first command you should understand is the TimeDelay (seconds) command. If you run the previous macro by running WinBatch, it will probably finish before you know what's happening. In order to simulate user interaction, you need to slow it down considerably. The TimeDelay (seconds) command lets you put delays in the script between keystrokes to simulate user typing rates. Also, remember that users are rarely typing in the application 100 percent of the time. The amount of delay you put in the script is up to you to judge.

You can introduce two types of delay: user-interaction delay and usage delay. User-interaction delay is the delay between keystrokes and between switching screens. User-interaction delay should be set up to mimic the average typing rate of the users and the speed with which the users normally switch through screens in the application when they're actively using it.

Usage delay is much more subjective and difficult to determine. Usage delay should represent the general level of application activity of all the users. Usage delay is the delay between repetitions of the script. If you're going to roll out the application to a busy data center where users are typing nearly constantly into their terminals, your usage delay should be very short. If you're going to roll out the application to users who will be using it only on brief occasions to gather or enter information, your usage delay could be several minutes or more. Be sure to qualify the results of your testing by the amount of usage delay you put into the scripts.

The other WIL command you'll need to know is the GOTO *label* command. This command is identical to the DOS batch file GOTO command. Use a GOTO statement at the end of the macro to loop back to the top and repeat it.

Putting this all together, here's the finalized testing script:

```
UsageDelay = 5
InteractionDelay = 2
:Start
SendKey(`The{SPACE}quick`)
TimeDelay (InteractionDelay)
SendKey(`{SPACE}brown{SPACE}`)
TimeDelay (InteractionDelay)
SendKey(`fox{SPACE}jumped`)
TimeDelay (InteractionDelay)
SendKey(`{SPACE}over{SPACE}the`);
TimeDelay (InteractionDelay)
SendKey(`{SPACE}lazy{SPACE}dog.`)
TimeDelay (InteractionDelay)
;Highlight the text (Shift+UpArrow) and delete it
SendKey(`+{UP}{DELETE}`)
TimeDelay (UsageDelay)
Goto Start
```

This script simulates a user typing rate of approximately 60 words per minute by using a user interaction delay of two seconds. The script also has a usage delay of five seconds between repetitions. Note how the TimeDelay (seconds) statements are evenly placed throughout the macro. This is important in order to simulate user interaction. If you do not space out the keystrokes using delays, they'll be sent all at once to the Terminal Server. This causes a false spike in utilization, which would not occur if an actual user were typing in the same data. By spacing things out, server utilization will more accurately reflect what it would be if an actual user were typing in the data.

Setting Up the Performance Test

Now that you know how to simulate user interaction and understand how your coworkers use the application, it's time for the actual performance test. For most projects, the best and easiest way to carry out a performance test is through *scaling*. This involves doing accurate load testing from a small number of Terminal Server stations and then scaling the results to the actual number of users who will be on the system. The advantage of scaling is that it's quick, easy, and provides a good feel for how an application will perform on the large scale. The disadvantage is that it's more inaccurate than full-scale testing. There's an underlying assumption with scaling that performance will scale linearly. This is not always the case (it can depend on many factors, such as how the application is written to perform under heavy use). To help eliminate these factors, your sample group should be at least three workstations. The more workstations in your sample, the more accurate your final results will be.

Here's one way to do a scaling test:

1. Install the application on the server and create three test users (for example, apptester1, apptester2, and apptester3) who have the application icon on their desktop or Start menu.

2. Install the Terminal Server client on three or more typical workstations. Make sure you use the exact same client settings on all the workstations, such as video resolution, encryption, and compression. Try to choose workstations that will be part of the final rollout. If that's not possible, use machines with the same operating system and basic hardware capabilities. A conference or training room is a great place to set up a performance test environment.

3. To simulate the connection, connect the machines to Terminal Server using the connection type and speed that will be used in the final rollout. If you're going to connect your clients to Terminal Server across a 100Mbps LAN in the final rollout, set up a separate 100Mbps network segment for doing the performance test. If you're going to distribute the clients across a WAN, either simulate the WAN link in your testing lab or choose a site on the WAN that's close to the main office to set up the test. For more information on simulating WAN links, see Chapter 17, "Terminal Server and Wide Area Networks."

4. Prepare to capture the data. You should have utilities prepared to measure the amount of memory being used by each client, the amount of processing time, the amount of paging file use, and the amount of network bandwidth. All these parameters can be measured and recorded using Performance Monitor. Techniques for capturing this information are covered in "Performance Monitor," toward the end of this chapter.

5. Using the scripts you've created, simulate user interaction on a single workstation, then on two workstations, and then on three. Record the results for each. It's normally best to run the script from the workstation, as noted earlier. If you run the script on the server, the server processing time taken to run the script will affect the results. You should see a roughly linear increase in usage at the server. If not, try the test with more workstations. Be sure all the client settings are the same. Because WinBatch only simulates keystrokes, not mouse movements, the location of the client window on the desktop is not relevant.

However, keeping both your desktop resolution setting and your client resolution, color, protocol, compression, and encryption parameters the same on all the clients is important for accurate results.

Try varying one or more of the settings on the client or the hardware configuration of the server to see how the change affects the results. Many of the settings that will affect performance are covered in the "Top Ten Performance Tips" section.

The two primary items you need to watch out for are average processor utilization and memory use. If you find that the average processor utilization scales to over 90 percent constant utilization per processor, and you're sure the high utilization is not due to lack of memory, you'll likely need to get higher performance hardware or more processors. Make sure the usage delay parameter in your scripts is realistic for your environment. Usage delay should reflect the average use you expect in your environment. It will have a direct effect on processor utilization. Bursts of heavy processor use are normal for any environment, but constant heavy use should be avoided. Constant heavy use means that all users will get slow response times when working with their applications.

Another important factor is memory use. By looking at the memory available while adding more users to the system, you should be able to get a good feel for how much memory each user requires. Not having enough memory can bring your server to a crawl. As the server runs out of memory, it will start swapping out memory to the system paging file. This constant use of the disk is called *thrashing*, and it will slow down your server to the point that it's nearly unusable.

You should note that 32-bit applications are reentrant. What this means is that once a 32-bit application's code and DLLs are loaded into memory, they can be used by all users of the application on your Terminal Server. This means that with 32-bit applications, you mainly need to be concerned about how much memory each user uses. Because 16-bit and DOS applications are not reentrant, the application's code needs to be reloaded for every user of the application. This means you need to be concerned about how much memory the application and user data take up for each user.

Author's Note: Performance Testing

Proper performance testing is a subject of much debate. The material in this chapter is intended to give you the tools and techniques you need to get started on performance testing of your server. Although no single perfect way exists for testing Terminal Server performance for every environment, there are many ways you can improve on the accuracy of these tests in your environment.

Top Ten Performance Tips

You can do several things to increase the performance of Terminal Server. However, there are also several things you should avoid doing so as not to severely degrade the performance of your server. The following are some of the most important tips for keeping your server running fast:

1. *Use multi-processors*   You may quickly find through testing that the biggest bottleneck is processing. Instead of increasing the processing speed you might try adding more processors. Terminal Server scales well across multiple processors. Even for small implementations (< 30 users), having at least two processors is a good idea. With a single processor, one user on the system can easily max out the processor utilization with a lot of activity.

2. *Don't skimp on memory*   By properly performance testing your server before implementation you can get a good idea of how much memory you will need. You can count on needing roughly 10MB per user if not more. This can vary considerably depending on your applications. Always keep a close eye out for applications with memory leaks. Because of the possibility of memory leaks with applications it is always a good idea to roll out the application to a small pilot group before rolling it out to everyone.

3. *Test different protocol combinations*   With the addition of MetaFrame to Terminal Server there are a large variety of protocol choices. During your performance testing make sure you try different protocol combinations, such as RDP on TCP/IP, ICA on TCP/IP, ICA on NetBEUI, or ICA on IPX. Depending on your environment you will likely find significant differences in performance and bandwidth usage between the protocol combinations. Be wary though that there may be a tradeoff between network bandwidth usage and processor utilization. In other words, if you find that one of the protocol combinations uses less bandwidth than another one, it may also use more processing power when handling that protocol.

4. *Use Windows 32-bit applications*   Terminal Server is designed to efficiently run 32-bit applications. If you are using Windows 16-bit or DOS applications, you can expect a large drop in performance. You will not be able to run as many users simultaneously using 16-bit or DOS applications as you would users who run 32-bit applications.

5. *Simplify the desktop, and eliminate complex graphics*   Remember that everything on the desktop needs to be compressed by the server and sent across the line. By reducing the complexity of the desktop, the compression algorithms will be able to compress the graphics much more efficiently.

6. *Reduce colors*   With Terminal Server you can use up to 256 colors simultaneously. If you can get by with 16 colors instead, use 16. The less colors used, the less bandwidth will be taken up sending your desktop across the wire.

7. *Never use animated screen savers or applications with animated graphics*   Make sure that users do not have the option of using an animated screen saver or the option of installing one from their Terminal Server desktops. You can lock down the ability to change screen savers with policies or even simpler, do not install any screen savers on your Terminal Server except the blank screen saver. Also, even small animated graphics within applications can take up surprisingly large amounts of network bandwidth. Many applications, such as Web browsers, allow you to disable animated graphics. If you see animated graphics or cursors in any of your applications, check with the publisher to find out how they can be disabled.

8. *Run applications locally*   Applications will run faster if the programs and their data are local instead of across the network. Unless you have a client/server application where you do not have a choice, always try to copy the applications and data to the Terminal Server.

9. *Use high performance network cards in your server*   Using a top-of-the-line, high-performance network card in the server can make a huge difference in Terminal Server performance. Also, make sure the network itself is designed to handle the heavy traffic that will be going in and out of the Terminal Server. Connecting your Terminal Server directly into a high-performance switch is always a good option.

10. *Use policies to restrict users to the applications they need*   With Terminal Server users are in competition for resources. Desktops should be thought of as terminals. They should be dedicated for specific tasks if possible. Reducing the number of applications a user can run will reduce the amount of processing time and memory that each user takes up.

Measuring and Monitoring Performance

It's difficult to improve the performance of your server unless you have a way of measuring it. This section covers several techniques for measuring the performance of your server. You'll learn how to use several tools, including Performance Monitor and Task Manager, in order to gain insight into bottlenecks. You'll also discover how to monitor your performance over the long run to prevent problems from occurring.

Realize that performance-monitoring tools themselves can affect the results of any performance testing. Try to run your performance tests from the console and not through a remote Windows session. If you do run the tests from a remote terminal, make sure to keep the performance-monitoring window minimized during the tests. The quickly changing parameters and performance results on the screen will, by themselves, eat up large amounts of processing time and network bandwidth as they are transferred across the line.

Task Manager

Included with Terminal Server is a very simple but powerful tool called *Task Manager*. Task Manager can provide quick, on-the-fly answers to your server performance problems. Although you'll not get the level of detail you can get with Performance Monitor, it provides a good summary view of the state of the server. It works best when being used for ongoing monitoring of the server. If you experience a performance problem, the first place to look is Task Manager. Once you've assessed the nature of the problem, you can isolate it further using Performance Monitor.

While we're covering the many performance parameters you can monitor with Task Manager, bring up Task Manager on your workstation and follow along. To run Task Manager, select NT Security from the Start menu and click the Task Manager button. If you're at the console, you can also press Ctrl+Alt+Del and then click Task Manager.

The Performance Tab

One of the most useful parts of the Task Manager is the Performance tab (see Figure 13.1). The parameters under the Performance tab provide a global view of how your server is doing. Under Performance, you'll find a graphical view of the CPU utilization and memory usage. When you double-click the Performance tab, the CPU utilization and memory usage graphs will fill the entire window, and you can size it as you wish. This window offers a quick view of the status of the server and can be kept open on the console.

> **Real-World Tip: Microsoft's Systems Management Server**
>
> By loading the network monitor agents on your Terminal Server, you can monitor many performance-related parameters remotely using Microsoft's Systems Management Server. This method has less of an effect on the performance results than running Performance Monitor, because the server does not have to store data locally. For more information on the capabilities of Systems Management Server, refer to the product information on Microsoft's Web site (www.microsoft.com).

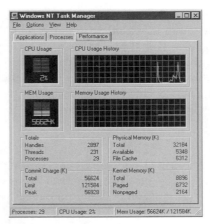

Figure 13.1   Task Manager's Performance tab.

Beneath the graphs in the Performance tab are several useful memory- and processor-related parameters:

- *Totals*   This gives you an idea of the workload on your processors. In Chapter 3, "Terminal Server Architecture," you learned that totals tell you how many handles, threads, and processes are currently running on the server.

- *Physical memory*   Physical memory is simply how much memory is installed in your server. It's a good idea to keep an eye on the Available count. The physical memory available is the amount of physical memory left after it has been committed to use for the applications and processes loaded on the server.

- *Commit charge*   The commit charge total, limit and peak are the most important memory parameters on the window. The commit charge total reflects the total virtual memory that has been committed to processes running on the system. The commit charge is what you need to watch as you add more users onto the system to get an idea of how much memory each user is taking up. The limit reflects the total virtual memory available on the system without expanding the paging file. The final parameter is the commit charge peak. The peak is the maximum memory that was committed during the session.

- *Kernel memory*   Kernel memory parameters refer to memory that is available to programs running in the privileged kernel mode. Paged is the part of the total memory that can be swapped to disk.

With all these parameters, which is the most important one to watch? It really depends on what you're looking for. One indicator that you need more physical memory is if your committed bytes are significantly greater than your physical memory. Although this may be normal for some server situations, this normally means that your system is relying heavily on the paging file. To verify this, check the paging file usage using Performance Monitor. If it's being heavily used during normal server activity, you have a good indication that you may need more memory.

You can also watch how much the committed bytes parameter increases as users log on and run their applications. In a controlled testing environment, you can use this parameter to get a good handle on how much memory each user and his applications will take up on the server. It's also a good idea to have the user work with the application for awhile and then compare the peak committed bytes to the committed bytes before the user logged on. You might find that some applications use significantly more memory than what they started with, depending on what procedures are run with them.

Beside memory use, the utilization parameters can also be very handy. With the utilization graph, you can gain a quick understanding of the current and recent utilization of the server.

The Processes Tab

Although the parameters in the Performance tab give you a good idea how the system as a whole is running, they don't provide you with the details you need to isolate the source of any performance problems. With the information under the Processes tab, you can quickly find which processes are using up the most memory, which ones have the highest utilization, and which ones have used up the most CPU time (see Figure 13.2). This real-time information is very valuable when troubleshooting performance problems. It's also good for periodic checking of the performance of your servers and finding out which applications and users are using up the most resources on your servers. Each process is broken down by user and image name, making it very easy to spot users who are running applications that hog system resources.

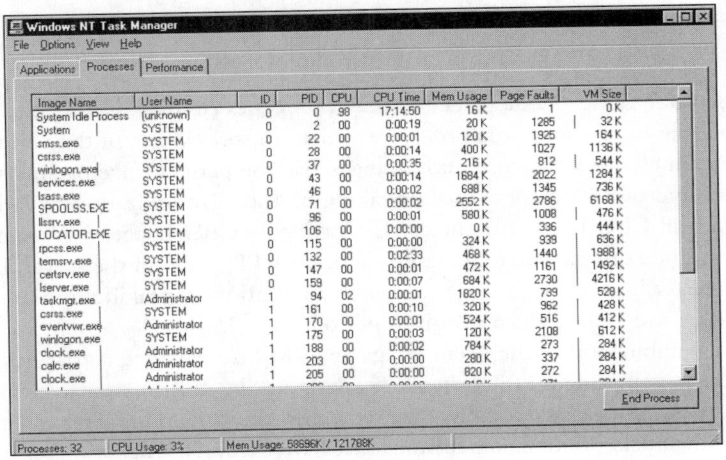

Figure 13.2 The Processes tab.

By default, under the Process tab, you're shown the image name, user name, ID, process ID (PID), CPU time, CPU utilization, and memory usage. Besides these default parameters, you can add several more by selecting Select Columns from the View menu. The following is a list of all the process parameters you can monitor with the Task Manager:

- *Image Name*   The name of the process. Processes usually go by the name of the application that started them.
- *PID*   Unique process ID number assigned to each process running on the system.
- *CPU Usage*   Percentage of CPU time used by the process's threads.
- *CPU Time*   Total processor time used by the process since the process began.
- *Memory Usage*   Amount of system memory used by the process.
- *Page Faults*   Number of instances where the disk had to be accessed to retrieve data because it was not in memory.
- *Page Faults Delta*   Change in page faults since the last update.
- *VM Size*   Size of the section of the paging file currently in use by the process.
- *Mem Usage Delta*   Change in memory usage.
- *Paged Pool*   Amount of memory in use by the process that's available to being swapped out to the paging file.
- *Nonpaged Pool*   Amount of operating system memory in use by the process. This memory is not available for paging.
- *Base Priority*   The relative priority of the process—either low, normal, or high. The priority of the process can be adjusted by right-clicking the process and selecting Set Priority.
- *Handle Count*   The number of object handles the process has opened.
- *Thread Count*   The number of threads the process has running.

Because there can easily be several hundred processes running at the same time, you need to be able to sort out which ones are which. To sort by one of the performance parameters, simply click the column heading above the performance parameter.

You can find out which processes are taking up the most utilization by looking at CPU Time and CPU Usage parameters. By sorting by CPU Usage, you can quickly find which process is currently taking up the most CPU time on the server. The CPU Time parameter is good for comparing which applications are taking up the most CPU time on the average during a given period.

Use the combination of the Mem Usage and VM Size parameters to quickly find which processes running on the system are taking up the most memory. Mem Usage represents physical memory, and VM Size represents the paging file. This is a good technique for quickly finding applications that have memory leaks or are using excessive amounts of memory.

One of the more useful but least used parameters is the Page Fault count. A page fault occurs every time a program tries to retrieve something from memory but ends up going to the paging file on the disk. Page Fault can be a very good indicator of application activity and thus processor utilization. Excessive page faults can also indicate a need for more system memory.

Performance Monitor

Performance Monitor is the premier tool included with Terminal Server for both short-term performance testing and long-term performance monitoring. With Performance Monitor, you can view performance, write performance parameters to log files for later analysis, and even run programs based on when a selected performance threshold has been exceeded.

This section shows you techniques for capacity testing your servers in a test environment and monitoring your server in the long run for performance problems.

Testing Your Server's Capacity Using Performance Monitor

During the testing stage of your server, one of the most important questions to answer is whether you have enough server power to meet the needs of the clients. Using Performance Monitor and the techniques described at the start of the chapter, you can come up with a solid answer to this question. The key is careful, methodical testing and close observation for performance bottlenecks.

The following section recommends a small set of performance parameters that you need to keep a close eye on during performance testing. Although these parameters will detect a wide range of performance problems, they will not necessarily detect all possible problems on the server. Keep in mind that you can monitor hundreds of different performance parameters with Performance Monitor. Once you've identified a performance problem, you can narrow down the problem further using some of the more specific performance parameters. It's recommended that you do some of your own experimentation to determine which performance parameters you should monitor. The Performance Monitor tool is such a feature-rich and flexible tool that you'll likely find several good techniques that work for you, beyond what's suggested in this chapter.

Defining Acceptable Performance

The key to any successful performance testing is defining acceptable performance. As you go through the different tests and stress test the server, you'll see how the response times of your applications will vary. The question to be answered is what is acceptable as a response time and what is not. Remember that when you're using user-simulation scripts, you're simulating active users on the system. In the real world, your server will likely see random peaks of heavy user activity throughout the day. It's the duration of these peaks that matter. If your server cannot keep up with the average level of activity of users, you need to add more hardware or more servers.

Before implementing your server, you should assess the workload of users. Say you have a small office that needs to be able to enter handwritten reports into a corporate database. Before even doing the performance testing of the server, ask some of the users at the office how many reports they enter per day on average. If you're going to roll out Windows-based Terminals to several offices, make sure to ask key people at each of the offices how much time per day they spend entering information into their Windows terminal.

Once you determine the average projected use of the Terminal Server, you can set up your performance tests properly to make sure your server has the capacity to handle this use. Your user-simulation script should reflect the tasks users will perform, on average, each time they use the server. The usage delay parameter in the scripts should reflect the time between these task performances. If a user says he will be entering roughly 80 reports per day, that equates to 10 reports per hour, or one report every 360 seconds. For testing, you should have the user-simulation script simulate the entering of a single report and have a Usage Delay parameter of 360 seconds. Always make sure you plan for capacity and document your reasoning behind the testing. The more accurate the simulation of the worker's actual workload, the more accurate your final results will be.

Another key to accurate performance testing is locking down the desktop. Users should only have access to the applications they need. In this way, you're aware of exactly what they will be doing with the server, and you can set up adequate performance tests to ensure the server has enough capacity.

Using Performance Monitor

The performance test is intended to gather the data you'll need to judge the performance of your server during user simulation. This performance information will also make an excellent baseline of performance for future comparison. Be sure to record exactly how the tests were set up and what parameters were measured so that in the future you'll be able to duplicate the results. In this way, when you make performance enhancements to the server, you'll be able to see the true effects of the enhancement.

Performance Monitor is available in the Administrative Tools group. When you run the application, it will come up with a blank chart. If you're not familiar with Performance Monitor, add a counter, such as processor utilization, to the chart by selecting Add to Chart from the Edit menu and watch. Figure 13.3 is a snapshot of Performance Monitor after adding the processor utilization counter. Note the statistics at the bottom of the window. For each counter, Performance Monitor keeps track of the maximum value, minimum value, and average over the tracking period. These statistics will be important as we begin measuring Terminal Server performance.

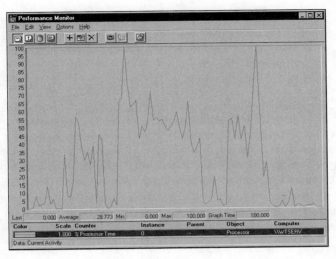

Figure 13.3 The Performance Monitor.

Performance Monitor comes with a plethora of counters, which are broken up into groups or objects. The following objects are some of the most useful and will be the ones we're the most concerned with in this chapter:

- *Session* Session is a collection of Terminal Server–specific counters. Under Session, you'll find counters such as Processor Utilization, Total Bytes, Input Errors, and Output Errors. One of the best things about the Session counters are that you can assign counters for individual or groups of connections. In this way, you can watch which users are taking up the most system resources.

- *Processor* Processor and the rest of the performance objects covered here are the same as the ones included with standard Windows NT Server 4.0. Under Processor, you'll find things such as Processor Utilization and Interrupts/Sec. You can track individual processors in the system.

- *Memory* Memory is a very important collection of counters. Under Memory, you'll find counters for things such as Pages/Sec, Page Faults/Sec, and Memory Available. One of the problems with memory counters is they only give you a picture of the memory status for the system as a whole; to understand which parts of the system are using the most memory, you'll need to use counters under Process or Session.

- *Process* Process counters provide the finest level of detail of activity and resource usage on the system. Once you've determined that there's a system bottleneck using the Global Memory and Processor counters, you can narrow in on which process or processes are using the most resources. Under Process, you'll find counters for such things as Processor Utilization, Virtual Bytes, and Page Faults. You can watch these counters for individual processes by selecting the process from the instance window.

- *System*   Under System are several system-wide counters. The counters under System are a good place to start your search for system bottlenecks.

- *Logical Disk*   Logical Disk performance counters let you see performance results such as Disk Bytes Read, Queue Length, and Disk Bytes Written. To record disk performance parameters you first need to enable them using the DISKPERF -Y command from the command prompt. Disk performance parameters are disabled, by default, because they can degrade system performance. In general, you should do disk performance testing separately from your main testing. Always make sure to disable disk performance counters (DISKPERF -N) when you're finished.

So far, we've discussed how to simply view performance counters in real time. The power of Performance Monitor, however, is its capability to both log performance parameters and send alerts. To understand how logging works, go into Performance Monitor and select Log from the View menu. In the Edit menu, select Add to Log. In the Performance Monitor's log window, shown in Figure 13.4, you can see all the objects you can log. When you add the objects to the log, what you're actually recording are all the counters under that object.

Once you've added the counters to the log, you need to assign the log a filename and start it. To do this, select Log from the Options menu. In the Log Options window, you need to enter the filename of the log and the update interval. By default, the log will be updated every 15 seconds with a sample of all the counters from all the objects you've selected. You can change this to any interval you wish or select Manual Update if you want to take manual samples of the parameters.

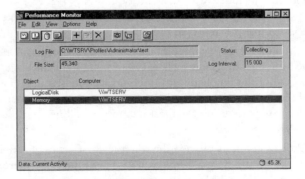

Figure 13.4 Performance Monitor's log window.

Once you've entered this information, you can select Start Log to start the logging. The log file will begin filling with samples of the counters at the specified time intervals. When you're done, select Stop Logging from the Log window.

Now that you have the sample information saved into a file, it's time to view it. By default, Performance Monitor is set for you to view current activity. Follow these steps to view this information:

1. Switch to the chart view by selecting Chart from the View menu.

2. Select Data From from the Options menu.

3. Select Log File and then enter the name of your log file. This prepares Performance Monitor to receive its data from the counters you recorded in the log instead of from current activity on the server.

At this point, all you need to do to see a particular counter is add it to the chart by selecting Add to Chart from the Edit menu. This will graph the values of the counter you selected for the time period you logged it.

If you want to work with a smaller section of the charted values, you can select the start and ending log times in the Input Log File Timeframe window by selecting Time Window from the Edit menu (see Figure 13.5). As you change the timeframe, the average, minimum, and maximum values will also change to reflect the data in the timeframe.

For even better analysis of your data, you can export the data into comma- or tab-delimited format. You can then import it into programs such as Microsoft Excel or Lotus 1-2-3, to take advantage of their better analysis and graphing capabilities. To export the data, follow these steps:

1. Enter chart view by selecting Chart from the View menu.

2. Add all the counters to the chart that you want to export by selecting Add to Chart from the Edit menu.

3. Select the timeframe for the data you want by selecting Time Window from the Edit menu.

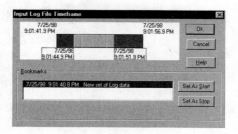

Figure 13.5 Input Log Timeframe window.

4. Save the data in comma-delimited (CSV) or tab-delimited (TSV) format by selecting Export Chart from the File menu. In Figure 13.6, you can see the actual Performance Monitor data from a processor utilization test after it was imported into an Excel spreadsheet.

Setting Up a Performance Test

Although this section provides some possible techniques for setting up a performance test, the exact manner in which you set up the test is up to you. In general, the steps to setting up the test are as follows:

1. Load the Terminal Server client on three or more workstations that will be involved in the load testing of the server. Connect them to the server using the same means of communication as will be used when the project is rolled out. For example, if most of the users will be dialing in, you should set up modems and modem lines so that the test machines are dialing into the server. The speed of the connection will definitely affect the final results of the test.

2. At the console, set up Performance Monitor logging. You should log the Session, Processor, and Memory counters. Choose your time interval for the logging. With any type of performance monitoring, you need to be careful how much monitoring, itself, affects the results. Having too short a time interval can affect the results, because it will increase processor utilization. Using the console for performance monitoring is also important. If you use a Terminal Server session instead, the results can be affected because the screen will be constantly changing during logging, thus causing an increase in processor and network utilization.

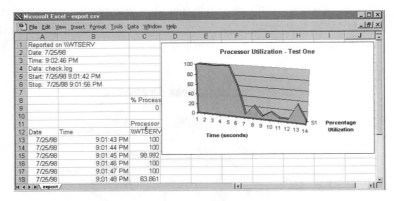

Figure 13.6 Importing Performance Monitor data into Excel.

3. Start the logging and then start the user-simulation script on the first machine. Let it run long enough to gather a good amount of data and then stop the logging. Change the data source to the log you just created by selecting Data From from the Options menu; then switch to chart view. Start adding the performance counters you want to look at to the chart. Set the timeframe to just the time when the user simulation was occurring by selecting Timeframe from the Edit menu. Finally, export the data to a comma- or tab-delimited file.

4. While the user simulation is still running and the logging is stopped, log onto the server from another workstation. Is the performance acceptable or are there unacceptable delays? As you continue to add more simultaneous users, always check to ensure that the general performance of the server is still at an acceptable level.

5. Start up the user simulation on the next workstation and continue the logging process. Keep doing this until you have tested all the workstations simultaneously. You should now have a collection of log files and exported data files for at least one to three simultaneous users.

6. As a control to the testing, also take a log file of the server with no users on it. This will help you eliminate any effects that the monitoring itself is having on the performance data.

Once you've collected all this data, it's time to analyze it. Here are some of the counters you want to be looking at:

■ *Processor, Processor Utilization* If you find that your processor utilization is averaging over 90 percent during the testing period, you'll likely need more processors in your server. Take a look at the difference in processor utilization between having one user, two users, and three users to see how utilization scales. You can use this to predict the amount of utilization with all the users you project will be using the system. Remember to make sure your usage delay parameter is realistic, because this will have a direct effect on the results. For a more detailed view of utilization, take a look at the Processor Utilization counters under Session. This will tell you how much processor time each session is using up.

■ *Memory, Available Bytes* The Available Bytes counter is the amount of memory, including virtual memory, available on the system. This counter will give you a good idea of how much memory each session is using. Watch this counter as you add more simultaneous users. Like processor utilization, you can scale the change in this parameter to predict how much memory you'll be using when all users are on the system. Memory Available Bytes should not increase significantly over time during a single-user simulation. If you find that the amount of memory a session takes up keeps increasing, there may be a memory leak in the program.

- *Memory, Pages per Second*   Pages per second is the number of pages read from disk to resolve memory references. If this counter remains high, your system will be very slow. Try adding more memory to your system.

- *Session, Total Bytes*   Session Total Bytes is the total number of bytes a particular session is transmitting or receiving from the network. This is a good counter to check to get an idea of network utilization.

Remember that if you want to log any of the disk-related counters, you need to first enable them using DISKPERF -Y. This will require a reboot of the server.

The advantage of recording your performance in this manner is that you've created a baseline. By documenting exactly how you set your tests up, what equipment was used, and what the server configuration was, and by saving all the performance results, you'll be able to repeat these tests in the future. The most powerful advantage to this is that you'll be able to see exactly how performance improves as you make improvements to the server, such as adding more processors, memory, or faster peripherals.

You can change several server parameters that will affect performance. One simple example is changing the protocol that you're using for the connections. To fine-tune performance, try changing server/workstation parameters such as the protocol, compression, and bitmap caching (MetaFrame only) and then repeat the testing. If used properly, these tests can be a great tool for fine-tuning the performance of your server.

Monitoring Performance Over the Long Run

Once you've determined that your server is up to the job of handling all the projected users, and the system is in place and running well, there are a couple of things you can do to ensure it keeps running this way. One way is to simply take periodic performance checks on the server and save the logs. You can review these over time and watch for any unusual rises in server usage. You can also set up constant logging at the server with a high interval rate, such as 3,600 seconds or an hour. By monitoring the server over a period of a couple weeks, you can get a good idea of what the busiest times of the day or week are.

The final technique is using alerts. Included in Performance Monitor is the Alert tool, one of the most powerful tools for long-term monitoring of your server. With the Alert tool, you can set up programs to be run if, for example, your available memory falls below 50MB. Besides running the program you set up, the Alert tool will also log the alert. Figure 13.7 shows an example of an alert for low memory. When memory drops below 50MB, the server will send a message to the administrator using the NET SEND ADMINISTRATOR LOW MEMORY command. To add an alert, select Add to Alert from the Edit menu and then select the counter you want to watch.

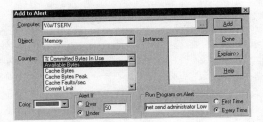

Figure 13.7 Sending alerts for low memory.

Real-World Terminal Server and MetaFrame Solutions

14

Terminal Server and Remote Access

ONE OF THE MOST POPULAR USES for Terminal Server is to provide secure remote control of networked applications through secure remote access to the network. The problem with many remote control products on the market today is that they put the control of network security in the hands of the users. However, with Terminal Server, network security is centralized at the server, and in the hands of those who have the experience and training to handle it properly. Centralizing remote access helps eliminate the modem proliferation that occurs at many corporations as modems are installed on desktops for both dial-in and dial-out applications. Terminal Server also helps make the best use of the analog lines you have available by sharing them between remote users.

This chapter covers some of the many ways you can set up remote access to both Terminal Server and MetaFrame servers. First, you see an overview of the three main remote access options: Remote Access Services (RAS) dial-in, remote access devices, and dial-in ICA. Next, you learn details of how to set up and use RAS and dial-in ICA for every client situation you are likely to encounter.

Remote Access Solutions for MetaFrame and Terminal Server

The remote access solutions you have available depend on whether or not you have MetaFrame. MetaFrame not only supports all means of remote access supported by Terminal Server alone, MetaFrame offers an additional type of remote access called dial-in ICA. The following sections describe the remote access options you have available and the advantages and disadvantages of those options.

Differences Between Remote Node and Remote Control

When it comes to remote access to network resources, there are generally three types of solutions: remote node, remote control, and remote node plus remote control. Before you delve into the details of the solutions that are available, you need to understand the differences between these types of solutions.

Remote Node Solutions

Remote node refers to a solution in which the remote workstation becomes a node on the network. A true remote node solution allows the remote workstation the same access to network resources as if it were plugged directly into the network. A remote node user is able to do things such as log on to servers on the network, send print jobs directly to network printers, and transfer files to and from hosts. Both RAS and most dedicated remote access devices are remote node solutions.

The main disadvantage of remote node solutions is normally speed. The user will usually connect to the network at a speed of less than 64KB. Trying to log on to a server and access files takes a long time at this speed because all data has to travel at this speed to the client. Simply opening up an application could take several minutes because the executable and all related files must be downloaded to the client. On the other hand, simpler networking operations such as pinging hosts or telneting can easily be accomplished at these speeds.

Remote Control Solutions

Remote control refers to a solution in which, rather than becoming a node on the network, you remote control an existing node on the network. When you try to bring up an application, only the screen updates are sent to you across the wire, instead of the entire application, making it feasible to run applications remotely. This is the concept on which Terminal Server is based.

The main disadvantage of remote control solutions is that you no longer have direct access to network resources as you do with remote node. If you need to access something such as a NetWare server, network printer, UNIX host, or some other network resource, you must have the correct client software loaded on the node you are remotely controlling. If the node does not support access to that resource, you are out of luck. Because of the huge amount of software available for the Windows platform, there are very few things you will not be able to access or run from a remotely controlled Terminal Server session.

Dial-in ICA, which is available only with MetaFrame, is purely a remote control solution. The details of this solution are presented in a little bit.

Remote Node plus Remote Control

Using RAS dial-in or a remote access device to remotely control a Terminal Server session is referred to as a remote node plus remote control solution. What this means is that two things happen when you use RAS to attach to a remote Terminal Server. First, your machine becomes a node on that network, just as if your machine were plugged directly into it. Second, you remotely control a Windows session on the Terminal Server.

RAS Dial-In

RAS dial-in is the standard remote access dial-in solution for Windows NT Server, and works the same on Terminal Server. RAS works with both Terminal Server and MetaFrame. It provides direct access to the network for remote users so that they can access both Terminal Server and other network resources as if they were locally connected to the network.

Security must be carefully implemented with RAS. Although your remote users need to authenticate using their domain name and password in order to gain access, after authenticated the users have the same level of access as a workstation that is connected locally to the network. This may be more access then you want to give. You may want to consider restricting their access to just the server.

Because Terminal Server alone works only with TCP/IP, you can access Terminal Server only using RDP over a RAS connection from remote Windows 95 or Windows NT clients. Windows for Workgroups only supports the NetBEUI protocol for RAS connections. To use Windows for Workgroups remotely with Terminal Server alone, you need to go with a remote access device solution that supports TCP/IP, which is discussed in the following section.

For some networks, RAS may be the best solution for remote access to Terminal Server. For one reason, it is inexpensive. The RAS software comes with Terminal Server out of the box, and setting it up is relatively easy. Because there is a large base of RAS users and because it is a Microsoft product, support for RAS is easy to find.

RAS can also be a good solution in situations in which users need access to more than just Terminal Server. As a node on your network, your remote users can do anything that a person on the network can do. They can access hosts directly through telnet, print directly to printers on the network, and access any other type of network resource your local network users can, providing they have the correct software on their remote machines. Although all of these types of resources can be accessed through a Terminal Server desktop, RAS gives users more choices. After they have established the connection and are a node on the network, they can determine what they want to access.

Suppose a network administrator wants to access the network remotely. With RAS, after the administrator establishes the connection, he is actually a node on the network. At that point he can run any software on his desktop that he would normally run at work, including the ICA MetaFrame client, MS Terminal Server client, terminal emulation software, network administration tools, and even network monitoring software. This is a great means for an administrator to check on the status of the network or resolve problems remotely while traveling or at home.

Remote Access Devices

Remote access devices are network devices that are dedicated to providing dial-in access to your network. One example of this type of device is the Shiva LANRover. After remote users have dialed in to and authenticated with a remote access device, the device connects them to the network, where they can access Terminal Server or MetaFrame as if they were locally connected.

The disadvantage of these devices is that after remote users are on your network, they can also access other devices on your network as if they were connected locally. Again, you need to be careful to choose a secure solution. Many remote access devices allow you to restrict a remote user's access to a single IP address, such as that of the Terminal Server.

Another disadvantage is that the security system used is often separate from any current security system on the network, such as the NT user domain database. There are ways around this, using authentication methods such as RADIUS, but keep this possible limitation in mind when looking at these types of solutions. Users will not only need a username and password to access the network, but also another username and password for the NT domain.

MetaFrame

Dial-In ICA Connection (MetaFrame Only)

Dial-in ICA works only with MetaFrame. Dial-in ICA allows you to put a communications board, such as a Digiboard, inside your server for incoming calls. You then set up MetaFrame connections to receive them. For smaller implementations, you can also use the server's built-in serial ports. For this solution to work you will also need modems to plug into the Digiboard's serial ports. Some solutions on the market have modems built in.

All of the following ICA clients have the ability to dial-in remotely to the MetaFrame server: DOS ICA, 16-bit ICA (Win 3.1/3.11), and 32-bit ICA.

This solution has some strong security advantages. Rather than connecting to your network first and then connecting to your server, users can only access the network through the server. This means that network security is controllable through server security.

Dial-in ICA has been highly optimized for speed and efficiency with remote connections. This is important in bandwidth-limited, remote-access solutions. Although the Dial-in ICA has been highly optimized, it is not guaranteed to be the fastest solution for your hardware setup. As always, make sure you test the different remote access solutions available to ensure that performance is adequate for your needs.

Although RAS is a good solution when you need a remote node solution in addition to remote control, dial-in ICA is a simpler solution than RAS. Establishing a RAS connection requires two steps: establishing the connection and then running the client, whereas dial-in ICA only requires setting up the connection once.

Installing and Using RAS

You can install RAS either during the initial install of the server or later through the Network Control Panel. RAS installs as a standard network service in the Network Control Panel. Before installing RAS make sure all of the communications equipment that you want to use are installed and working.

Most communications adapters, such as Digiboards, install as network adapters and create COM ports in the system for each new communication port they add. For example, to install an 8-port Digiboard, you would normally get the network adapter driver for the board from Digi. After you install this, it adds eight additional COM ports to your system. These COM ports can be configured through RAS to send and receive calls.

After you have installed your communications equipment, including all modems, installing RAS is a breeze. The steps to install RAS on the server are as follows:

1. Install the Remote Access Service by selecting Network from Control Panel. From the Network window select the Services tab and click Add. Choose Remote Access Service from the list in the Select Network Service window.

2. The RAS installation process lists any modems already defined on the system in the Add RAS Device window. Select the device you want to add for RAS from the drop-down list and click OK. If there are no modems installed, you are asked if you want to launch the Install New Modem Wizard. Modems are

installed into the system using standard Windows NT 4.0 TAPI method for installing modems into the system (by selecting Modems in Control Panel). Remember that you need to have first installed your communications card and drivers. If not, the COM ports will not be there to assign the modems to.

3. After you have selected your first modem for RAS, you are taken to the Remote Access Setup window, where all the modems currently enabled for RAS access are listed. At this point, you have the options of adding more modems for RAS by clicking Add; configuring the modems for dial-out, dial-in, or both dial-out and dial-in by clicking Configure; or setting the network parameters for your RAS connections by clicking Network. After you are finished, click OK. (See the next section for details on the network configuration parameters.)

4. If you have not set the network configuration parameters for your RAS connection by clicking Network, you are prompted for the parameters for each protocol as it is bound to RAS.

   After RAS has finished installing, you return to the Services tab in the Network window.

5. Click Close from the Network window and restart the system when prompted.

By default, no users have been granted access to dial-in. Although the RAS service may be started if users tried to dial-in, they would be given a message that they do not have dial-in permission. See the "Administering RAS" section for instructions on how to enable dial-in.

Table 14.1   **Common Case I/O Ports and IRQs**

COM Port	Base I/O Port	IRQ
COM1	3F8	4
COM2	2F8	3
COM3	3E8	4
COM4	2E8	3

Real-World Tip: Installing COM Ports

Often Windows NT will not correctly detect the system's built-in COM ports. You can manually install a COM port by selecting Ports from Control Panel. Select Add and then select the COM port number, base I/O port address, and IRQ. Table 14.1 shows the common base I/O ports and IRQs for COM ports 1 to 4.

Be careful to choose the correct IRQ and base I/O for your COM port. The settings in Table 14.1 are the defaults for COM 1 to 4, but on many systems you can change these settings in the system BIOS.

Configuring the RAS Network Parameters

In step 3 of the RAS installation process, you had the option of configuring the network parameters. Although most steps of the RAS installation process are simple, configuring the network parameters correctly can be challenging. In this section you learn how to set these parameters correctly for your network.

To configure the network parameters, click Network from the Remote Access Setup window in step 3. You can get back to the Remote Access Setup window after RAS has been installed by doing the following:

1. Select Network from Control Panel.

2. Click the Services tab.

3. Highlight Remote Access Services and click Properties.

From the Network Configuration window (select Network from the Remote Access Setup window) you have several options that affect how the remote clients will be communicating with the server. Take a look at Figure 14.1. These options apply for all of the modems that you have configured in the Remote Access Setup window.

There are three protocols that you can use across a RAS communication line: IPX/SPX, TCP/IP, and NetBEUI. By clicking the Configure button, you can configure each protocol's RAS settings independently. All protocols allow you to specify whether the remote client has access to just this server or the entire network. This is an important security setting. By default, the remote client will have access to the entire network, including your Terminal Server. This means she could directly log on to any host on your network, which can be a big security risk. It is recommended to always set up RAS connections for access to the Terminal Server only. From a Terminal Server session she can still access hosts on the network, but she will have to log on to the Terminal Server first. This makes your Terminal Server the first line of security.

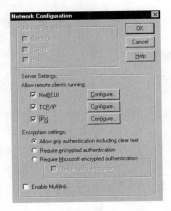

Figure 14.1 Network Configuration window.

Configuring IPX/SPX

To configure the IPX/SPX protocol, click the Configure button next to IPX/SPX in the Network Configuration window. The RAS Server IPX Configuration window, shown in Figure 14.2, appears.

With IPX/SPX, every node on the network has a network address and a node address. When a remote user dials in, he must have a network address and node address before he can access any IPX/SPX network resource. RAS, by default automatically assigns the remote user an open network address and node address. In some situations, such as if you have a NetWare network with several remote IPX/SPX networks, you need to be careful that the network number Terminal Server assigns does not conflict with any other IPX/SPX networks. In cases like this, you have the option of specifying which network number is used for your remote clients by selecting Allocate Network Numbers in the RAS Server IPX configuration window and filling in a range. If you want all of your remote clients on separate networks, you must uncheck the Assign the Same Network Number to All IPX Clients box.

Configuring TCP/IP

To configure TCP/IP options, click the Configure button next to TCP/IP in the Network Configuration window. The RAS Server TCP/IP window, shown in Figure 14.3, appears.

With TCP/IP, addresses are assigned to dial-in clients in one of three ways: through DHCP, through an address range, or manual assignment. By default DHCP is used, which of course requires a DHCP server on the network. If you do not have a DHCP server, your clients do not receive any IP address when they log on. Although they do not have IP addresses, your clients can still access the Terminal Server using IP because the server knows which connection the client is coming in from.

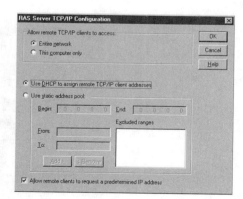

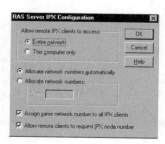

Figure 14.2   RAS Server IPX Configuration window.

Figure 14.3   TCP/IP Configuration window.

For better control of IP addresses, you can assign an address range by selecting the Use Static Address Pool option button and assigning a range.

Your clients can also manually assign their own IP addresses in their Dial-Up Networking window. Because this option puts the control of the IP addresses in the hands of the clients, this could easily cause you security problems. Suppose a client accidentally uses an IP address that conflicts with one of your mission critical servers; this mishap could cause communication problems with that server. In general, it is best to uncheck the Allow Remote clients to Request a Predetermined IP Address box and to assign addresses solely through DHCP or an address range.

Configuring NetBEUI

When you click on the Configure button next to NetBEUI in the Network Configuration window, a dialog box appears with only two options: Allow Remote NetBEUI Clients to Access Entire Network or Allow Access to This Computer Only. Again, for the best security select Allow Access to This Computer Only and click OK.

Administering RAS

The main tool for administering your RAS server is the Remote Access Admin tool. Located under the Administrative Tools group, this tool allows you to perform the following tasks:

- Start, stop, and pause the RAS service
- Set dial-in and callback options for users
- View port statistics
- View current users and send messages

In the following sections you learn about each of these capabilities in detail.

Starting and Stopping the RAS Service

By default, the RAS service is set to automatically start when you start up your server. If you want RAS enabled only for occasional remote access use, you can set the service to manually start by going into Control Panel and selecting Services. Highlight Remote Access Service and select the Startup button. Change the Startup type to Manual. The next time you reboot your server you must start the Remote Access Service manually. The Remote Access Service can be started, stopped, and paused using the Remote Access Admin Tool. These options are all under the Server menu on the main window.

Setting Dial-In Permissions and Callback Options

By default, no user has dial-in permission. Dial-in permission can be granted in one of two places: either in the Remote Access Admin tool or in User Manager. In the Remote Access Admin tool, select Permissions from the Users menu. In the Remote

Access Permissions window that appears (see Figure 14.4), you can enable dial-in access for anyone in the domain. For instructions on how to set remote access permissions using User Manager see Chapter 7, "Creating Users and Groups in Terminal Server," in which User Manager is covered in detail.

Another important RAS feature is callback, which is good for both security and for lowering the telephone bills of users who have to dial in remotely from long distance sites. You will find the callback settings in the Remote Access Permissions window along with the ability to grant dial-in access. There are two types of callback options:

- *Set by Caller*   If you set the callback options to Set by Caller, when users dial in they receive a dialog box asking for their callback number. After they enter the number, the server hangs up the connection and call the user back. Meanwhile, the RAS client on the user goes into auto-answer mode in order to receive the incoming call from the server.

- *Preset*   By defining a preset number, the RAS server automatically breaks the connection when the user first attaches and then calls back the preset number. This offers the highest level of security, but allows the user to call in from a single location only.

Checking Port Status

You can get a lot of good information about the connection by selecting Communications Ports from the Server menu, highlighting the port of interest and clicking Port Status. The error counters in the Port Status window that appears, as shown in Figure 14.5, can be useful for determining the connection quality. In addition, the compression status and bytes counters can be useful for quick performance or bandwidth usage checks.

Figure 14.4   Remote Access Permissions window.

Figure 14.5   Port Status window.

Viewing Current Users and Sending Messages

To view the users that are currently on the server, select Active Users from the Users menu. In the Remote Access Users window that appears, as shown in Figure 14.6, you will see a list of all active users along with the time that they connected to the system. From this window, you can also send messages to individual users. Note that this feature does not work for all types of clients; you are better off using the Send Message feature in the Terminal Server Administration tool.

Troubleshooting RAS Connections

RAS has been around for a long time and has become increasingly reliable over the years. The most difficult part of setting up RAS is the initial installation—after RAS is set up and working, you can count on long and reliable service. If you are having problems setting up RAS, perform the following checks:

- *Make sure RAS dial-in permission is enabled*   This permission is commonly overlooked because it is disabled by default for all users. Users normally get an error message saying that they do not have dial-in permission. Simply enable the permission in either User Manager or Remote Access Admin.

- *Try another modem type such as one of the Standard types*   Sometimes you find yourself in a situation in which RAS fails during connection with no plausible cause. You might want to try another modem type or a slower-speed modem to see if you can connect it.

- *Try to access the modem with Hyperterminal*   One good test to ensure your modem is communicating properly is to attach to it with Hyperterminal. First, you must stop the RAS service by going into the Remote Access Admin tool and selecting Stop Remote Access Service from the Server menu. Next bring up Hyperterminal, create a test connection, and attach to the COM port of your modem. Click Cancel when it tries to dial so that you can get to the communications window. Type **AT** and press Return: This is the standard Hayes Attention command. With most modems, you should see your characters echoed back from the modem and the modem should respond OK. If you have an external modem you can also watch the send and receive data lights. They should blink rapidly as you type characters to the modem. If none of these are the case, double-check that your COM port settings are correct and the modem is cabled properly. Until you can get to the point where you can communicate with your modem, RAS will not work at all.

- *Make sure DTR is held high (on) and the modem is in Autoanswer mode*   With most modems you need DTR held high and the modem to be in Autoanswer mode before it will answer the line. If you have a situation in which you dial but the modem never answers, check to ensure that this is the case. You also might try a different modem type. For more information on how to set DTR high and put your modem in Autoanswer mode, refer to your modem manufacturer.

Figure 14.6   Remote Access Users window.

In addition to these basic troubleshooting steps, there are a few lesser-known ways to troubleshoot RAS. The first is using the RAS `device.log` file, which when enabled keeps track of communications between the server and the modems. You can review this file to see if there are any problems in the modem initialization strings. To enable logging to the `device.log` file you need to set the following Registry entry to one (1):

```
HKEY_LOCAL_MACHINE\SYSTEM\CurrentControlSet\Services\RASMan
➥\Parameters\Logging
```

If the `Logging` value does not exist, you must add it (select Edit | Add Value in the REGEDT32). It is type `REG_WORD` and String Value 1. After the `Logging` value has been added, stop and restart the RAS service by using the Remote Access Admin Tool.

The second troubleshooting method is using the `ppp.log` file. This file keeps track of the PPP negotiation commands that occur during the establishment of a connection into RAS. To enable PPP logging, set the following Registry entry to one (1).

```
HKEY_LOCAL_MACHINE\SYSTEM\CurrentControlSet\Services\RASMan\PPP\Logging
```

As with the `device.log` Registry entry, if the `Logging` value does not exist you need to add it. After you stop and restart the RAS service, the log should be enabled.

The final troubleshooting tip is to use the `IPCONFIG /ALL` command. `IPCONFIG` is useful in situations in which the connection has been established but you are still having problems accessing IP resources on the network. With `IPCONFIG`, you can see all of the IP parameters that have been assigned to the incoming RAS connection. By default, a Dial-Up Networking connection into RAS will take many of the server's parameters for itself, such as default gateway and primary and secondary DNS and WINS entries. If you need your remote users to be able to use DNS or WINS, or to get out of the network through a gateway, make sure all of these parameters are set in the Network Control Panel on your server. After the parameters have been set, double-check that the dial-in clients are receiving these parameters by using the `IPCONFIG` command. You can manually specify the DNS and WINS entries in Dial-Up Networking configuration if necessary.

Dialing In to a Terminal Server with RAS Using Windows 95

Both Windows 95 and Windows NT 4.0 use Dial-Up Networking to establish a PPP connection with RAS. The procedure to set up a Dial-Up Networking connection varies between the two but the general idea is the same. After the connection is established, the Windows 95 or NT 4.0 client can use NetBEUI, IPX/SPX, or TCP/IP to communicate with the remote Terminal Server. Both the Terminal Server client and Citrix's ICA client can communicate with the remote Terminal Server across the established RAS connection.

Setting up a Dial-Up Networking connection with Windows 95 is relatively easy:

1. Open the Dial-Up Networking Control Panel by going to Accessories and selecting Dial-Up Networking. If Dial-Up Networking has not been installed, add it by selecting Add/Remove Programs | Windows Setup from Control Panel Dial-Up Networking under the Communications component.

2. In the Dial-Up Networking window, select Make New Connection. When the Make New Connection window appears, define the name of the new connection and select the modem you wish to use. Click Next.

3. In the telephone setup screen, enter the telephone number and area code for the Terminal Server. Click Next one more time, verify the information, and click Finish to create the Dial-Up Networking entry.

Although Dial-Up Networking has several parameters you can change, the default parameters are really all that you need to connect to a RAS server. The IP address, default gateway, DNS servers, and WINS entries are all automatically assigned by the RAS server after you are connected.

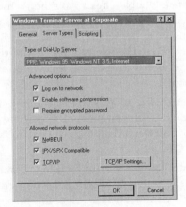

Figure 14.7   Server Types tab.

Before establishing the call, right-click on the connection entry in the Dial-Up Networking window and select Properties. In the Properties window for the connection, select the Server Types tab. Under this tab, ensure that only the protocols you need to communicate with the Terminal Server are selected. Also, make sure that the Server Type selected is PPP, as shown in Figure 14.7. RAS uses PPP for communication. If you will be using TCP/IP and you want to manually assign your IP address, or DNS or WINS entries you can click the TCP/IP Settings button in this window. You are taken to a window where you have the option to manually enter these parameters. By default, the system is set to learn the parameters from the RAS server.

To establish the connection, double-click on the new Dial-Up Networking entry. Enter your username and password for the Terminal Server domain and click Connect. After the connection has been established, you can start either the Citrix ICA or the Terminal Server client to attach to your server.

Dialing In to RAS Using Windows NT 4.0

The procedure for setting up a Dial-Up Networking connection with Windows NT 4.0 is similar to setting up one under Windows 95. The main difference is that Dial-Up Networking is installed as part of RAS on the Windows NT workstation. For the initial part of the installation, follow the instructions earlier in this section; the steps used for setting up RAS on the server are the same as on the workstation.

Be careful, however, when you are adding modems in the Remote Access Setup window; make sure to enable them for dial-out access by selecting either Dial Out Only or Dial Out and Receive Calls under Port Usage. If you already have RAS installed on your workstation, you can get to this window by selecting Network | Services from Control Panel. Double-clicking on the Remote Access Service brings up the Remote Access Setup window. Double-clicking on the modem you want to check brings up its port usage window.

After RAS has been set up on the workstation, reboot the workstation and make sure the Remote Access Service is started. The following instructions guide you through the rest of the setup:

1. In Accessories, select Dial-Up Networking. You first need to create a new phonebook entry. Because the phonebook is currently empty, it should prompt you to create a new entry and then take you to the New Phonebook Entry Wizard window.

2. You can either go through the wizard by using default options and entering the phone number for the server, or select the I Know All About Phonebook Entries button. It is recommended to select this button because there are a few options that need to be double-checked that cannot be set through the wizard. If you select the I Know All About Phonebook Entries button, the New Phonebook Entry window appears.

3. Click the Basic tab in the New Phonebook Entry window, and enter the Entry name and Phone number. Also, ensure that the Dial Using parameter is set for the modem that you want to use.

4. Select the Server tab and ensure that the Dial-up server type is set to PPP. Also, ensure that only the protocols you need for this connection are enabled. If you will be using TCP/IP, you may want to review the options by clicking the TCP/IP Settings button. In general, it is best to leave the options at their defaults. By default, all of your TCP/IP settings for the client are determined by the RAS server you dial in to.

Just as with Windows 95 Dial-Up Networking, you must establish the connection first. To establish the connection, go into Dial-Up Networking, select the phonebook entry you just created and then select Dial. You are prompted for your username, password, and domain. After these items have been entered, the workstation attempts to dial the Terminal Server, establish a connection, and log on to the server. After the connection has been established, you can run either the Terminal Server or Citrix ICA clients across the RAS connection.

Dialing In to RAS Using Windows for Workgroups (MetaFrame Only)

MetaFrame

One of the last options for accessing Terminal Server remotely by using RAS is with Windows for Workgroups. Windows for Workgroups has a built-in RAS client that is very easy to set up and use. The one limitation of the client is that you can only use NetBEUI to communicate with the Terminal Server. This setup, consequently, works only with MetaFrame using NetBIOS over NetBEUI because Terminal Server works with TCP/IP only.

Because NetBEUI is a simple and thus very efficient protocol, it is an excellent choice for accessing Terminal Server remotely. By using NetBEUI strictly for accessing the Terminal Server, you can leverage the more sophisticated network capabilities of the Terminal Server from the simplest of clients, Windows for Workgroups. Windows for Workgroups supports machines with as little as a 386 with 4MB. From a 386 with 4MB you can run, using NetBEUI across RAS, any 32-bit application which runs on Terminal Server.

The following instructions guide you through connecting to RAS running on Terminal Server from a Windows for Workgroups client:

1. In the Networks program group select Remote Access. The first time you select this, you are taken into the RAS setup. After you select to install RAS services, several files are copied to your PC. Because RAS relies on Windows for Workgroups networking services, these are installed first.

2. After the appropriate files are installed, the Remote Access Configuration window appears (see Figure 14.8). In this window, you can select the modem and

the COM port it is attached to. The modem list is the original list that came with Windows for Workgroups. Because of this, there is a good chance that your modern modem will not appear on the list. In this situation, you have two options. The first is to select a modem that is close to your modem model. The Hayes-compatible modems work well for this. The second is to modify the `modem.inf` file.

The `modem.inf` file is located under the `C:\WINDOWS\SYSTEM` directory. The modems in this file are what make up the list of modems you can select from in the RAS Configuration window. Following, you see the section for the Hayes Compatible 9600 modem. Before you modify the `modem.inf` file with the settings for your particular modem, make a backup copy of the modem.inf file. The main items you need to change are the `maxcarrierbps`, `maxconnectbps` and `command_init`. The recommended initialization string for your modem can normally be found in the modem's instruction manual. Otherwise, the following Hayes Compatible string will work for most modems:

```
[Hayes Compatible 9600]
<speaker_on>=M1
<speaker_off>=M0
<autodial_on>=ATDT
<autodial_off>=ATX3D
CALLBACKTIME=10
DEFAULTOFF=compression
MAXCARRIERBPS=9600
MAXCONNECTBPS=9600

COMMAND_INIT=AT&F&C1&D2 V1 S0=0 S2=128 S7=55<speaker><cr>
COMMAND_DIAL=<autodial><phonenumber><cr>
COMMAND_LISTEN=ATS0=1<cr>
```

3. After you select your modem, you are prompted to reboot your machine for the RAS settings to take effect.

Figure 14.8   Remote Access configuration.

4. After rebooting, go back into Network and select Remote Access. Because the phonebook is empty you are prompted to create a new one. Enter the connection name and phone number. After you finish, the Remote Access window appears. The setup is now complete.

To establish a connection with Terminal Server, simply go to the RAS phonebook entry window, select the entry for the server and select Dial. You will then need to enter the username and password for the Terminal Server domain. Windows for Workgroups dials the server, establishes the connection, and logs on. After the connection has been established, you can run Citrix's ICA client across the RAS connection. Be sure to configure it for NetBIOS (which is actually NetBIOS over NetBEUI).

Dial-In ICA Connections

Dial-in ICA connections, also referred to as ICA asynchronous or dial-in remote control connections, are the most efficient means for remotely accessing your MetaFrame server. Although you can remotely access your server by using RAS, dial-in ICA has less overhead.

The steps to setting up a dial-in ICA connection are very similar to those of setting up a network connection. First, you create the connection at the server to receive the call. Dial-in ICA uses a special type of connection type called *async*. Next, you create a dial-in connection entry on the remote workstation's ICA client and dial in.

The following sections cover the steps for setting up dial-in access at the server and client in more detail. These sections also go over how to troubleshoot problems establishing dial-in connections.

Setting Up Dial-In ICA Access at the MetaFrame Server

The steps for setting up dial-in access are simple:

1. In the Administrative Tools folder (Start | Programs), select the Terminal Server Connection Configuration tool. Create a new connection by selecting New from the Connection menu in the Terminal Server Connection Configuration main window.

2. From the New Connection window that appears, select transport type async. Select the modem you will be assigning the connection to from the Device list box. You can install a new modem, if it is not in the list, by clicking the Install Modem button.

3. Enter the Name for the connection and click OK to create it.

There are several other options you can set on a connection level by clicking the Client Settings, Advanced, and ICA Settings buttons in the New Connection window. These are covered in more detail in Chapter 9, "Installing Clients." Remember that these settings apply for the current modem connection only. Any user who dials in to this modem is affected by the options. In situations in which you have only one modem, changing these settings on a connection level makes sense. In general, it is better to control these settings at a user level using User Manager because the settings will apply no matter what modem the user dials in with.

Connecting the ICA 32-bit Client to MetaFrame

For a Windows 95 or Windows NT workstation to dial in to a MetaFrame server, you must first install the ICA 32-bit client. This client has the ability to establish several different types of connections to MetaFrame servers. Chapter 9 covers how to set up the ICA 32-bit client to connect to a MetaFrame server across a network. This section covers how to connect across an asynchronous phone line.

The steps to set up a dial-in connection are very similar to the steps for setting up a network connection:

1. Install the ICA 32-bit client software. You can create the ICA client disks by using the ICA Client Creator tool (select ICA Client Creator from MetaFrame Tools).

2. After you have created the ICA client disks, install the client by running SETUP.EXE off the first disk. Other than the client name, which needs to be unique, there are very few choices you have to make during the installation.

3. After the client is installed, run the ICA Remote Application Manager. When you first run the program, it asks whether you want to create a new connection. If you already have the client software installed, you can create a new connection by pressing Ins or by selecting New from the Entry menu.

4. Choose Dial-in Connection for the connection, type Choice, and click Next.

5. Enter the connection description and click Next. The modem list is generated from the modems that are installed in your system. If you have not installed your modem yet, you need to select Modems from Control Panel and install it before you can continue setting up the dial-in connection.

Real-World Tip: Restricting Remote Access

Because of the high security risk with providing remote access, remote access must be closely controlled. One of the simplest ways to control remote access is by setting permissions in the Terminal Server Connection Configuration tool. To set permissions, from the Terminal Server Connection Configuration Tool main window, highlight the modem connection for which you want to modify permissions and select Permissions from the Security window. From the Connection Permissions window that appears, you can control which groups and users have access to this connection.

6. Enter the phone number for your Terminal Server and click Next.

7. Following the phone number screen, you have the choice of several more options, which are covered in Chapter 9. Unless you need to change the screen size, set up automated logon, change compression and bitmap settings, or set up an application to be run with this connection, you can keep the defaults and skip past these screens. By default, compression and bitmap caching are enabled on a dial-in connection. This ensures the most efficient use of the limited bandwidth of the dial-up line.

After you create your new connection, it shows up in the list of connections in the Remote Application Manager window. Double-clicking on the connection starts the process for establishing it.

Connecting the ICA 16-bit Client to MetaFrame

You will find that both the modem setup and the connection setup with the ICA 16-bit client are surprisingly similar to the setup under either Windows 95 or Windows NT. This is a definite plus, especially for WinFrame administrators who may be used to adding new modems by manually editing configuration files. Not only are the setups similar, but you can even use the UNIMODEM driver files with the 16-bit client. The UNIMODEM files are the ones that are included with most new modems for Windows 95 and Windows NT.

The following steps guide you through setting up a remote connection using the ICA 16-bit client:

1. Create the client disks by using the ICA Client Creator tools (select ICA Client Creator from MetaFrame Tools).

2. Run SETUP.EXE from the first disk to start the install of the client. There are few choices during the install of the client. The install creates a Citrix ICA Client program group in Program Manager with icons for the client.

3. To start the client and set up the connection, run the Remote Applications Manager from the Citrix ICA Client group.

4. Select New from the Entry menu to create a new connection.

5. Select Dial-in Connection. If there are no modems set up, the Modem Setup Wizard automatically appears. If this screen does not appear but you need to add another modem, you can add it from the main client window by selecting Modems | Add from the Options menu.

6. From here, you have the choice of either having the client software automatically detect your modem or manually choosing it from a list. If your modem was not detected or if you do not see your modem in the list, try one of the Standard modems that match the baud rate. These general-purpose modem drivers work with most modems on the market.

7. After installing your modem and clicking Next, you are taken to a screen in which you must enter a unique description for the connection and select the modem you want from the list. When you're finished, click Next.

8. When the screen for entering the phone number of the MetaFrame server appears, enter the phone number and click Next.

The rest of the screens are the same as if you were setting up a network connection. You have choices for screen resolution, application launching, autologon, compression, and bitmap caching. Using the defaults works fine for most cases.

To begin the connection, double-click on the New Connection entry in the Remote Application Manager window.

Connecting the ICA DOS Client to MetaFrame

The final client type is DOS. The ICA client for DOS makes remote connection to Terminal Server very easy. Because even the DOS client supports UNIMODEM modem configuration files, you can use modem drivers that are meant for Windows 95.

1. Select ICA Client Creator from MetaFrame Tools to create the client disks by using the ICA Client Creator.

2. From Disk 1, run INSTALL.EXE. This creates a WFCLIENT directory on the C: drive that contains the ICA DOS client files.

3. Run WFCLIENT.EXE from this directory to start the DOS-based Remote Application Manager.

4. To configure a new dial-in entry, select New from the Entry menu in the main screen of the ICA DOS client.

5. Enter the description for the connection and then select Standard COM port for the Transport type. If your modem has not been added, click the down arrow at the Device prompt and select New Device. The Add Device screen appears.

6. In the Add Device screen, select the COM port, baud rate, and modem. You have the option of allowing the client to try to auto-detect your modem by selecting Detect. You can also add the modem to the modem list if you have the UNIMODEM driver disk by selecting Import. Remember that the UNIMODEM drivers are the Windows 95 modem drivers that you can obtain from the manufacturer.

7. After you have added your modem, the Entry Properties screen reappears. Fill in just the phone number and you are finished. There are several other choices that can be made, but the defaults work best for most situations.

After the connection is installed, it is added to the client connection list. To dial the MetaFrame server and establish the connection, simply highlight the connection and press Return.

15

Terminal Server and NetWare

F OR ALL THE ADMINISTRATORS OUT THERE trying to integrate Terminal Server into existing NetWare networks, this chapter is for you. Terminal Server works very well with NetWare networks and has specific features and tools that are designed to make the integration with NetWare as easy and seamless as possible.

This chapter begins with a discussion of both the differences and similarities between NT Server and Terminal Server, in terms of NetWare integration. For those who are already used to integrating NT with NetWare, there are some possible limitations with Terminal Server that you need to be aware of. Next, you'll learn how to install and use the basic Microsoft service required for NetWare connectivity: Gateway Services for NetWare (GSNW). Those already familiar with this service on NT may want to skip ahead to the final section, "Advanced NetWare Integration," which provides several different tips and techniques to help you successfully integrate your Terminal Server with NetWare.

NetWare and NT Versus NetWare and TS

Integrating Terminal Server into a NetWare network is much like integrating an NT 4.0 workstation into the same network. Here are two things you need to do:

- Install and configure Gateway Services for NetWare (GSNW). GSNW supports both bindery and NetWare Directory Services (NDS) logins.

- Keep your Terminal Server usernames and passwords synchronized with NetWare. If not, users will have to log on twice, once to Terminal Server and once to NetWare.

Although some differences exist between TS and NT, which we'll cover next, the basics have remained the same.

Novell's Client for IntranetWare

As of this writing, the major difference between Terminal Server and NT 4.0, in terms of NetWare access, is the lack of support for Novell's IntranetWare client for NT. Although you can still attach to NetWare using the Microsoft client for NetWare (included in the GSNW), you can't make use of the advantages provided by Novell's client, such as full support for the NDS API. Novell has promised to fix this limitation in the NetWare 5 (Moab) release of the IntranetWare client for NT. This client is due out sometime in the fall of 1998.

For most users, the limitations will be negligible. You'll still be able to access NetWare volumes and printers just as you would normally under NT. However, for administrators who want to be able to run NetWare utilities such as the NetWare Administrator, use NDS directory maps, run the NT Workstation Manager, or make use of any other utility that relies on the NDS API, the Microsoft client for NetWare will not work. In this chapter, you'll learn the best techniques for resolving these types of problems.

The main reason why Novell's client will not work with TS is that Novell's client changes the GINA or login program used by Terminal Server. Although this is a normal and accepted practice with standard Windows NT, the GINA in Terminal Server has special functionality in order to support a multiuser environment. If the GINA is replaced with Novell's GINA, this functionality is lost and Terminal Server will not work correctly. Although version 4.11 of Novell's client for NT will "autosense" the presence of both Terminal Server and WinFrame and will not replace the GINA, this is not a full solution. Because of the necessity of the Novell GINA for many of the client's features, Novell will not provide support for the client without the correct GINA.

> ### Author's Note: Support for NetWare-Related Issues
> An important thing to note is how support works for NetWare-related issues with Terminal Server. Those who have worked with Citrix WinFrame will recall that if you had a problem integrating it with a NetWare server, you would usually call Citrix for support. However, with Terminal Server, any problem related to a core function of the Terminal Server operating system, such as support for NetWare, is handled through Microsoft. The Citrix MetaFrame add-on does not add any NetWare-specific enhancements to Terminal Server; therefore, Citrix is not responsible for NetWare-related connectivity problems. Although this policy is subject to change, currently you should call either Microsoft or Novell for problems involving the integration of Terminal Server into a NetWare environment.

Similarities and Additional Features

NT Server 4.0 and Terminal Server have many more similarities than differences when it comes to integrating them with NetWare. The following are some of the many similarities:

- *Login script processing*   Both NT and TS fully support NetWare login script processing, including container, profile, and user login scripts.

- *Drive mappings and printers*   With NT and TS you can connect any drive letter to any directory on a Novell volume through both the Explorer and MAP commands in the Novell login script. Novell print queues can also be set up using the Printer control panel and can be captured from DOS.

- *Passthrough authentication*   Users are automatically logged on to their preferred server or tree in the background after they log on to the NT domain. The logon name and password entered at the logon screen will be used for authentication to both the NT domain and NetWare.

- *NetWare migration*   A migration utility comes with both NT and Terminal Server that allows you to migrate your NetWare users and groups into the user database, as well as your NetWare volumes into shares.

- *Password changes*   You can still change your password from the Windows NT Security window, across all the servers you're logged on to, including NetWare servers and the tree.

- *Compatibility with Novell's NDS for NT (member server only)*   As long as your Terminal Server is a member server and not a PDC or BDC, you can use it in a domain that has been incorporated into NDS using NDS for NT.

In addition, the following new features have been added to Terminal Server to make NetWare integration even easier:

- *NetWare validation*   By default, Terminal Server will validate your password first, and then you'll be validated against your NetWare preferred server or tree. With this option, you'll be validated against NetWare first and then against Terminal Server. If your Terminal Server password does not match, it will automatically be changed. This feature is good for environments where NetWare passwords are frequently changed.

- *Map root of the home directory*   You can map-root a drive to the user's home directory on the NetWare server, just as you normally would with NetWare.

These additional features and more are to be covered in the "Advanced NetWare Integration" section in this chapter. For now, we'll cover how the Gateway Service for NetWare is installed under Terminal Server.

Installing and Using GSNW

The first step to integrating Terminal Server into a NetWare network is installing the Gateway Services for NetWare (GSNW). The name is somewhat deceptive. Besides providing gateway services to NetWare servers, this service also installs Microsoft's Client for NetWare. This client is what you need to attach to both bindery and NDS-based NetWare servers. This section covers the basics of how to install and use GSNW.

Installing GSNW

GSNW installs just like any other service on Terminal Server. The following is a quick coverage of the steps you need to follow:

1. Open the Network Control Panel (Control Panel | Network) and select the Services tab.

2. Click the Add button on the Services tab to add a new service.

3. In the Select Network Service window, highlight Gateway (and Client) Services for NetWare and click OK.

4. Enter the path to your Terminal Server CD-ROM's install directory in the Windows NT Setup window (normally D:\i386).

5. After the file install has finished, click Yes to shut down and restart.

   The server will now reboot. When it comes back up, the Gateway Service for NetWare will be started.

6. At the logon window, log on as the user for whom you need to set up NetWare access.

   The first time you log on after GSNW has been installed, you'll be presented with a window that requests your preferred server or preferred tree. It also asks whether you want to run your NetWare logon scripts.

7. (Preferred Server) If you're going to be logging on to a NetWare 3.12 server or an NDS server in bindery context, select the server from the drop-down list under Preferred Server.

8. (Default Tree and Context) If you're going to be logging on to a NetWare tree, select the Default Tree and Context radio button and enter your tree and context.

   Although typeful naming is supported for the context, it is generally easier to use typeless naming instead (in other words, acct.acme.corp).

9. Select the check box next to Run Login Script if you want Terminal Server to process your bindery or NDS login scripts when you first log on.

10. Click OK to accept your settings and continue.

At this point, Terminal Server will attempt to log on to the NetWare server or tree you specified using the username and password you initially logged on with. The service is now installed and ready to use.

Setting Preferred Server or Default Tree

One important feature of the client is that it keeps track of NetWare settings separately for each user. In this way, two different users can log on to Terminal Server, each with a different preferred server or tree.

The disadvantage of this feature is that each user will be prompted for the preferred server or default tree that he or she wishes to attach to the first time he or she logs on to Terminal Server. For users who are not NetWare aware, this prompt will be confusing. If you have a small number of users, you may choose to simply reset their passwords, log on to the server as each user, and set their NetWare parameters manually. Once these parameters have been set, the users will not be prompted for them again. If you opt instead to have users enter the information based on written or verbal instructions, you can double-check that the parameters they enter are correct by running the Registry Editor (REGEDT32) and viewing the following Registry key:

```
HKLM\System\CurrentControlSet\Services\NWCWorkstation\
➤Parameters\Option\[User SID]
```

A SID entry under the Option key will be created as each user logs on and sets the NetWare parameters for the first time. Under the User SID key will be values for `PreferredServer`, `LogonScript`, and `PrintOption`. Out of these values, the `PreferredServer` value is of most interest. If the user chose a preferred server, this value will be set to its name. If instead the user chose a default tree and context, `PreferredServer` will be set to `*[Tree Name]\[Context]`. Notice the preceding asterisk. This differentiates it from a preferred server.

This Registry key can also be handy to know if you need to change your server's name or a tree or container name in the future.

Real-World Tip: The NDSPSVR Utility

Even if users set their preferred trees and contexts to the correct ones, the question of which server they will be authenticating into NDS with still remains. It's important to know this information, because this server is the one on which a NetWare connection license will be used. Microsoft has provided the NDSPSVR utility to handle this need. To set the preferred server for an NDS logon, type the following at the command prompt:

```
NDSPSVR /ENABLE:[Preferred server name]
```

Note that this is a global setting and will affect all users who log on.

Using GSNW

Installing the GSNW is the easy part; using it correctly can be a little more challenging. The following subsections cover how to configure and use the many different features that are a part of the Gateway Services for NetWare.

Changing GSNW Options

When you install GSNW, it creates an extra icon labeled GSNW in the Control Panel. When you click this icon, the Gateway Service for NetWare window shown in Figure 15.1 appears. From here, you change the preferred server as well as the default tree and logon script execution options you set previously. You can also find additional options for printers and the gateway service.

Printer Options

The printer options and their explanations are as follows:

- *Form Feed*   By turning on the Form Feed option, an extra form feed will be appended to the end of every print job.
- *Notify When Printed*   When this option is on, a message window will pop up to notify you when a job has finished printing.
- *Print Banner*   This option places a separator page at the start of every print job.

Gateway Services

When you click the Gateway button in the Gateway Service for NetWare window shown in Figure 15.1, you'll be taken to the configuration screen. The gateway service allows you to make a NetWare server's files and printers look like NT shares and NT printers to remote Microsoft clients. For example, you can have your NetWare SYS volume appear as a SYS share under your Terminal Server.

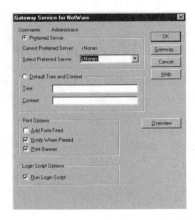

Figure 15.1 Gateway Service for NetWare.

If you find that this functionality is needed on your network, you should use another NT server as your gateway to NetWare instead of Terminal Server. The extra processing overhead caused by the gateway translations can slow your Terminal Server down. It's usually more efficient to simply access the NetWare servers directly using Microsoft's client for NetWare, which is a part of the GSNW.

Mapping Drives to NetWare Servers

Once you've authenticated with the NetWare server or tree, you can map drives in the same manner as you would with NT servers and shares. NetWare servers are looked at by Terminal Server as servers with volumes, as opposed to NT servers, which are viewed as servers with shares. There are three primary methods for mapping drive letters to NetWare: manual mappings using Explorer, mappings through the NetWare login script using the MAP command, and mappings using the built-in NET USE command.

Mapping NetWare Drives Using Explorer

Mapping NetWare drives using Explorer is similar to mapping drives to NT shares, with one important difference: You can map-root a network drive to any directory in a NetWare volume, whereas with NT shares you can map-root a drive only to the root of the share itself. Map-rooting a drive makes it much easier to hide the complexities of the directory structure from the user. To map-root a drive letter to a directory on a NetWare volume, simply follow these steps:

1. Run Explorer (go to the Start menu and choose Programs | Windows NT Explorer).

2. Click the NetWare server you want to map to in Network Neighborhood; then go to the volume and directory you want.

3. Right-click and select Map Network Drive.

4. Select the drive letter you want to map-root to the selected directory and check whether you want to have the drive automatically reconnected at logon.

Mapping Drives Through the NetWare Logon Script

One advantage of mapping drives through the NetWare logon script is that you can create both search drives and standard mappings. To map a search drive to a server, add the following line to your NetWare login script:

```
MAP INSERT S1:=[Server]/[Volume]:\[Directory]
```

This drive will automatically be added to your search path and be available from the command prompt.

This may be self-explanatory for most NetWare administrators, but what you may not realize is that you can also easily incorporate mappings to NT servers and shares in your NetWare logon script using the following syntax:

```
#NET USE [Drive letter]: \\[NT server name]\[Share name]
```

The leading pound sign (#) means to treat this as an external command.

By incorporating both the MAP ROOT and NET USE statements into your NetWare logon script, you can fully control all your drive mappings from one central location.

Mapping Drives Through the NET USE Command

The syntax for the NET USE command for mapping drives to NetWare volumes is as follows:

```
NET USE [Drive letter]: \\[NetWare server name]\[Volume name]\[Directory]
```

Remember that the NET USE command will map-root the drive letter to that directory.

Printing to NetWare Printers

By adding the GSNW, you also give users the ability to print to NetWare printers. Although adding a printer to the desktop is the same with Terminal Server as it is with NT, remember that whatever printers you add at the server will be global in nature. In other words, adding a printer for a user will make that printer available in everyone's printer list.

Adding a NetWare Printer Using the Printer Control Panel

Using the Printer Control Panel is the standard method for adding a printer under NT. Here's how:

1. Go to Start menu and choose Settings | Printers.

2. Select Add Printer from the Printer window.

3. From the Add Printer Wizard, select the Network Print Server radio button and click Next.

4. In the Connect to Printer window, expand the NetWare or compatible network by double-clicking it.

5. Expand the NetWare server that has the print queue you want to print to by double-clicking it and then double-click the queue name. You can also find the queue under the tree for NDS users.

6. You'll receive a message warning that the queue does not have printer drivers associated with it; click OK.

7. Select the manufacturer and model of your printer from the list in the Add Printer Wizard printer selection window and click OK.

The printer drivers will now be installed, and the printer will be added to the printer window. Users with appropriate permissions should now be able to print to this printer.

NetWare Printers and MetaFrame (MetaFrame Only)

MetaFrame

MetaFrame allows you to automatically incorporate your clients' current printers, including NetWare printers, into their Terminal Server desktop as they log on. This gives you better control of the printers, because you can control them at the client instead of having to add everyone's printer to the server. If your clients log onto the MetaFrame server and they have the Connect Client Printers at Logon option set, the NetWare printers that they currently have on their desktops will automatically become part of their MetaFrame desktops. The printers will appear in their printer lists as [client name]#[queue name]. You'll recall from Chapters 6, "Creating the Connections," and 7, "Creating Users and Groups in Terminal Server," that the Connect Client Printers options can be set at either a user level using User Manager or a connection level using the TS Connection Configuration Tool. By default, this option is enabled for all MetaFrame users.

On the other hand, if you have a NetWare printer that is used by a large group of people on your Terminal Server, you may instead want to add it to the server. By adding the printer to the server, print jobs will be sent directly to that printer instead of to the client and then to the printer.

Printing from DOS to NetWare Print Queues

The easiest ways to print to a NetWare printer from a DOS-based program is to either capture a port to the printer in the logon script or use NET USE command. To capture a port in the logon script, add the following command to it:

```
#CAPTURE Q=[Queue name] L=[LPT port number]
```

This is the standard Novell NetWare CAPTURE command. This command will capture all output from the LPT port number you specified to the queue. For more information on the available settings, refer to your NetWare manual. Although the CAPTURE command will work from the logon script, you may have problems running it from the command prompt (see the following Real-World Tip for suggestions).

Here's the second method for capturing your LPT ports to a NetWare print queue using the NET USE command:

> **Real-World Tip: NetWare Utility Behavior Under Terminal Server**
>
> You may notice that several of the NetWare utilities, such as NETADMIN, may not work from the command prompt as expected. Remember that the NetWare API is not fully implemented in the Microsoft GSNW. Until NetWare's client for NT is available and fully working for Terminal Server, you may have to find workarounds to the functionality of some of the tools.
>
> An example of this is the CAPTURE/SHOW command. Normally CAPTURE/SHOW lists which ports have been mapped to which printers. Because of the way in which the NetWare API has been implemented, the CAPTURE/SHOW command under IntranetWare will not list the printers captured as expected. To see which printers you have connected, type NET USE and press Enter instead. Also, if you use the CAPTURE command in any batch files to capture printers, replace the command with the NET USE statement shown in this section.

```
NET USE LPT[n]: \\[NetWare Server Name]\[Queue name]
```

This command will map the queue to the port you specified. As with the NET USE command shown previously, if you wish to add this command to your NetWare logon script, put a pound sign (#) in front of it.

Advanced NetWare Integration

For those administrators who want more advanced integration tips than how to install and use GSNW, this section is for you. This section contains a collection of useful tips on many different aspects of NetWare integration with TS. Read the titles and pick which ones sound the most useful to you. We'll start with one of the most important topics: user and password synchronization.

Synchronizing Users and Passwords

One of your first concerns when integrating NetWare with Terminal Server will be synchronizing users and passwords. You need a user created on your NetWare servers for every user on Terminal Server who needs access to them. As long as the username and password are both the same between NetWare and Terminal Server, logons will be seamless. In other words, your Terminal Server users will be able to log on once at the main logon prompt and be mapped to whatever NetWare and TS resources they need without having to log on again. This section is all about tips and techniques for synchronizing the users and passwords in the first place and keeping them synchronized in the future.

Importing NetWare Users Using NetWare Migration Tool

The NetWare Migration Tool is a great tool for bringing your NetWare users and groups into the NT domain in a hurry. If you have a lot of TS users who need access to NetWare resources, this is one of the best ways to do it:

1. Run the NetWare Migration Tool from the Start menu by selecting Programs|Administrator Tools.

2. In the Migration Tool for NetWare main window, click the Add button.

3. From the Select Servers for Migration window, click the ellipsis (...) next to From NetWare Server; then select the NetWare server you want to migrate the users from and click OK. If you're not currently logged on as an admin or supervisor equivalent, you'll be prompted for a username and password.

4. Click the ellipsis next to To Windows NT Server and select the PDC of the domain you want to migrate the users to and click OK.

5. Click OK to return to the main window.

    The servers you just selected should appear under Servers for Migration in the main window. Keep adding servers by following the preceding steps until all the NetWare servers you want to migrate users and groups from are shown in the Servers for Migration list.

6. Click the File Options button.

7. Unless you intend to also transfer files from NetWare to NT, uncheck the Transfer Files option in the File Options window, shown in Figure 15.2, and click OK.

8. From the main window, click the User Options button.

9. Under the Passwords tab in the User Options window, select how you want the passwords to be handled. You may also want to investigate the other options available under the User Names, Group Names, and Defaults tabs. Once you're finished, click OK.

10. Select Start Migration from the main window.

The users and groups from NetWare will now be migrated into your domain database. Once the migration is complete, you'll be shown the error logs so that you can check for any problems, such as duplicate user or group names. After a successful migration, when you go into User Manager you'll now see all your NetWare groups and users.

When users log on for the first time, they'll be prompted to change their passwords. Instruct users to make their passwords the same as their NetWare passwords. In this way, the passwords will now be the same between NetWare and Terminal Server, meaning that future logons will be seamless.

Real-World Tip: File Transfer Options

Although transferring users and groups is the priority here, take note of the file transfer options shown in Figure 15.2. These options can be very useful for copying large amounts of files and directories from NetWare to NT. Note how the tool is automatically set up to transfer your NetWare volumes to directories on NT. The directory names will be set to the volume names by default. The tool also creates shares of the same name on the NT server.

By clicking the Modify button, you'll be taken to a window where you can check which directories you do and do not want to copy across. Even if your intention is not to bring an entire volume into NT, this tool can be very useful in the future for bringing over one or more large directories.

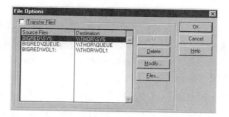

Figure 15.2 File Options window.

Bindery Context and the NetWare Migration Tool

You may be thinking that this will work great for bringing NetWare 3.12 users into NT, but how will it handle users who are part of an NDS tree? The answer is through *bindery context*. Bindery context is an IntranetWare server console setting that controls how your IntranetWare server's users and groups will be viewed by bindery-based applications and clients, such as the NetWare Migration Tool. By setting bindery context, you can migrate as many users and groups from as many containers as you wish into NT.

Bindery context is set by typing the following command in at the server console. Because this command will directly affect your bindery user's ability to log on, you should only run this command after hours, preferably from a server in the tree that's not often logged onto. Here's the syntax for the command:

```
SET BINDERY CONTEXT = [Container context 1]; [Container context 2]...
```

Here's an example:

```
SET BINDERY CONTEXT = eng.acme.corp; hr.acme.corp
```

When you migrate the users from this server, you'll get all the users and groups that are part of the `eng.acme.corp` and `hr.acme.corp` containers.

Real-World Tip: Migrating Passwords from NetWare to NT

The fact that passwords are not migrated from NetWare to NT is one of the main disadvantages of this tool. If you have a largely NetWare environment and you've implemented NDS, you may want to consider using NDS for NT instead of migrating users into NT in this fashion. In the following section, we'll go over some of the advantages and caveats for NDS for NT.

Your other option is to have Terminal Server validate against NetWare first and then change your NT password to match. To set up this option, follow the instructions given in the "NetWare Option in User Manager," later in this chapter.

NDS for NT

If you have a primarily NetWare NDS network with only a handful of NT servers, and if none of your Terminal Servers are PDCs or BDCs, then NDS for NT may be a solution worth looking into. NDS for NT allows you to bring all the users from an NT domain into the NDS tree. This centralizes your NT management by allowing you to control both NT and NetWare users with the NetWare Administrator Tool. Although you won't learn how to install this product here, you will learn how it works.

NDS for NT works through authentication redirection. Normally when you log on to Terminal Server, Terminal Server authenticates with the domain by sending an encrypted logon request to either the domain's PDC or a BDC. This request will be handled at the PDC or BDC by SAMSRV.DLL. This DLL takes the username and password hash and matches it against the username and password hash in the domain database. If they match, the user is then logged on to the server and receives the rights to the domain resources that have been assigned.

NDS for NT, on the other hand, replaces SAMSRV.DLL with its own version of the DLL. This version authenticates with NDS instead of with the NT user database. In this way, all NT authentications on that domain are redirected to the NDS tree.

For more information on the features of the NDS for NT product and how to integrate it with your network, go to www.novell.com.

NetWare Option in User Manager

Yet another way to keep passwords in sync is through the NetWare option in User Manager. This option allows you to enter a domain administrator and password that will be used for synchronizing your domain password with NetWare's. Normally when you log on, you're validated against the domain first. With the NetWare option in User Manager, you'll be validated against your preferred NetWare server or tree first and then against the NT domain database. If this validation fails, your NT password will be changed to match your NetWare password and then you'll be logged on. This is a good option to use if users tend to change their passwords in NetWare first or if you have your NetWare passwords set to expire periodically. Here's how to set this option:

> ### Author's Note: Approach NDS for NT Installation Carefully
>
> Because NDS for NT makes changes to critical NT operating system components and because it requires the installation of Novell's NetWare client on all the PDCs and BDCs in the domain, do not attempt to install it on your Terminal Server's domain if your Terminal Server is a BDC or PDC.
>
> An NDS for NT installation should be approached with caution; be sure you're aware of how it works and test it thoroughly before implementing it in a production environment.

1. Open User Manager for Domains (in the Start menu, select Programs | Administrator Tools | User Manager for Domains).

2. Double-click the user whose passwords you want synchronized. You can also select several users using either the Shift+click or Ctrl+click techniques shown in Chapter 7.

3. Click the Config button.

4. Click NetWare.

5. Enter the name and password for a domain administrator, as well as the server name of the NetWare server that the user will authenticate against.

Changing Passwords

The easiest and most important way to keep users' passwords in sync is to instruct users on the best method for changing them. Terminal Server users should normally change their passwords through the NT security windows. The old method of getting to the NT security window was to press Ctrl+Alt+Del at the workstation. With Terminal Server, this has changed slightly:

1. From the user's desktop, select Windows NT Security from the Start menu. The Windows NT security window will appear.

2. Click the Change Password button.

3. Enter both the old and new passwords for the domain.

4. Click OK to change the password on the other servers that you're attached to (NetWare servers, for example).

The NT Security utility changes the password on all servers you're currently attached to. This is the best method for keeping passwords in sync across platforms.

IPX Networks and MetaFrame (MetaFrame Only)

MetaFrame

Because many NetWare networks make strong use of the IPX protocol, this chapter ends with some information on IPX that may be of use to you when integrating a MetaFrame server into an IPX network.

Determining Frame Type, Network Number, and MAC Address

By default, MetaFrame will first try to autodetect the frame type and network number of the network it's attaching to. If it cannot determine the type, it will normally set its network number to 0 or 1 and the frame type to Ethernet 802.2.

Using the IPXROUTE command, you can verify that MetaFrame is detecting the network number and frame types correctly. Besides just frame type and network number information, the IPXROUTE command can offer you a wealth of information on your IPX network, especially if you have RIP installed on your NT server.

Go to the command prompt and type the following to see a list of the options available with the `IPXROUTE` command (note that this command is installed only if you already have the IPX protocol loaded on your server):

```
C:> IPXROUTE /? ¦ MORE
```

One of the most useful `IPXROUTE` commands is `IPXROUTE CONFIG`. When you type `IPXROUTE CONFIG`, you'll get the following information:

```
C:> IPXROUTE CONFIG
Net 1: network number 00000100, frame type 802.2, device NE20001
➥(0040332525b9) <-MAC Address
```

If you're ever having problems connecting to your MetaFrame server on an IPX network, use the information from the `IPXROUTE COMMAND` to check the following at the client:

- *Frame type* Is the client using the same IPX frame type as the MetaFrame server? By default, MetaFrame will autodetect the frame type on the network. If your network has a mix of IPX frame types, you may run into connection problems. You can lock down the IPX frame type that your MetaFrame server is using in the Network Control Panel (Control Panel | Network). Select the Protocols tab, highlight NWLink IPX/SPX, and select Properties. Change it from Autodetect to Manual and then specify the frame type and network number shown earlier.

- *Network number* Does the network number match the network number of the NetWare servers that your client logs on to? The network number and frame type shown with `IPXROUTE CONFIG` both need to match the network number and frame type on your NetWare servers that are part of the same network segment. You can check what your NetWare servers are set to by typing `CONFIG` at the server console. Again, once you find the correct network number and frame type, you should manually specify them in the Network Control Panel.

- *MAC address* If you cannot see your MetaFrame server from your client, you may need to enter the IPX network address of the server. The address consists of the network number and the MAC address and can be typed in as follows:

  ```
  [Network Number]:[MAC Address]
  ```

  The IPX network number for this example would be `100:0040332525b9`. Enter this number in the server dialog box when adding a new remote application to your ICA client.

RIP and SAP

For those familiar with IPX networks, RIP and SAP will be no strangers. RIP stands for *Router Information Protocol*. It's the default routing protocol used on current NetWare IPX networks. SAP stands for *Service Advertisement Protocol*. It's how devices on the network advertise which services they currently have available on IPX. RIP listens for the SAP advertisements and creates a list of services that are available on the network from them. It then can be configured to pass the list of services to other RIP routers in the network so that all routers know about all IPX services that are available.

Although we could go into much more depth concerning these protocols and how they're configured, what you need to know as a MetaFrame administrator is that MetaFrame uses SAP number 0x083D in order to advertise itself on IPX networks. If you'll be connecting a client to a MetaFrame server across an IPX WAN, you need to make sure that the MetaFrame SAP is not filtered. If it is filtered, you still may be able to connect to the MetaFrame server by typing in the full IPX network address shown previously, but you'll not be able to list the MetaFrame servers that are available from the remote client.

16

Terminal Server and the Internet

I F YOU'RE AN ADMINISTRATOR WHO WILL be integrating your Terminal Server with the Internet or your corporate intranet, this chapter is for you. It begins with topics that apply to both Terminal Server and MetaFrame, such as the TCP/IP ports they use and how to access them through a firewall. The chapter also covers Virtual Private Networks and how to use them for remote access to either Terminal Server or MetaFrame. You can also build on your knowledge of MetaFrame application publishing in Chapter 20, "Application Publishing and Load Balancing with MetaFrame," where you will learn how you can publish applications off your corporate Internet or intranet Web server. The chapter ends with coverage of the Java ICA client, which is a very popular client for use on the Internet because most Web browsers and operating systems can run it.

Accessing Terminal Server and MetaFrame Across the Internet

When setting up access to your Terminal Server from the Internet, your first concern should be security. Any access that you provide needs to be carefully evaluated in terms of its security risk to your corporation. A person accessing your Terminal Server across the Internet can have the same access to your corporate network as someone sitting at an NT workstation one cubicle away from you. Access to both the Terminal Server and the Terminal Server itself should be locked down tightly.

In this section, two methods of accessing a Terminal Server across the Internet will be covered—access through a firewall and access through a Virtual Private Network. For each method, you'll be shown the advantages and disadvantages, how to implement it, and what security is provided.

Accessing Terminal Server and MetaFrame Through a Firewall

Accessing internal network services through a firewall is one of the most common methods for providing access to corporate resources from across the Internet. Firewalls provide protection to internal network resources by tightly controlling which resources are made available to users on the Internet. Most firewalls can be set up to allow either RDP access to Terminal Server or ICA access to MetaFrame from across the Internet. Although many firewalls have additional security features, such as the ability to audit access or to control which IP addresses on the Internet can go through, you should realize that once a user is through your firewall, he or she has access to Terminal Server, just as if this person were accessing it locally.

To access Terminal Server or MetaFrame through a firewall, you first need to know which TCP/IP ports are used. TCP/IP ports identify which application layer protocol a TCP/IP packet is intended for. Particular port numbers have been reserved for use by many different types of TCP/IP application protocols, such as mail protocols (IMAP4, POP3, and SMTP), file transfer protocols (FTP and SFTP), Web protocols (HTML, Real Audio, and VRML), and, of course, Terminal Server protocols (RDP and ICA). Port numbers are between 1 and 65534. Table 16.1 lists the ports that are used by the RDP and ICA protocols. Take, for example, an RDP packet. Inside that packet is a field for both the destination port and the source port of the packet. This allows two applications to communicate with each other across the network. When a Terminal Server client first contacts Terminal Server, the destination port in its packets will be number 3389. In this way, Terminal Server will know that these packets are RDP packets and can begin establishing an RDP connection with the client.

Table 16.1 **TCP/IP Ports Used by RDP and ICA**

Protocol	Port	TCP or IP
RDP	3389	TCP
ICA	1494	TCP
ICA browsing and ICA gateways	1604	IP

Note that the ICA protocol has two ports—one for standard ICA and the other for ICA browsing. ICA browsing is only used by clients when browsing for available Citrix servers or by ICA gateways when communicating with each other. If you have two ICA gateways attempting to communicate with each other across a WAN, make sure that the ICA browser port (1604) has not been filtered out between them. The standard ICA port (1494) is used for all initial client communication to a Citrix server.

When a client wishes to connect to a Citrix server, it will address the server on port 1494. The server will respond to the client on 1494 and assign it a port number in the "high port" range (1023–65534) for further communication. Depending on your firewall, you may have to manually open up this "high port" range to your Citrix server in addition to the standard ICA port (1494) to communicate with the server.

Changing the ICA Port Number

If you need to change the port that's being used by ICA, run the `icaport /port:[new port number]` command from the command line. When connecting to the MetaFrame server from the client, you'll have to do one of two things to connect using the new port number:

- Append the new port number by using a colon to the address or server name in the Server field. For example, if you changed your MetaFrame server to port number 2000 and its IP address is 10.1.1.1, you would need to enter either `[server name]:2000` or `10.1.1.1:2000` in the Server field when setting up the connection entry at the client.

- Add `ICAPortNumber=[port number]` to either individual server/application sections or to the `[WFClient]` section in the `appsrv.ini` file. You'll find the `appsrv.ini` file in the directory where you installed the ICA client.

Controlling Which Users Have Access from the Internet

By default, when you open access on the Internet to your Terminal Server through a firewall, all users on the domain can log on just as if they were accessing the server on the local network. The first security measure you should take is to control which domain users have access to the available connections. To do so, follow these steps:

1. Create an INTERNET_ACCESS group (or similar group) using User Manager for Domains.

2. Add all the users to the group who you want to have access to the server from the Internet.

Real-World Tip: Placing a Server on Its Own Network

If your server is strictly for demonstrative purposes (for example, application demos) or does not require access to resources on your internal network, you might want to put the server on its own network with a separate firewall between it and the Internet. In this way, if a security breach occurs, the hacker can access the server itself, but nothing on the internal corporate network.

Real-World Tip: Remote Access for Administrators

Do not add administrative-level users to the Internet access group, if possible. If an administrator needs remote access, either set up a user-level account with the applications and access that he or she needs remotely or set up dial-in remote access. Both methods are significantly more secure than allowing administrative-level access to your Terminal Server from across the Internet.

3. Go to the Start menu and select Programs | Administrative Tools. Then run the Terminal Server Connection Configuration Tool.

4. Highlight either the rdp-tcp or ica-tcp connection to which you'll be granting access from the Internet.

5. Select Permissions from the Security menu on the main window of the TS Configuration Tool.

6. From the Connection Permission window that appears, remove all groups and users except SYSTEM, by highlighting each one and clicking the Remove button.

7. Click the Add button.

8. From the Add Users and Groups window, highlight the INTERNET_ACCESS group listed under Names.

9. Select Guest Access from the drop-down list next to Type of Access.

10. With the INTERNET_ACCESS group still highlighted, click Add and then click OK.

The INTERNET_ACCESS group will now be added to the access list in the Connection Permissions window with guest access. Guest access only gives the members of the INTERNET_ACCESS group the ability to log on and log off the Terminal Server.

Remember that connection permissions are not related to NTFS security, user rights, or any other type of Terminal Server security. They are mainly used to control which users or groups have permission to log on using a particular connection. Once logged into your server, these users will still have access to their files just as before.

This initial security measure is only a start. For more complete security information and additional security tips, refer to Chapter 11, "Securing the Server."

Accessing Terminal Server Through a Virtual Private Network

For even more secure access to your Terminal Server from the Internet, you may consider a Virtual Private Network (VPN) solution in addition to a firewall. Literally hundreds of different VPN solutions are available on the market from various manufacturers; there's even one included with Terminal Server called *PPTP*. In this section, you'll learn what a VPN is, in what situations you would want to use one, and where to look for VPN solutions that will fit your needs.

Real-World Tip: Separating Connections

You have several methods available for separating your internal connections from the connections for your Internet users. One recommended way is to put a second network adapter in your Terminal Server. Dedicate this network card to Internet traffic by networking it with the inside adapter of your firewall. You can now assign either RDP or ICA connections to just this adapter and control their security separately from your internal network adapters. See Chapter 6, "Creating the Connections," for more information on how to set up connections for a particular LAN adapter. Make sure you also unbind NetBIOS from the Internet-connected adapter. Having NetBIOS bound to this adapter can both hamper performance and compromise the security of the server.

What Is a VPN?

A *VPN* is a secure packet tunnel that's established by a VPN client across the Internet or public network to a private network. Using VPN technology, you can give your remote users (and even remote offices) access across the Internet to your Terminal Server. Because VPNs use standard TCP/IP, they're a secure tunneling technology that can work across almost any TCP/IP connection, including a corporation's internal network. In this capacity, VPNs can be used for enhancing internal security on large networks.

When used across the Internet, the VPN connection is normally started by the client by connecting to the Internet Service Provider using standard PPP, such as provided with Windows 95/98 Dial-Up Networking or Windows NT RAS. After this connection to the Internet has been established, a special VPN client is run that communicates across the Internet connection to a VPN server or VPN–capable firewall on the corporate server. The user then authenticates with the corporate VPN server. After the user has been authenticated, the VPN server establishes an encrypted packet tunnel between the remote user and one or more devices on the internal corporate network.

Why Use a VPN?

You may be wondering what the real advantages are to using a VPN with Terminal Server. Out of the box, Terminal Server supports up to 128-bit compression using RDP alone; therefore, even without the additional encryption provided by a VPN, Terminal Server with RDP is already a securely encrypted solution. In addition, a VPN adds additional overhead that can slow response time, especially across low bandwidth connections to the Internet. Finally, a VPN normally requires the user to authenticate twice, once to the VPN and once to Terminal Server.

The exact advantage of a VPN solution depends mainly on which VPN solution you choose. In general, though, a VPN's greatest advantage is simply additional security. When making your corporate network resources available on a public network, any additional security you can get is a good thing, even at the cost of some convenience. The following are some of the many advantages of a VPN/firewall solution versus a firewall solution alone:

- *Most VPN solutions allow you to audit on a user level*   Whereas firewalls generally allow you to audit which IP addresses have accessed your network, with VPNs, you can normally list the users who have accessed your network and what time they accessed it.

- *VPNs are a remote node solution*   VPNs are remote node solutions because you can have direct access to more than one device on your corporate network from a remote location, just as if you were a node on the local network. With most VPNs, you can finely control which internal network devices external users have access to. Firewalls, on the other hand, restrict your access to internal devices to particular TCP/IP ports.

- *VPNs can often encapsulate other protocols*   Some VPN solutions, such as PPTP from Microsoft, can encapsulate other protocols, such as IPX/SPX. In this way, you can access both IPX/SPX and TCP/IP devices across the same VPN connection. Firewalls, on the other hand, normally have no support on their own for tunneling unless they're VPN enabled.

- *VPNs offer many very secure methods of authentication*   Many VPNs give you a choice of authentication methods. For example, instead of simple username and password logons, you can choose to give your remote users special electronic keys. Many VPNs also support authentication through a RADIUS server, which is an industry standard authentication method.

If you already have a firewall solution that you're satisfied with, check with the firewall manufacturer for which VPN solutions it recommends for its firewall. Because firewalls are so closely related to VPNs, you'll find that your firewall manufacturer may already have a VPN solution that either plugs into or works directly with its firewall.

Another good resource for more information is the International Computer Security Association (ICSA). The ICSA, formerly known as the *National Computer Security Association*, is an independent organization dedicated to improving global computing security. It has a certification program in which it performs rigorous security testing on security-related products such as firewalls, VPNs (IPSec), and biometric devices. The devices that have passed its rigorous certification processes are listed on its Web site at www.ncsa.com.

Publishing Applications on the Web (MetaFrame Only)

MetaFrame

One of the more powerful features of the MetaFrame add-on product is the ability to embed applications in or launch applications from your corporate Internet or intranet Web pages. In this way, your Web site can offer static information as well as interactive applications to its users. The following are some of the many different uses for this feature:

- *Providing corporate applications on an intranet*   The ability to publish applications on the corporate intranet can greatly add to its usefulness. One idea would be to publish a corporate phonebook database so that users can look up phone numbers quickly through the intranet site.

- *Offering custom in-house applications to major customers or suppliers*   Setting up an "extranet" is easy with Web publishing. You can set up a secure Web site for your major clients or suppliers with embedded applications. One example of this is a help desk application where clients can enter trouble tickets directly into your help desk system.

- *Software demonstrations*   Web publishing is a good tool for developers who want to be able to set up secure demo sites of their software for potential customers.

■ *Quick application distribution*   By publishing an application on the Web, it's instantly accessible to anyone who can connect to the Internet, thus eliminating costly time spent distributing applications through traditional methods.

This section discusses how to implement Web-based application publishing for uses such as these. We'll start with the basics of how Web-based publishing works. After you've gained a basic understanding, you'll be shown the steps you need to take to implement Web-based publishing on your Web server. This section is written for administrators who already have a working knowledge of the Web server on which they will be publishing the applications and who are familiar with HTML.

Web Publishing Basics

Web administrators already familiar with embedding content in their Web pages will find few surprises with how ICA clients are embedded. The basic steps are as follows:

1. Publish the application you want to embed in your Web page using the Application Configuration Tool (see Chapter 20).
2. Create an ICA file for the published application.
3. Make that ICA file available to your Web page ICA clients using HTML.

Note that the essential piece is the ICA file. The ICA file contains the instructions—such as the IP address of the MetaFrame server and the application executable name—that the ICA Web clients need to connect with the server.

Creating ICA Client Files

ICA client files are built using the Application Configuration Tool. To create an ICA file, you must first have a published application defined for the application that you want to embed. For more information on how to publish applications, refer to the instructions in Chapter 20.

Here's how you create an ICA file:

1. Go to the Application Configuration Tool under Start | Programs | MetaFrame Tools; then publish the application for which you want to create the ICA file.
2. Highlight the published application and select Write ICA File from the Application menu in the main Application Configuration Tool screen.
3. At the Choose Your Path window, select "A lot!..." and click Next.
4. In the ICA File Window Size and Colors window, enter either the screen size for the embedded application or the relative percentage of the desktop to be taken by the application screen.
5. Select either 16 or 256 colors and click Next.
6. In the ICA File Encryption window, select the level of encryption for the connection and click Next.

7. Enter the filename for the ICA file in the ICA Filename window and click Next.

8. Select No in the Write HTML File window and click Finish. You can create an HTML file at a later time.

The Application Configuration Tool will now generate an ICA file based on the instructions you provided. The following is an example of the contents of a typical ICA file:

```
[WFClient]
Version=2
TcpBrowserAddress=10.1.1.1
IpxBrowserAddress=0:0040332525B9

[ApplicationServers]
clock=

[clock]
Address=clock
InitialProgram=#clock.exe
DesiredHRES=640
DesiredVRES=480
DesiredColor=2
TransportDriver=TCP/IP
WinStationDriver=ICA 3.0
```

Note the key information that's included in this file: the IP address of the MetaFrame server, the application executable name (clock.exe), and the window size and colors. This is the information that the Web client needs to connect to your server across the Net.

Setting Up the ICA File on the Web Server

The last step in publishing your application on the Web is to set up the ICA file on the Web server. The first thing you need to do is register the ICA MIME type on your server. This makes the Web server aware of the ICA file type and relates it to the .ICA file extension. The instructions for doing this vary considerably across different Web servers. See the instruction manual for your server to register the ICA file type on your server.

Once this is registered, you need to place the HTML code for the ICA file into the appropriate Web page. You generally have two different ways to run the published application, as described in the following list:

- *Launching* When the application is set up for launching from the Web page, it will be run in a new window once the user clicks the application icon or hyperlink on the page.

- *Embedding* This refers to incorporating the application into the current Web page instead of a new window. As the page is loaded, so is the embedded application.

MetaFrame can generate sample HTML code that you can incorporate directly into your Web page for either launching or embedding the application. Here's how to create it:

1. Highlight the published application for which you just created the ICA file in the Application Configuration Tool.

2. Select Write HTML File from the Application menu in the main window.

3. Select "A lot!…" in the Choose Your Path window and then click Next.

4. Select Use an Existing ICA File from the Create New ICA File? window and then click Next.

5. Enter the filename of the ICA file you created previously and click Next.

6. In the HTML Appearance window, select either Embedded or Launched, depending on how you want the application to run from the Web page. From here on, the steps will vary slightly depending on whether you choose Embedded or Launched.

7. (Embedded only) Select either Java Client or Netscape Plug-in/Active X Control, depending on what you want the user to use for the application. Click Next.

8. (Embedded Only) Enter the size of the window that will be embedded in your Web page for the application at the HTML Embedded Window Size screen and click Next. Generally, you should use the same window parameters you used for the ICA file.

9. Check Verbose Page at the Verbose Page window if you want the HTML file to be heavily commented. Click Next.

10. Enter the name for the HTML file you want generated and click Finish to generate it.

We won't get into the details of the generated HTML code here. In general, though, the code generated is intended to make the ICA file available to whatever Web client is used. At this point, you need to copy the ICA file you generated earlier to a published directory on your Web page. You then need to integrate the pertinent HTML code that was generated for you into the Web page from which you want to launch the application; otherwise, you need to embed the code.

HTML Code for the Netscape Plug-in/Active X Control

If you choose Netscape Plug-in/Active X Control, the Application Configuration Tool generates HTML code that will first "autosense" what browser type you have. If you do not have the plug-in or control, the tool takes you to the download page for whichever one is appropriate for your browser.

Troubleshooting Tips

Remember that while the launching or embedding of an application into a Web page is a more seamless way to integrate an application with the Internet, you still need to open the ICA port on your firewall to the Citrix server. Make sure the IP address that's defined in the ICA file matches the IP address the Internet user will have access to. In other words, if your firewall does address translation, make sure the ICA file has the address that will be used on the outside of the firewall to represent your MetaFrame server. By default, when you create the ICA file, it will put the current internal address for the server into the ICA file. You can easily edit the ICA file with any text editor.

One quick way to check whether the ICA file is working properly is to run it directly from a client on the Internet. Make sure that when you run it, you're on the same side of the firewall as your normal users will be on. The command line to run the ICA file from the 32-bit ICA client is wfica32 [ICA filename].

Also, make sure the directory of the ICA file referred to in the HTML code matches the directory on your Web server into which you put the ICA file.

The Java ICA Client

To run the Java ICA client, you need a Java Virtual Machine (or JVM). JVMs have been created for most operating systems and are also built into most Web browsers. Because of this, the Java ICA client is the most widely usable of all the ICA clients. The Java ICA client is the client you would normally use on network computers, because network computers include a Java Virtual Machine.

The Java ICA client can either be run from a Web server as a Java applet using a Java-enabled Web browser or run locally on the client as a Java application using a JVM for that client's operating system. Whether it's run as an applet on the Web or as a local application, the features and appearance of the client remain the same.

Installing the Java Client as a Local Application

Two Java ICA clients are available for you to download from Citrix's Web site: the Java client for Java Developer Kit (JDK) 1.0 and the Java client for JDK 1.1. Most modern Java Virtual Machines will support both versions of the Java SDK; older JVMs may only work with version 1.0. No matter which client you download, the installation filename will be setup.class. This is actually a compiled Java program that needs to be run from your JVM. The following installation instructions apply for a Windows 95 or Windows NT 4.0 machine:

1. Change to the directory where you downloaded the setup.class installation file. You can also find a copy of this file for JDK 1.1 under the \icaclient\java directory on the MetaFrame CD-ROM.

2. Run c:\windows\jview setup.

Jview is the name of the JVM program from Microsoft. This program is normally located at the root of the Windows directory. Although the previous instructions apply for only Windows 95/NT 4.0, you can run the `setup.class` Java program from any JVM. Refer to technical support for your particular OS to determine what the JVM executable is and how to run a Java program with it.

Once you install `setup.class`, regardless of the platform, you'll go to the ICA Java Client Installation Wizard's Welcome screen. From here you need to take the following steps to finish the installation of the client:

1. Click Next in the Welcome screen.

2. Read the agreement, check that you accept all the terms, and click Next.

3. Enter the destination path for the ICA client at the Choose Destination Location screen and then click Install.

   The installation program will now start copying files to the user's hard drive. Once this is finished, you'll be taken to the Installation Complete window.

4. Click Finish in the Installation Complete window.

Using the Java ICA Client as an Application

To attach to your MetaFrame server, first check your TCP/IP connectivity by pinging the server. Once this has been established, run the following command from the directory where you installed the Java client:

```
jicasession "address:[hostname or ip address of the server]
```

This will launch a regular ICA session with MetaFrame using Java. If you need to run a published application off of MetaFrame, use this syntax instead:

```
jicasession "address:[Pub app name] "tcpbrowseraddress:[hostname or ip
➥address of server] "InitialProgram:#[Pub app name]
```

Installing the Java ICA Client as an Applet

To install the Java ICA client as an applet, you first need to create a Web page that either has the applet embedded in it or launches the applet from it. In "Setting Up the ICA File on the Web Server," earlier in this chapter, you were shown how to use the Application Configuration Tool to create the HTML code to do this. In step 7, you select Java Client. The Application Configuration Tool then creates the HTML code necessary.

> **Real-World Tip**
>
> One of the best places on the Internet to get Java information is at `java.sun.com`. This is where the Java movement really started. At this Web site, you can download JDKs for both Win32 platforms as well as for Solaris.
>
> Another good Java resource page is the Java Centre at `www.java.co.uk`, where you can find tons of Java information and links to other sites on the Internet.

Three different Java applets are available. These applets are included with the Java ICA client for JDK 1.1, which is available for download from Citrix's Web site. The following is a list of the Java applet files available in the Java ICA client and which Web browsers they were designed to work with:

- *JICAEngJ.jar* This applet can be used by any browser that fully implements JVM 1.1. HotJava is one popular browser in which this applet will run.

- *JICAEngN.jar* This applet is designed to work with Netscape Navigator and is signed using Netscape's authentication method.

- *JICAEngM.cab* This applet contains a signed cabinet file (.CAB) that's signed using Microsoft's authentication method. It will work with both version 3.02 and 4.x of Microsoft's Internet Explorer.

17

Terminal Server and Wide Area Networks

THIS CHAPTER ADDRESSES TWO PRIMARY ISSUES about wide area networking (WAN). The first is WAN access to the Terminal Server. In a WAN environment, broadcast packets do not normally go across the WAN. Because Terminal Server advertises itself using broadcasts, users at remote sites cannot see the server in their Terminal Server client or ICA client browse lists. In the first major section, "WAN Access to Terminal Server and MetaFrame," you learn techniques to get around this issue, such as using WINS servers and ICA gateways, to enable browsing from remote networks.

The second issue is WAN performance. When accessing Terminal Server on a local area network (LAN), the bandwidth usage of the clients is not of as much concern as the amount of processing power and memory the clients are using on the server itself. With wide area networks, however, network bandwidth utilization is of primary importance. In the second section of this chapter, "Prototyping the WAN," you learn several different methods of prototyping your WAN in order to measure performance. These methods build on those you learned in Chapter 13, "Measuring Performance," with specific emphasis on measuring network bandwidth utilization.

WAN Access to Terminal Server and MetaFrame

How you connect to Terminal Server across a WAN is similar in many ways to how you connect to MetaFrame across a WAN. Both products support browse lists that are maintained by a master browser on the network. Because both products accept either network addresses or hostnames when filling in the server address at the client, you are not required to see the server in the client's browse list in order to connect to it. In the following sections you learn some of the options that are available for enabling browsing at the client, and in what ways your client can connect if it cannot see the server in its browse list.

Connecting Across a WAN with the Terminal Server Client

The Microsoft Terminal Server RDP client, referred to as the Terminal Server client, has a simple browsing mechanism. When you first start the client, it will make a broadcast to retrieve a list of all Terminal Servers on the network from the master browser. Since broadcasts do not travel across routers, you have three options on a WAN in order to connect your clients to a remote Terminal Server—static addresses, hosts file, and dynamic name resolution. With the exception of WINS, all of the options will also work with MetaFrame.

Static Addresses

The first option, static addresses, means simply typing in the TCP/IP address of the remote server at the client. When using either the Client Connection Manager or the Terminal Server client, type in the TCP/IP address in the Server field. In the Client Connection Manager you find the Server field on the first screen when you create a new connection (File | New Connection from the main window). On the Terminal Server client you can find the Server field at the top of the main Terminal Server client window. Providing a TCP/IP address forces the client to connect to this IP address. Although using static addresses is a simple solution, if you ever need to change the IP address of the Terminal Server you must change the IP address at all the remote clients that had connected to it.

Hosts File

Another option is to create a hosts file on each user's workstation that maps names to IP addresses. Creating this file makes it easier for the users because they must remember only the name of the host, not the IP address. However, you must still change the host entry in the hosts file on all the remote clients if the IP address of the Terminal Server changes. The following steps instruct how to set up a host file on a Windows 95 or Windows NT client:

1. Open the hosts.sam, or hosts, file if it exists, from the C:\WINDOWS directory on a Windows 95 workstation or the C:\WINNT\SYSTEM32\DRIVERS\ETC directory on an NT workstation using Notepad or any other text editor.

2. Add the following entry to the bottom of the host file:

   [IP Address]   [Host Name]

   Substitute the IP address of the remote Terminal Server for [IP Address] and the name you want to assign to it for [Host Name]. Note that the hostname should not have any spaces in it.

3. Save the `hosts.sam` file as `hosts` in the `C:\WINDOWS` directory on Windows 95 or the `C:\WINNT\SYSTEM32\DRIVERS\ETC` directory on Windows NT. The `hosts.sam` file is a sample file, hence the .sam extension. For Windows 95 or Windows NT to recognize the `hosts` file, it must be named just `hosts` with no extension.

4. From the command prompt, try pinging the host name you just added to the host file using the `PING [Host Name]` command.

Dynamic Name Resolution (DNS and WINS)

There are two primary options for name resolution in a Windows network: WINS and DNS. Putting either a WINS or DNS server (or a combination of the two) at your central office is the best solution for connectivity across the WAN. When you set up the clients, you need to point them to the central name server. You can normally enter the addresses of your WINS or DNS servers in the properties for the TCP/IP protocol in the Network Control Panel on the client. They must then type only the name of the Terminal Server in the Server field in order to connect to it. The DNS or WINS server handles resolving that name into an IP address. If the address of the Terminal Server ever changes, the WINS server updates automatically. The DNS server can also be easily changed to reflect the new address. In general, implementing dynamic name resolution is the best long-term solution for most networks.

Connecting Across a WAN with the ICA Client

As with the Terminal Server client, you can use static addresses, a hosts file, or dynamic name resolution to connect to a MetaFrame server using TCP/IP with an ICA client. Simply fill in the address or the name of the server in the Server field on the ICA client as you create the new entry for the client. The ICA client can resolve a name using a DNS server or hosts file into an IP address.

The ICA client differs from the Terminal Server client in its capability to connect using more than just the TCP/IP protocol. The following sections address some of the more complex issues involved in connecting to a MetaFrame server with an ICA client.

Connecting to MetaFrame by Using IPX/SPX

A MetaFrame server advertises itself on an IPX/SPX network by using the Service Advertising Protocol (SAP). With SAP, each type of service available on a network uses a unique SAP number to advertise itself. MetaFrame uses SAP number 0x83D. As long as your network is set up so that the SAP list reaches the remote site's router, you should be able to see the MetaFrame server from the remote ICA client's browse list. Many times network engineers block certain SAPs on the routers in order to reduce WAN traffic. If this is the case, you must ensure that SAP 0x83D is let through. For more information about the SAP protocol, refer to the discussion on SAPs in Chapter 15, "Terminal Server and NetWare."

If you still cannot browse the MetaFrame servers when setting up a new entry at the client, there are a few additional techniques you can try. First, make sure you are using the same frame type. By default, MetaFrame attempts to auto-detect the frame type of the network it is attached to. If it does not sense a frame type, MetaFrame uses frame type 802.2. It can also be manually set for other IPX/SPX frames such as 802.3 and Ethernet II in the Network Control Panel, as follows:

1. Open the Network Control Panel from the Start menu | Settings | Control Panel.

2. Click on the Protocol tab in the Network window.

3. Highlight NWLink IPX/SPX Compatible Transport under the Protocol tab and click the Properties button.

4. In the NWLink IPX/SPX Properties window that appears, select Manual Frame Type Detection and click Add. The Manual Frame Detection window appears.

5. Select the Frame Type that you want to bind to the server, enter the IPX Network Number for that frame type, and click OK to return NWLink IPX/SPX Properties window. The Frame Type you selected is shown in the Frame Type list in this window.

6. If you want to bind more frame types to the server, click the Add button and repeat step 5; otherwise, click OK.

7. Click Close from the Network window to finish binding the new IPX frame types to the server.

8. Shut down and restart the server.

To double-check the frame type being used at the MetaFrame server, run the IPXROUTE CONFIG command from the command prompt. Running this command displays the following information:

```
C:> IPXROUTE CONFIG
NWLink IPX Routing and Source Routing Control Program v2.00
net 1: network number 00000000, frame type 802.2, device IEEPRO1
(00aa00a13711)
```

Note that this command shows not only all bound frame types, but also the IPX network number (0) and the MAC address of the card (00aa00a13711).

Windows clients generally use 802.2, by default, unless they detect another frame type on the network. The method of checking which frame type is selected varies with each type of client. If you are using Windows 95, you can check the frame type that is selected in the Network Control Panel under the Advanced Properties for the IPX/SPX protocol. A setting of Auto means that the client will auto-detect the protocol on the network. If you have a Novell server on the network using 802.3, then Windows 95 chooses 802.3. If the MetaFrame server is only running 802.2, you will not be able to see the frame type. To get around these problems, change either the server or client to the same frame type.

If you are still having a problem bringing up the list of MetaFrame servers, try entering the IPX/SPX address directly when setting up the connection at the client.

The IPX/SPX address of the server is formatted as [network number]:[MAC Address]. You can get this address by using the IPXROUTE CONFIG command. For the server in the previous example of IPXROUTE CONFIG, you would enter 0:00AA00A13711 in the Server field when setting up the ICA client connection.

Connecting to MetaFrame by Using NetBIOS

The first thing you need to know about NetBIOS is that it is not routable. To connect to a MetaFrame server across a WAN using NetBIOS, you must set up a bridge to the remote office instead of a router. You also must ensure that NetBIOS broadcasts are enabled across the bridge. The advantages of using NetBIOS are low overhead and simplicity. If you have more than a few remote offices, it is highly recommended to use a routable protocol such as IPX/SPX or TCP/IP.

Publishing Applications Across the WAN

One of the trickiest items to get working properly is a published application across a WAN. With a server connection across a WAN, all you really need to type in while setting up the connection on the ICA client is the address of the server. You do not have to be able to browse the server list in order to establish a connection as long as you have the server's network address. With published applications, however, you must be able to browse the application list from the ICA client or you will not be able to set up up the connection to the application. To understand what you need to do to make this work, you must understand how ICA browsing works.

ICA browsing is much like standard Windows NT browsing, but it is completely separate from it. All MetaFrame servers on a local network hold an election to determine which server will be the ICA Master Browser. Once it is selected, the ICA Master Browser begins building a list of all MetaFrame servers on the network, all published applications, and the servers or server farms that the published applications run on. The ICA Master Browser maintains this list for every protocol that it is bound to.

When you create a new connection entry on the ICA client (select New from the Entry menu on the Remote Application Manager) and click on the down arrow to browse for published applications, you are actually reading a list from the ICA Master Browser. If your client cannot reach the ICA Master Browser, you cannot see the applications available and create the entry.

> **Real-World Tip: To Bridge or Not to Bridge**
>
> Often the decision must be made whether to set up a bridge to a remote office or a router. The main advantage of bridging is its simplicity. A bridge is very easy to set up and you do not have to worry about complex protocol issues. The disadvantage of most bridges is that there are few ways to control the traffic over the bridge. Bridging generally works best when you have a small number of remote offices. On large WANs, you are likely to find that the added control provided with most routers is beneficial for managing your WAN traffic.

Browsers rely on broadcasts to exchange information. Because broadcasts do not normally travel across WANs, an ICA Master Browser maintains a list of the MetaFrame servers on the current network segment only. For your clients to connect to the ICA Master Browser across a WAN and retrieve this list, you must define the addresses of your MetaFrame servers on the client:

1. From the main window in the 32-bit ICA client, select Settings from the Options menu.

2. From the Settings window that appears, click the Server Location tab to see the Network Protocol and the Address List. By default, all protocols are set to Auto-Locate. This means that when you try to browse for published applications or servers, the client sends out broadcast packets to find the ICA Master Browser.

3. From the list, select the network protocol you are using.

4. Add to the list the network addresses of all the MetaFrame servers at the corporate site.

Now when you try to browse with your selected protocol, it searches each listed server in sequence for the one acting as the ICA Master Browser. Your protocol then obtains the list of applications from that server and allows you to choose one.

It is important to enter the IP addresses of all your MetaFrame servers in this list on the clients. You cannot readily predict which server will become the ICA Master Browser in an election.

ICA Gateways

Normally, each network segment has its own ICA Master browser that maintains a list of the servers and published applications on that segment alone. Suppose, however, you have two MetaFrame servers that are across a WAN from each other, and you want your clients to be able to see and run published applications off both of them. Because the servers are on their own network segments, you can see the published applications on only the server whose segment your workstation is on. To see the list of published applications available on the other server, you can either manually enter the address of the server in your Server Location list, as shown in the previous section, or establish an ICA gateway between them. An ICA gateway synchronizes the browse lists across two or more segments. After an ICA gateway has been established, your clients can browse servers and applications from both sides of the WAN.

To set up an ICA gateway, follow these steps:

1. Select the Application Configuration tool from the MetaFrame Tools folder.

2. Select ICA Gateways from the Configure menu. The ICA Gateways window appears.

3. Click Add to add a new ICA Gateway.

4. In the Add ICA Gateway window that appears, select either IPX/SPX or TCP/IP for the gateway protocol. Select the local servers on which to store information from the gateway, and enter the network address or hostname of the remote server with which you want to synchronize the local servers. When you're finished, click OK to create the gateway.

After you have created the gateway, the ICA Master Browsers on both sides of the WAN synchronize their browse lists with each other. The result is that each ICA Master Browser now can provide the clients with a list of servers and published applications on both sides of the WAN.

Prototyping the WAN

In this section, you will learn techniques for estimating how much network bandwidth your clients will be using. Although many of the techniques are based on those covered in Chapter 13, the focus here is on network bandwidth rather than processor utilization or memory usage. One thing that many may not realize is that Terminal Server has its own built-in network analyzer! The following sections teach you how to set up this analyzer and use it effectively for predicting future performance, how to resolve wide area networking problems, and how to monitor your wide area network in the long term.

There are two main decisions that you need to make when setting up Terminal Server on the WAN. First, you must determine what protocol to use. With Terminal Server, the choice is obvious—TCP/IP. With MetaFrame, you can use TCP/IP, IPX/SPX, or even NetBEUI, assuming you are bridging. This choice is not always obvious and may depend on many factors. For one, you need to consider performance. TCP/IP, IPX/SPX, and NetBEUI vary in their performance and network bandwidth utilization.

Second, consider protocol standardization. There are many advantages to standardizing on a single protocol corporate-wide. The protocol of choice for this need is TCP/IP. It has become the de facto primary protocol for major network operating systems today. Even Novell's NetWare, the most well-known operating system whose primary protocol has been IPX/SPX, has native TCP/IP support in its latest release. Protocol standardization is very important for effective network monitoring. The focus of most major network monitoring packages is the monitoring of TCP/IP. You will find support for other protocols such as IPX/SPX and NetBEUI often lacking, in comparison with the robust monitoring features available for TCP/IP.

Setting Up the WAN Lab

To effectively test the various WAN options available to you, you must set up a lab or test environment. The first part of every Terminal Server project plan should be dedicated to prototyping. Prototyping in a lab or test environment is critical for the success of any Terminal Server project because in the prototyping stage you can best make the decisions about protocol type, necessary WAN bandwidth, and acceptable performance for your environment. Unfortunately, with WANs a true test environment is somewhat difficult to set up. Here are some options:

- *Imitate a WAN link using a crossover cable* Many types of WAN links can be imitated in a test environment by using a simple crossover cable between two CSU/DSUs with routers or bridges on each side. This technique works well for both T1 links and DDS (such as 56K). This is a good technique for offline testing before actually bringing your equipment into the WAN environment. Although this technique works well for dedicated links, it may not be as accurate a performance predictor for switched links, such as frame relay. The reason concerns the ways in which switched technologies handle circuit utilization. You learn more about this topic in a little bit.

- *Establish a WAN link to the site closest to you for testing* If you have a hub-and-spoke type WAN configuration—in other words, a large corporate office with many branch offices—this option will probably work best for you. Setting up tests in this scenario gives you a very realistic picture of what to expect during the final rollout. Unfortunately, this works well only for new installations. Setting up testing across a WAN link that is already being relied on for daily use is not a good plan. Your testing could easily knock off current WAN users.

- *Perform after-hours testing on the WAN* For many corporations, after-hours testing, when WAN utilization is low, is the only real testing option. The results of this testing provide real-world performance results that you can rely on for predicting the success of the actual rollout.

Whatever option you choose, the important thing is doing enough testing to ensure that when the project is finally rolled out, the level of performance across the WAN will be acceptable to users.

Setting Up the Lab by Using a WAN Crossover Cable

You may have heard of a network crossover cable—but a WAN crossover cable? They do exist, can be made easily, and work well for testing. Much like making an Ethernet crossover cable, making a WAN crossover cable involves swapping the send and receive pairs. By creating a cable in which these pairs have been swapped, transmit to receive, you have created a crossover.

Which pairs have the transmit and receive signals vary between circuit types. CSU/DSU manufacturers should be able to provide instruction on how to create a WAN crossover cable for their equipment.

Remember, this technique works only for point-to-point links, such as T1 or 56K. You should try this technique only if your CSU/DSU's manufacturer is willing to support it for testing. For dial-up links such as ISDN or even modems, your only real option to test them locally is to set up two lines locally, and have one dial into the other one. Crossovers do not work for these types of lines.

Because typically the circuit provider provides the clock, you may also need to set up one of the CSU/DSUs to provide the clock and the other to receive it. This is a test environment, so you have the opportunity to try all the different speeds that the CSU/DSU supports.

Of course, for any testing to occur, you also need either a router or a bridge on both ends. The router or bridge typically has a network connection (10 Base-T/100 Base-T) and a serial connection for the CSU/DSU (V.35 cable). Many modern routers can be ordered with internal CSU/DSUs. This option makes the job of setting up a WAN link much easier by reducing the number of different types of cables you need. Simply connect your network to the network port on the router and the WAN to the CSU/DSU WAN port.

Switched Circuits and Crossovers

The problems of simulating a switched WAN connection using a simple WAN crossover cable were discussed earlier. With a point-to-point link, simulation using a crossover cable is an accurate test because you have the full bandwidth available to you. If you purchase a 56K line, that link has been dedicated for your exclusive usage across their network.

With frame relay and some other switching technologies, you are essentially renting bandwidth on the carrier's switches. With frame relay in particular, there is a concept called CIR, the committed information rate, by the carrier. Although you may have a link rate of 320KB, if your CIR is 256KB and the switches are congested, your excess bandwidth usage may simply be discarded by the switch! Frame relay's main advantage over other switching technologies such as the older X.25 is low overhead. With low overhead comes higher speed but also a loss in reliability. You should keep a close eye on frame relay circuits. The performance you get out of frame relay can depend greatly on how well your carrier has planned for the load on their switches. If their switches are overloaded, you could start to see high packet loss on your routers. This high packet loss results in intermittently slow or possibly lost connections to your Terminal Server.

There are two suggestions for handling this situation. First, always test for the CIR in your frame-relay WAN simulations. Although CIR is not a guaranteed transmit rate, it is the most reliable rate estimate your carrier will provide. Beyond this rate, your packets have a much higher chance of being discarded. The second suggestion is to carefully watch your frame relay connection for lost packets, especially during busy times of the workday, such as early morning or afternoon. You may even want to do a load test during these times over a couple of days to see how your carrier's switches handle your packets. If you find a significant amount of packet loss, address the problem with your carrier to ensure that they are not experiencing bandwidth problems in your area.

Because frame relay and other switching technologies can span the world, the path between your office and a remote one is not always a simple one. Often your packets are sent through several switches, even switches from different carriers, before reaching their destination. Understanding the routes that your packets take and whose equipment is involved along the way is critical for pursuing circuit problems. Be sure to get this information from your carrier when they install your new circuit. They should be able to tell you the location of all switches between you and the destination and any other equipment in between.

For mission-critical WAN, links always have a backup. A dial-up ISDN line works very well as a backup WAN link. Most major router manufacturers have equipment options that support ISDN as a backup WAN link. A major problem at your carrier can easily result in several hours of downtime for the sites on your WAN.

Using Existing WAN Links for Testing

Using existing WAN links can be the most accurate method for performance testing, but you must be careful about interfering with existing traffic. If the WAN links have not been set up yet and you plan to roll them out specifically for Terminal Server connections, you are fortunate. In this situation, make sure to roll out a site close to the main office first during the prototyping stage of the project. This site will become your test site, and you can run your performance tests to it. In this way, you can accurately estimate the amount of bandwidth that your Terminal Server application requires. This is important to know early in the project. Without accurate estimates of the amount of bandwidth Terminal Server will be using, you may quickly run into a situation in which there is not enough bandwidth for your Terminal Server needs at the sites. Depending on the type of line you ordered, you may end up being stuck ordering new routers and/or CSU/DSUs to increase the speed.

If you are like most administrators, however, you do not have the luxury of new installations. Instead you are probably trying to incorporate a Terminal Server solution into an existing WAN environment. In this situation, you will likely have to do two things. First, you must estimate the amount of current usage of the WAN. There are many ways to do this, depending on what equipment and network monitoring software you have at your disposal. Your local carrier often can be of great assistance by providing detailed wide area network utilization information—check with them first. Obtain the following information from them:

- The average bandwidth you are using
- The usage patterns during the week

This information will help greatly when planning for the additional traffic load caused by Terminal Server.

The second thing you must do is estimate this additional traffic load. Because this is a live WAN, you should probably do your testing after hours. Based on your traffic analysis, choose an off-peak time during which the testing results will not be skewed by background traffic.

To set up the actual test environment, you must deploy one or more test work-stations to the remote site upon which you will be running performance tests. Try to use machines that are similar in capability to the ones you will be using in the rollout phase of the project. You should, of course, set up the Terminal Server client and protocol of choice on each workstation and establish connectivity to the Terminal Server.

A particular difficulty with this arrangement is ease of access. Every time you want to change a parameter on the workstation to test its effect on performance, you will probably need to dispatch someone to the site. If you are testing several different parameters, this can become tedious very quickly. One solution is to implement a remote control product such as pcANYWHERE or Remotely Possible with dial-in access. In this way, you can dial in to the remote PC, set up the network and Terminal Server client the way you want, and commence the test, all without leaving the office! Be sure to close out of the remote control session after the tests have started. The screen updates for the remote control session can also affect the results because they take up processing time at the client.

Measuring WAN Bandwidth and Performance

After you have set up the testing environment, it is time to get some of the actual testing work done. Chapter 13 covers how to set up user simulation scripts in detail. It is recommended that you use these scripts to simulate user interaction across the WAN. Remember to keep the timing of these scripts realistic to mimic users' average use during the day. If the remote user will be using Terminal Server all day long, the amount of WAN bandwidth used is greater than if the user only occasionally needs access to the central office applications. Also, be certain to set up simulation scripts that include all of the applications that you will be rolling out to the remote sites in user simulation scripts.

Although Chapter 13 covers in detail how to measure the usage of nearly every major server resource, it did not provide much coverage of how to measure network bandwidth utilization. There are several methods that you can use with Terminal Server to measure network bandwidth utilization. The three primary methods covered in the following sections are using the Terminal Server Administration Tool, Network Monitor, and Performance Monitor.

Measuring Network Utilization Using the Terminal Server Administration Tool

Using the Terminal Server Administration Tool is a quick way to get a rough picture of your network utilization. You can watch the packet's input and output from your server using the Status of Logon window shown in Figure 17.1.

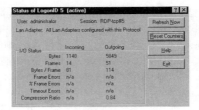

Figure 17.1   Connection status window.

In this window, you can see not only how many bytes have been transmitted into and out of your server, but also the average frame size, any network errors, and the compression ratio of the connection. To use the information in this window to determine your network utilization, you need to do the following:

1. Log on to Terminal Server from the test workstation across the WAN or simulated WAN connection.

2. Open up the Connection Status window from the console by running the Terminal Server Administration Tool, highlighting the test connection (as shown in Figure 17.2), and selecting the Status from the Actions menu. It is important to do all of the connection monitoring and bandwidth measurement from the console. If you monitor the connection remotely, your monitoring will greatly influence the results.

3. Start the user simulation script on the workstation that you created in Chapter 13. If you did not have time to create the script, you can have a user onsite work with you to simulate application activity.

4. Select Reset Counters from the Status window and start your stopwatch or an equivalent type of timer.

5. At the end of ten minutes of user simulation, or however long you have decided to run the test, click the Print Screen button. This trick captures the screen to the clipboard at the moment the clock stops. This makes it much easier to read the input and output byte totals.

6. Run the clipboard view to see the results. To obtain an estimate of the network bandwidth utilization over the tested period of time, add the input and output bytes together and divide the total by the number of seconds you ran the test for:

    (input + output)/number of seconds

    This gives you bytes/second bandwidth utilization.

Measuring Network Utilization Using Performance Monitor

Performance Monitor is a great tool for getting a good picture of your network utilization pattern. You can use Performance Monitor for the following tasks:

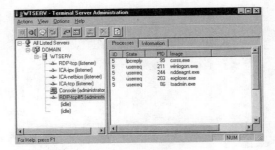

Figure 17.2 Selecting the test connection.

- Testing to get a better idea of which application operations take the most network bandwidth
- Long-term network monitoring
- Baselining your network utilization over a long period of time
- Watching your traffic patterns throughout the day

Although there are many useful network-related parameters you can monitor, the one you should be most concerned with is Total Bytes. In Figure 17.3, you see that the Total Bytes counter, which is located under the Session object, is added to the chart view. To add this counter to the chart, follow these steps:

1. Run Performance Monitor from the Administrative Tools folder located in Start menu | Programs.
2. Select Add to Chart from the Edit menu.
3. Select Session from the Object drop-down list.
4. Select Total Bytes from the Counter list.
5. Select the Instance for which you want to get a count for from the Instance list. Each Instance represents the Total Bytes from a different active session on Terminal Server.
6. Click OK to add the counter to the chart.

By default, the Total Bytes being transmitted are sampled every second, providing you with a good short-term picture of the network utilization patterns. For a longer sample rate, select Chart from the Options menu and raise the sample rate.

For more useful long term testing, go into the Performance Monitor logging section by selecting Log from the View menu. Here you can set up Performance Monitor to start logging the counters under the various objects. Again, the main object of concern is the Session object for network utilization. It is recommended to log the Session counters while you are doing your performance testing. The best thing about the log is that you can view the results in the chart view at any time after they are recorded. You can also view any session counter from any instance. This level of flexibility is great for obtaining an accurate picture of the application's network usage.

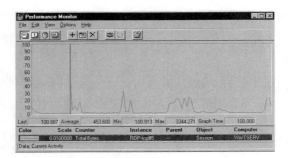

Figure 17.3 Total Bytes counter.

To get an idea of your network utilization patterns throughout the day or week, try changing the logging interval to something in the neighborhood of 15 minutes (900 seconds). Continue logging the session parameters for several days at this interval. By importing the results into a spreadsheet program such as Excel, you can generate traffic utilization charts. These charts can be very beneficial for future planning. For example, you can use the first chart you create as a baseline. By sampling the network utilization every couple of months and overlaying the charts, you can watch how your utilization changes as the network grows. You might also want to include processor and memory object counters in your logging. Long-term logging is covered in more detail in Chapter 13.

Measuring Network Utilization Using Network Monitor

The final technique for monitoring or measuring network utilization is using Network Monitor, which is Microsoft's network analyzing software. The version included with Terminal Server and NT Server 4.0 does not have as many features as the full-fledged Network Monitor that comes with Microsoft's SMS. The TS version only monitors traffic going to and from the Terminal Server. On the other hand, it still can give you a ton of useful network information on your Terminal Server and it is free! To install and use Network Monitor you need to do the following:

1. Go to Control Panel and select Network | Services. Select Add and then select the Network Monitor Tools and Agent service, as shown in Figure 17.4. After this service is added and you exit from the Network Control Panel, Terminal Server installs the new service and prompts you to reboot the server.

2. When the server comes back up, select the newly created Network Monitor shortcut from the Administrative Tools folder in Start menu | Programs.

3. Start the user simulation script on the remote workstation.

4. To capture the packets from the remote workstation, select Start from the Capture menu in the Network Monitor window. Network Monitor begins capturing packets going to and from the Terminal Server into a local file. It also starts gathering statistical information on the network traffic.

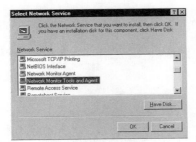

Figure 17.4 Selecting a network service.

5. To finish the test, select Stop from the Capture menu. The duration of the test is up to you. Remember, however, that there is a lot of information being gathered and the database can quickly begin taking up a lot of space on the hard drive. To change the buffer size, select Buffer Settings from the Capture menu. The buffer size is limited to 24MB in this version.

Figure 17.5 shows the results of a typical capture. On the bottom part of the window, notice the network address on the left, followed by frames sent, frames received, and other statistics. These statistics represent the packet activity to and from each of the network addresses listed on the left.

If you are on a test network with only the Terminal Server and the test station, it is simple to determine which network address belongs to which device. If you need help determining which network address is which, right-click on the address in question and select edit address. You are taken to the window in Figure 17.6; the grayed-out value next to Address is the MAC address of the network card.

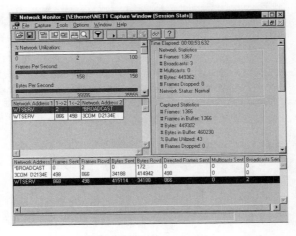

Figure 17.5 Capture results.

Figure 17.6 Network MAC address.

You now need to determine the MAC address of the PC. Under Windows 95, you can get the MAC address by running WINIPCFG. Under Windows NT, run IPCONFIG/ALL from the command prompt. For other operating systems, refer to the manufacturer of your network card. By matching up this MAC address to the one in the capture window, you can determine which machine is yours.

The main parameters of concern are the packets that are going between your PC and the Terminal Server. In the Capture window you can see the bytes sent and received from each network address. Using these statistics, you can determine the network bandwidth utilization of the connection.

For a more detailed view of the packets, select Display Captured Data from the Capture menu. The window shown in Figure 17.7 appears, in which you can view the individual packets down to a byte level.

Because both RDP and ICA packets are encrypted, you cannot translate the packet types. On the other hand, you can gain valuable information about the TCP/IP port being used, where the packet is coming from, what its destination is, the packet size, and how much overhead there is in the packet. Network Monitor also works with IPX/SPX and NetBEUI, which makes it very useful for troubleshooting ICA network problems.

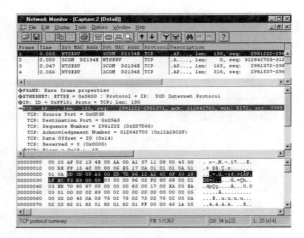

Figure 17.7 Packet capture.

Other Ways to Measure Network Utilization

To measure network utilization, you must determine the number of bytes that have gone between the client and the server over a period of time. Most of the methods discussed so far use utilities that run from the server itself. Because the server has to waste extra processing time monitoring the network with these utilities, this can have an effect on the results. Although the effect should be minimal, there are some non-intrusive means to monitor network traffic:

- Run a packet sniffer and protocol analyzer on a separate box to capture the packets going between the test workstation and Terminal Server. You can use Network Monitor, but you will need the full version included with SMS.

- If your test workstation is plugged into a switch, most switches keep statistics on the bytes sent and received for each port.

- If your workstation is at a remote small office, and it is the only workstation at the office going across the WAN, you can use the statistics in the router. Most routers maintain traffic statistics.

Real-World Tip: Capturing ICA Packets at the ICA Client

If you are interested only in seeing what's inside of an ICA packet or would like to do some quick network troubleshooting on the client side, do a simple packet capture using the ICA client:

1. Load the ICA client and select Settings from the Options menu.

2. Scroll sideways to the Event Logging tab by using the arrows in the upper-right corner.

3. Select the Data Received, Data Transmitted, and/or Keyboard and Mouse Data Log Events and click Apply.

Although access is very slow, you can now make a connection and start capturing packets to the log file. After you are done with the capture, turn the Log Event options off. You can then view the packets you captured in the wfcwin32.log file located under the ICA Client directory.

18

MetaFrame and UNIX Clients

Ｉｎ many corporations, UNIX workstations have been the operating system of choice for particular applications or needs. Bringing those UNIX workstations into the corporate application fold, however, has often been challenging for network administrators. Although many high-end applications, such as CAD programs, have been written to work across most UNIX platforms, other more widely used corporate applications have been written only for Windows.

MetaFrame bridges this gap between the UNIX and Windows worlds by allowing you to run Windows applications on most of today's UNIX platforms. Besides being able to run Windows applications, MetaFrame's ICA UNIX clients can also access their local drives, print to their local printers, and even transfer objects to their UNIX clipboards, all from a MetaFrame session.

In this chapter, you'll first learn how to install the ICA UNIX client. Once it's installed, you'll learn how to incorporate your UNIX workstation's local drives and printers into a MetaFrame session. In the second half of the chapter, we'll consider more advanced UNIX integration topics, such as printing to a UNIX LPD (Line Printer Daemon) print server from MetaFrame and setting up your MetaFrame server as an FTP server so that you can more easily transfer files to your UNIX workstations.

Although this chapter is mainly about running MetaFrame sessions on UNIX graphical workstations, administrators who currently have text-based UNIX terminals may instead want to replace them with Windows-based Terminals (WBTs). In this chapter, you'll learn how easy it is to do this by replacing the text terminal with

WBTs that access a Terminal Server across the network or that are directly connected to a MetaFrame server using existing serial lines.

UNIX Basics for NT Administrators

For administrators who are new to the UNIX world, we'll start with the basics. This section provides you with some introductory UNIX material may be of assistance when you're installing the ICA UNIX client.

Basic UNIX Commands

Table 18.1 lists the UNIX equivalents to some basic DOS commands that you may need during installation. Note that the UNIX commands are all in lowercase. Almost everything in UNIX is *case sensitive*, including filenames, directory names, commands, usernames, and passwords. If you find that a particular command you've typed does not work, check to see whether the case is correct first. Also note that the back slash for directories in DOS is replaced with a forward slash in UNIX.

To enter the UNIX commands listed in Table 18.1, you need to be at a command prompt. Much like the DOS command prompt in NT, the UNIX command prompt allows you to type in commands to interact with the operating system. Usually when you log in to UNIX, you're brought to or shown a command prompt right away. On some systems, you may have to make a menu selection from the graphical interface to open up a command prompt window. Exactly how this done varies from system to system, and it also depends on how the workstation is set up.

Accessing the Install Files from the CD-ROM

The first step in installing the client is getting the install files to the UNIX workstation. The install files for all the ICA UNIX clients are included on the MetaFrame CD-ROM under the /icaclients/icaunix directory. Those used to the DOS/Windows world of drive letters may be surprised to learn that drive letters do not normally exist in the UNIX world. Therefore, you cannot just insert the CD-ROM into the drive on the UNIX workstation and access it from a drive letter. Instead of drive letters, directory structures, such as that of the CD-ROM, need to be "mounted" into the current file system onto a *mount point*. The mount point is normally set to a directory off the root of the file system. Once you mount the CD-ROM under the mount point, you'll be able to see all the files in the CD-ROM underneath this directory, just as if the directory was your D: drive on your Windows workstation.

Table 18.1 **UNIX Equivalents to Basic DOS Commands**

Command Description	DOS	UNIX
Change directory	CD \[directory]	cd /[directory]
View directory	DIR	ls
Make directory	MD or MKDIR	mkdir
View text file	TYPE readme.txt	more readme.txt or cat readme.txt

Table 18.2 shows the mount commands that you need to enter to mount a CD-ROM on various UNIX operating systems underneath the /cdrom directory off the root.

Accessing Install Files from the Web

The other option you have for installing the client is to download the latest installation files from Citrix's Web site for the ICA UNIX client for your operating system. You'll find these files at www.download.citrix.com.

The files on the Web site are usually available in one of two compression formats, indicated by their filename extension: either .Z or .gz. The .Z compressed install file can be uncompressed using the widely available uncompress [filename].Z UNIX command. The .gz or "zipped" file needs to uncompressed using the gunzip [filename].gz command. Although the gunzip command has been ported to many UNIX OSs, it's not always included with a base UNIX install. Although some differences exist in the efficiency between the two compression schemes, your main consideration should be whether you have the uncompress or gunzip decompression commands installed on your workstations.

Generally, it's easiest to simply download the install file directly from the Web site through a browser on your UNIX workstations to the local drive. If you do not have a browser available, one easy way to get the file to the workstation is to use FTP. In the "Advanced UNIX Integration with MetaFrame" section, toward the end of the chapter, you'll learn how to set up your Terminal Server as an FTP server that's accessible from your UNIX workstations.

Within of the compressed install file you download from the Web, you'll find a UNIX .tar file. This tar file contains the install files you need. To expand the tar file, run the tar -xvf [filename].tar command from the directory on your UNIX server where you want the files installed. The tar command will expand the tar file into the files and directories it contains. The most important file for the installation is setupwfc. This file will be expanded into the current directory. As you'll see in the installation instructions, this is the file you need to run to install the ICA UNIX client.

> ### Real-World Tip: Using WinZip
>
> If you want to download and decompress the files on your Windows workstation first before transferring them to UNIX, one utility you can use to do this is WinZip. WinZip is a shareware compression/decompression utility that works with many different compression formats, including .zip, .tar, .Z, and .gz. You can find this utility at www.winzip.com.
>
> Once the .gz or .Z file has been expanded into a .tar file, you can make the file available to your UNIX workstations using FTP.

> ### Real-World Tip: The man Command
>
> If your operating system is not listed, try typing **man mount**. If your operating system has the text manuals loaded, the man command will show you the syntax you need to use on your system for the mount command. The man command can also be very handy for looking up specific information on other commands you want to use.

Table 18.2 **Mounting the MetaFrame CD-ROM**

Operating System	Command
Solaris	`mount -F hsfs -o ro /dev/dsk/c0t6d0s0 /cdrom`
HP-UX	`mount -t cdfs -o ro /dev/dsk/c1d1s0 /cdrom`
SunOS	`mount -t hsfs -o ro /dev/sr0 /cdrom`
General	`mount [CD file system] /dev/[CD device name] /cdrom`

Installing and Using the ICA UNIX Client

This section covers the basic steps for installing the ICA UNIX client and the many different ways you can use it.

Installation Requirements

The MetaFrame ICA UNIX client has been ported to several different UNIX platforms, with more to come in the future. Here's the current list of supported versions of UNIX:

- Digital UNIX v3.2 or greater
- HP-UX v.9.x or greater
- IBM-AIX v.4.1.4 or greater
- SGI IRIX v6.2 or greater
- Sun Solaris 1.0 (SunOS 4.14) or 2.5.1 (SunOS 5.5.1)

If your UNIX operating system is not listed, you still may be able to access MetaFrame using the ICA Java client. ICA Java clients are available for both version 1.0 and 1.1 of the Java Developer Kit. Because Java has been ported to most UNIX platforms, you'll likely be able to run it.

Remember that the ICA UNIX client requires support for graphics on the UNIX workstation. Although MetaFrame makes it easy to replace text terminals, no support is built into MetaFrame for running text-based applications on text terminals. To run the ICA UNIX client, your UNIX workstation needs to meet the following hardware requirements:

- 12MB of disk space available for the install
- TCP/IP connectivity to the MetaFrame server
- 16- or 256-color display

Author's Note: Before Installing the ICA UNIX Client...

Before installing the ICA UNIX client on version 1.0 of the SunOS, you need to download and install patch `100444-76.tar.Z` from SunSolve Online (`www.sunsolve.sun.com`).

Currently, some of the ICA UNIX clients (in particular, the Solaris/x86 client) do not support 24-bit graphic workstations. Because UNIX workstations are often used for high-end graphic applications, this can be a major limitation. If you find that the ICA client will not run in the graphics mode that your workstation needs to run in, try the ICA Java client instead.

Installing the ICA UNIX Client

The sections that follow contain general instructions that are mainly intended to be followed by UNIX administrators who are familiar with the specific operating system on which the ICA UNIX client is being installed. If you haven't worked significantly with UNIX before, many basic tips have been included in the instructions.

Obtaining the ICA UNIX Client

The first step to installing the ICA UNIX client is obtaining the correct one for your system and accessing it from the UNIX workstation onto which you want to install it. ICA UNIX clients for all the operating systems listed previously are included on the MetaFrame CD-ROM under the \icaclient\icaunix directory. If you want to use these versions of the client, simply mount the CD-ROM onto your UNIX workstation.

Installation Steps

The following are the steps you need to take to install the ICA UNIX client:

1. Log in as root.
2. Get to the command prompt. The method of doing this will vary from system to system.
3. Either mount the CD-ROM as shown previously and change to the ICA-CLIENT/Icaunix directory or change to the directory where you expanded the install files obtained from the Web site (remember that the command for changing directories in UNIX is cd).
4. Run the setup program by typing **./setupwfc**.

   The period and forward slash combination (./) in front of the command is necessary to indicate to UNIX that you want to run the command from the current directory.
5. Select "1. Install Citrix ICA Client" from the main installation menu by entering **1** and pressing Enter.

> **Real-World Tip: Gaining Root Access**
> The root user has full access to the UNIX system, just as the administrator user has full access in NT. To gain root access to the system, normally you can either log out and then log back in as root or simply type **su** at the command prompt. The **su** (or *super user*) command will prompt you for the root password and then grant you root access on most systems.

6. The program will then prompt for the directory in which you want to install the ICA UNIX client. Either type in the full directory path or press Enter to accept the default (/usr/lic/ICAClient).

7. Type **y** for "yes" to proceed with the installation when prompted.

8. Type **y** again to accept the license agreement.

   The actual installation will now begin. Once the installation is complete, you'll return to the main installation menu.

9. Press **3** to quit the Citrix ICA client setup and return to the command prompt.

Using the ICA UNIX Client

Now that the files have been installed, it's time to use the client. In this section, you'll learn how to run the client, access your local drives, and access your local printers from the MetaFrame session.

Running the Client

If you installed the client into the default directory (/usr/lib /ICAClient), you can run the client by typing **/usr/lib/ICAClient/wfcmgr** at the command prompt.

If you installed the client into a different directory, you'll first need to set the ICA-ROOT environment variable to the location of that directory. On most systems, the command to do this is **set ICAROOT = [ICA Client directory]**.

Creating a Connection Entry

Running the client will bring up the ICA UNIX client manager window. This window looks very similar to the main window you see with the 32-bit and 16-bit ICA client. From this window, you can create connection entries to your MetaFrame server. The following instructions guide you through the process:

1. Select New from the Entry menu.

2. In the Properties page that appears, enter the description for the connection in the Description field.

3. Select either Server or Published Application, depending on whether you want to create an entry for a server connection or an entry for running a published application.

4. Click the ellipsis (...) button next to the Server or Published Application field to obtain a list of the servers or applications that are available on the network; then select the one you want the connection to be made to. You can also type in the IP address of the server or the name of the published application in the field if you want.

5. If you want this connection to automatically log on to the MetaFrame server, enter the username, domain, and password for the user. Leaving these blank will cause the standard Terminal Server logon prompt to come up when the connection is first made.

6. Click OK to save the new connection entry.

Before attempting to connect with the new entry you just made, try pinging the MetaFrame server first using the `ping [IP Address]` command. You need to have TCP/IP connectivity to your MetaFrame server before you can connect to it with the ICA UNIX client.

Once you've established that the MetaFrame server is reachable, run the connection entry by double-clicking its description in the Citrix ICA client manager window. This will start your Windows session on MetaFrame.

UNIX Hotkeys

You'll find that access to your Windows applications through the ICA UNIX client is nearly identical to the other ICA clients. One thing that's slightly different is the default session hotkeys with UNIX. To view and/or change the default hotkeys, follow these steps:

1. Select Settings from the Options menu at the Citrix ICA client manager main window.

2. Select Hotkeys from the pull-down menu in the upper-left corner.

A window will appear with all the current hotkey mappings. From here, you can change them to whatever you want.

Accessing Your Local Drives from MetaFrame

Because UNIX does not support drive letters for accessing your local files from your MetaFrame session, you need to map drive letters to the local directories on your UNIX workstation. The following instructions guide you through doing this:

1. From the Citrix ICA client manager main window, select Settings from the Options menu.

   A window appears showing drive letters on the left and blank fields for each drive letter on the right. Each field corresponds to the directory on your UNIX workstation that you want to map to a particular drive letter on a MetaFrame session.

2. Enter the directory path in the blank field next to each drive letter you want to map to a local directory; then select the Enable check box next to it. You can also click in the blank field and then click the Modify button to browse for the directory you want to map the drive letter to.

3. Select whether you want to be able to read and/or write to the drive from MetaFrame by selecting/deselecting the read (spectacles) or write (pencil) icons next to the Enable button for the drive letter.

4. Select the Enable Drive Mapping button and then click OK.

The next time you log on the MetaFrame server, the UNIX directories you just mapped will be available as drive letters in your session. Remember that if the drive letters you've selected conflict with any of MetaFrame's drive letters, MetaFrame will automatically remap them higher in the alphabet, starting with drive V.

Accessing Your Local Printers from MetaFrame

By default, your locally defined printers should automatically be incorporated into your MetaFrame printer list when you log onto MetaFrame. You can view your local printers from the Printer control panel (Start menu | Settings | Printers). Your local printers will have the name [workstation name]([username])#[printer name]. When you print to any of these printers from an application, the print job will be redirected to your local printer.

If you do not see your local printers listed in the Printer control panel, you can map them manually using the following instructions:

1. Go to the Printer control panel (Start menu | Settings | Printers) and double-click Add Printer.
2. Select Network Printer Server and click Next.
3. Expand Client Network by double-clicking it; then double-click Client.

   Client Network will expand to show all the printers you have available on your UNIX workstation.
4. Select the printer from the list and click OK.
5. Select Yes if you want this to be your default printer. Click Next.
6. Click Finish to finish the install.

Your local printer should now be listed in the Printer control panel.

Advanced UNIX Integration with MetaFrame

For many, the integration of UNIX with MetaFrame does not end with the simple installation of the ICA UNIX client. In this section, we'll go over some of the more advanced integration techniques for bringing together the UNIX and Windows worlds.

Setting Up UNIX Printers in MetaFrame

Accessing the locally defined UNIX workstation printers is one thing, but what if several of your UNIX clients need to be able to print to a UNIX (LPD) printer from their MetaFrame sessions? The easiest way to do this is to define the LPD printer in MetaFrame.

For those who are not used to LPD printing, basically what happens is that a device on the network, such as a UNIX server or network print server, runs a small application called the LPD (Line Printer Daemon). This application listens on the network for print jobs that are directed to it and then spools them and sends them to the requested print queue. One LPD can have multiple print queues assigned to it. To set up a Terminal Server printer to print to a queue off of an LPD print server, you need to know two things: the IP address or hostname of the LPD print server and the name of the queue or printer that you want to print to.

Here's how to set up an NT printer to print to an LPD print queue:

1. Go to the Network control panel (Start menu | Settings | Control Panel | Network) and select the Services tab.

2. Click the Add Service button.

3. Select Microsoft TCP/IP Printing from the Select Service window and then click OK.

4. Enter the location of the Terminal Server install files if prompted.

   The LPD compatible printing system will now be installed on your server, and you'll be brought back to the Network control panel window.

5. Click Close from the Network control panel window.

6. Select Yes to restart the computer.

After the computer has restarted, you'll be able to set up the LPD printer as an NT printer, as follows:

1. Go to the Printer control panel (Start menu | Settings | Printer) and double-click Add Printer.

2. Select My Computer from the initial Add Printer Wizard window.

3. Select Add Port.

4. From the Printer Ports window, select LPR port. This port type was added to the list when you installed the Microsoft TCP/IP printing service.

5. In the Add LPR Compatible printer window, enter the IP address or hostname of the LPD print server next to the field labeled Name or Address of Server Providing LPD.

6. Enter the queue name or printer name on the server that you want to print to in the field labeled Name of Printer or Print Queue on That Server.

   The new LPD port will now be added to the list of ports in the Add Printer Wizard port window.

7. Click Next in the Add Printer Wizard port window.

8. Select the correct make and model for the printer and click Next.

9. Enter the printer name and click Next.

Author's Note: Support for LPD Printers

MetaFrame provides the same support for LPD printers as that included with NT Server 4.0. This support is based on the LPD printing scheme defined in RFC1179, which is supported by most LPD network print servers today.

The instructions provided for setting up an NT printer to print to an LPD queue can also be used to set up UNIX printers on Terminal Server alone.

Real-World Tip: Special Queue Names

Some LPD print servers, such as HP Jet Direct's print server, use special queue names to define how the data should be handled (for example, "raw" for no formatting). Refer to the manufacturer's instructions on which queue name to choose.

10. Select the Share radio button and enter the share name if you want to share the printer on the network. Then click Next.

11. Select whether you want to print a test page and then click Finish.

The printer you just created will now be available in the printer lists for the clients on MetaFrame.

Setting Up FTP Services on Terminal Server

FTP (File Transfer Protocol) originated in the UNIX world as a means to access files on remote systems. To access files on a remote FTP server from UNIX, you would normally type the `ftp [IP address or host name of FTP server]` command. From here, you can use standard FTP commands such as `ls`, `get` and `put` to list files on, retrieve files from, and send files to the FTP server.

Out of the box, Terminal Server is capable of being configured as an FTP server. By providing the FTP service to your UNIX clients, you can make files and directories on your Terminal Server available to them. One good use for this is for making the ICA UNIX client available for download for your UNIX workstations.

For your Terminal Server to become an FTP server, you must first install the Internet Information Server (IIS), which is included on the Terminal Server CD-ROM. The following instructions guide you through installing IIS 3.0 and setting up a directory on Terminal Server for anonymous access through FTP:

1. Run the IIS setup program by either double-clicking the Install Internet Information Server icon on the desktop or running the `C:\WTSRV\SYSTEM32\INETINS.EXE` program (Start menu | Run).

2. When prompted, enter the location of your Terminal Server install files (for example, `D:\I386`).

3. Click OK at the Microsoft Internet Information Server 3.0 Setup window.

4. Under Options, select FTP Service and Internet Service Manager for installation. Click OK.

5. By default, the IIS server will be installed under `C:\WTSRV\SYSTEM32\INETSRV`. If this directory does not yet exist, you'll be prompted whether you want to create it. Click Yes to create the directory and continue.

6. At the Publishing Directory window, enter the directory on the Terminal Server that you want to publish to your UNIX clients. By default, the directory will be `C:\InetPub\Ftproot`. This directory and its subdirectories are the only directories that the remote FTP clients will be able to see.

7. Click Yes to create the directory if it does not already exist.

The files for the IIS server will now be copied to your hard drive, and the FTP service will be started.

8. Click OK at the final setup window.

At this point, the FTP service has already been started on your server. Any files that are now placed under `C:\InetPub\Ftproot` (or whatever publishing directory you set up in step 6) will immediately be available for download through anonymous FTP by your UNIX clients. Your UNIX clients will need to type `ftp [IP address or host-name of your Terminal Server]` to attach. They will be prompted for a username and password. Have them type **anonymous** for the username and their email address or leave the password field blank. They can now enter standard FTP commands to list, send, and retrieve files from the Terminal Server published directory.

By default, the only type of access that's enabled to your server is anonymous access. A special IIS user is created during the installation of IIS—`IIS_[server name]`. This user is considered the anonymous user. By controlling this user's access to the FTP publishing directory, you control the access of all users who use anonymous access. If you want to increase the security on the files you publish, you can change the NTFS permissions for the `IIS_[server name]` user to the FTP publishing directory and its files.

The FTP server included with Terminal Server has many more options you may be interested in using. Although these options are beyond the scope of this book, you can view which of them are available by running the Microsoft Internet Service Manager tool (Start menu | Programs | Microsoft Internet Server | Internet Service Manager), highlighting the FTP service, and then selecting Service Properties under the Properties menu.

Replacing UNIX Terminals with Windows-based Terminals

This section if for administrators who are interested in replacing their text-based UNIX terminals with Windows-based Terminals, but yet still retain user access to the UNIX hosts. Although specific guidelines for particular systems is beyond the scope of this book, you'll be provided with general guidelines to help get you started. These general guidelines will also be of use for replacing other types of text-based terminals with WBTs, such as 3270 and VT-100 terminals.

The IP Address Test

Because you'll be replacing all your text-based terminals with WBTs and because all the WBTs will be running terminal emulation sessions on Terminal Server, the application on the host you're accessing must be able to differentiate the sessions running on Terminal Server.

> **Real-World Tip: Using Web Browsers to Access Files**
>
> For those who are not familiar with or do not want to type the FTP commands, you can also use a Web browser that supports access to FTP servers to access the files on your Terminal Server. For example, if your UNIX clients are using Netscape Navigator, they would type in the following address to access the files on your Terminal Server through FTP:
>
> `ftp://[IP address or hostname of the Terminal Server]`
>
> They could then browse directories and retrieve files just as they would on any FTP server on the Internet.

For example, suppose you have a UNIX server running a text-based accounting application, and you have ten VT-100 text terminals attached to it through direct serial connections. You want to replace these ten terminals with WBTs running off of a single Terminal Server whose IP address is `10.1.1.1`. Each WBT will be running a VT-100 terminal emulator from a Terminal Server session. The problem here is that every WBT that accesses the UNIX server will be accessing it using the same source IP address (`10.1.1.1`). As long as your UNIX application does not think that each IP address represents a single client, you'll have no problem. If, instead, the UNIX application assigns such things as security rights to the user by IP address, you'll likely have difficulties running it from Terminal Server.

Before investing much time or money, perform this simple test to help ensure that you can run multiple simultaneous user host sessions from one machine with one IP address:

1. Load the terminal emulator you intend to use on an NT 4.0 workstation.

2. Open up two or three simultaneous sessions to your UNIX host.

3. Log into your UNIX server from each session using a different username.

4. Test the UNIX application that users will normally be running to ensure you have no problems running it from two or three simultaneous sessions from the same IP address.

A key indicator that an application will be a problem is if you're required to enter the client's IP addresses into a table on the host before new users can fully access it. Also check with the publisher of the application to see if any problems are involved with accessing the application using multiple sessions from the same IP address.

Choosing Your WBTs

You have several options available when choosing your Windows-based Terminals. If you're going to use RDP-based WBTs and Terminal Server, you'll need to network them. Some shops have already replaced the serial cables going out to their text terminals with network cables to make it easier to replace them with networked devices such as PCs, Network Computers, or WBTs.

If you still have serial cables running out to your terminals, you may want to consider purchasing MetaFrame. With MetaFrame, you can directly connect the ICA-based WBT's to a multiport serial communications card (for example, Digiboard) that's installed in your MetaFrame server. Make sure, of course, that the WBT you choose supports direct serial links to a MetaFrame server.

For more information on WBTs and their manufacturers, see Appendix B, "Windows-Based Terminal Manufacturers."

Setting Up the Server

On the Terminal Server, you'll need to install your chosen terminal emulation program and make shortcuts available for everyone who will be using it. For more information on how to set up applications on Terminal Server, see Chapter 10, "Installing Applications on Terminal Server."

Be careful of user settings such as screen color, text size, key mappings, and so on when using terminal emulators in a multiuser environment. You need to make sure these settings are kept in separate locations for each terminal emulator user so that one user's settings does not overwrite another's. If your terminal emulator program has a definable directory for terminal settings, make this directory the user's home directory. As long as the home directory has been mapped to the base of the user directory using the SUBST command, as shown in Chapter 10, users should have no difficulty keeping their settings separate. If the settings are all kept in one location, you might want to consider either making them read–only or, if the terminal emulator is small, installing a copy under each user's home directory.

Replacing the Terminals

As long as you've planned appropriately, replacing the terminals should go very smoothly. Because the cabling should already be in place, you can simply replace each user's text terminal with a WBT, one at a time. Because you don't need to take down the UNIX server to do this, only the user whose terminal you're currently replacing will be affected by the transition.

As more WBTs access the Terminal Server simultaneously, keep a close eye on the server's performance. If the server usage is scaling over what you had planned, you may need to purchase more hardware or an additional server. It's better to catch an unexpected performance problem now then after all the WBTs have been rolled out. For more information on measuring the performance of your server, see Chapter 13, "Measuring Performance."

MetaFrame and Macintosh

WINDOWS 32-BIT AND 16-BIT APPLICATIONS as well as DOS applications running on a Macintosh? Yes! Although running these applications on a Macintosh has been done by using many different methods in the past, using the MetaFrame ICA client for Macintosh tops the list as being the most seamless and easy way. You may be surprised at the ease with which the Macintosh ICA client brings together the disparate worlds of Macintosh and Windows.

This chapter starts out with the installation and use of the Macintosh ICA client. In this first section, you'll learn how to install the client, incorporate your Macintosh printers into your Terminal Server desktop, and how to access your local Mac drives. The second half of this chapter is dedicated to advanced Macintosh integration topics, such as setting up Macintosh-accessible volumes on Terminal Server, printing directly to AppleTalk printers from TS, and accessing TS remotely by using MacPPP.

For those administrators who do not often work in the world of Macintosh, you'll find many introductory tips to help you as we go along.

Installing and Using the Macintosh ICA Client

This section covers the installation and use of the standard Macintosh ICA client, which runs as a normal application from your Macintosh desktop. With this client, you can access MetaFrame just as you would with any other ICA client.

Installing the Macintosh ICA Client

The installation of the Macintosh ICA client is actually very simple. Many of the features that you find in the 32-bit or 16-bit version of the ICA client are also available in the Mac version. Before getting into the installation process, we need to go over the minimum requirements that you need to meet for the Macintosh ICA client to work:

- *Operating system*   You need version 7.1 or later of the Macintosh OS. If you have version 7.1, you'll also need to download and install the Thread Manager extension, which is available at Apple's Web site (www.apple.com).

- *Processor*   The client was written to work on 68030/040 or PowerPC processors.

- *TCP/IP*   The Macintosh ICA client only works with TCP/IP, not AppleTalk. You need either MacTCP or Open Transport TCP/IP version 1.1 or later.

- *Memory*   At least 4MB available.

- *Disk*   At least 2MB free.

- *Video*   Requires either a 16- or 256-color video display.

The Citrix Macintosh ICA client is included on the MetaFrame CD-ROM in the \clients\icamac folder off the root. It's also available for free download on Citrix's Web site at www.download.citrix.com. Here's how to install it:

1. Copy the MACICA_SEA.HQX file from either the CD-ROM or Citrix's download page to your Mac's local hard disk. Expanding this file directly from the CD-ROM can cause freezing on some systems.

2. Decompress the MACICA_SEA.HQX file using Stuffit Expander or a similar decompression utility. Note that the filenames may differ slightly if you're using the version from the Citrix's Web site.

3. Double-click the Citrix ICA Client 2.6.SEA file that was expanded from the HQX file. The files inside of the SEA file will be put into the temporary folder on your Macintosh.

4. Double-click the installer icon from the temporary folder and follow the directions.

Real-World Tip: The HQX Extension

For those who have not worked much in the Macintosh world, the HQX extension may be unfamiliar. The HQX extension means that the file has been compressed by using the BinHex compression algorithm. Just as zip files are the most common type of compression in the PC world, most Mac files available for download on the Internet use the HQX extension.

The most common method for decompressing HQX files is to download, install, and use the freely available Stuffit Expander utility from Aladdin Systems (www.aladdinsys.com). The install program will create an icon on the Macintosh desktop. To decompress an HQX file, you need to drag and drop it onto the Stuffit Expander icon.

A Citrix ICA Client folder will now be created with icons for the Citrix ICA client, the ICA client editor, the ICA client guide, and the ICA client editor guide. Normally, the next step is to create connection icons using the ICA client editor:

1. From the Citrix ICA Client folder, double-click the Citrix ICA Editor icon.

2. In the Citrix ICA Client Editor dialog box that appears, select either Server or Published Application. With the Macintosh ICA client, you can access both. Publishing applications is covered in detail in Chapter 20, "Application Publishing and Load Balancing with MetaFrame."

3. In the Server field, either enter the IP address of the MetaFrame server or select the server or published application from the drop-down list.

4. If you want to have the connection automatically log onto the server, you can optionally enter the username, domain, and password for logon.

5. Click Save to save the connection icon for later use or click Connect to connect directly to MetaFrame without creating a connection icon.

Using the Macintosh ICA Client

Now that you have the connection up and running, it's time to go over how to use some of its main features, such as access to the Macintosh client's local drives and printers as well as the Clipboard.

Connecting to MetaFrame

You can connect to your MetaFrame server by double-clicking the connection icon you created in the previous section. This will open a standard Terminal Server session on your Macintosh desktop. You'll first be taken to a Terminal Server logon screen where you need to enter your Terminal Server username and password. If you entered these already when creating the connection, this screen will not appear. After you've logged on, your Terminal Server desktop appears. You'll be able to access the Terminal Server and its applications in a manner nearly identical to other ICA clients.

Real-World Tip: The MacPing Utility

For the connection to work, you must have TCP/IP connectivity to your MetaFrame server. The easiest way to ensure that you have TCP/IP connectivity is to ping it. You may be surprised to know that unlike most other operating systems, Mac OS has no built-in ping utility. To resolve this need, Apple has made available a MacPing utility for free download from its Web site (www.apple.com). Download this utility and keep it in a centrally accessible location for quick TCP/IP troubleshooting.

Author's Note: The Option Key

Because the Alt key is not available with most Macintosh keyboards, use the Option key instead.

Accessing Your Local Drives from MetaFrame

Just as with most other ICA clients, your local Macintosh drives can be automatically incorporated into your MetaFrame desktop. With this capability, you can open files from your Macintosh, work on the files using Windows applications running on MetaFrame, and then save the files back to your local Mac drive. Here's how to set it up:

1. Open the Citrix ICA editor from the Citrix ICA Client folder.

2. Select Default Settings from the Options menu.

3. Select Drive Mappings from the drop-down list at the top of the Citrix ICA client editor window.

   The window will now change to show you the default drive letter mappings that will be used on MetaFrame to represent your local Macintosh drives. Note that if you choose a drive letter that already exists on the MetaFrame server, MetaFrame will automatically remap the drive to a letter higher in the alphabet.

4. To change any of the default mappings, select a mapping and click Modify.

5. Select the drive letter you want the resource to be mapped to.

6. Once you're finished modifying the drive mappings, click Save.

The next time you connect by using one of the ICA connections, you'll be able to see and use your local Macintosh drives just as you would any other drive letter on the MetaFrame desktop.

Printing to Your Local Printers from MetaFrame

Besides accessing local drives, you can also print to your local printers from MetaFrame. When set up correctly, your local Macintosh printers will automatically become a part of your available printer list in MetaFrame.

For this feature to work, the printer must be attached directly to your Mac. Also, make sure that the printer you want to print to from MetaFrame is listed in the Macintosh Chooser dialog box and that you can print to it locally from the Mac workstation.

Follow these steps to make your Macintosh's local printers accessible from MetaFrame:

1. Open the Citrix ICA editor from the Citrix ICA Client folder.

2. Select Default Settings from the Options menu.

3. Select Printer Setup from the drop-down list at the top of the Citrix ICA client editor window.

4. Select either PostScript if your printer supports PostScript or Direct Printer if it does not.

5. (Postscript only) Select your Postscript printer from the drop-down list or select Generic Postscript if your particular model is not available.

6. (Direct Printer only) Select your printer from the list or type the name exactly as it would appear in the Add Printer Wizard in MetaFrame. You can get to the Add Printer Wizard by going to the control panel and selecting Printers | Add Printer from the MetaFrame console.

7. Select Enable Local Printer and click Save.

When you next connect to the MetaFrame server, the local printer that you just set up will be available from any printer selection list. Your local printer will appear as follows:

```
[Macintosh name]#[Printer name]
```

The Macintosh name can be set in the Macintosh Sharing Setup control panel.

Clipboard Integration

By default, objects that you cut and paste to the Clipboard on your MetaFrame session will also be available to other applications running on your Macintosh. An example of the use of this feature would be to copy a graphic from your Internet browser running on MetaFrame so that you can work with it in a graphics program, such as Photoshop, running on your Macintosh.

Advanced Macintosh Integration

For those who want more than just basic integration tips and instructions, this section is for you. You'll learn how to set up your Terminal Server as a Macintosh file server, how to print to networked AppleTalk printers from MetaFrame, and how to connect your Mac to MetaFrame using dial-up PPP connections.

Quick Overview of Macintosh AppleTalk Networking

For those who are new to Macintosh networks, this section will provide a quick overview of the concepts you'll need to know about when integrating your Macintosh network with Terminal Server using AppleTalk. Keep in mind that this discussion is only pertinent to the AppleTalk protocol. The Macintosh ICA client does not use AppleTalk—it uses MacTCP or Open Transport TCP. AppleTalk will only be used with Terminal Server if you plan to make either Terminal Server files or printers available directly to Macintosh clients, outside of any Terminal Server session.

The AppleTalk Protocol

Macintosh computers use a protocol called *AppleTalk* to communicate with each other as well as with other devices on a network. AppleTalk has gone through various iterations since its initial development; however, the version that you'll most likely be working with is either EtherTalk or TokenTalk:

> **Real-World Tip: Non-PostScript Drivers**
>
> PostScript drivers are included with Macs. However, if you need to print to a PC printer that does not support PostScript, you might need to download and install the correct driver first. You'll find a good collection of non-PostScript drivers available in the PowerPrint package available from InfoWave Wireless Messaging at www.infowave.com.

- *EtherTalk* is AppleTalk designed to work over Ethernet networks using the Ethernet 802.3 frame type.

- *TokenTalk* is AppleTalk designed to work on Token Ring using the standard 802.5 frame type.

Both TokenTalk and EtherTalk are extensions to the AppleTalk protocol and therefore share the same fundamental AppleTalk design concepts that will be explained next.

AppleTalk Zones

AppleTalk networks are logically divided into units called *zones*. For NT administrators who are not familiar with zones, you can think of a zone as an NT workgroup that has been spanned across network segments. Every AppleTalk node on a particular network needs to become part of either the default zone or a particular predefined zone when they first attach to the network. You can have devices that are part of different zones on the same network segment.

Zones are normally used to keep network resources together. For example, suppose you want just two Macintosh users on one segment and three users on another segment to be able to see an AppleTalk printer. By assigning all five workstations and the printer to the same zone, only the workstations in that zone will be able to see the printer. Note that as with NT workgroups, this is not as much a security measure as a logical division of network resources. Workstations can still freely switch zones if needed.

Zones are defined on a particular segment by what is called a *seed router*. Seed routers normally advertise the zones they're aware of on all network segments to which they're attached. When setting up AppleTalk networking on a Macintosh, you'll need to choose which zone the Macintosh will be a part of. This zone list is retrieved from the seed router on that segment.

Network Numbers

Although zones can span network segments, each segment is assigned a unique range of network numbers, called a *cable range*, to keep it addressable from other segments. This way, routers that support AppleTalk, such as Terminal Server (which is capable of AppleTalk routing), know where to send AppleTalk packets that are destined for networks other than their own.

Each network number can be from 1 to 65,279. Up to 253 devices can be assigned to one network number, hence the need for a cable range to support more than 253 devices on one segment. Unless you have an unusually large number of devices on one segment, a cable range of one network number should be plenty.

AppleTalk Addressing

If you could look inside of an AppleTalk packet, you would find two primary identifying pieces of information that allow it to reach its intended destination: the network number and the node number. An AppleTalk device's network address is normally written like this:

```
[network number].[node number]
```

For example, a Macintosh that's part of network 101 and has node number 15 would have a network address of 101.15.

When an AppleTalk device first attaches to the network, it will retrieve its network number from that segment's AppleTalk router. It will then randomly generate a node number, check whether that node is available on the segment, and then use it as part of the address. This unique method of automatic address assignment makes setting up AppleTalk networks very easy.

Setting Up Macintosh-Accessible Volumes on TS

For an all-in-one Terminal Server networking solution for Macintosh, you can set up your Terminal Server or any NT Server on the network as a Macintosh file server. You can only make NTFS volumes accessible to Macintosh users; FAT volumes cannot store the required additional file information necessary to work with Macs. The following instructions will guide you through setting up the services for Macintosh on Terminal Server:

1. Go to the Network control panel (Control Panel|Network) and select the Services tab.

2. Click the Add button to add a new service.

3. Select Services for Macintosh from the Select Network Service window and click OK.

4. Enter the location of your Terminal Server setup files if prompted.

5. At the AppleTalk Protocol Properties window, which appears next, select the AppleTalk zone that each network card is to be made a part of. The Terminal Server resources to be made available to Macintoshes will appear on the zone that you configure.

   Note that the zone list is pulled from whichever AppleTalk router is currently attached to that network segment. If no routers are attached, no zones will be listed. The card becomes part of the default zone instead.

   If you wish to make this server into an AppleTalk router or seed router, select the Routing tab from the AppleTalk Protocol Properties window. Otherwise, click OK.

> **Author's Note: Socket Numbers**
>
> Mac gurus may notice the omission of sockets. Socket numbers are also part of the identifying information in the AppleTalk packets. However, in terms of Terminal Server, node and network numbers are the most pertinent. In addition, this discussion primarily focuses on the features of AppleTalk Phase II.

At this point, you'll be prompted to restart your server. The server needs to be restarted to begin the Macintosh service and continue the installation.

After the reboot, you'll notice a new shortcut and a new control panel available on your Terminal Server. Under the Start menu's Programs | Administrative Tools selection, you'll see a new shortcut for File Manager. File Manager is the same file manager you may have used with NT 3.51. It has been enhanced with the additional menu—the MacFile menu. Under this menu are options for setting up and administering Macintosh volumes. In addition to File Manager, you'll also notice a MacFile control panel in the Control Panel window. The MacFile control panel allows you to monitor the usage of the Macintosh-accessible volumes that you've set up. The following instructions will guide you through the setup of a basic Macintosh-accessible volume on Terminal Server:

1. Open File Manager from the Start menu by selecting the Programs | Administrative Tools group.

2. Select Create Volume from the MacFile menu.

3. In the Create Macintosh-Accessible Volume window, shown in Figure 19.1, fill in the volume name and path. Note that the path should point to a directory on an NTFS volume on one of your Terminal Server's local drives.

Author's Note: Terminal Server As an AppleTalk Router

To make your Terminal Server into an AppleTalk router or seed router, perform the following steps with the Routing tab selected:

1. Click Enable Routing to enable AppleTalk routing.

2. To make this server into a seed router, check Use This Router As a Seed Router. For each network card in the drop-down list, you need to define a network number range and assign zones.

3. Click OK when you're finished.

Author's Note: Setting Up a Mac-Accessible Volume on TS

The instructions guide you through setting up a directory on your Terminal Server as a Macintosh-accessible volume with guest access (and therefore no password). This guest access has nothing to do with the Guest account on NT; it instead refers to Macintosh guest access. Because of the fundamental user authentication differences between Macintosh and NT, setting up a volume for access using encrypted passwords involves several more steps. For more information on these steps, see the README.UAM text file, located in the AppleShare folder in the Microsoft UAM volume (which is made accessible to Macintosh, by default, by Terminal Server when the services for Macintosh are first installed).

Figure 19.1 Creating a Macintosh-accessible volume.

4. Leave the password blank and make sure the Guests Can Use This Volume check box is checked.

5. If you want to make the volume read-only, check the This Volume Is Read-Only check box.

6. Select OK to create the volume.

In the Chooser window on your Macintosh, you should see your Terminal Server listed under AppleShares. By connecting to it with Guest access, your Mac users should be able to see and use the volume that you just created. You'll also see the Microsoft UAM Volume.

Printing to AppleTalk Printers

With Terminal Server, you can set up and print directly to any AppleTalk printer on your network. This is a very handy feature if you have AppleTalk-only printers on the network that you want Mac users to be able to print to from their MetaFrame sessions. Printing to an AppleTalk printer requires the services for Macintosh, so make sure they're loaded before continuing. Here's how to set an AppleTalk printer up on Terminal Server:

1. Go to Control Panel|Printers and double-click the Add Printer icon.

2. Select My Computer.

3. Click the Add Port button to add a port for an AppleTalk printer.

4. Highlight AppleTalk Printing Device from the Printer Ports window and click OK. If you do not see this port listed, the services for Macintosh are not installed.

5. From the Available AppleTalk Printing Devices window, select the zone that the printer is a part of and then select the AppleTalk printer that you wish to print to.

Author's Note: My Computer
Make sure you select My Computer and not Network Printer Server. AppleTalk printers install as a new type of printer port off your computer.

6. You'll be prompted whether you wish to capture the AppleTalk printer device. Click Yes if you want to prevent Macintosh users from printing directly to the printer.

7. The AppleTalk printer you just created should now appear in the Add Printer Wizard window. Make sure the check box for it is checked. Click Next.

The rest of the installation is identical to setting up a standard NT printer. Select the make and model, assign the printer a name, and then optionally share it. Once the AppleTalk printer has been set up on Terminal Server, all your Terminal Server clients on this server, including non-Macintosh ones, will be able to print to it from their sessions.

Connecting to TS Using PPP

Using PPP, you can connect your Macintosh to a Terminal Server using several different remote connection options, such as using either analog or ISDN modems. Because of the popularity of using PPP to connect to the Internet, several different PPP options are available that you can use to connect your Macintosh to a Terminal Server network. Covering the specific steps of what you need to do for each of these options is beyond the scope of this book; however, here's what you need to do in general:

1. Select and install a PPP client on your Macintosh and configure it to dial into the MetaFrame server using a modem.

2. Configure the Terminal Server with Remote Access Services using TCP/IP with a modem that's set up to receive the incoming Macintosh calls. For further information on setting up RAS, see Chapter 14, "Terminal Server and Remote Access."

3. Establish a PPP connection to Terminal Server by dialing into it with the MacPPP client. Test the connection by pinging your Terminal Server using MacPing (available at www.apple.com).

4. Once a TCP/IP connection has been established, run your Macintosh ICA client connection to attach to MetaFrame.

For a list of some commonly used or recommended MacPPP clients, go to either www.apple.com or www.macorchard.com. At the Mac Orchard site, you'll find a large collection of useful Internet-related Macintosh software, including a listing of the various PPP clients available for the Macintosh.

Author's Note: The PPP Protocol

Microsoft RAS fully supports the PPP protocol for both dial-in and dial-out access. With the default options set and TCP/IP enabled, you can use either PAP or CHAP authentication from the MacPPP client. Header compression is also enabled by default. Knowing these settings may help you when setting up your MacPPP clients.

20

Application Publishing and Load Balancing with MetaFrame

MetaFrame

IN THIS CHAPTER, YOU'LL LEARN about two very powerful features of MetaFrame: application publishing and load balancing. *Application publishing* is an application-centric view of thin-client computing. With application publishing, you set up your servers to publish a set of applications to your users. Instead of the traditional concept of choosing the server first and then running the applications from a desktop, you first choose the applications and then log on to the server and run them directly. As you'll learn in this chapter, application publishing is the method of choice when it comes to providing both applications and desktops to users.

Load balancing is an add-on feature for MetaFrame that's available for purchase from Citrix. Load balancing and application publishing are closely related. Load balancing allows you to evenly spread your published application users across a group of servers, called a *server farm*. When a user attempts to run a particular load-balanced published application, the server farm will decide which server is currently being used the least and will connect the user to it. In this chapter, you'll learn how to setup a load-balanced server farm and how you can tune its performance.

Advantages of an Application-Centric Approach

Although at first it might seem that the change from server-centric to application-centric access is not very significant, publishing applications have many benefits:

- *Security*   When you set up published applications, you can control which groups or users can use them. This is a very simple and easy way to secure access to your server's applications.

- *Seamless Windows*   This is a great but often misunderstood feature that is designed to integrate well with published applications. When you run a published application in a Seamless Window, it appears as just another application on the desktop. This seamless integration into the user's desktop is a boon to the administrator and to the user. Normally, a user has two different desktops—his or her own desktop and the MetaFrame desktop. This doubles the work of the administrator and complicates the thin-client connection. With seamless windows, the users only have to worry about their own desktops. Applications running on the MetaFrame server are seamlessly integrated into it, just as if they were any other Windows application. Seamless Windows also ensures that only a single MetaFrame license is taken at the server, even if the user is running several applications on it at once. We'll get further into the many benefits of Seamless Windows in this section.

- *Load balancing*   Load balancing only works with published applications. This provides you with the highest level of performance and reliability for running applications in the enterprise. When the client chooses an application, the master MetaFrame server in the load-balanced server farm decides which server you should run it on, based on several adjustable parameters. Remember that this is an add-on option. By default, MetaFrame can publish only applications from individual servers, not as part of a server farm.

- *Publishing applications on the Internet*   The Application Configuration Tool allows you to create a publishable HTML or ICA file for use on your Web page. We'll go into detail about this feature in Chapter 16, "Terminal Server and the Internet."

Publishing an Application from the Server

Applications are published by using the Application Configuration Tool. To publish an application, follow these steps:

1. Choose Start | Programs | MetaFrame Tools folder, and then Application Configuration.

2. Select New from the Application menu to create a new application.

3. Enter the application name in the Enter Application Name dialog box. This name will be advertised on the network and is what the clients will see.

4. At the Choose Application Type screen, you have two application types you can choose: explicit or anonymous. The main purpose of anonymous users is to provide access to applications from the Web. Unless you're publishing an application on the Web, choose the Explicit option. For more information on anonymous users, see Chapter 16. At this point, select Explicit and click Next.

5. The Define the Application dialog box appears, as shown in Figure 20.1. Enter the command line and working directory for the application you're publishing. If you want to publish a desktop instead, leave the command line and working directory blank. Click Next when you're finished.

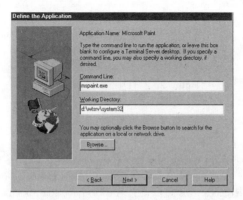

Figure 20.1 Filling in the command line.

6. At the Specify Application Window Properties screen, you can choose to hide the application's title bar and start it maximized. Choose the options appropriate for your needs and click Next to continue.

7. In the Configure Groups and Users screen, choose the groups or users who will be allowed access to the application. You should create specific groups for specific applications to control access to the server. Users who do not have access to an application will receive the message shown in Figure 20.2 after they try to log on to the application. Click Next when you're finished.

Real-World Tip: Keeping the Name Unique

When you publish an application from any server on a network, that application is automatically added to the browser list of all the applications available on that network. Suppose you have two separate MetaFrame servers on a network. On the first server, you publish Application A; on the second server, you publish Application B. When your clients try to create a connection, they'll see Application A and Application B in the list of applications available.

For this reason, you should keep application names unique. One suggestion is to always put the server name in front of the application (Server 1- Application A). This way, your users will know which server they're running the application from. If you're using a load-balancing server farm, put a name that represents the farm in front of the application (Cluster 1 - Application A).

Note for WinFrame Administrators: Publishing Applications in a Mixed WinFrame/MetaFrame Environment

You can set up a load-balancing server farm with a mix of WinFrame 1.7 and MetaFrame servers and publish a common set of applications. Because both servers handle publishing applications nearly identically, the client should notice little difference as long as the application runs well on both NT 3.51 and NT 4.0. On the other hand, publishing desktops will not work too well because the WinFrame desktop is NT 3.51 based and the MetaFrame desktop is NT 4.0 based. Therefore, your clients could get either desktop, depending on which one the ICA master browser chooses. Also, you should be aware of the incompatibility of profiles between WinFrame and MetaFrame.

Figure 20.2 Denial of access.

8. The next window, Add the Application to Citrix Servers, is only of concern if you're using load balancing. Load balancing is an additional option pack you need to purchase from Citrix and install on your MetaFrame server. It allows you to publish a single application from multiple servers. If you do not have load balancing installed, skip this screen. If you do have load balancing, you need to select the servers in the server farm on which the application can execute. By default, only your current server is in the Configured list. Only servers that have load balancing enabled and are on the local network will be listed. For more information on load balancing, see the "Load Balancing" section at the end of this chapter. Click Next when you're finished.

Publishing Desktops

Publishing applications makes good sense in terms of reliability and performance, because you can have multiple servers publishing the same set of applications. If one server goes down, users can still get to the applications, because they're still being published by the other servers.

What if a user needs a desktop on the server and not just a single application? Publishing desktops is a good option for power users who need access to several different applications on Terminal Server. An example of this is an administrator who needs access to several different administrative applications on the server. Publishing these applications and running them in separate sessions would take more server resources than publishing a desktop for the administrator and running the applications from there.

To set up a published desktop, create a published application called MetaFrame Desktop by using the Application Configuration Tool, as shown in the previous section. Leave the command line and working directory blank for the published application.

Once the published application is created, your users will be able to select MetaFrame Desktop for their connection. When they click this, they'll be taken to a logon prompt and then to their own desktop. To increase security, you may want to create a Desktop_Users group and give this group rights to run only the MetaFrame Desktop application.

For greater reliability, you can set up a server farm by using load balancing and publish the desktop on the servers. Then, if one server goes down, the users on that server only need to reattach to a working server to receive another desktop.

Connecting to a Published Application at the Client

As soon as you publish an application from the server, the server adds it to the browse list for the clients. To connect to a published application from an ICA client, follow these steps:

1. From the ICA client, create a new entry (select New from the Entry menu on the 32-bit ICA client). Select Network for the connection type and click Next.

2. At the next window shown in Figure 20.3, select Published Application instead of Server. When you click the down arrow next to Published Application, the client will send a broadcast packet out to the network in search of the list of published applications available. You can then select the application that you need from this list. After you're finished, click Next.

3. At the next screen, make sure Seamless Windows is selected in order to take advantage of its advanced features. The rest of the options are the same as if you were setting up a server connection. For more information on these options, see Chapter 9, "Installing Clients."

Creating an Icon for the Published Application

At this point, the application is not completely seamless. The user first needs to run the ICA client and then select the application that he or she wants. To make the connection seamless, you can create an icon or shortcut on a user's desktop for the connection. The program you need to create the shortcut for is WFCRUN32.EXE [Application Name], where the application name matches the application description in the Remote Application Manager.

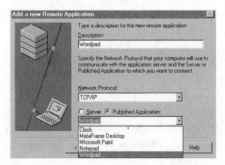

Figure 20.3   Description window.

Advantages of Seamless Windows

The Seamless Windows feature has several advantages besides making applications appear as if they're running locally. One of the lesser known ones is how Seamless Windows sessions take up MetaFrame licenses. Suppose you're running two published applications on your workstation—Application A and Application B. Because these are published applications, you have two connections opened with your MetaFrame server, one for each application. How many MetaFrame licenses are you taking? The answer is only one if you're using Seamless Windows for both applications. There are some exceptions to this rule: First, the applications must both have all the same settings, including the same settings for encryption, protocol, disk cache, and bitmaps. Second, they must both be running from the same server. If you're running the applications from different servers, they take up two licenses. These limitations may be fixed in future hot fixes or service packs for MetaFrame.

Load Balancing

Load balancing is perhaps the most powerful add-on feature for MetaFrame, and the reason many corporations will choose it over Terminal Server alone. Load balancing allows you to publish an application for execution on any one of a group of MetaFrame servers. This group of servers is called a *server farm*. In this section, we'll go over how load balancing works and how to set it up.

Setting Up Load Balancing

The first step in setting up load balancing is installing the option pack license. This option pack needs to be purchased and installed on all the servers in the server farm that will be participating in the load balancing. As with the standard client licensing process for MetaFrame, the license code you obtain from the option pack needs to be installed using the MetaFrame licensing tool.

Once you've installed the license on all servers in the server farm, it's time to publish your applications. Publishing an application to be load balanced is nearly identical to publishing a single server application. The exception is when you come to the step of choosing the servers on which the application can be run. Follow the steps listed under the "Publishing an Application from the Server" section in this chapter. When you get to the step in the Add Application to Citrix Servers window where you choose which servers the application can execute on, select all the servers in the server farm and add them to the Configured list on the right.

If one of the servers is not listed, make sure that load balancing is installed on that server and that it's connected to the network. Also, make sure that all the servers, including the one you're on, are running the same protocols. If you need to bring up one of the servers during the installation, you can click the Update List button in the Add Application to Citrix Servers window once the server is up in order to add it to the Available list.

After you've followed all the steps and created the published application, it should be immediately available to your clients.

IV

Appendixes

A The History of Terminal Server

B Windows-Based Terminal Manufacturers

C Disaster Recovery Kit

D Terminal Server Resources

The History of Terminal Server

ALTHOUGH HAVING A GOOD TECHNICAL grasp of Terminal Server is essential, it can also be beneficial to understand the technology from a historical perspective. This appendix gives you a good understanding of where the product has been and where it is headed.

The Terminal Server Story

The story of Terminal Server begins with a south-Florida software company called Citrix, founded by Ed Iacabucci and twelve programmers in 1989. With the help of Mr. Iacabucci's strong OS/2 background at IBM, Citrix set to work on a DOS/Windows terminal server based on OS/2.

The resulting WinView product was a significant technological accomplishment. It was the first product on the market that gave administrators the capability to distribute multiple Windows 3.x desktops to remote users from a single server. This new technology became an excellent remote-access solution for many networks. From home, users could dial in to the WinView server and access a Windows desktop on the corporate network as though they were sitting at the server itself.

In November 1992, Citrix licensed the source code for Windows NT 3.51. Its intention was to rewrite core sections of the operating system to make it work as a

Windows NT 3.5x terminal server. In 1995, they released their first version of this product, called WinFrame.

WinFrame

WinFrame quickly gained industry-wide attention. The product split the user interface from the Windows applications running on the server, packaged it, and sent it across the network to a WinFrame client. It offered businesses the capability to simultaneously run multiple remote Windows NT desktops off a central NT-based server, on nearly every type of client in their enterprise. Even legacy computers could run 32-bit Windows applications with the robust power of a Pentium-based server.

The secret was the remote-control protocol called Independent Computing Architecture (ICA), which split the user interface from the application, compressed it, and sent it over the wire to the Windows terminal. ICA was specially designed to work well over low-bandwidth connections, such as modem links. The Windows terminal only received screen updates, and did not actually process the applications, allowing a low-end terminal to leverage the high-end capabilities of a server.

Windows NT Server 4.0, Terminal Server Edition

It did not take long for Microsoft to realize the potential of Windows terminals, especially with the rise of competing technologies such as Java. With Citrix's technology, Windows applications could run on nearly every desktop in the enterprise, including UNIX, Macintosh, and OS/2. Citrix was also interested in working with Microsoft for several reasons, including access to large enterprise class organizations and enhanced support.

In early 1997, a team of Citrix representatives, led by Mr. Iacabucci, went to Redmond to negotiate with Microsoft. In May 1997, the announcement was made: Microsoft had licensed significant portions of the WinFrame technology from Citrix and released it as Windows NT Server 4.0, Terminal Server Edition. This product incorporated much of the current WinFrame MultiWin code, which enables a single Citrix server to support multiple Windows sessions. Microsoft, with the assistance of Citrix, integrated this technology into Windows NT Server 4.0.

Because Microsoft did not license the ICA protocol from Citrix, Microsoft also developed its own version of Citrix's ICA protocol, called the Remote Desktop Protocol (RDP), which Microsoft based heavily on the communications protocol it was already using with its NetMeeting product.

MetaFrame

The RDP protocol was designed to work across TCP/IP. For those who needed Terminal Server to work with more protocols and platforms, Citrix offered an add-on product to Terminal Server called MetaFrame, which allows the base Terminal Server product to work across IPX/SPX and NetBEUI, using the ICA protocol. It also allows a much larger variety of clients, such as Macintosh and UNIX X Window, to connect to Microsoft's Terminal Servers. This, along with several other features, makes MetaFrame an attractive alternative for many companies, especially enterprise organizations.

The Future of Terminal Server

Microsoft is already working on a new version of Terminal Server that will work with the next version of NT Server, version 5.0. Citrix continues to work on making ICA clients for an even larger variety of operating systems and platforms than they currently support.

The legal agreement between Citrix and Microsoft prevents Microsoft from creating non-Windows clients for Terminal Server for a period of time. As a result, you can expect this functionality to continue to be provided by Citrix. However, Microsoft has the freedom to add other functionality to the product, such as load balancing and more integrated access to client-side drives and printers. Expect to see many new Terminal Server innovations from both companies.

To keep up to date on the latest product happenings, refer to each respective company's Web page:

■ *Citrix MetaFrame* `www.citrix.com`

■ *Microsoft's Terminal Server* `www.microsoft.com/ntserver/basics/terminalserver`

B

Windows-Based Terminal Manufacturers

THE FOLLOWING IS A LIST of some of the major manufacturers of Windows-based Terminals (WBTs). The company's home page is usually the best place to start to find out more about their WBT offerings. From time to time you will also find WBT comparisons in computer trade magazines. Keep your eyes open for new WBT offerings, for the WBT market is a new one and is growing rapidly.

Boundless Technologies
100 Marcus Blvd.
P.O. Box 18001
Hauppauge, NY 11788-3762
1-800-231-5445 or 516-342-7400
info@boundless.com
www.boundless.com

Javelin Systems, Inc.
17891 Cartwright Rd.
Irvine, CA 92614
949-440-8000
sales@jvln.com
www.jvln.com

Ketronics
P.O. Box 14687
Spokane, WA 99214-0687
509-928-8000
www.keytonic.com

Neoware
400 Feheley Dr.
King of Prussia, PA 19406
1-800-NEOWARE
info@neoware.com
www.neoware.com

Network Computing Devices, Inc.
350 North Bernardo Ave.
Mountain View, CA 94043-5207
1-800-800-9599
info@ncd.com
www.ncd.com

Tektronix, Inc.
Corporate Headquarters
P.O. Box 1000
Wilsonville, OR 97070-1000
1-800-TEK-WIDE
www.tek.com/vnd

Wyse Technology, Inc.
3471 N. First St.
San Jose, CA 95134
800-GET-WYSE
info@wyse.com
www.wyse.com

Disaster Recovery Kit

THE DISASTER RECOVERY KIT (DRK) is an important part of your administrative arsenal. If your Terminal Server ever goes down, you need to be prepared to quickly bring it back to life. The Disaster Recovery Kit will help you do this by providing you with the critical information you need to restore your server. The DRK can additionally serve as an administrative and troubleshooting tool for your server.

In this appendix, you will learn how to create a DRK.

Creating the Disaster Recovery Kit

The best time to create your DRK is while you are installing Terminal Server. It is critical to record such information as license key codes, hardware configuration, and installation notes so that you are prepared if you ever have to reinstall your server in a hurry in the future. The Disaster Recovery Kit (DRK) is intended to serve this purpose and more.

The DRK can take many forms, depending on what you find the most useful for your environment. You could keep all the information in the DRK in electronic form on your local drive or on the drive of another server on the network. You could also print out all the information for the DRK and keep it in a binder in safe storage.

No matter which option you choose, it is important to gather sufficient information in order to quickly rebuild your server from scratch.

Gathering Server Information

Out of all the information you will be gathering, detailed server information is perhaps the most critical. Included with Terminal Server is an often-overlooked utility for gathering server information—the Windows NT Diagnostics program. With the Windows NT Diagnostics program, you can gather all the following information into either a printed report or text file (see Figure C.1):

- *Version*   Provides version information, including to whom Terminal Server is registered, the product number, and the service pack level.

- *System*   Includes the loaded HAL, system processors, processor speed, and BIOS version.

- *Display*   Provides information on the current resolution, VGA BIOS version, display adapter, and display drivers.

- *Drives*   Shows the total and free space of all system drives.

- *Memory*   Provides a large variety of information on memory, including total memory and memory available.

- *Services*   Lists the services and device drivers that are currently loaded.

- *Resources*   Shows the system resources currently being taken, including I/O ports, IRQs, DMAs, and memory ranges.

- *Environment*   Displays both the user and system environment variable settings.

- *Network*   Provides detailed network information, including logon domain, workstation name, protocols loaded, network adapter MAC addresses, network statistics, and network settings.

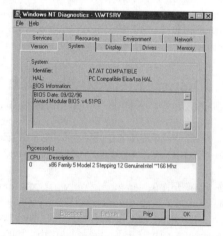

Figure C.1   Windows NT Diagnostics program.

To create a report on your server with the Windows NT Diagnostics program, follow these steps:

1. Run the Windows NT Diagnostics program from Start Menu, by selecting Programs | Administrative Tools.

2. In the Windows NT Diagnostic program main window, click Print. The Create Report window appears.

3. In the Create Report window, select All Tabs under Scope. Selecting All Tabs creates a report with all the information listed previously.

4. Select Complete under Detail Level in order to create as detailed a report as possible on your server.

5. Select either File, Clipboard or Default Printer under Destination, depending on the media format in which you want the report.

6. Click OK to create the report.

Besides the Windows NT Diagnostics program, there are often utilities available from your server's manufacturer for gathering server information. COMPAQ, for one, makes a survey utility for gathering detailed information on their servers. This utility is freely available on their web site (`www.compaq.com`). The survey utility can generate a report with COMPAQ-specific information, such as the model of all installed COMPAQ components, which is lacking in reports from the Windows NT Diagnostic program.

Application Installation

Because of the unique manner in which applications are installed on Terminal Server, it is important to maintain good records of their installation techniques. These records will help in both the administration and troubleshooting of your server. They will also make it easier for you to delegate server responsibilities, such as setting up new users with applications. The following is a list of some of the pertinent information you should keep on the applications installed on your server:

- Application basics, including a description of the application, its purpose, and who makes it.

- Any notes taken from application testing, such as memory used by the application and any problems encountered.

- Detailed installation steps of the initial application install, and instructions for setting up new users on the application.

- Application troubleshooting tips.

- Application technical support information, such as telephone numbers, contact names, and hours of operation for technical support.

Other Information

The following are some of the many other pieces of information that should be kept on your server and network as part of the DRK:

- Take the time to record the licensing key codes for all the products that you will be installing on Terminal Server. It is especially important to record the MetaFrame license and product codes if you will be installing it.
- Any driver disks you needed during the installation should be kept with the DRK.
- Any unusual BIOS or jumper settings.
- Network diagrams.
- Maintenance logs for keeping track of server maintenance and for making notes on troubleshooting.

Server Images as a DRK

Experienced administrators may want to consider simply taking an image of their server using an imaging product such as Ghost. Restoring a server using an image is one of the quickest and most reliable means of disaster recovery. Some administrators go as far as making a bootable CD-ROM that holds the server image and completely automates its installation. Of course, if you use this technique, you need to make sure that changeable data, such as user data, is kept on other servers on the network.

Imaging is one of the best techniques to use in a load balancing or load sharing setup. Data is normally already stored centrally with this setup because users can log on to either server.

D

Terminal Server Resources

WITH SUCH A DIVERSE PRODUCT as Terminal Server, it is impossible to do it full justice in print. Every day new products come out that add to or enhance its robust capabilities. In this appendix, you will learn about some of the many resources that are available to you as a Terminal Server administrator.

Resource List

The following are some of the many Web sites on the Internet that have information that will be of use to you as a Terminal Server administrator:

- *www.citrix.com* Citrix's Web site has loads of useful troubleshooting information, including a knowledge database and online forum. Even if you will not be installing the add-on product MetaFrame, this Web site is worth a look.

- *www.microsoft.com/ntserver/basics/terminalserver* This is Terminal Server's home page at Microsoft. Here you will find links to several additional Terminal Server resources. Microsoft's support site (support.microsoft.com) also has a growing collection of Terminal Server troubleshooting tips.

- *www.technotips.com* A periodically updated collection of Web site links, tips, and other useful information for Terminal Server administrators maintained by the author.

- *www.thinergy.com* Citrix will be updating this page with information about their Thinergy conference. Thinergy '98 was one of the first conferences dedicated entirely to thin-client technology. While this conferences will likely occur only once a year, you can currently obtain names of many of the companies that are most involved with thin-client technology by looking at this Web site.

- *www.thinworld.com* This site is a good place to go for information on thin clients in general. They also do an interesting monthly piece called "Thinworld's ThinMan," where they interview leading business people involved in the thin-client movement.

- *www.winntmag.com* *Windows NT* magazine currently sponsors a Terminal Server community at their Web site, where you can post and read Terminal Server–related messages.

With this list, the book has come to an end. Good luck in all your Terminal Server endeavors and, as always, think thin!

Index

Symbols

A

I

M

Q-R

S

V

W-Z

Books for Networking Professionals

Windows NT Titles

Windows NT TCP/IP

By Karanjit Siyan
1st Edition Summer 1998
500 pages, $29.99
ISBN: 1-56205-887-8

If you're still looking for good documentation on Microsoft TCP/IP, then look no further—this is your book. *Windows NT TCP/IP* cuts through the complexities and provides the most informative and complete reference book on Windows-based TCP/IP. Concepts essential to TCP/IP administration are explained thoroughly, then related to the practical use of Microsoft TCP/IP in a real-world networking environment. The book begins by covering TCP/IP architecture, advanced installation and configuration issues, then moves on to routing with TCP/IP, DHCP Management, and WINS/DNS Name Resolution.

Windows NT DNS

By Michael Masterson, Herman L. Knief, Scott Vinick, and Eric Roul
1st Edition Summer 1998
325 pages, $29.99
ISBN: 1-56205-943-2

Have you ever opened a Windows NT book looking for detailed information about DNS only to discover that it doesn't even begin to scratch the surface? DNS is probably one of the most complicated subjects for NT administrators, and there are few books on the market that really address it in detail. This book answers your most complex DNS questions, focusing on the implementation of the Domain Name Service within Windows NT, treating it thoroughly from the viewpoint of an experienced Windows NT professional. Many detailed, real-world examples illustrate further the understanding of the material throughout. The book covers the details of how DNS functions within NT, then explores specific interactions with critical network components. Finally, proven procedures to design and set up DNS are demonstrated. You'll also find coverage of related topics, such as maintenance, security, and troubleshooting.

Windows NT Registry

By Sandra Osborne
1st Edition Summer 1998
500 pages, $29.99
ISBN: 1-56205-941-6

The NT Registry can be a very powerful tool for those capable of using it wisely. Unfortunately, there is very little information regarding the NT Registry, due to Microsoft's insistence that its source code be kept secret. If you're looking to optimize your use of the Registry, you're usually forced to search the Web for bits of information. This book is your resource. It covers critical issues and settings used for configuring network protocols, including NWLink, PTP, TCP/IP, and DHCP. This book approaches the material from a unique point of view, discussing the problems related to a particular component, and then discussing settings, which are the actual changes necessary for implementing robust solutions. There is also a comprehensive reference of Registry settings and commands, making this the perfect addition to your technical bookshelf.

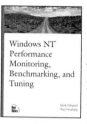

Windows NT Performance Monitoring, Benchmarking, and Tuning

By Mark Edmead and Paul Hinsberg

1st Edition Fall 1998

400 pages, $29.99

ISBN: 1-56205-942-4

Performance monitoring is a little like preventative medicine for the administrator: No one enjoys a checkup, but it's a good thing to do on a regular basis. This book helps you focus on the critical aspects of improving the performance of your NT system, showing you how to monitor the system, implement benchmarking, and tune your network. The book is organized by resource components, which makes it easy to use as a reference tool.

Windows NT Terminal Server and Citrix MetaFrame

By Ted Harwood

1st Edition Winter 1998

500 pages, $29.99

ISBN: 1-56205-944-0

It's no surprise that most administration headaches revolve around integration with other networks and clients. This book addresses these types of real-world issues on a case-by-case basis, giving tools and advice on solving each problem. The author also offers the real nuts and bolts of thin client administration on multiple systems, covering such relevant issues as installation, configuration, network connection, management, and application distribution.

Windows NT Security

By Richard Puckett

1st Edition Winter 1998

600 pages, $29.99

ISBN: 1-56205-945-9

Swiss cheese. That's what some people say Windows NT security is like. And they may be right, because they only know what the NT documentation says about implementing security. Who has the time to research alternatives; play around with the features, service packs, hot fixes, and add-on tools, and figure out what makes NT rock solid? Well, Richard Puckett does. He's been researching Windows NT Security for the University of Virginia for a while now, and he's got pretty good news. He's going to show you how to make NT secure in your environment, and we mean really secure.

Windows NT Administration Handbook

By Eric Svetcov

1st Edition Winter 1998

400 pages, $29.99

ISBN: 1-56205-946-7

Administering a Windows NT network is kind of like trying to herd cats—an impossible task characterized by constant motion, exhausting labor, and lots of hairballs. Author Eric Svetcov knows all about it—he's administered NT networks for some of the fastest growing companies around Silicon Valley. So we asked Eric to put together a concise manual of best practices, a book of tools and ideas that other administrators can turn to again and again in administering their own NT networks. Eric's experience shines through as he shares his secrets for administering users, for getting domain and groups set up quickly and for troubleshooting the thorniest NT problems. Daily, weekly, and monthly task lists help organize routine tasks and preventative maintenance.

Planning for Windows NT 5

By David Lafferty and Eric K. Cone
1st Edition Spring 1999
400 pages, $29.99
ISBN: 0-73570-048-6

Windows NT 5 is poised to be one of the largest and most important software releases of the next decade, and you are charged with planning, testing, and deploying it in your enterprise. Are you ready? With this book, you will be. *Planning for Windows NT 5* lets you know what the upgrade hurdles will be, informs you how to clear them, guides you through effective Active Directory design, and presents you with detailed rollout procedures. MCSEs David Lafferty and Eric K. Cone give you the benefit of their extensive experiences as Windows NT 5 Rapid Deployment Program members, sharing problems and solutions they've encountered on the job.

MCSE Core Essential Reference

By Matthew Shepker
1st Edition Fall 1998
500 pages, $19.99
ISBN: 0-7357-0006-0

You're sitting in the first session of your Networking Essentials class and the instructor starts talking about RAS and you have no idea what that means. You think about raising your hand to ask about RAS, but you reconsider—you'd feel pretty foolish asking a question in front of all these people. You turn to your handy *MCSE Core Essential Reference* and find a quick summary on Remote Access Services. Question answered. It's a couple months later and you're taking your Networking Essentials exam the next day. You're reviewing practice tests and you keep forgetting the maximum lengths for the various commonly used cable types. Once again, you turn to the *MCSE Core Essential Reference* and find a table on cables, including all of the characteristics you need to memorize in order to pass the test.

BackOffice Titles

Implementing Exchange Server

By Doug Hauger, Marywynne Leon, and William C. Wade III
1st Edition Fall 1998
450 pages, $29.99
ISBN: 1-56205-931-9

If you're interested in connectivity and maintenance issues for Exchange Server, then this book is for you. Exchange's power lies in its ability to be connected to multiple email subsystems to create a "universal email backbone." It's not unusual to have several different and complex systems all connected via email gateways, including Lotus Notes or cc:Mail, Microsoft Mail, legacy mainframe systems, and Internet mail. This book covers all of the problems and issues associated with getting an integrated system running smoothly and addresses troubleshooting and diagnosis of email problems with an eye toward prevention and best practices.

SQL Server System Administration

By Sean Baird, Chris Miller, et al.

1st Edition Fall 1998

400 pages, $29.99

ISBN: 1-56205-955-6

How often does your SQL Server go down during the day when everyone wants to access the data? Do you spend most of your time being a "report monkey" for your co-workers and bosses? *SQL Server System Administration* helps you keep data consistently available to your users. This book omits the introductory information. The authors don't spend time explaining queries and how they work. Instead they focus on the information that you can't get anywhere else, like how to choose the correct replication topology and achieve high availability of information.

Internet Information Server Administration

By Kelli Adam, et. al.

1st Edition Winter 1998

300 pages, $29.99

ISBN: 0-73570-022-2

Are the new Internet technologies in Internet Information Server 4.0 giving you headaches? Does protecting security on the Web take up all of your time? Then this is the book for you. With hands-on configuration training, advanced study of the new protocols in IIS 4, and detailed instructions on authenticating users with the new Certificate Server and implementing and managing the new e-commerce features, *Internet Information Server Administration* gives you the real-life solutions you need. This definitive resource also prepares you for the release of Windows NT 5 by giving you detailed advice on working with Microsoft Management Console, which was first used by IIS 4.

UNIX/Linux Titles

Solaris Essential Reference

By John Mulligan

1st Edition Winter 1998

350 pages, $19.99

ISBN: 0-7357-0230-7

Looking for the fastest, easiest way to find the Solaris command you need? Need a few pointers on shell scripting? How about advanced administration tips and sound, practical expertise on security issues? Are you looking for trustworthy information about available third-party software packages that will enhance your operating system? Author John Mulligan—creator of the popular Unofficial Guide to Solaris Web site (sun.icsnet.com)—delivers all that and more in one attractive, easy-to-use reference book. With clear and concise instructions on how to perform important administration and management tasks and key information on powerful commands and advanced topics, *Solaris Essential Reference* is the reference you need when you know what you want to do and you just need to know how.

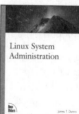

Linux System Administration

By James T. Dennis

1st Edition Winter 1998

450 pages, $29.99

ISBN: 1-56205-934-3

As an administrator, you probably feel that most of your time and energy is spent in endless firefighting. If your network has become a fragile quilt of temporary patches and workarounds, then this book is for you. For example, have you had trouble sending or receiving your email lately? Are you looking for a way to keep your network running smoothly with enhanced performance? Are your users always hankering for more storage, more services, and more speed? *Linux System Administration* advises you on the many intricacies of maintaining a secure, stable system. In this definitive work, the author addresses all the issues related to system administration, from adding users and managing files permission to internet services and Web hosting to recovery planning and security. This book fulfills the need for expert advice that will ensure a trouble-free Linux environment.

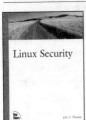

Linux Security

By John S. Flowers
1st Edition Spring 1999
400 pages, $29.99
ISBN: 0-7357-0035-4

New Riders is proud to offer the first book aimed specifically at Linux security issues. While there are a host of general UNIX security books, we thought it was time to address the practical needs of the Linux network. In this definitive work, author John Flowers takes a balanced approach to system security, from discussing topics like planning a secure environment to firewalls to utilizing security scripts. With comprehensive information on specific system compromises, and advice on how to prevent and repair them, this is one book that every Linux administrator should have on the shelf.

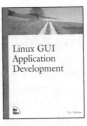

Linux GUI Application Development

By Eric Harlow
1st Edition Spring 1999
400 pages, $34.99
ISBN: 0-7357-0214-7

We all know that Linux is one of the most powerful and solid operating systems in existence. And as the success of Linux grows, there is an increasing interest in developing applications with graphical user interfaces that really take advantage of the power of Linux. In this book, software developer Eric Harlow gives you an indispensable development handbook focusing on the GTK+ toolkit. More than an overview on the elements of application or GUI design, this is a hands-on book that delves deeply into the technology. With in-depth material on the various GUI programming tools, a strong emphasis on CORBA and CGI programming, and loads of examples, this book's unique focus will give you the information you need to design and launch professional-quality applications.

Lotus Notes and Domino Titles

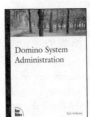

Domino System Administration

By Rob Kirkland
1st Edition Winter 1998
500 pages, $29.99
ISBN: 1-56205-948-3

Your boss has just announced that you will be upgrading to the newest version of Notes and Domino when it ships. As a Premium Lotus Business Partner, Lotus has offered a substantial price break to keep your company away from Microsoft's Exchange Server.

How are you supposed to get this new system installed, configured, and rolled out to all of your end users? You understand how Lotus Notes works—you've been administering it for years. What you need is a concise, practical explanation about the new features, and how to make some of the advanced stuff really work. You need answers and solutions from someone like you, who has worked with the product for years, and understands what it is you need to know. *Domino System Administration* is the answer—the first book on Domino that attacks the technology at the professional level, with practical, hands-on assistance to get Domino running in your organization.

Lotus Notes & Domino Essential Reference

By Dave Hatter and Tim Bankes
1st Edition Winter 1998
500 pages, $19.99
ISBN: 0-7357-0007-9

You're in a bind because you've been asked to design and program a new database in Notes for an important client that will keep track of and itemize a myriad of inventory and shipping data. The client wants a user-friendly interface, without sacrificing speed or functionality. You are experienced (and could develop this app in your sleep), but feel that you need to take your talents to the next level. You need something to facilitate your creative and technical abilities, something to perfect your programming skills. Your answer is waiting for you: *Lotus Notes & Domino Essential Reference*. It's compact and simply designed. It's loaded with information. All of the objects, classes, functions, and methods are listed. It shows you the object hierarchy and the overlaying relationship between each one. It's perfect for you. Problem solved.

Networking Titles

Cisco Router Configuration & Troubleshooting

By Pablo Espinosa and Mark Tripod
1st Edition Winter 1998
300 pages, $34.99
ISBN: 0-7357-0024-9

Want the real story on making your Cisco routers run like a dream? Why not pick up a copy of *Cisco Router Configuration & Troubleshooting* and see what Pablo Espinosa and Mark Tripod have to say? They're the folks responsible for making some of the largest sites on the Net scream, like Amazon.com, Hotmail, USAToday, Geocities, and Sony. In this book, they provide advanced configuration issues, sprinkled with advice and preferred practices. You won't see a general overview on TCP/IP—we talk about more meaty issues like security, monitoring, traffic management, and more. In the troubleshooting section, the authors provide a unique methodology and lots of sample problems to illustrate. By providing real-world insight and examples instead of rehashing Cisco's documentation, Pablo and Mark give network administrators information they can start using today.

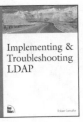

Implementing & Troubleshooting LDAP

By Robert Lamothe
1st Edition Spring 1999
400 pages, $29.99
ISBN: 1-56205-947-5

While there is some limited information available about LDAP, most of it is RFCs, white papers, and books about programming LDAP into your networking applications. That leaves the people who most need information—administrators—out in the cold. What do you do if you need to know how to make LDAP work in your system? You ask Bob Lamothe. Bob is a UNIX administrator with hands-on experience in setting up a corporate-wide directory service using LDAP. Bob's book is NOT a guide to the protocol; rather, it is designed to be an aid to administrators to help them understand the most efficient way to structure, encrypt, authenticate, administer, and troubleshoot LDAP in a mixed network environment. The book shows you how to work with the major implementations of LDAP and get them to coexist.

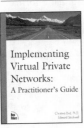

Implementing Virtual Private Networks: A Practitioner's Guide

By Tina Bird and Ted Stockwell
1st Edition Spring 1999
300 pages, $29.99
ISBN: 0-73570-047-8

Tired of looking for decent, practical, up-to-date information on virtual private networks? *Implementing Virtual Private Networks*, by noted authorities Dr. Tina Bird and Ted Stockwell, finally gives you what you need—an authoritative guide on the design, implementation, and maintenance of Internet-based access to private networks. This book focuses on real-world solutions, demonstrating how the choice of VPN architecture should align with an organization's business and technological requirements. Tina and Ted give you the information you need to determine whether a VPN is right for your organization, select the VPN that suits your needs, and design and implement the VPN you have chosen.

New Riders
How to Contact Us

Visit Our Web Site

www.newriders.com

On our Web site you'll find information about our other books, authors, tables of contents, indexes, and book errata. You can also place orders for books through our Web site.

Email Us

Contact us at this address:

newriders@mcp.com

- If you have comments or questions about this book
- To report errors that you have found in this book
- If you have a book proposal to submit or are interested in writing for New Riders
- If you would like to have an author kit sent to you
- If you are an expert in a computer topic or technology and are interested in being a technical editor who reviews manuscripts for technical accuracy

international@mcp.com

- To find a distributor in your area, please contact our international department at the address above.

pr@mcp.com

- For instructors from educational institutions who wish to preview Macmillan Computer Publishing books for classroom use. Email should include your name, title, school, department, address, phone number, office days/hours, text in use, and enrollment in the body of your text along with your request for desk/examination copies and/or additional information.

Write to Us

New Riders Publishing
201 W. 103rd St.
Indianapolis, IN 46290-1097

Call Us

Toll-free (800) 571-5840 + 9 + 4557
If outside U.S. (317) 581-3500. Ask for New Riders.

Fax Us

(317) 581-4663